Treasures of the Musée national de la Marine

This book was collectively produced by the staff of the Musée National de la Marine.

Authors of explanatory texts:
Frédérique Chapelay, Assistant Curator
Marie-Pierre Demarcq, Libraries Manager
Annie Madet-Vache, Assistant Curator
Angelina Meslem, Photographic Collection Manager
Marjolaine Mourot, Head Curator
Alain Niderlinder, Assistant Curator
Hélène Tromparent de Seynes, Curator

Authors of chapter introductions:
Virginie Duchêne, Murielle Machicot, Catherine Pinard and Bruno Ponsonnet of the Cultural Department, with the assistance of the Conservation Department and M.-P. Demarcq.

Bibliography:
Delphine Allannic-Costa, Documentalist

Picture research:
Patrick Dantec and Arnaud Fux, photographers
Dominique Salva and Karine Bomel, picture researchers
Jean-François Norget, computer specialist

Note

- The names of ships set in italics are given exactly as they appear on the model of the ship.
- Dimensions are given in centimetres (height x width x depth), except in the case of full-scale boats where dimensions are given in metres.
- In the case of composite models and objects, only the principal materials are given.
- The respective names Salle de Marine, Naval Museum, Musée de la Marine and Musée National de la Marine correspond to different periods in the history of the museum.

Names of collections:
Former Salle de Marine Collection: the Salle de Marine was opened at the Louvre Palace in 1748 in order to present a large collection of dockyard models of ships and dockyard machinery that had been given to King Louis XV by the Chief Inspector of the Navy Henri-Louis Duhamel du Monceau.
Former Trianon Collection: this collection was started in 1810 when Napoleon ordered the construction of a series of models of France's warships for display in the gallery of the Grand Trianon at Versailles. It was transferred to the Musée de la Marine in 1828.

Abbreviation (inventory numbers):
MnM: Musée national de la Marine

Treasures
of the Musée national de la Marine

Réunion des Musées Nationaux

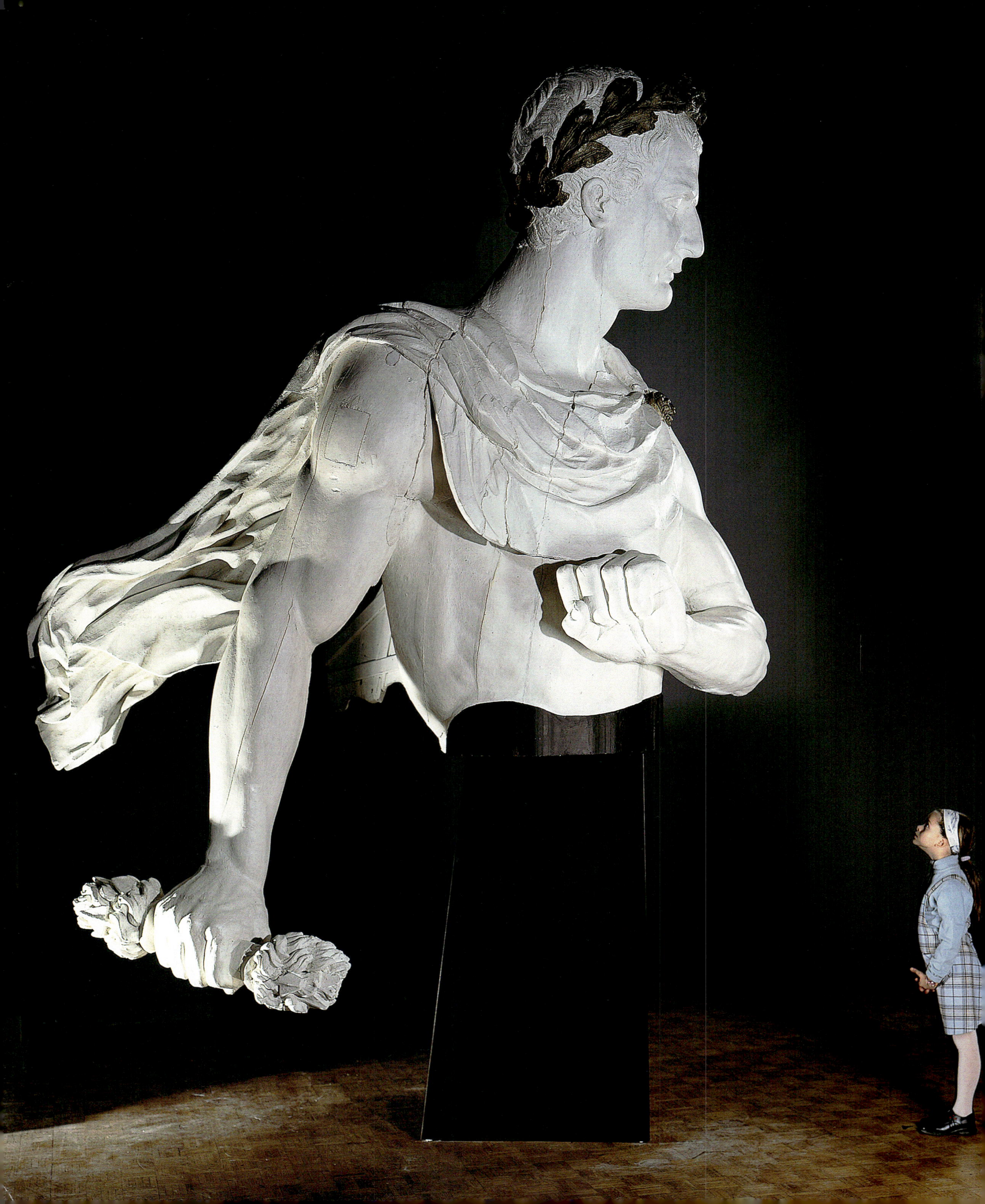

Foreword

In the pages of this book devoted to the treasures of the collection of the Musée National de la Marine, the reader will encounter major pieces such as the superb shipyard models of the 18th and 19th centuries, Joseph Vernet's 'Views of France's Ports' and the galley *Réale* with its impressive 17th-century carved ornamentation.

But the aim of this book is also to present, alongside these exceptional pieces, works that are lesser known but that have undeniable artistic, historical or documentary value. For example, that of Amiral François-Edmond Pâris, director of the museum from 1871 to 1893, rightly considered the father of maritime ethnography. This particular treasure is an extraordinary collection of documentary material – original drawings and models – pertaining to traditional boats, amassed in the 19th century.

The book also presents objects that are not usually displayed owing to their fragility, such as manuscripts and old photographs, or to their size, such as the yacht *Pen-Duick V*, with which Eric Tarbarly won the Transpacific Race in 1969, and which is today based at the French national sailing school.

Readers will gain an insight into the richness and diversity of the museum's collection. The Musée National de la Marine is revealed as a museum of fine arts and technology as well as a museum of history and popular traditions. The works are divided into sixteen thematic chapters highlighting the specificity and history of the museum. Founded in 1748, this collection reflects the development of a national navy from the 17th century on. There are few works from earlier centuries, or objects relating to the fishing industry, for example, whose history is charted in the many museums that have opened on the French coasts. This book does not claim to be a new illustrated history of the French maritime industry, but a faithful presentation of the museum's exceptional collection. It is one that continues to be enriched regularly thanks to purchases and donations.

Finally, extreme care has been given to the choice of pictorial material. The book was designed as a voyage of discovery in images, and emphasis is placed on correspondences and confrontations between works and on unusual viewpoints. Illustrations enable the reader to enter inside an 18th century model, and take a very close look at a detail of ornamentation.

These treasures provide a vision of man's adventure with the sea, immersing the reader into a world of labour, inventions, challenges and pleasure. May this book enable each and every one to make an enjoyable voyage around one of the finest and oldest maritime collections in the world.

Vice-amiral Jean-Noël Gard
Director of the Musée National de la Marine

Anonymous
Attributed to the sculpture workshop at the Brest dockyard
Bust of Napoléon I
Figurehead of the ship *Le Iéna*, ca. 1846 . Sculpture in the round, polychrome resinous wood . 369 x 230 x 235 cm . Entered museum collections 1949 . MnM 41 OA 87

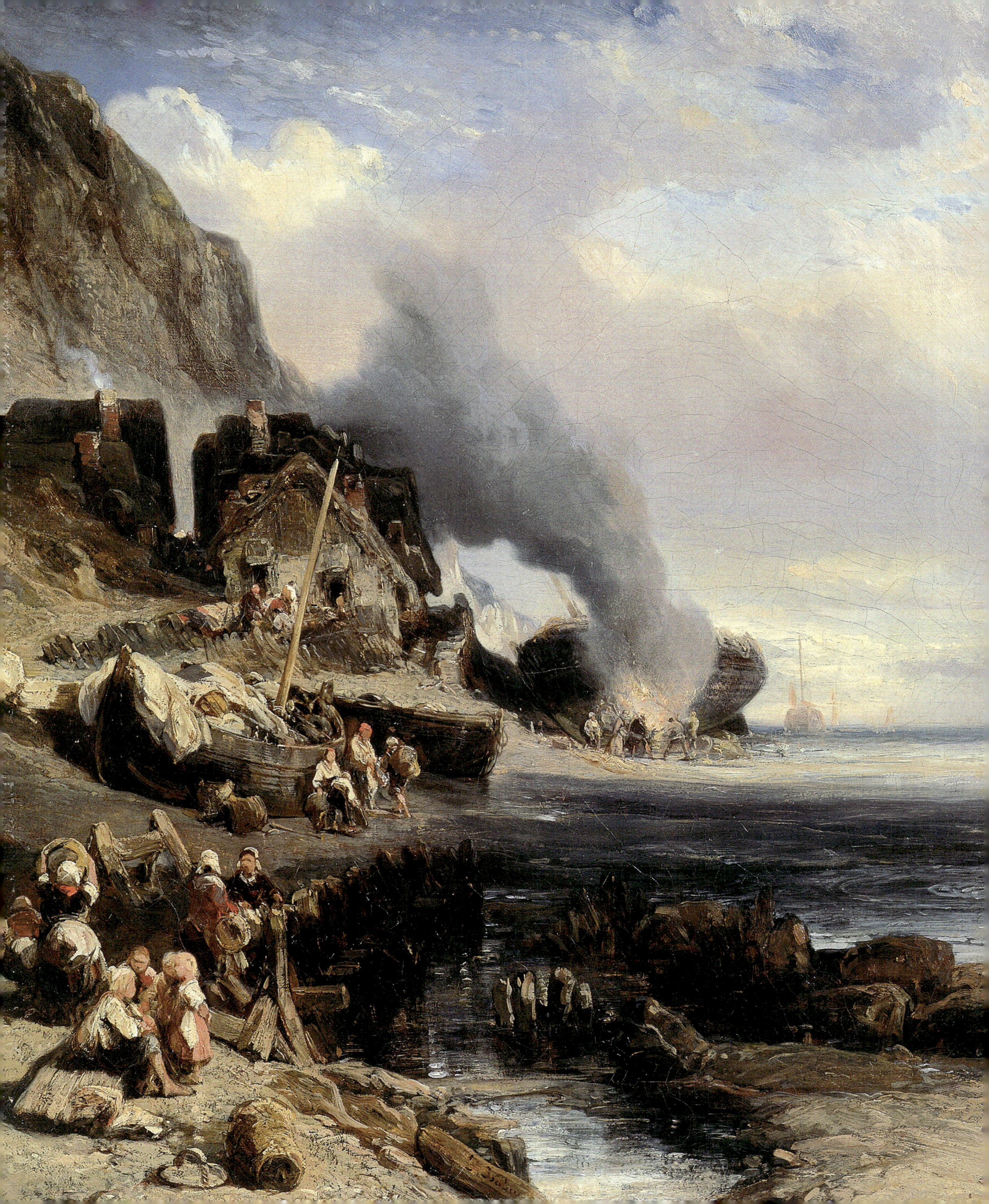

Contents

Eugène Isabey (1803–1886)
The Fishermen
19th century . Oil on canvas . 61 x 50 cm . Signed bottom centre .
Entered museum collections 1999 . MnM 9 OA 237

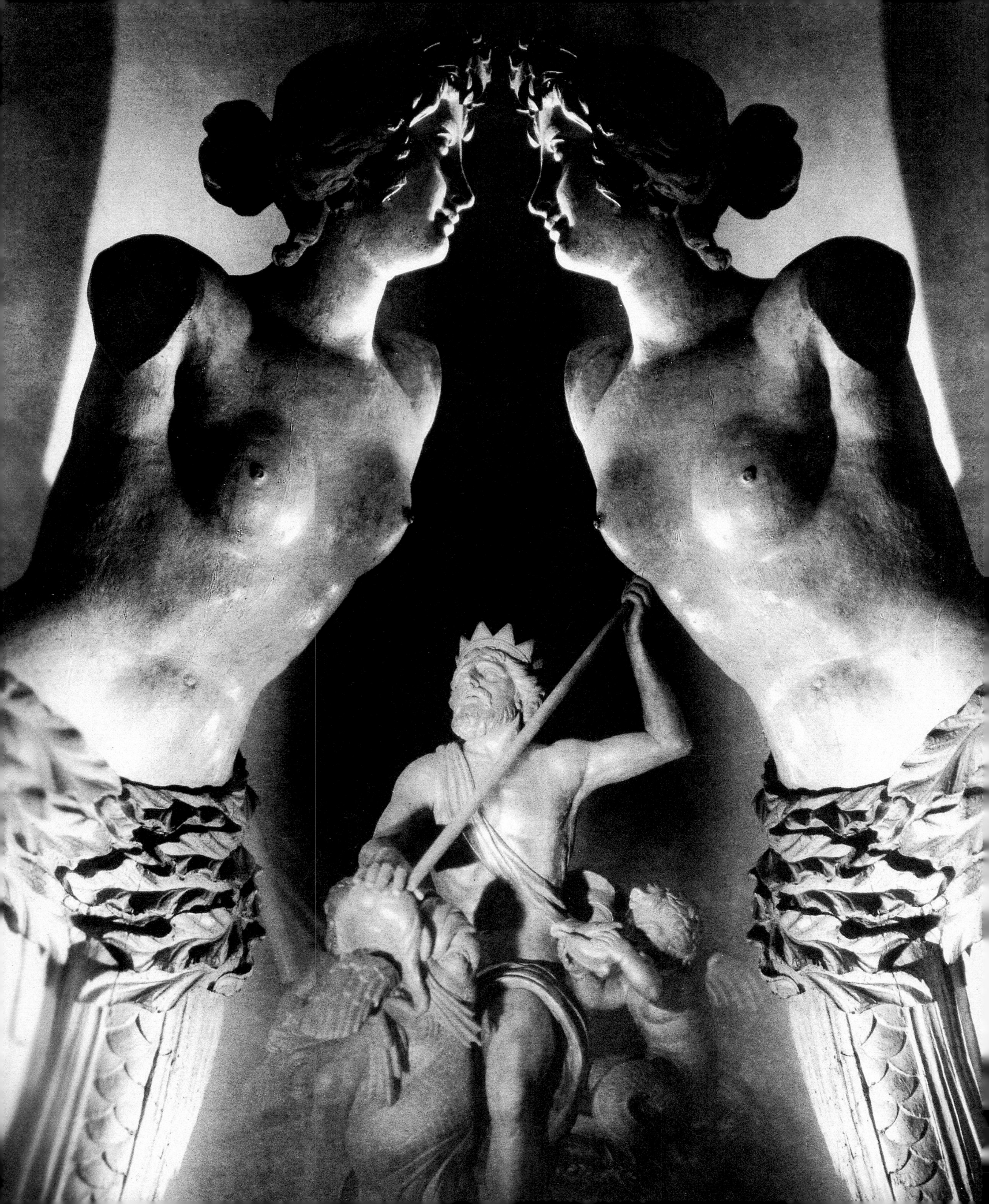

The history of a collection

The Salle de Marine at the Louvre

During the Enlightenment, enthusiasm among the elite for the great voyages of exploration and the spreading of scientific and technical knowledge led to the creation of collections of maritime objects. These included navigational instruments and technical objects, maps, engravings and paintings, and, naturally, models of ships. The successors of the templates used by shipwrights, scale models developed in France in the second half of the 17th century, when shipbuilding was not yet based on drawings. The models were constructed in the royal dockyards at the same time as the real ship, and enabled architectural information to be recorded. In the 18th century, they were considered as much as educational tools as art works. Extremely finely executed, built meticulously to scale using quality materials, these models were sophisticated and highly sought-after objects. The encyclopaedist and Chief Inspector of the Navy Louis Duhamel du Monceau built up the largest collection of model ships and harbour machinery of his time. In 1748, he gave his collection to King Louis XV. This gift was made on two conditions: the collections should be installed at the Louvre, and should serve to teach students at the naval construction engineering school, of which he was the director. A man of the Enlightenment and an enthusiastic supporter of technical progress, Duhamel du Monceau belonged to a small circle of learned men and officers who wished to improve the scientific training of the officers of the royal navy. It was for this purpose that he himself founded this naval construction engineering school in 1741 and helped to found the Académie de Marine in Brest in 1752.
The collection was installed on the first floor of the old Louvre palace near the Académie des Sciences room, and named the 'Salle de Marine', or Naval Room. Used for the students' practical work, it was also open to people interested in objects of technical or artistic value, rather like a cabinet of curiosities. In considering his collection to be of more use to the nation than to himself, Duhamel du Monceau established the cultural and institutional bases of a national maritime museum.

The vicissitudes of the Revolution

The period following the French Revolution proved paradoxical for this collection in a number of respects. With the closure of the Salle de Marine at the Louvre in 1793, when the Académies were abolished, a large part of Duhamel du Monceau's original collection was merged into a much larger ensemble. This included the former collections of the king and that of the navy ministry, as well as the Revolutionary seizures of the possessions of the émigrés, such as the collections of the Duke of Orleans. The existence of a ensemble of items related to a specific heritage, with a national vocation and placed under the responsibility of the naval administration was by then recognised; but this recognition, largely theoretical, did not immediately lead to the creation of a museum. The passing years and regimes saw a number of proposals for a maritime museum, but none came to fruition.

François Kollar (1904–1979)
Photomontage of the figurehead
of the Emperor's Barge and a caryatid
Circa 1948 . Gelatin silver print . Entered museum collections 1998 .
MnM, Photographs Collection

In 1801, a museum did open its doors to the public, in the new naval ministry on Place de la Concorde. It occupied three rooms and a gallery. Alongside the models of ships and technical objects were art works, including the Joseph Vernet's series of paintings 'Views of France's Ports'. But the museum closed in 1803. A few years later, in 1810, Napoleon decided to create a gallery of models at the Grand Trianon at Versailles, which was to glorify the naval power of the Empire. A magnificent ensemble of models was presented there, known to this day by the name 'Trianon Collection'.
The upheavals resulting from successive political and administrative reorganisations in turn brought together, mixed up and dispersed these fragile collections, causing some irreparable damage in the process. However, the continuous presence of the men in charge of these collections, in various capacities, partly compensated for these vagaries of fortune. Notable among them were the geographer Jean Nicolas Buache, the painters Jean-François Hue and Nicolas Ozanne, the great naval architect Jacques Noël Sané and the engineer Antoine Groignard, both former students of Duhamel du Monceau.

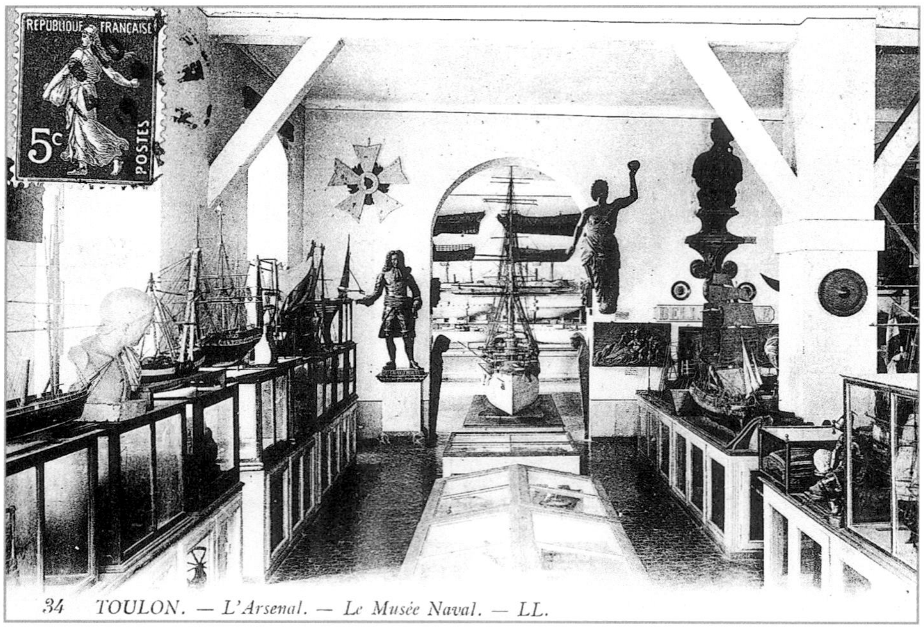

Anonymous
Toulon. The Shipyard.
The Musée Naval
Circa 1900 . Postcard . Private collection

1827, the creation of the Musée Naval at the Louvre

After thirty years of postponement, the Musée Naval was eventually opened in the Palais du Louvre in December 1827, by decree signed by Charles X. The first task of Pierre Zédé, a naval engineer and the new museum's first curator, was to reassemble the collections that had been scattered around the various official palaces and shipyards. He drew up the first inventory, ordered showcases from the best cabinet-makers and installed the museum exhibits. His work was foundational. It was also at this time that model rooms, or museums, and sculpture rooms were opened in the dockyards at Cherbourg, Brest, Lorient, Rochefort and Toulon, under the direct authority of the navy. From 1848 onwards the Musée Naval was considered the sixth department of the Musée du Louvre. Apollinaire Lebas, Antoine Léon Morel-Fatio and François Edmond Pâris succeeded each other at its head. In the late 19th century, the museum occupied nineteen small rooms on the second floor of the Cour Carrée on the Rue de Rivoli side. Works were presented as an accumulation of models, paintings, technical and ethnographical objects, as was the custom at the time. However, ill-accepted by the fine arts administration, which saw it as a primarily technical and military museum, the Musée Naval encountered numerous difficulties within the Louvre. A chronic lack of financial and human resources limited any initiative to develop and modernise the museum. It was on several occasions threatened with dispersion or removal elsewhere.
In 1905, the major ethnographical collections were assigned to other museums. In 1920, a new step was taken when Musée de la Marine ceased to come under the authority of the fine-arts administration and became attached to the French navy. However, from 1901 to 1929, the curator Jean Destrem completed the mammoth task inventorying, verifying and identifying the collections, which resulted in the publication of a catalogue raisonné.

The growth of the collections in the 19th century

The Musée Naval was originally designed as a museum of models. It presented the French navy of its time from a technical and historical angle. The collections grew with the models of contemporary warships that were built in shipyard workshops until the mid-19th century. These models charted the progressive yet utterly revolutionary transition from sail power to steam. The museum also received a number of prestigious models made for the World's Fairs, thereby opening up its collections to other fields such as merchant shipping,

L. Rouille (fl. 19th century)
Portrait of Amiral Pâris (1806–1893)
Last quarter of 19th century . Heliotype . 33.8 x 20.7 cm . Entered museum collections 1955 . MnM, Photographs Collection

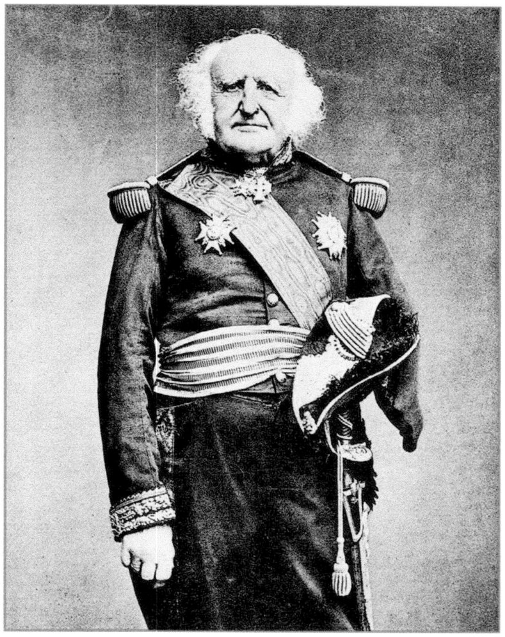

Jules Noël (1810–1861)
Musée Naval at the Louvre Salle La Pérouse, general view
Vol. 15, p. 12, in *Magasin Pittoresque* . 1847 . MnM J4030

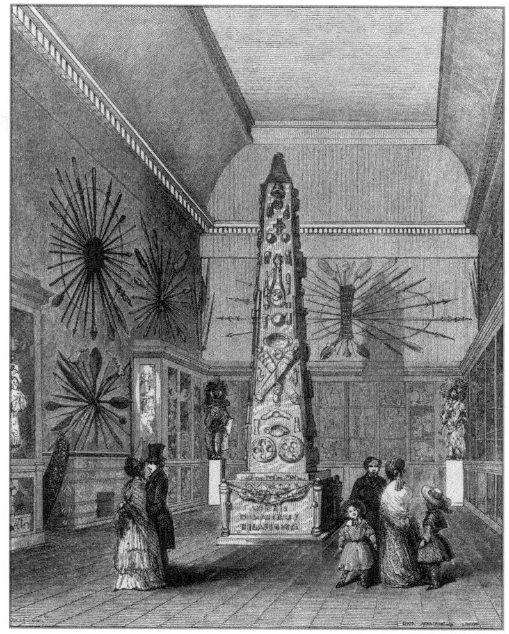

yachting and sea rescue. At the same time, the museum's own model-making workshop, with its talented craftsmen including Jean-Baptiste Tanneron (1833 to 1852) and Charles Hamelin (from 1872), also contributed to the development of the collections. From its opening, the workshop carried out extensive historical reconstruction work and filled certain gaps, executing, notably, models of the principal types of ship in use during the reign of Louis XIV. Amiral Pâris, director of the museum from 1871 to 1893, gave new impetus to the enrichment of the collections. Considered the founder of naval ethnography, Pâris had almost 230 models built by the museum's workshop, models of traditional craft from the coasts of Europe and, mostly, from Asia and Oceania, after records made by himself and his son in the course of their voyages. The exceptional Pâris collection, without equal in the world, preserves the memory of traditional navigation in the first half of the 19th century.
The history of the Musée de la Marine of the 19th century would be incomplete without mention of its significant collection of ethnographical objects brought back the great expeditions and colonial missions. The pieces, given to the museum either by the naval ministry – which administered the colonies until 1893 – or by the explorers themselves, or by private collectors, were registered in a separate inventory. They include Asian, African, American and Oceanian objects, which constituted the basis of the first French ethnographical museum. When the collection was divided up among various museums from 1905 on, the Musée de la Marine kept only objects directly related to the maritime context, notably those brought back by Dumont d'Urville after his voyage in search of Lapérouse.
During the same period, the museum also acquired works of art and sculpture. The fine arts were thus progressively associated with the models and objects of the historical collection. From the museum's opening, Pierre Zédé decided to present the decorative elements of the galley *Réale*, incorrectly attributed at the time to the famous Puget. He went on to commission works from sculptors of repute, such as Jean Antoine Houdon (1741–1828) and François Rude (1784–1855), notably marble busts of the great men who had made the glory of the navy. From 1875 onwards, in the context of his research work, Amiral Pâris asked the watercolourist François Roux (1811–1882) and later the painter Édouard Adam (1847–1929) to execute for the museum a large number of portraits of ships, warships, merchantmen and fishing vessels. History and marine painting made a later appearance in the collections: the paintings of Joseph Vernet, loaned by the Louvre Museum, were not registered in the inventory until 1903; Théodore Gudin, appointed First Official Painter to the Navy in 1830, used the museum models to compose his great historical canvases for Versailles.

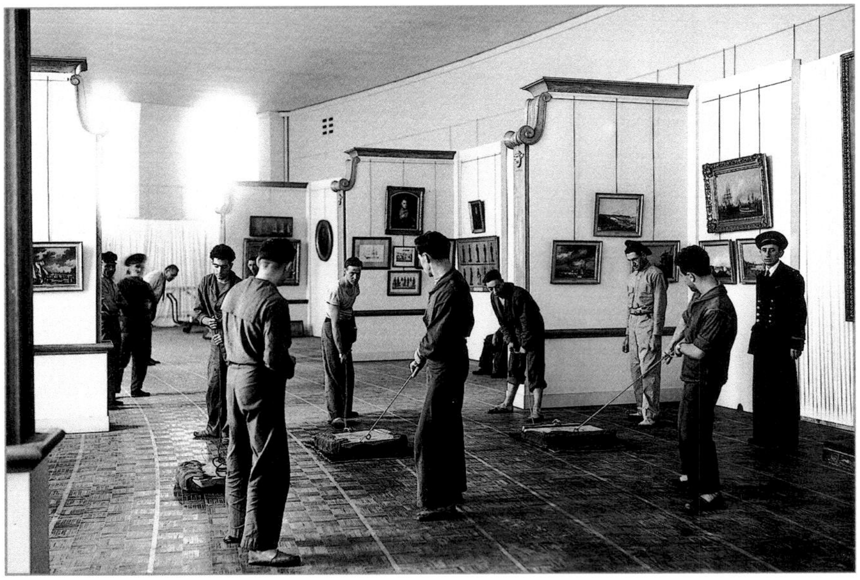

Anonymous
Military personnel on fatigue duty at the exhibition 'Vieille Marine'
1947 . MnM PH 4953

1937, the move to the Palais de Chaillot: a renaissance

The Musée de la Marine benefited from a major architectural programme related to the World's Fair of 1937: the new Chaillot, Tokyo and Iéna palaces were to house a number of museums. In 1935, an agreement between the various administrations concerned established that the Musée de la Marine would share the Passy wing of the Palais de Chaillot with the Musée de l'Homme (museum of mankind). The museum's move to the Palais de Chaillot, initially postponed for administrative reasons, was again held up by the outbreak of war. The collections were packed up and the most precious items sent to the provinces, notably to Chambord. The collections were progressively transferred to the Palais de Chaillot between 1939 and 1943, and in August of that year the museum opened its doors.

The museum's installation at the Palais de Chaillot was a renaissance: here, the Musée de la Marine attracted a new public. It occupied three times as much space as at the Louvre and could at last show the extent of its collections. A major research project was initiated by the director at the time, Jacques Vichot (1943–1971), with the creation of a very large collection of documents devoted to maritime iconography in all its diversity. The latest research techniques were adopted. The library was developed and opened to a large public of university scholars and amateur enthusiasts. In 1947, a national network was formed with the official attachment to the Paris museum of the 'port' museums, successors to the former shipyard museums. But these establishments (Brest, Rochefort, Toulon) suffered considerable damage under the bombings, when they were not entirely destroyed, as in Cherbourg and Lorient. Major restoration work of both the buildings and collections was carried out.

The museum offers an academic panorama of French maritime history; the history of battles won and of the great men – admirals, privateers, explorers and engineers – who made the naval heritage of France; dreams of glory and adventure that have inspired generations of children and adults alike. The port museums were designed as small-scale replicas of the Paris museum.

In 1971, the museum acquired 'établissement public à caractère administratif' (public service) status and was given the mission of ensuring the conservation, presentation and enrichment of its collections in all maritime fields: not just the military navy, the historical core of the collections, but also the merchant navy, the fishing fleet, oceanographic research, as well as nautical sports and yachting. The museum thus embraced the whole spectrum of maritime heritage and culture.

The museum's dynamic policy of hosting temporary exhibitions for an international market and cultural events have made it the centre of French maritime heritage, located both in Paris and on the coast thanks to its sister establishments. Operating as a network and present on both the Atlantic and Mediterranean coasts (where the themes and collections are today closely related to local history), the Musée National de la Marine is a precursor of cultural decentralisation.

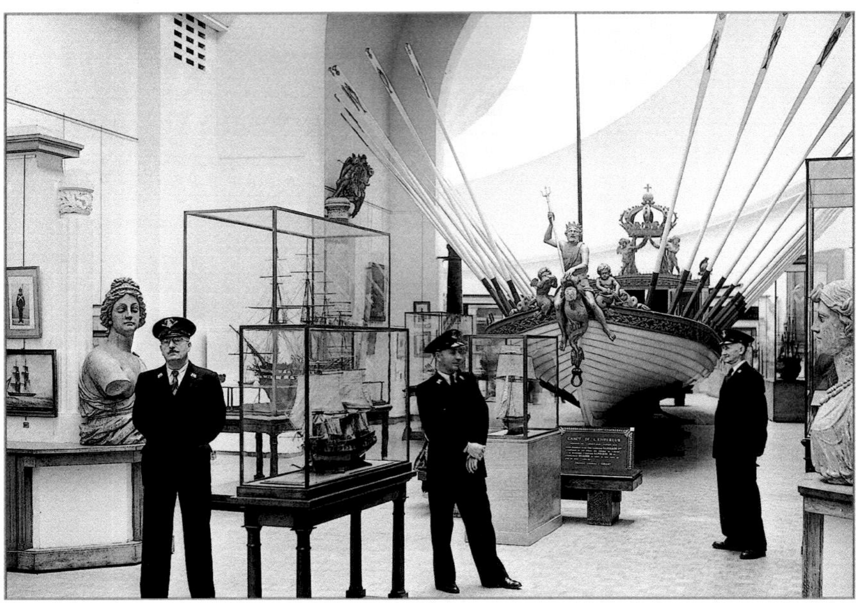

Anonymous
Attendants in uniform at the Musée National de la Marine
Circa 1950 . MnM PH 11508

The present day

Our predecessors made choices that have proven judicious. The museum is rightly proud to have conserved a considerable number of scientific instruments and maps from the past, a collection significantly enriched by deposits and transfers of items by the French navy's Hydrographical and Oceanographical Service, as well as sophisticated equipment from coastal lighthouses before their automation loaned to the museum by the Bureau des Phares et Balises in 1973. Maritime and shipbuilding companies have always supported the museum in the field of commercial and passenger shipping. Among these donators are the Compagnie des Messageries Maritimes in 1977, the Société d'Armement et de Navigation Charles-Schiaffino in 1991, and the Chargeurs Réunis in 2000. An exceptional donation was made by the Champigneulle family in 1997, in the form of Charles Champigneulle's preparatory work for the decoration of the ocean liner *Normandie*.

We are also indebted to Docteur Jean Pillet, whose enthusiasm, tenacity and extreme generosity enabled the opening in 2005 at Port-Louis of a room entirely dedicated to sea rescue. A new permanent exhibition space had already been opened at Port-Louis in 2002, 'Trésors d'Océans' (Ocean Treasures), devoted to underwater archaeology on the route to India, largely thanks to a major donation by Franck Goddio. Finally, since 1995, the museum has operated a policy of acquisitions to build up a collection of toys with a maritime theme. Following a number of isolated purchases, this project resulted in 2005 in the purchase of the Jac Remise collection.

Although in the last ten years the museum has chosen to focus on technical maritime heritage and so-called 'popular' art, it has not neglected its fine-arts collections. A increase in its budget enabled the acquisition of over thirty oil paintings, mostly genre scenes by minor masters of the 19th and 20th centuries. Drawings, prints and posters are regularly added to the collection. These works are systematically enhanced through restoration and presentation operations. This was the case for the collection of photographs relating to the national maritime heritage, recently disassociated from their strictly documentary context.

The maritime world and maritime techniques are continually evolving, in naval construction and technologies as well as ship design, means of navigation, port facilities and sea exploitation, to name but a few examples. The vocation of the Musée National de la Marine is to reflect this evolution through its exhibitions, and also through its collections. While continuing to enrich the latter with works and objects that evoke the past, the museum is acquiring contemporary records: a model of the aircraft carrier *Charles De Gaulle* and one of a recent container ship, for example. Likewise, the *Pen Duick V* was purchased by the museum in 1992. Éric Tabarly's historic boat, the prototype for several contemporary racing yachts, was restored with the support of the Fondation Jean-Pierre et Marie-Thérèse Le Roch–Les Mousquetaires. Today based at the national sailing school, it continues to sail and trains the skippers of tomorrow. Finally, a number of objets related to the construction of the liner *Queen Mary II* by the Chantiers de l'Atlantique have joined the museum's collections.

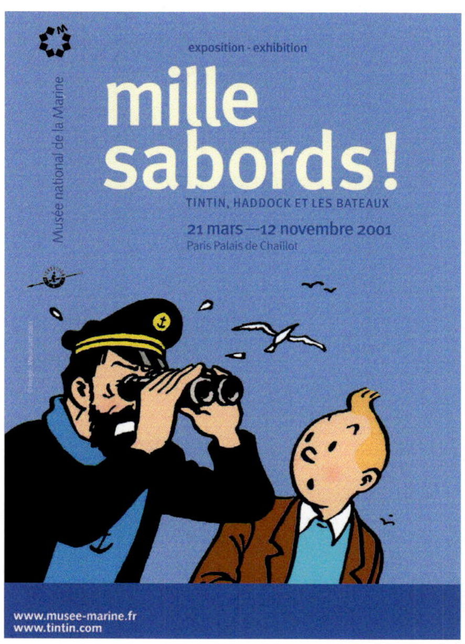

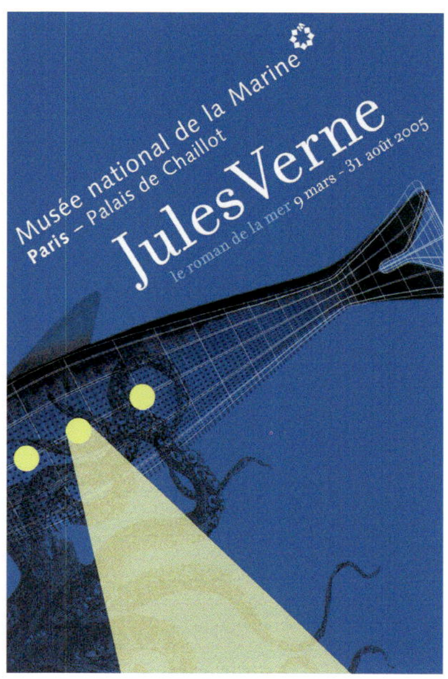

Two Musée National de la Marine exhibition posters
2001 and 2005

Shipyard models

Historical models constitute the jewel of the museum's collection of model ships, of which they are in many respects representative. These 350 or so models built in the 18th and 19th centuries, which all come from the shipyards or the navy ministry, exclusively represent French naval ships. Most of them are contemporary to the vessels they represent, hence their immense historical and aesthetic interest.

The construction of shipyard models served several purposes. The first models were made in the country's principal dockyards in the second half of the 17th century, at a time when ships were not built after drawings. Some of them served as a templates. More complete and more sophisticated prestige models followed during the 18th century. They were constructed to a uniform scale (1:36, 1:40 or 1:48 according to the period) at the same time as the real ships they represented, enabling architectural data to be recorded. Two or three centuries later, these models remain the chief documentary reference source for naval construction in this period.

Educational models were of a different kind. Made to a larger scale, they could be up to three or four meters in length. Designed to complete the training of students at the naval schools, they were used in the 18th and 19th centuries to teach the various parts of the ship, rigging, manoeuvres and related technical vocabulary.

From the mid-18th century on, these masterpieces of accuracy and craftsmanship, symbols of the industrial value of the dockyards and the power of the State, were also brought together in royal collections and other collections built up by enlightened scientists such as Duhamel du Monceau. For the gallery at the Palais de Trianon, Napoleon commissioned a series of models of the principal ships and vessels of his navy. This prestigious ensemble, built in precious materials, still goes by the name of the 'Trianon Collection'. Out of necessity as well as taste, the tradition of model making endured in the shipyards until the eve of the 20th century.

Le Louis Quinze

Model of a 110-gun ship, 1:36 scale ▪ Attributed to one of the shipyard model workshops ▪ Before 1720 ▪ Painted wood, gilded wood, cotton, bronze ▪ 216 x 220 x 95 cm ▪ Entered museum collections 1830, former Salle de Marine Collection ▪ MnM 9 MG 1

With its three superposed battery decks, this model is representative of the largest ships in the late 17th century. These enormous vessels carried the command of the squadron, made up primarily of smaller ships and frigates. Despite several archaic details, this model was crafted to a high level of accuracy, and its lavish, highly symbolic ornamentation reflected the prestige of the French royal navy. It was used in the 1720s for the education of the young Louis XV. H. T.

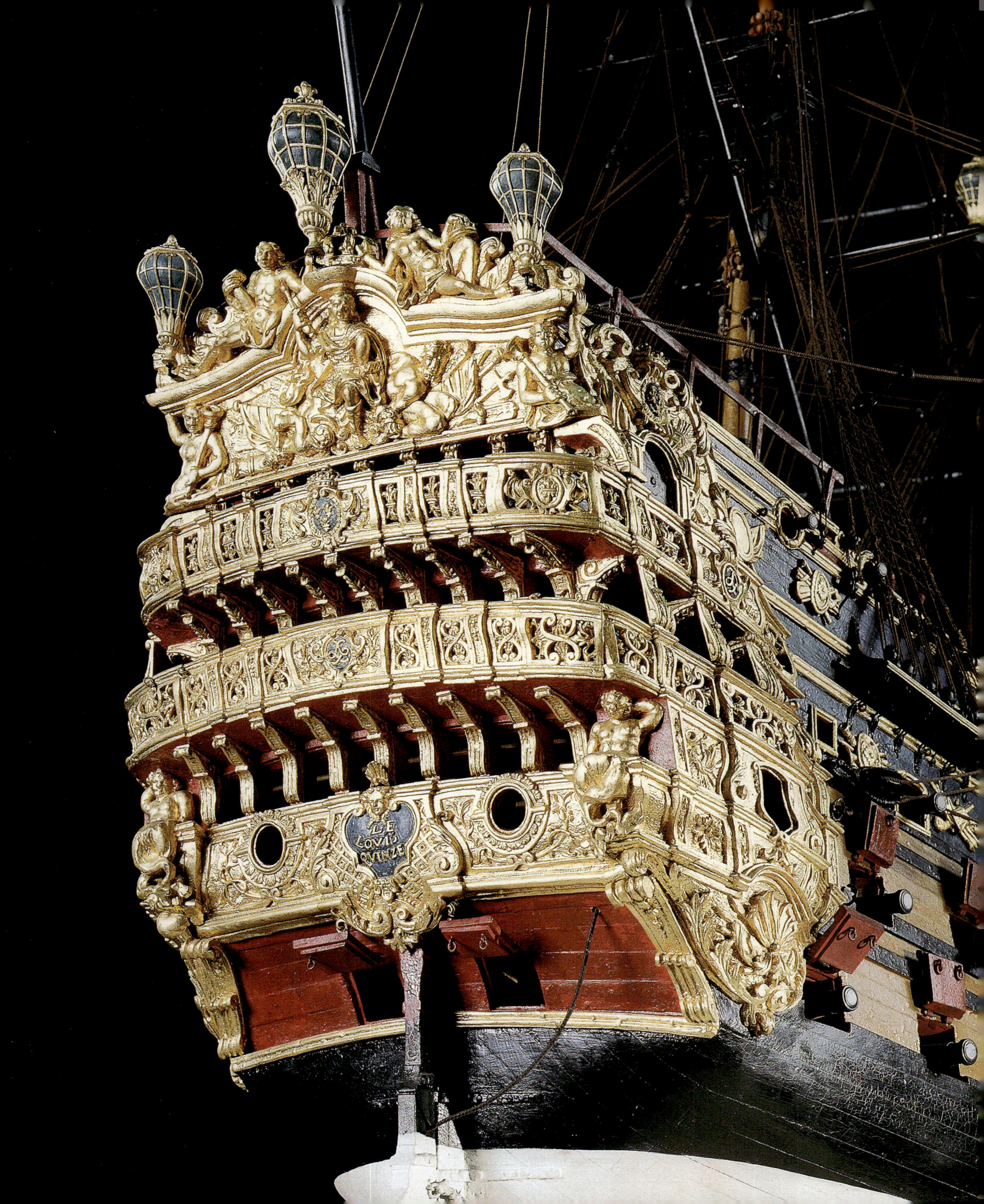
LE
LOVIS
QVINZE

Le Royal Louis

Model of a 124-gun ship, 1:18 scale . Attributed to the Brest dockyard model workshop . Circa 1770 . Wood, bronze, iron, brass, cotton . 445 x 520 x 240 cm . Entered museum collections 1949, former collection of the Brest dockyard . MnM 13 MG 32

Made for the training of officers at the 'Gardes de la Marine' school in Brest, this very large model with a closed hull shows the details of the rigging. It has pivots at the bow and stern which enabled it to be tilted for teaching purposes. It was based on a real three-deck ship, the *Royal Louis*, launched in Brest in 1759. H. T.

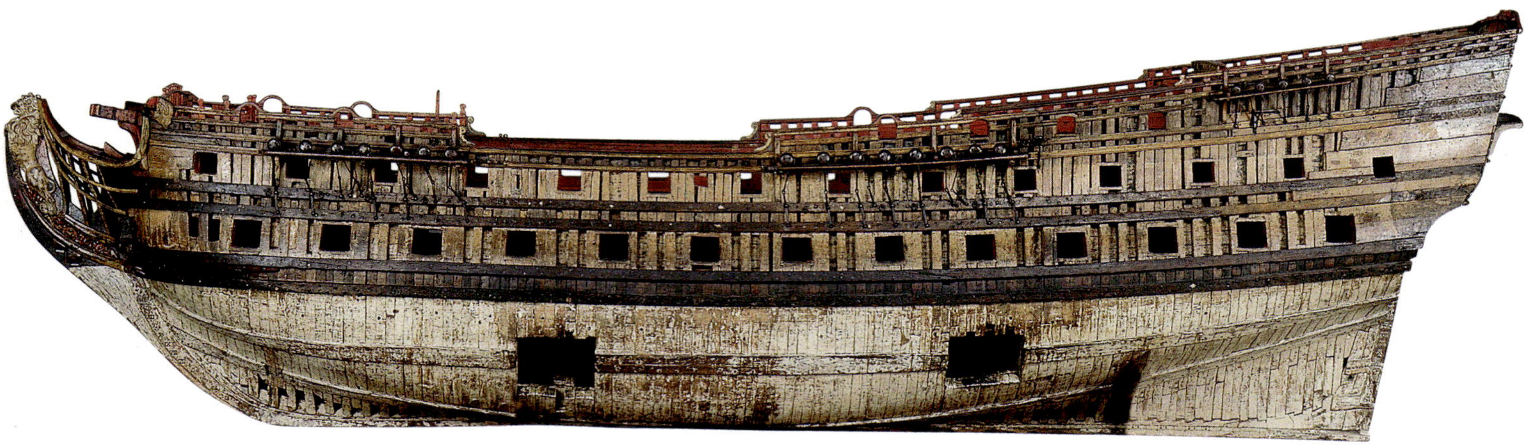

Le Royal

Unrigged model of a 74-gun ship, 1:12 scale . Constructed at the Rochefort dockyard by the model workshop . Circa 1720 . Wood, brass, iron . 134 x 461 x 115 cm . Entered museum collections 1953, former collection of the Rochefort dockyard . MnM 13 MG 34

In the 18th century, two-deck 74-gun ships were the most commonly used in Europe. This large-scale model has an open hull on the port side to show the details of the frame, reproduced with great accuracy. It was made for the instruction of naval officer students at the 'Gardes de la Marine' school in Rochefort. H. T.

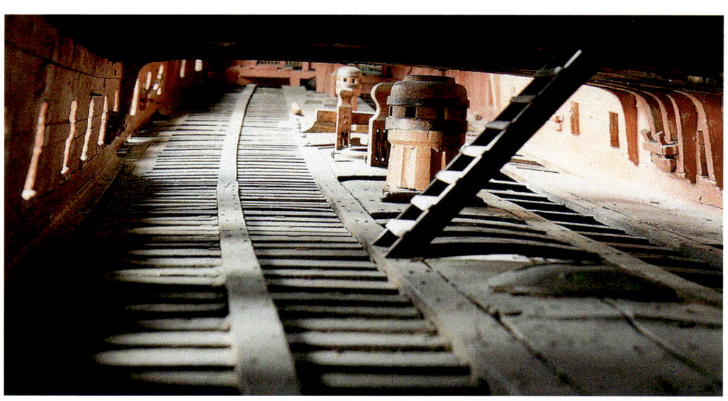

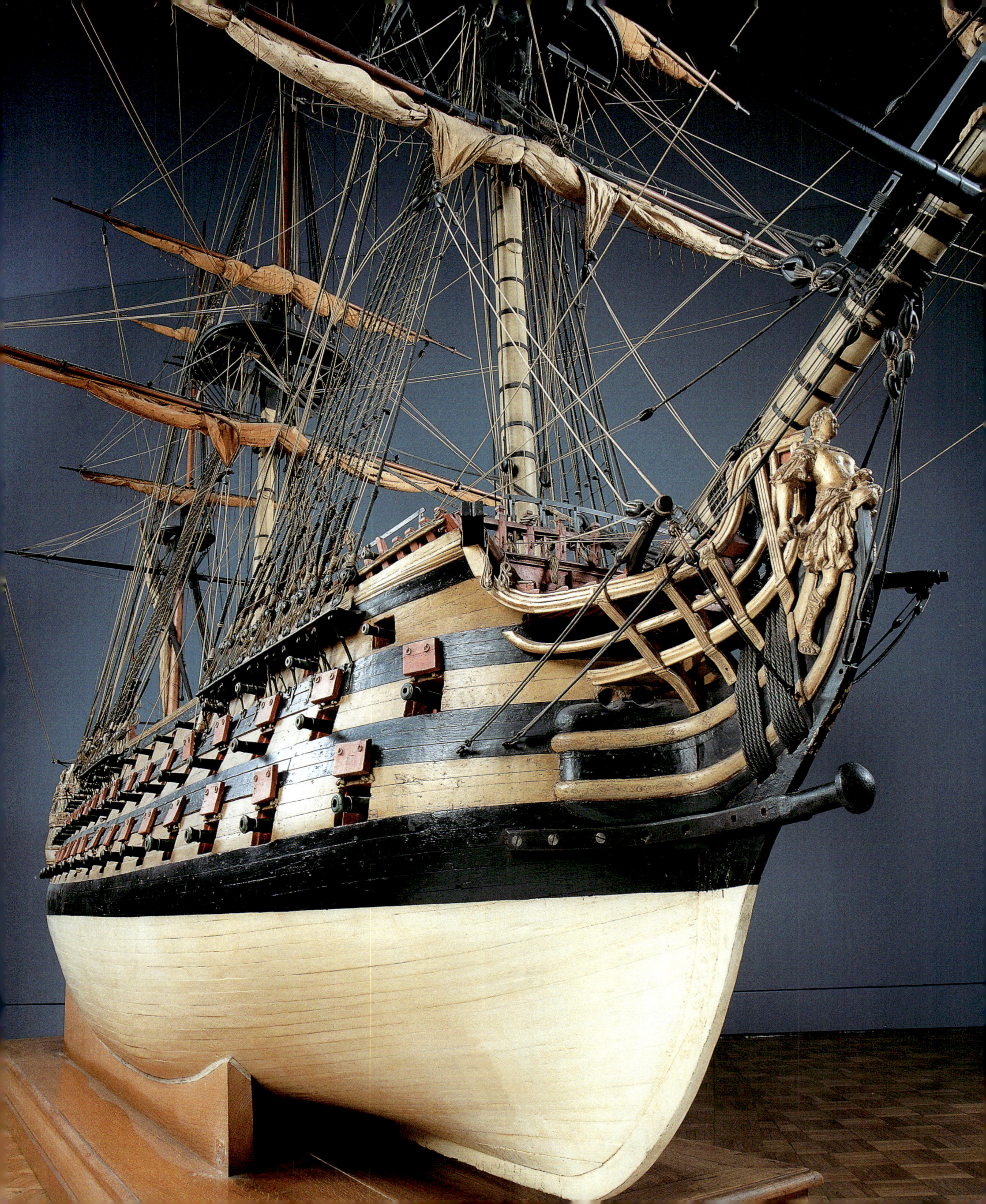

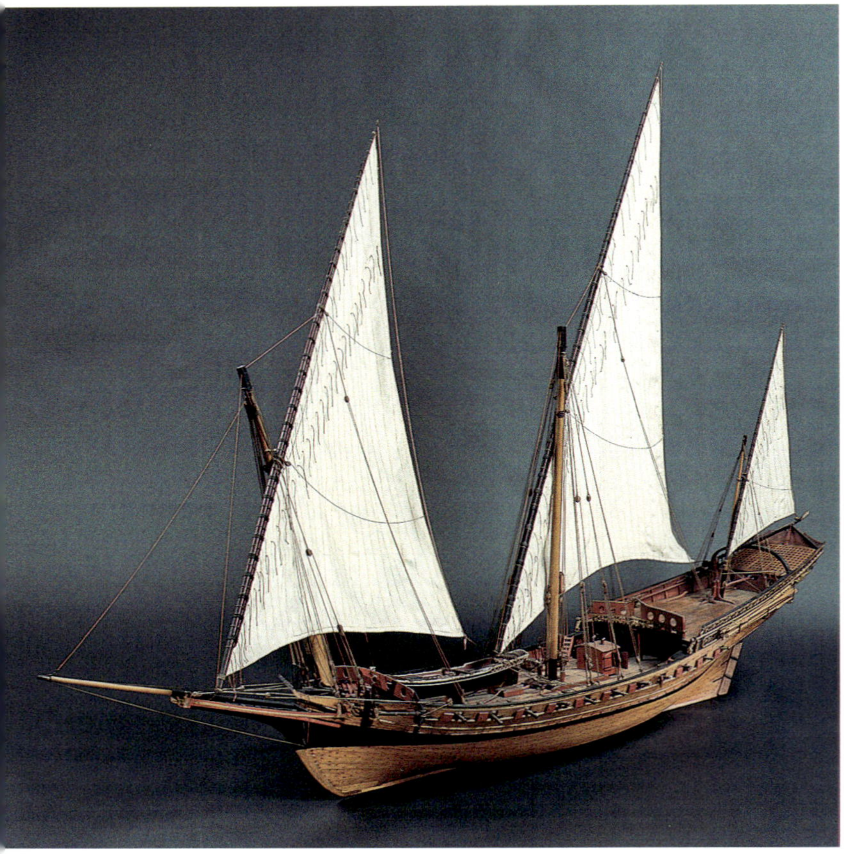

24-gun xebec

Model of a xebec, probably *Le Requin* launched in Toulon in around 1750, 1:24 scale . Constructed at the Toulon dockyard model workshop . Circa 1750 . Wood, cotton, bronze, brass . 153 x 213 x 47 cm . Entered museum collections 1830, former Salle de Marine and Trianon Collections . MnM 13 MG 13

Xebecs are small Mediterranean ships with a characteristic shape, much used in the 17th and 18th centuries by Barbary Coast pirates. Slim, fast and easy to manoeuvre, they could be both sail- and oar-powered.

In 1750, with a view to protecting French trade, the construction of four xebecs was begun in the port of Toulon, under the supervision of specialised shipbuilders from Majorca. This high-quality model is a reproduction of one of them. It is a rare and precise illustration of what was a new vessel for the royal navy at the time. H. T.

La Minerve (below and facing page)

Model of an 'ordinary' galley, 1:25 scale . Constructed by Augustin Pic (1722–after 1780) . 1741–1746 . Wood, cotton, brass . 130 x 227 x 37 cm . Entered museum collections 1836 . MnM Paris 3 MG 4

A youthful work of Augustin Pic, this model was finished in 1746 at Marseilles, where the royal galleys were based. Pic led a rather mediocre career as a shipwright in the dockyards, but excelled in the art of constructing models. He made remarkable reproductions of ships he dreamed of building, which explains why he signed and dated this galley near the prow, on a small silver plaque. H. T.

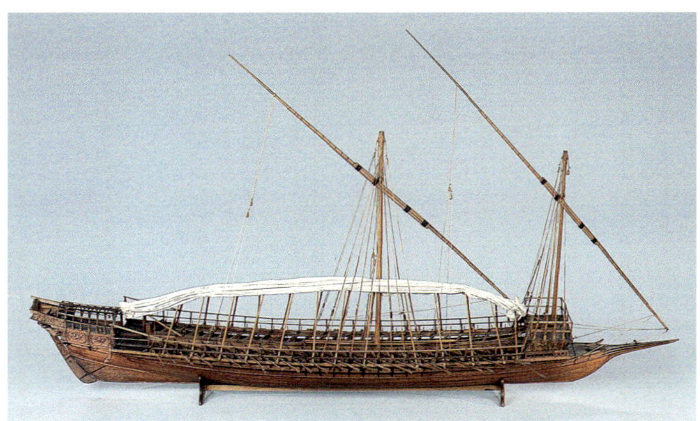

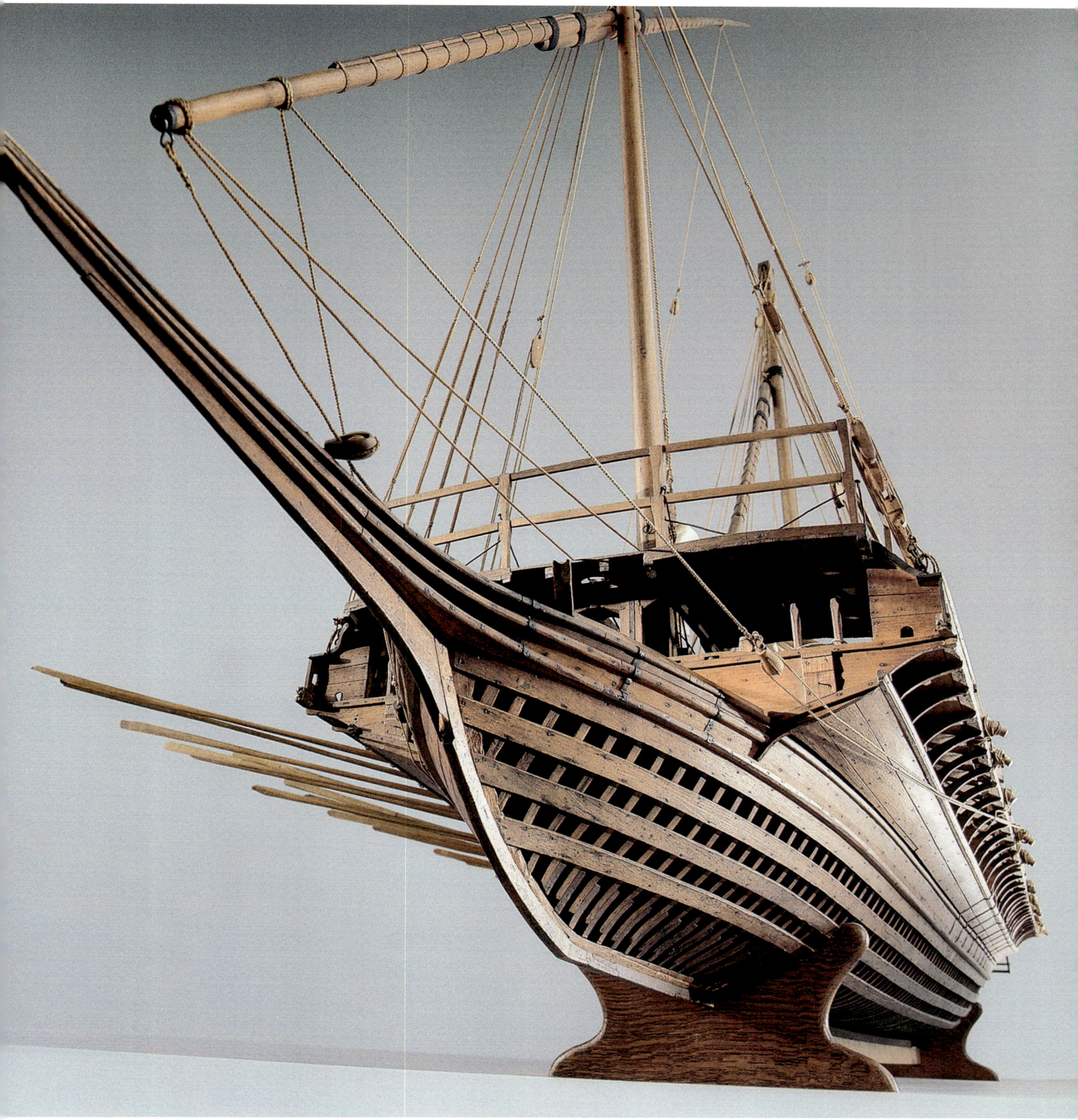

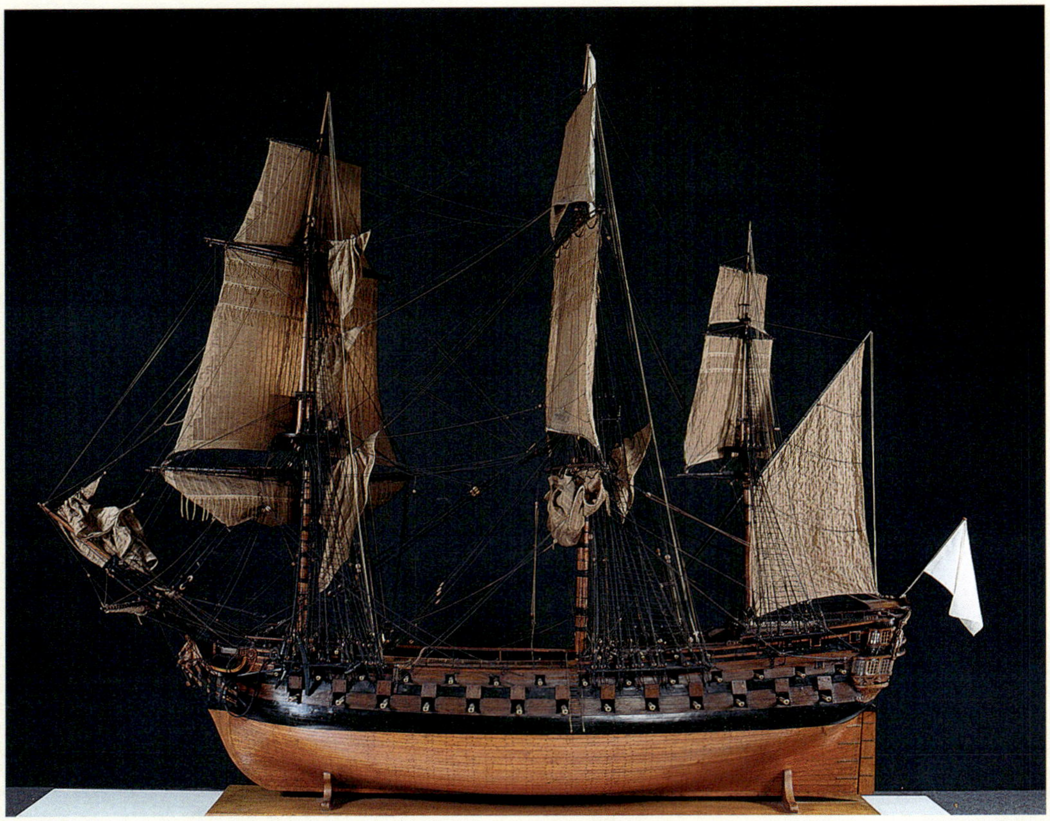

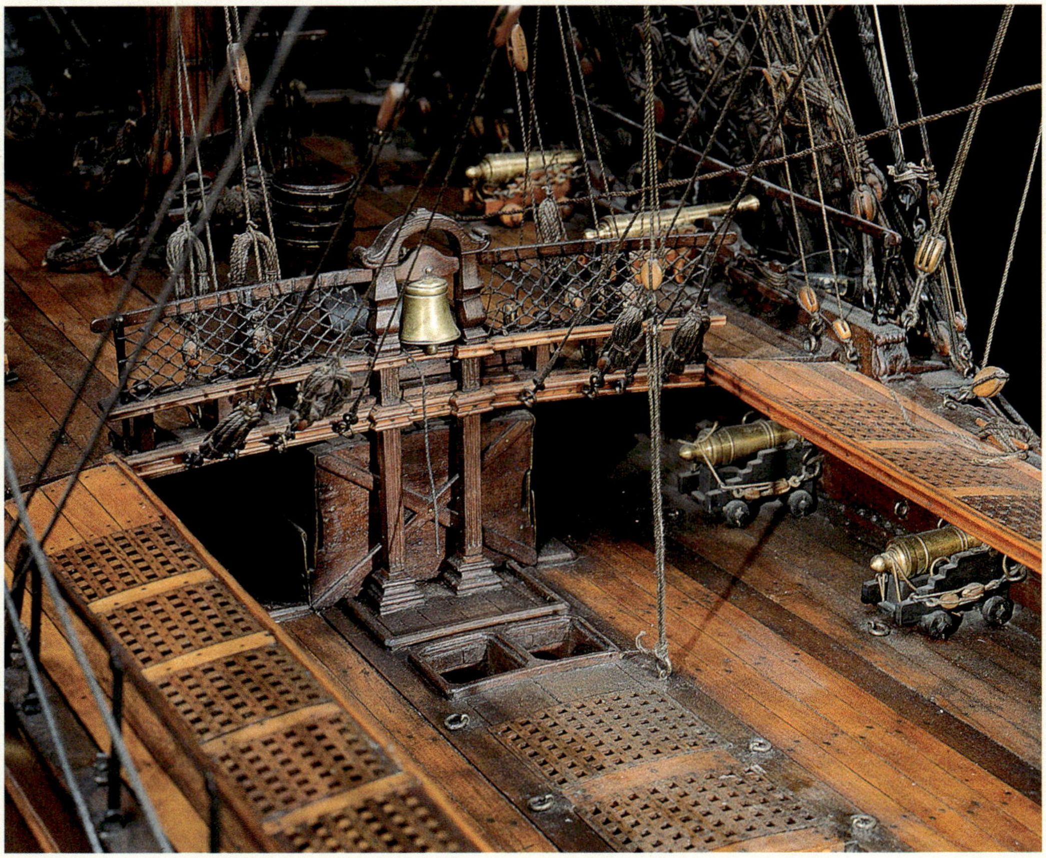

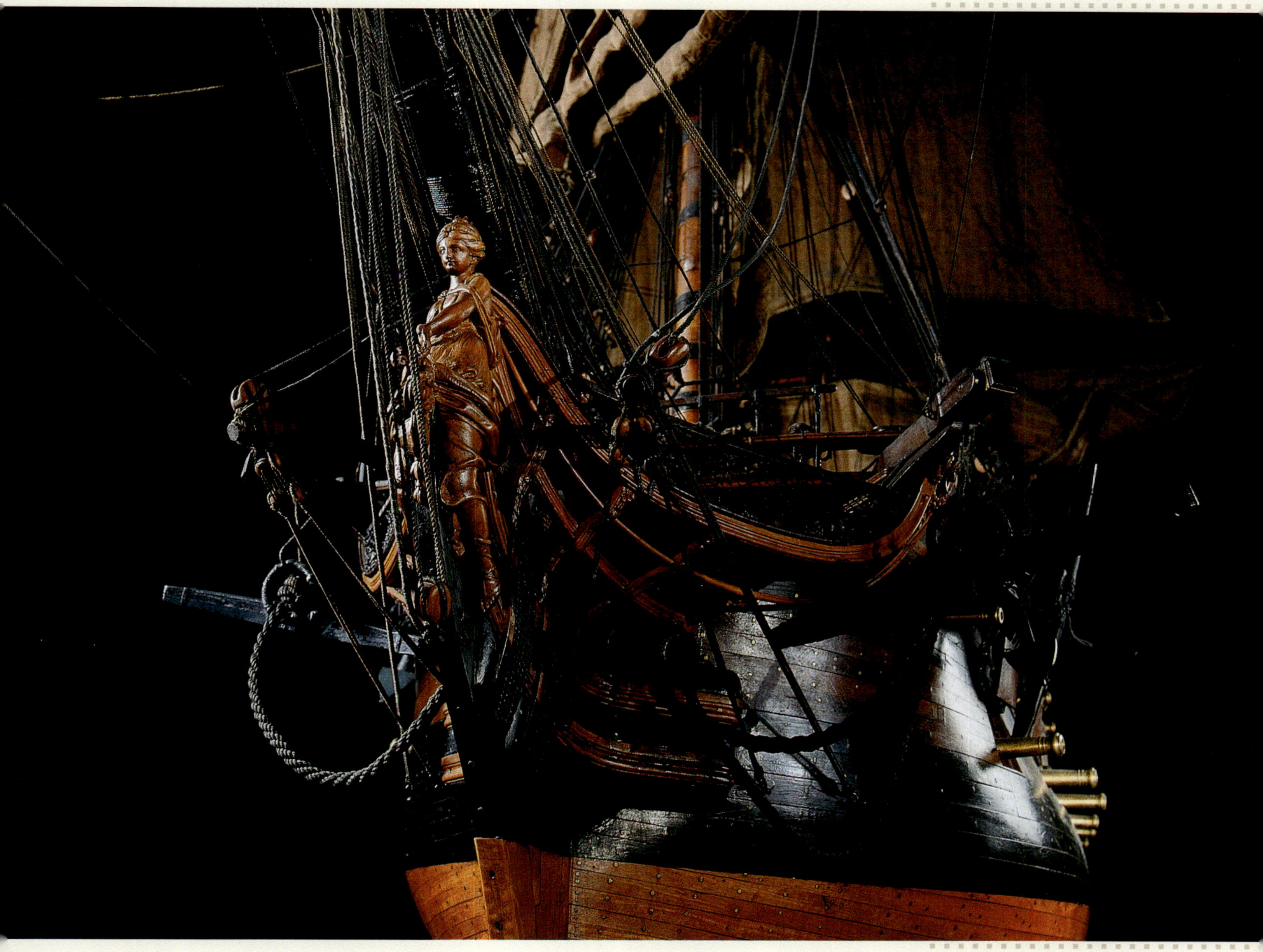

L'Artésien

Model of a 64-gun ship launched in Brest in 1765, 1:36 scale ▪ Constructed by Sébastien Cupin (fl. mid-18th century) and the Brest dockyard model workshop, after drawings by the shipbuilder Joseph Ollivier (1729–1777) ▪ Circa 1764 ▪ Wood, cotton, brass, bronze, iron ▪ 211 x 260 x 92 cm ▪ Entered museum collections 1828, former Trianon Collection ▪ MnM 13 MG 3

The 64-gun ship *L'Artésien* was presented to the king by the States of Artois and Flanders in the context of the effort to rebuild the royal navy. This model was sent to Versailles in 1765, probably as an official gift. It could originally be entirely dismantled, and was a marvellous teaching aid. Nicolas Ozanne, a naval draughtsman, used it from 1769 onwards in lessons he gave to the future Louis XVI and his brothers. **H. T.**

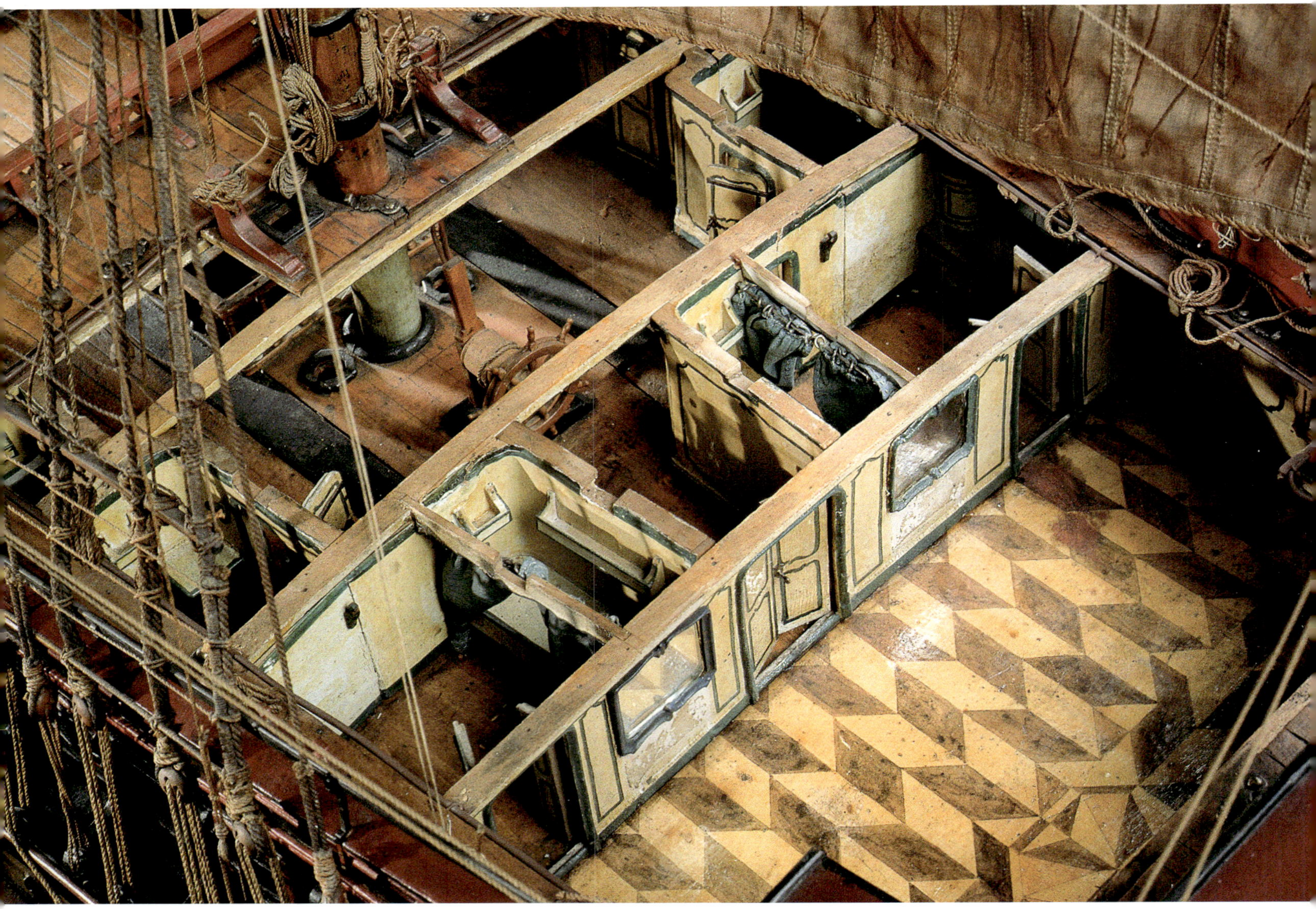

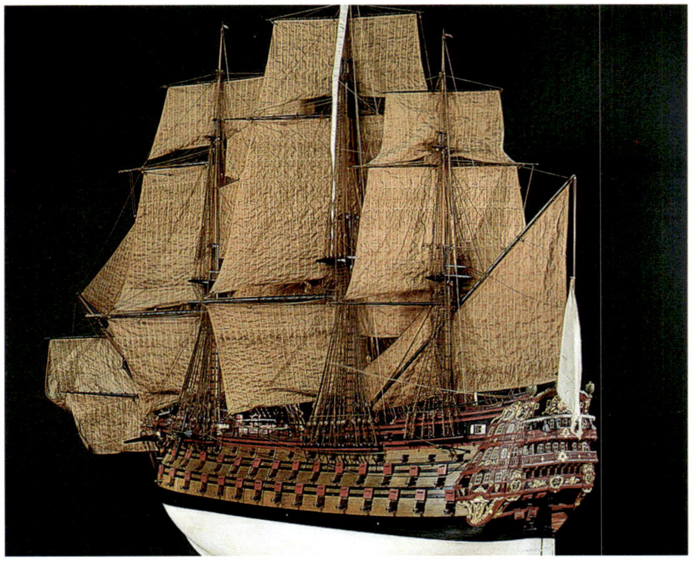

Le Sans-Pareil

Model of a 108-gun ship from the 1760s, 1:30 scale . Attributed to the Toulon dockyard model workshop . Second half of 18th century . Wood, cotton, brass, iron . 230 x 285 x 80 cm . Entered museum collections 1829–1830 . MnM 13 MG 1

Purchased by the French State in 1794 from a private individual for the 'Musée de la République', the model of the *Sans-Pareil* provides evidence of a project for a ship that was never built. The delicacy and accuracy with which it is executed, the complete sails and rigging, and the open hull on the port side showing the details of the fittings and stowage all put this model in a class of its own. The deck can be dismantled to show the officers' quarters. H. T.

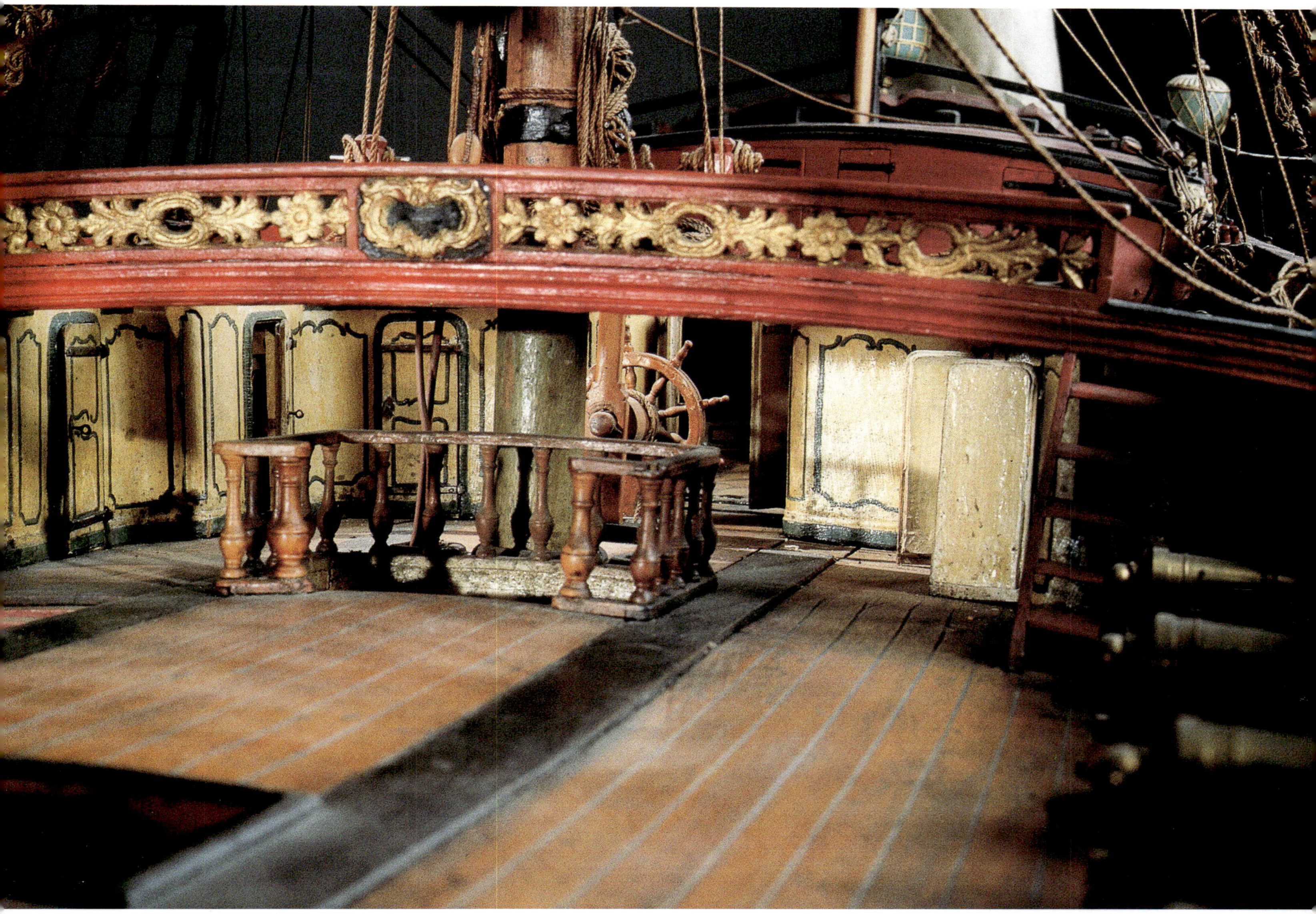

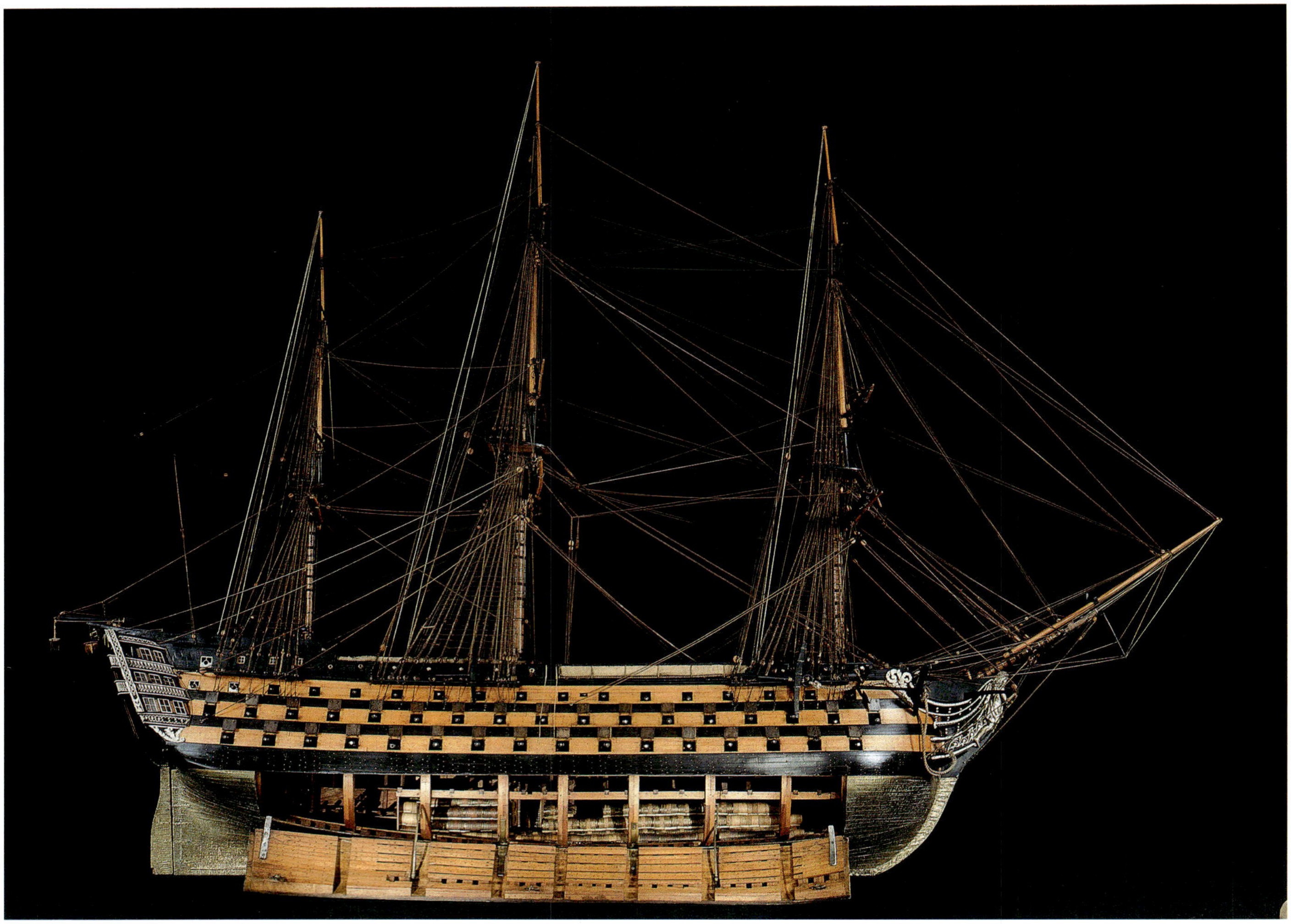

L'Océan

Model of a 118-gun ship launched at Brest in 1790, 1:48 scale ▪ Constructed by the Brest dockyard model workshop after drawings by the engineer Jacques Noël Sané (1740–1831) ▪ Before 1793 ▪ Wood, cotton, ivory, ebony, copper, brass ▪ 155 x 210 x 78 cm ▪ Entered museum collections 1828, former Trianon Collection ▪ MnM 13 MG 20

This model has an illustrious story to tell. Built in Brest at the end of the Ancien Régime, it was transferred to the Convention Nationale in Paris in 1793, and selected in 1810 to be displayed in the gallery of models that Napoleon had ordered for the Palais de Trianon at Versailles. On this occasion it was transformed by model makers from the shipyards who worked at a studio that had been set up in Paris especially for the purpose. The model was restored and adapted to show modifications carried out in 1804 on the ship itself. The use of ebony and ivory in the decor reflects the valuable nature of this collection created for the emperor.

L'Océan illustrates the peak of French shipbuilding in the late 18th century, a period when France, in the light of lessons learnt from the American War of Independence, was building up a powerful, modern navy, thanks to the adoption of standard construction drawings that were used until the late 1840s. H. T.

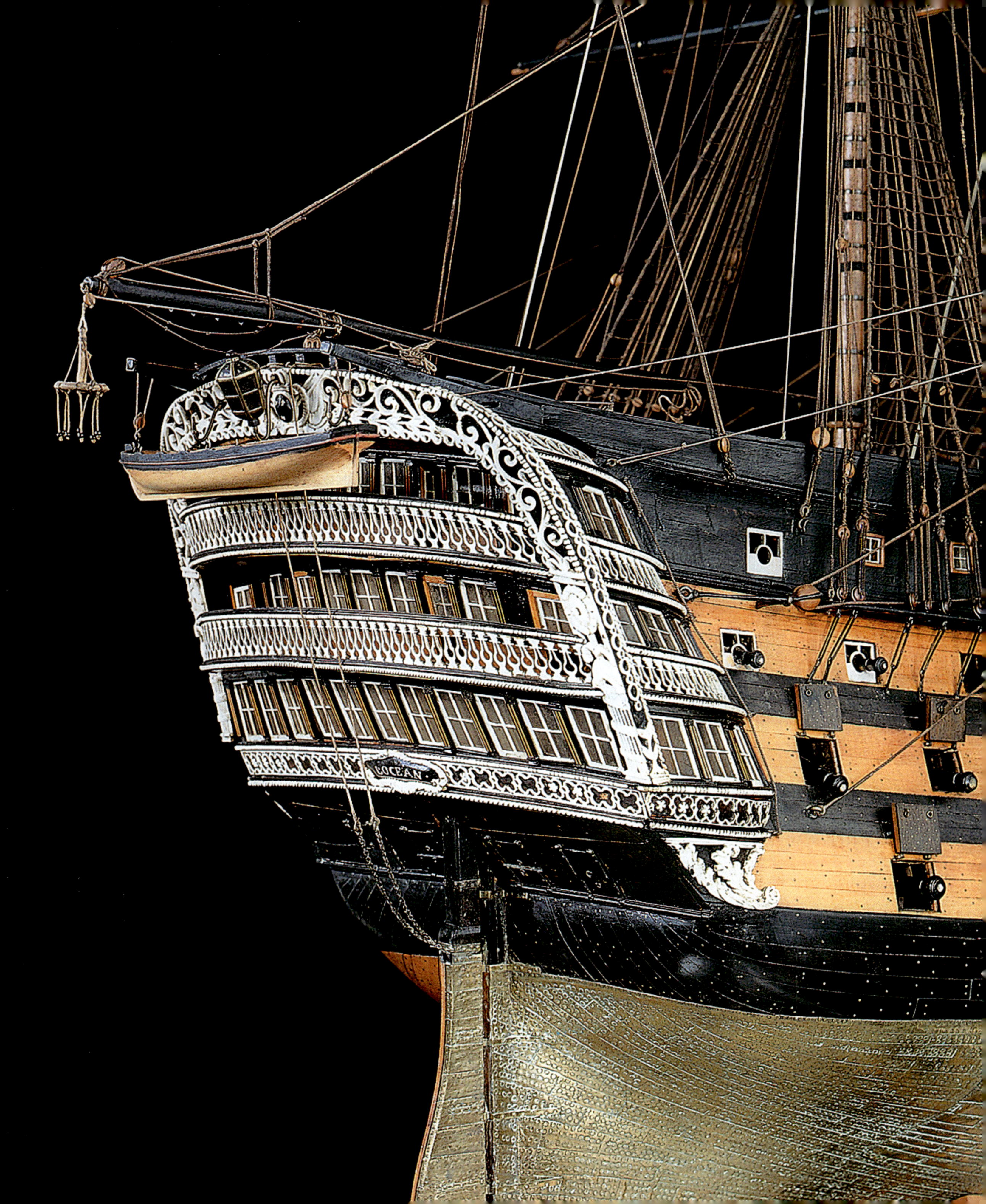
LOCEAN

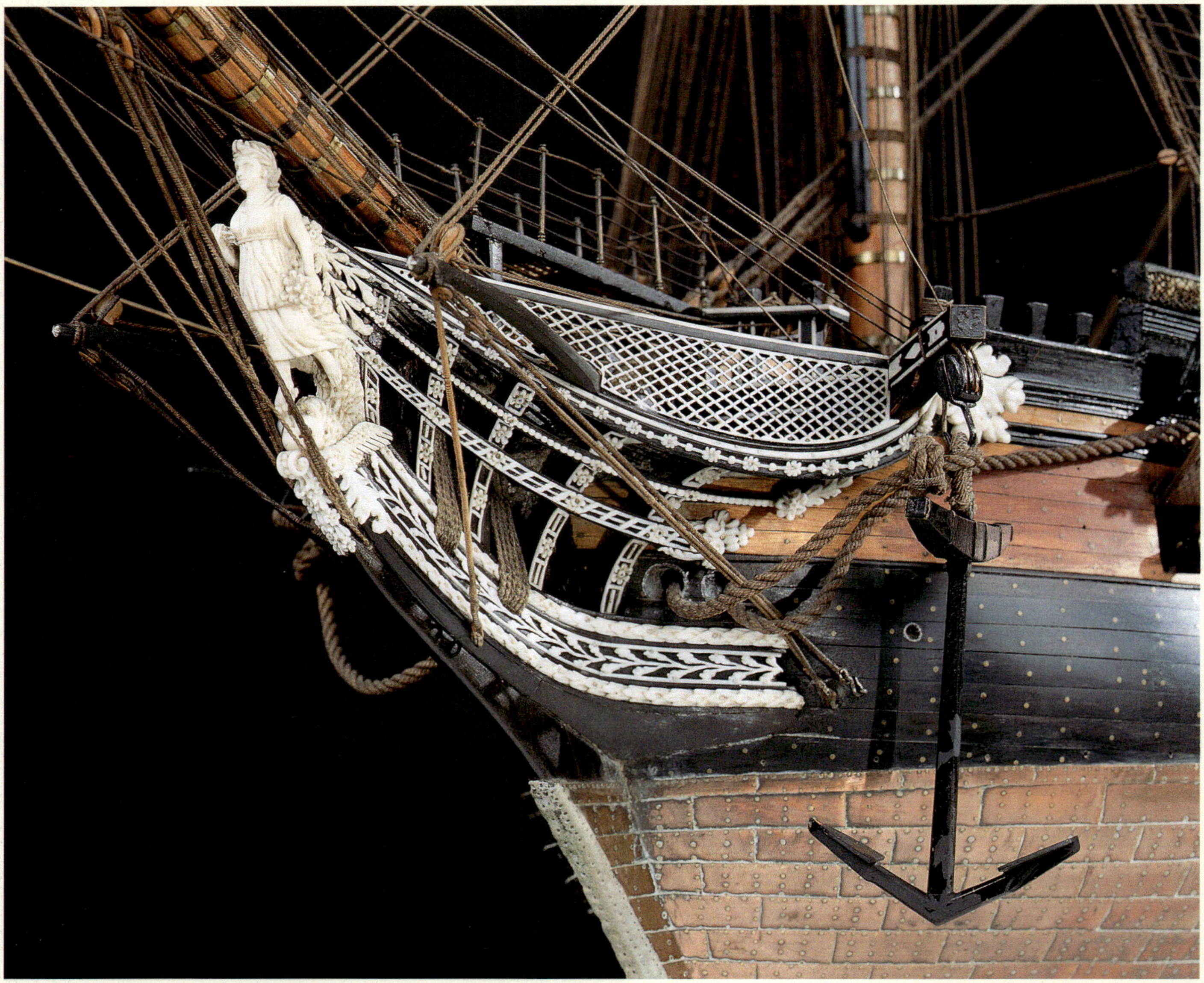

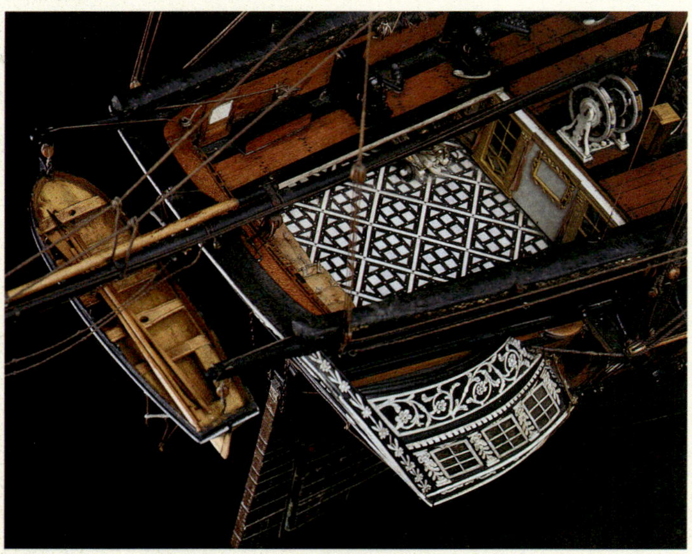

La Flore

Model of the 44-gun frigate launched at Rochefort in 1806, 1:48 scale . Constructed by the model workshop in Paris after drawings by the engineer Pierre Rolland . 1816 . Wood, cotton, ivory, ebony, brass . 124 x 169 x 56 cm . Entered museum collections 1828, former Trianon Collection . MnM 17 MG 10

In keeping with the quality and particular style of the models made for the model gallery at Trianon, *La Flore* was constructed to a high degree of technical accuracy. Its finely carved ivory ornamentation and certain remarkable details, such as the large chamber in gilded wood with ivory and ebony inlay, make it truly a work of art. This model served to represent the frigates armed with 18-pound cannons that were characteristic of the French navy under the Empire. H. T.

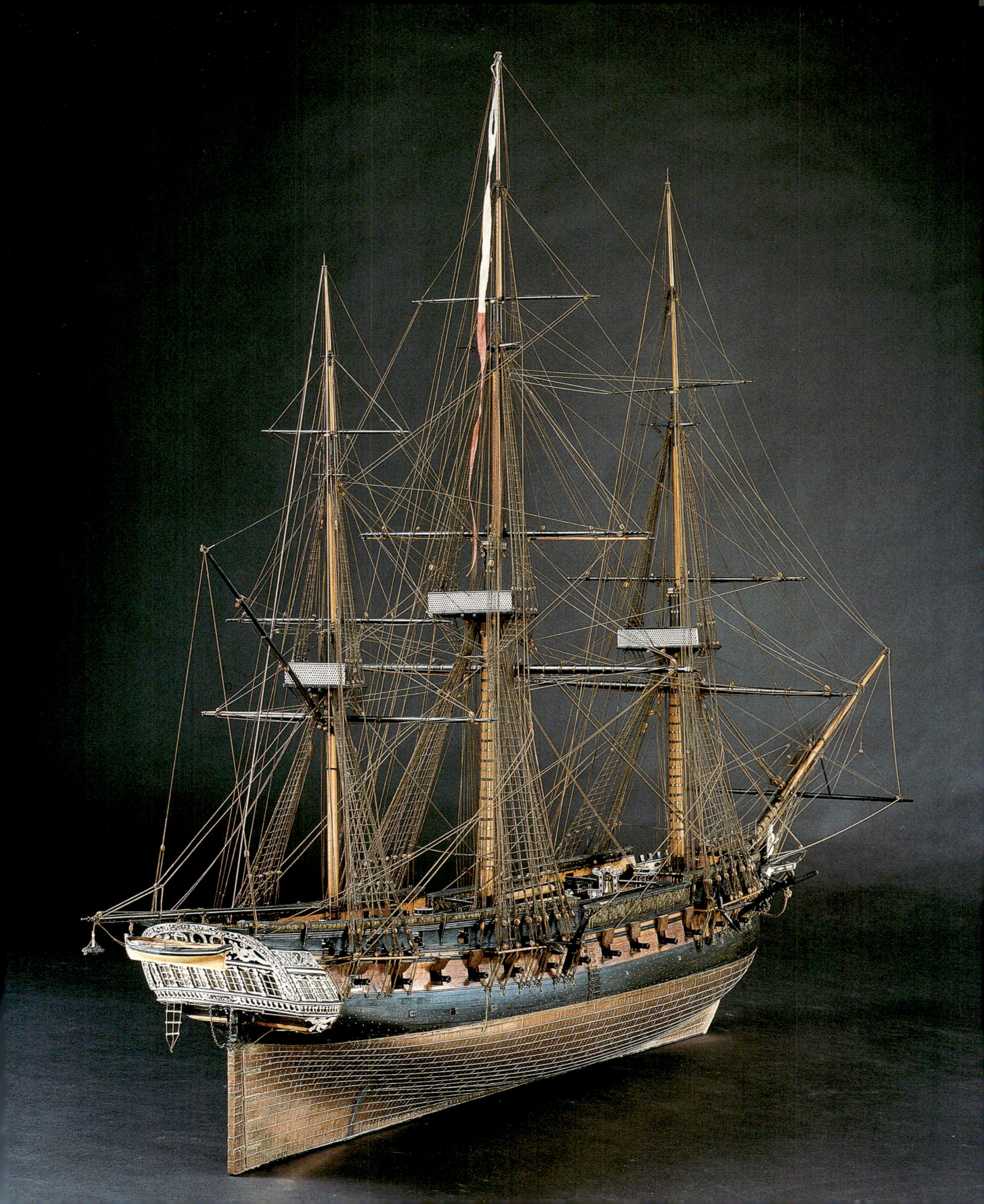

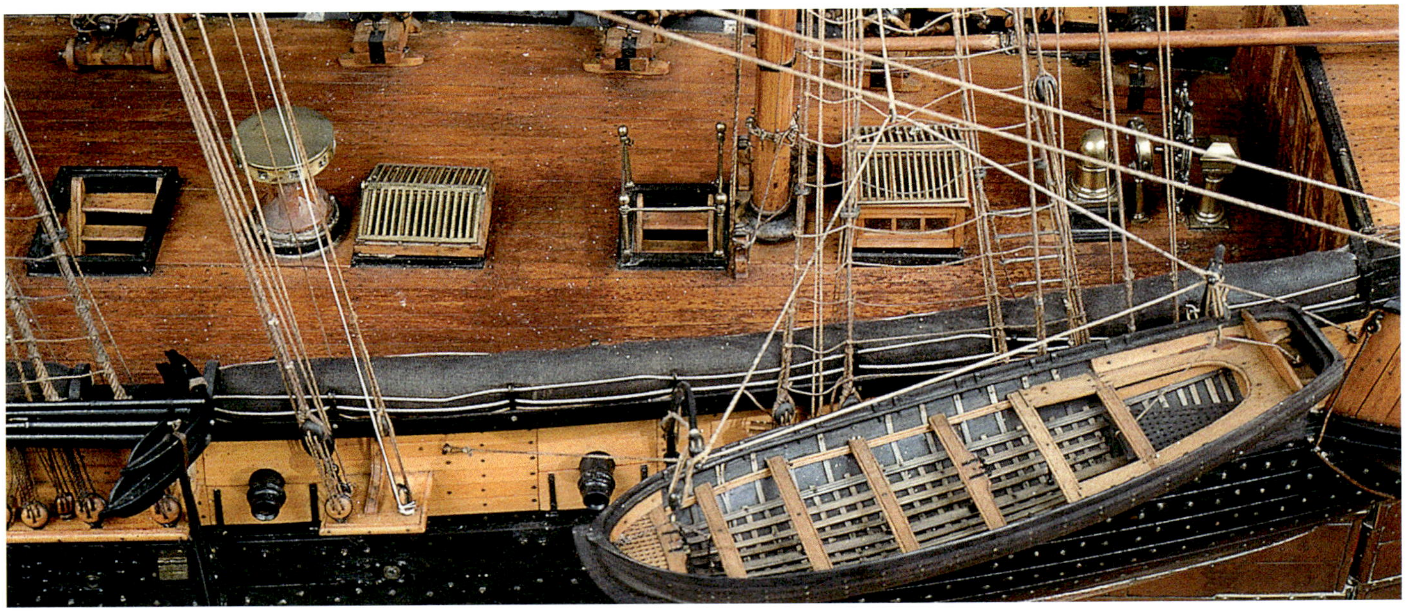

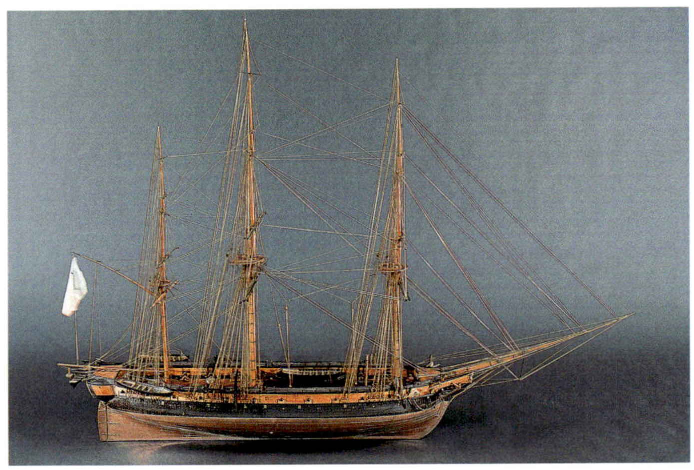

The *Créole*

Model of a 24-gun corvette launched at Cherbourg in 1829, 1:40 scale . Constructed by the Cherbourg dockyard model workshop after drawings by the engineer Pierre Leroux . Circa 1828 . Wood, ebony, copper, brass . 122 x 166 x 56 cm . Entered museum collections 1829–1830 . MnM 21 MG 25

The model of the *Créole*, built at the same time as the corvette of which it is a reproduction, shows many finely executed technical details, such as a new type of helm, visible on the deck. It illustrates the exceptional documentary value of the shipyard models, as well as the virtuosity of the model makers. H. T.

The *Belle Poule*

Model of a 60-gun frigate launched at Cherbourg in 1834, 1:40 scale . Constructed by the Cherbourg dockyard model workshop after drawings by the engineer Mathurin Boucher . Second quarter of 19th century . Wood, bronze, iron, brass, cotton . 165 x 240 x 85 cm . Entered museum collections 1844 . MnM 21 MG 16

In 1840, the *Belle Poule* was sent to Saint Helena to bring back the ashes of Napoleon, under the command of the Prince de Joinville, third son of Louis-Philippe. On the occasion of this funerary mission, the entire outside of the hull above the waterline was painted black. This is how the ship is shown in the Musée National de la Marine model, which is of great symbolical and technical value. It stood with the model of the *Créole* in the Prince de Joinville's study at the Palais des Tuileries, before it was transferred to the museum in 1848. H. T.

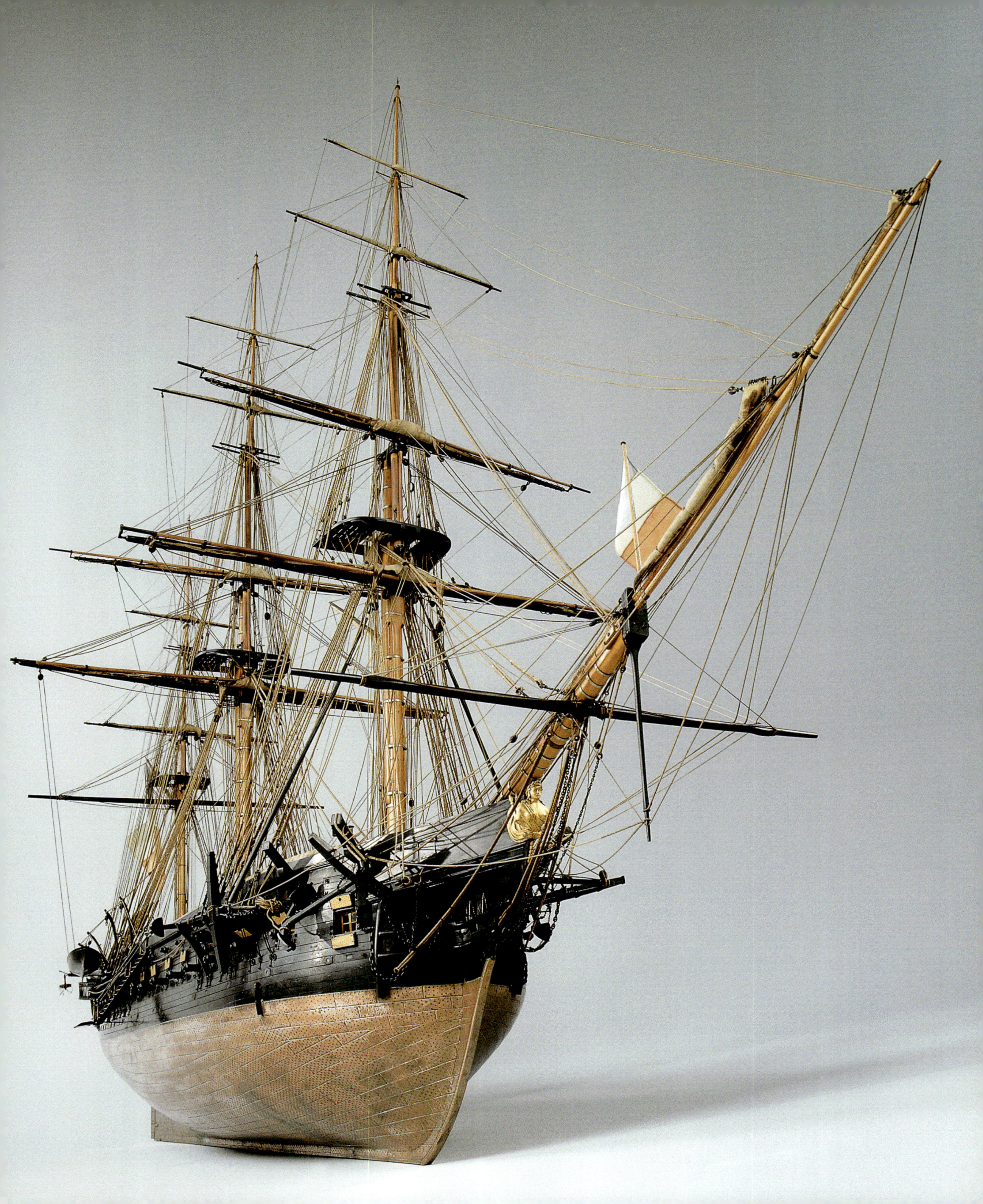

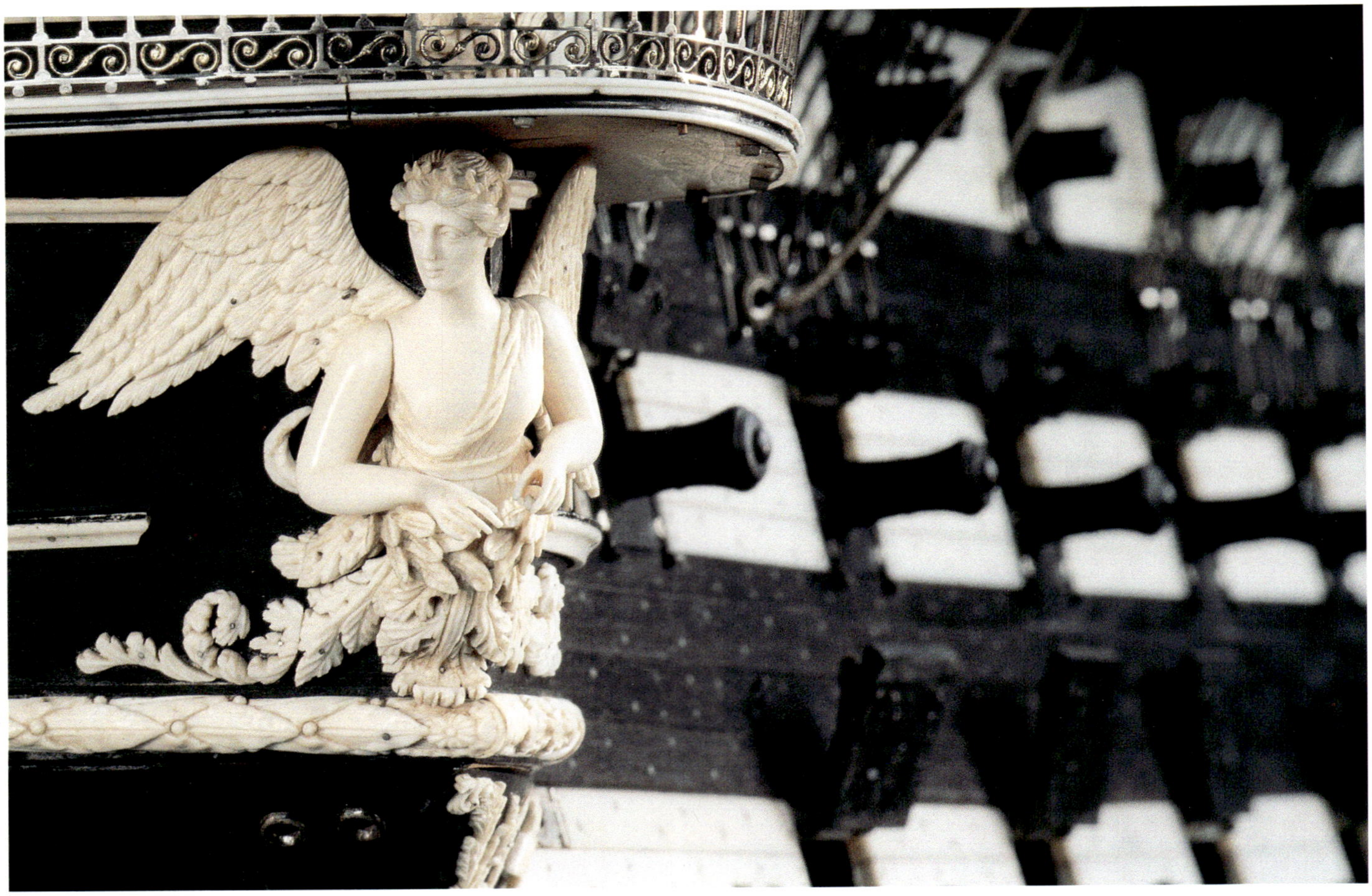

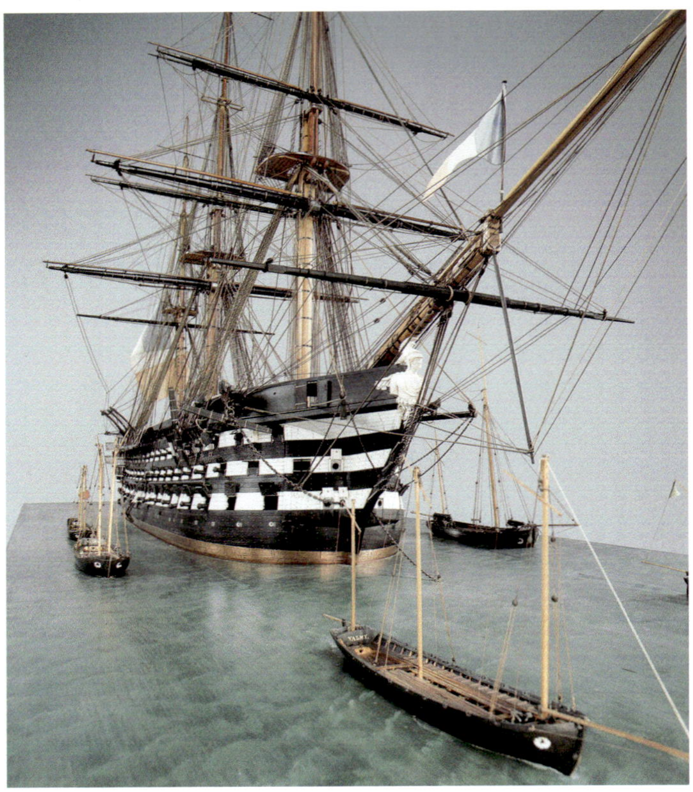

The *Valmy*

Rigged model of a 120-gun ship launched at Brest in 1847, 1:40 scale . Constructed by the Brest dockyard model workshop after drawings by the engineer Pierre Leroux . 1838–1842 . Wood, cotton, ebony, ivory, silver . 210 x 281 x 92 cm . Entered museum collections 1842 . MnM 21 MG 4

The *Valmy* was the last triple-deck ship in the sail-powered navy. On its construction, two models were made in Brest, exceptional in the quality of their workmanship and the precious materials used. It took six shipyard craftsmen five years to complete them. The one shown here is a reconstruction of the complete ship, with its rigging and ten regulation boats. The other was a building model, with an open hull revealing the interior arrangements of the ship.

The rigged model of the *Valmy* reflects the educational approach of the museum developed by Amiral Pâris, curator of the Musée de la Marine from 1871 to 1893. It was at this time that the model was placed 'in context' on an artificial sea, surrounded by its launches and boats. H. T.

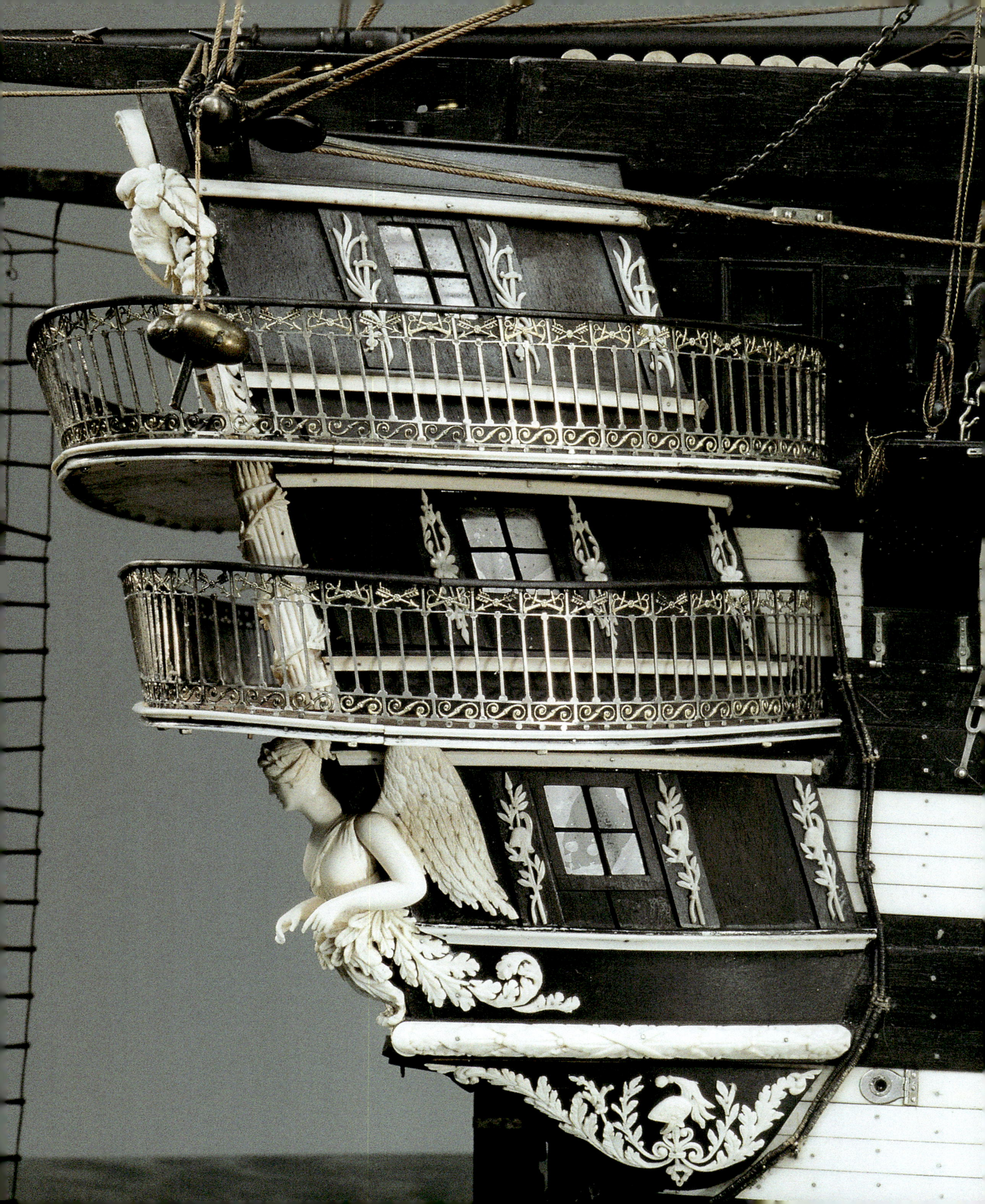

Naval decoration

For the greater glory of the king, emperor or nation, naval sculpture, which includes not only figureheads but also sumptuous stern decors and ornamentation for ceremonial barges, drew largely from mythological, allegorical and historical themes. It was in France, between the reigns of Louis XIV and Louis-Philippe, that this rich, refined form of decoration became an art in its own right. It is no surprise, therefore, that the Musée National de la Marine houses the largest collection of naval sculpture in the world.

This collection is remarkable in the quality and diversity of the works conserved. From preparatory drawings to finished decors, it illustrates the genesis of this art form. The museum notably possesses wax figures, the oldest of which date back to the 1750s. Despite their extreme fragility, these rare projects for ship carvings have stood the test of time, while the decors for which they served as models have disappeared for ever. A major piece in the museum, the stern ornamentation of the galley *Réale*, executed in the late 17th century and contemporary to the great decors at Versailles, was a symbol of royal power.

After engaging the services of Puget and Le Brun, Colbert summoned the most illustrious decorator of the time, the court artist Jean Bérain. Bérain drew up a decorative scheme for the king's ships characterised by harmonious proportions and the use of allegorical references. Ship carvings were subject to very particular constraints: firstly, this was an ephemeral art form, for it was usually destined to disappear with the ship it adorned; secondly, the weight and position of the decorations should not hamper the ship's manoeuvres; finally, the ornamentation had to be visible from afar, whence the exaggerated lines and use of gilt and paint.

These monumental, highly refined pieces created in the naval dockyards between the 17th and 19th centuries, the only vestiges of ships of the past, compel our admiration and respect.

After Jean Mathias (?–1706)
Sculpture workshop at the Marseilles dockyard

Stern ornamentation of the galley *Réale*

1688 and 1694 . Bas-reliefs and sculptures in the round, gilded walnut, lime and poplar . Entered museum collections 1830 . MnM 37 OA 5

This sculptural ensemble, miraculously preserved from the ravages of the sea and time, is representative of the style of ship decoration in the time of Louis XIV, when it served to 'shine forth at sea the magnificence of His Majesty'. Here, the pictorial scheme centres on the figure of Apollo, god of Light, who reigns over the seasons as the Sun King reigned over the world. The frequent use of this metaphor in diverse forms reached its height on the French ship *Réale*. M. M.

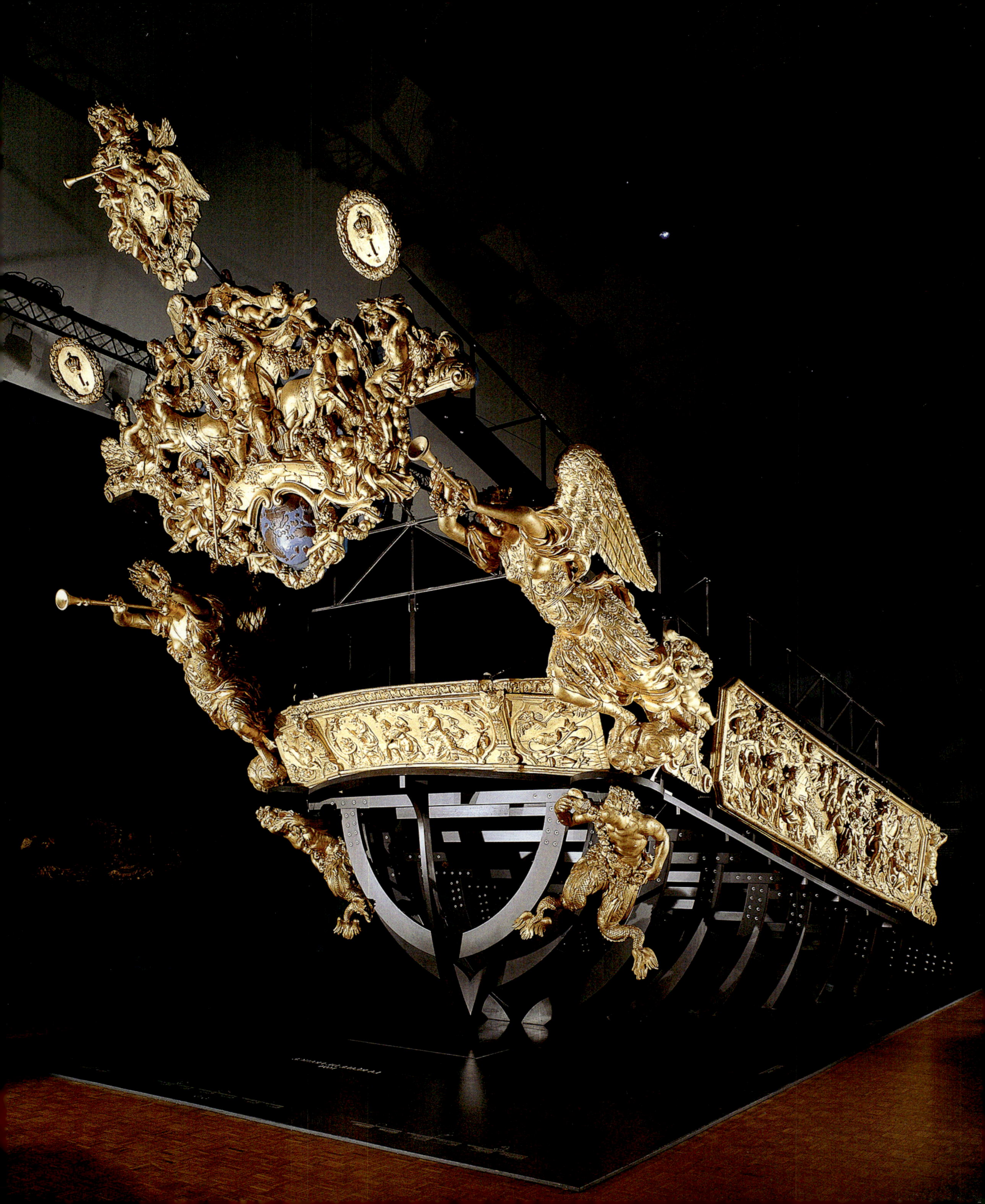

Attributed to François Caravaque (?–1698)
After Jean Mathias (?–1706)
Sculpture workshop at the Marseilles dockyard

Triton Blowing a Conch

**Stern ornament (left side) from the galley *Réale* . 1694 .
Sculpture in the round, gilded walnut . 160 x 110 x 58 cm .
Entered museum collections 1830 . MnM 37 OA 5.3**

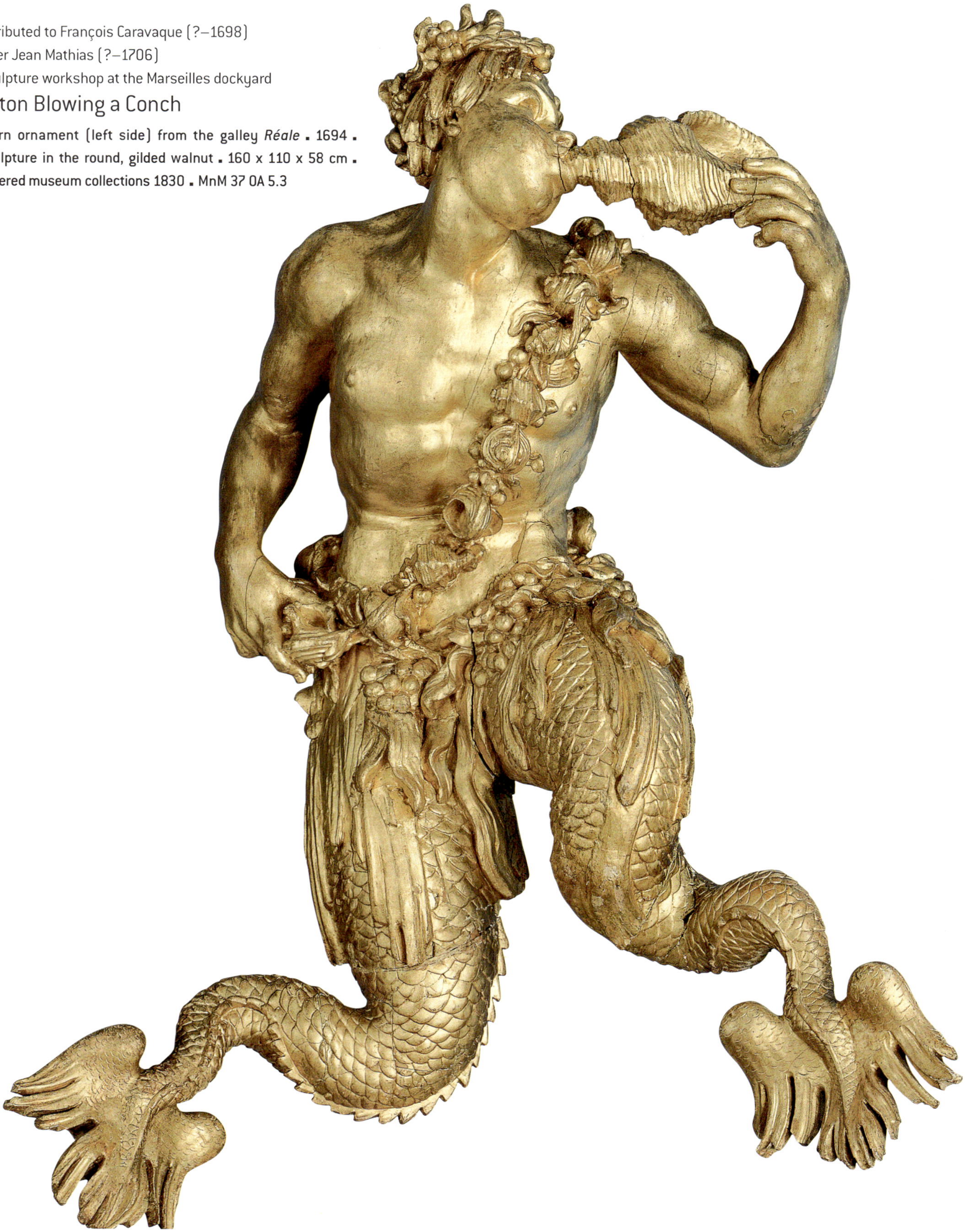

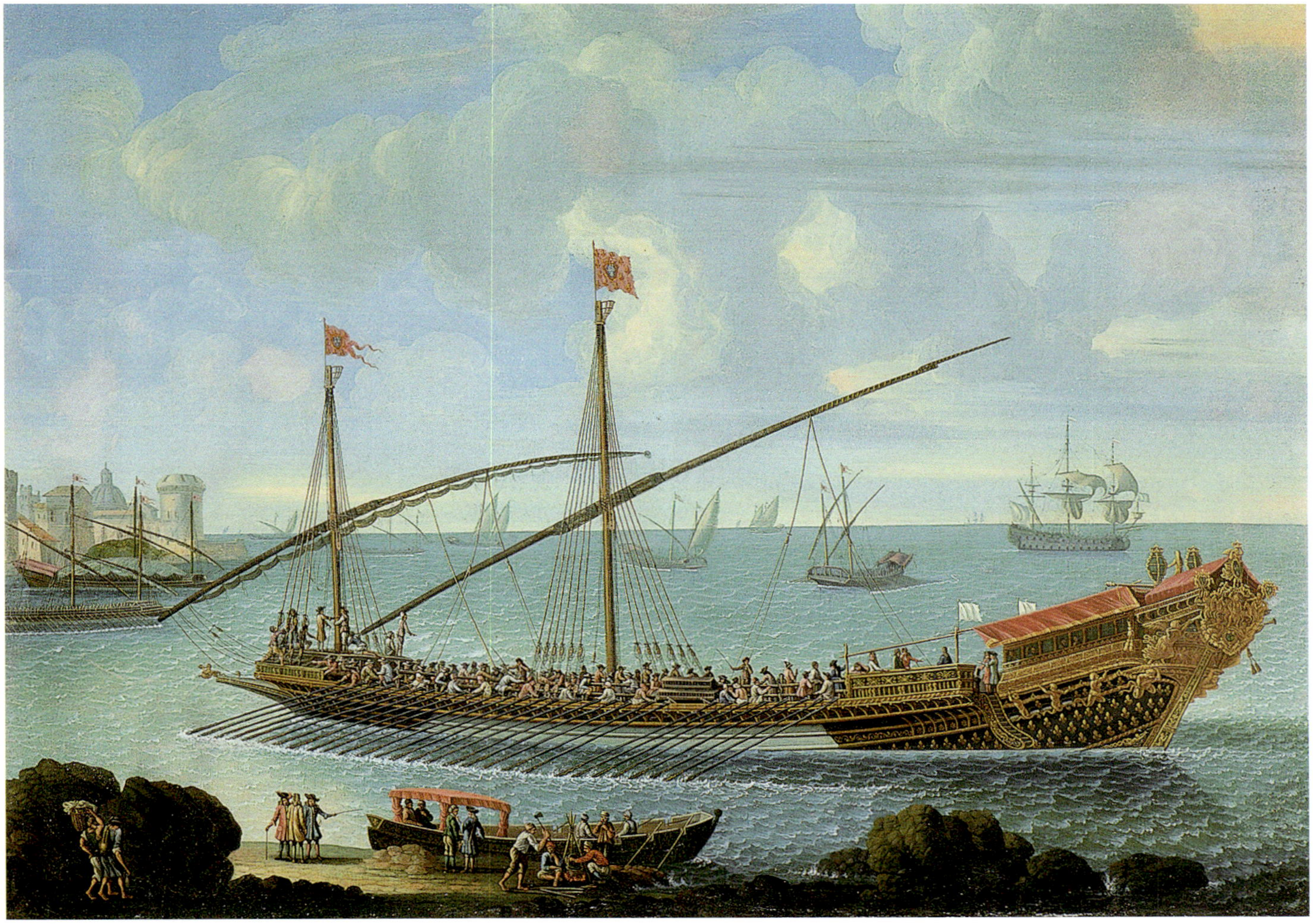

Anonymous, 17th century French school

The Réale Returning to Port

Circa 1694 . Oil on canvas . 73.5 x 99.5 cm . Entered museum collections 1989 . MnM 1 OA 23

Attributed to Jean-Baptiste Olérys (fl. Marseilles in 1688)

After Jean Mathias (?–1706). Sculpture workshop at the Marseilles dockyard

Spring

Stern ornamentation (detail of the left side panel) from the galley *Réale*, 1688 and 1694 . Bas-relief, gilded walnut . 114 x 500 x 16.5 cm . Entered museum collections 1830 . MnM 37 OA 5.8

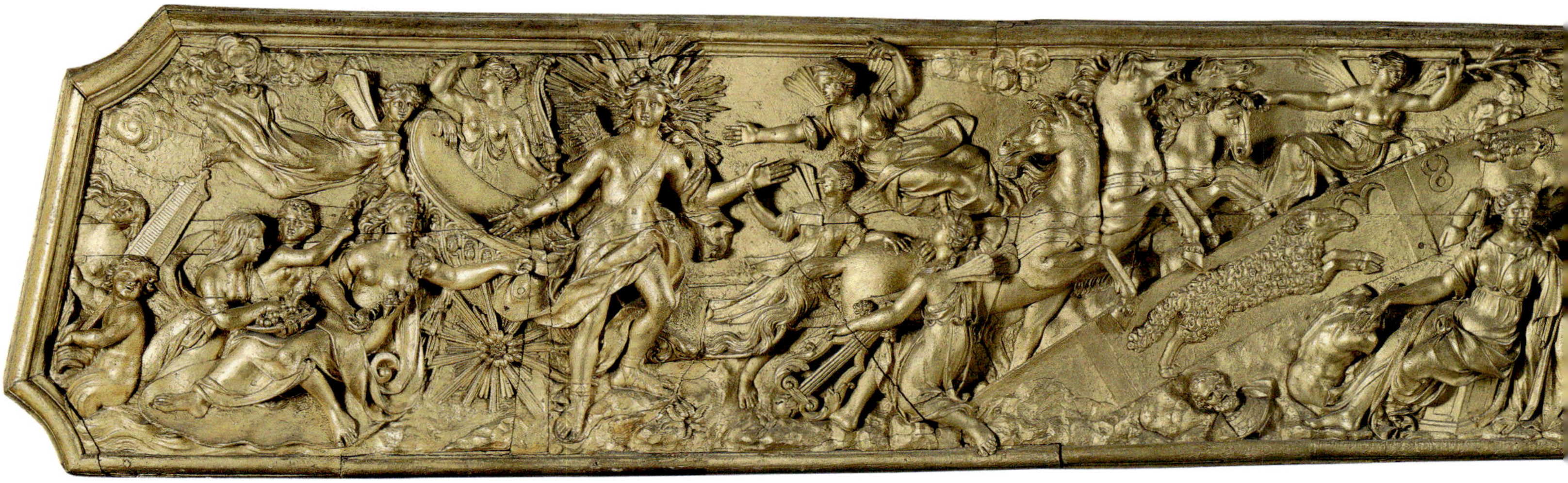

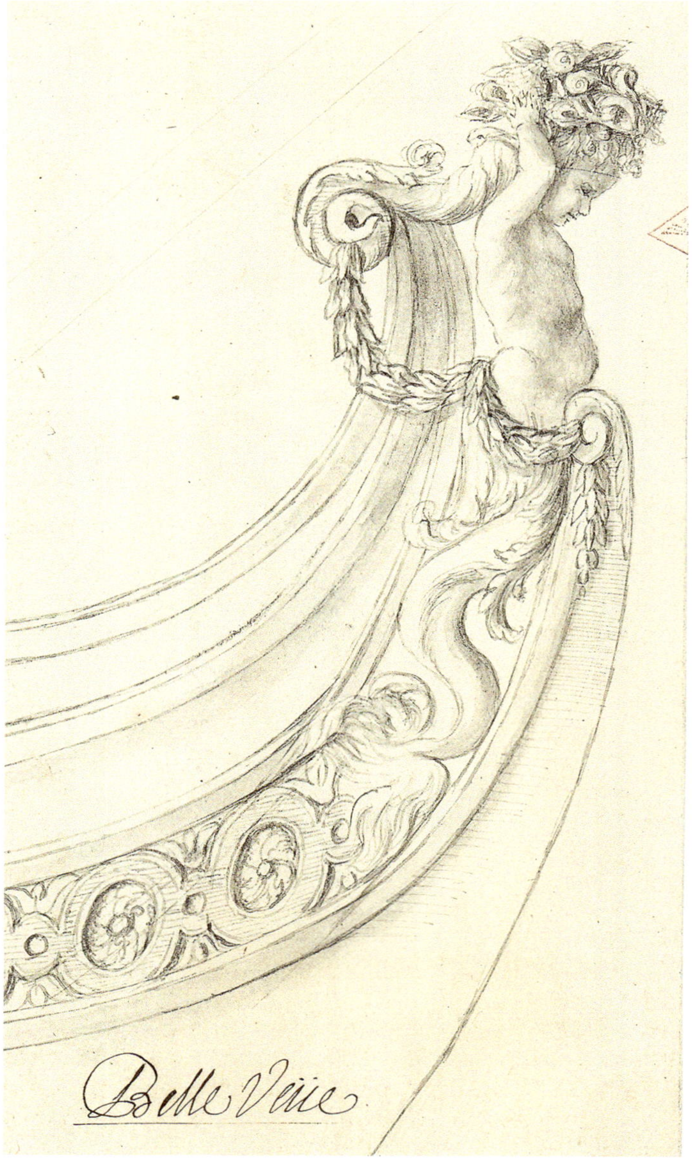

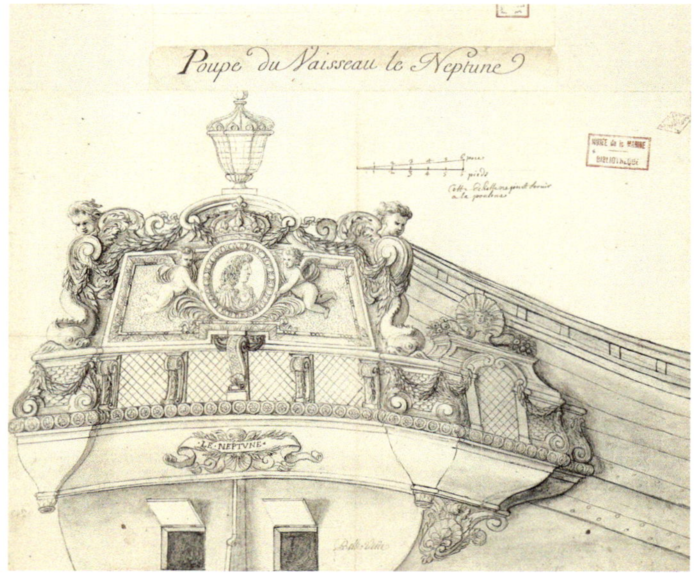

René d'Augère, sieur de Belle-Veüe (1642–1703)

Stern and bow ornaments of the ship 'Le Neptune'

1679 . Black chalk, black ink and grey wash on paper . 32.5 x 46.5 cm; 27 x 20 cm . Entered museum collections before 1946 . MnM Ico 10901.1, 10901.2

In the naval dockyards, artists rivalled each other in imagination in their adornment of the king's ships with allegorical sculptures. Colbert, however, requested that they confine themselves to simple ornamentation in order to avoid topweight. In Brest, René d'Augère, known as Belle-Veüe, proposed two designs for *Le Neptune*, a third-class ship built by Laurent Hubac in 1678–1679. His narrative figures were modest yet refined in style in keeping with the taste of the times. M. M.

Attributed to Jean Bérain (1640–1711)

Stern ornamentation of the ship 'La Renommée'

1698 . Graphite, black ink and grey wash on paper . 50 x 37 cm . Entered museum collections 1909 . MnM 25 OA 68

Seeking to control artists' 'itch to create fine figures', while unable to standardise ship decoration, Colbert put one artist in charge of this task, Jean Bérain, who was 'Designer to the King's Chamber'. 1685 to 1711, Bérain designed the ornamentation of almost one hundred ships, practically the entire fleet of Louis XIV. For *La Renommée*, a small ship built in Bayonne by Antoine Tassy in 1697–1698, Bérain proposed a single figure, directly related to the name of the ship, repeated on each part bearing a carved decor: the bow, the stern and the roundhouses. M. M.

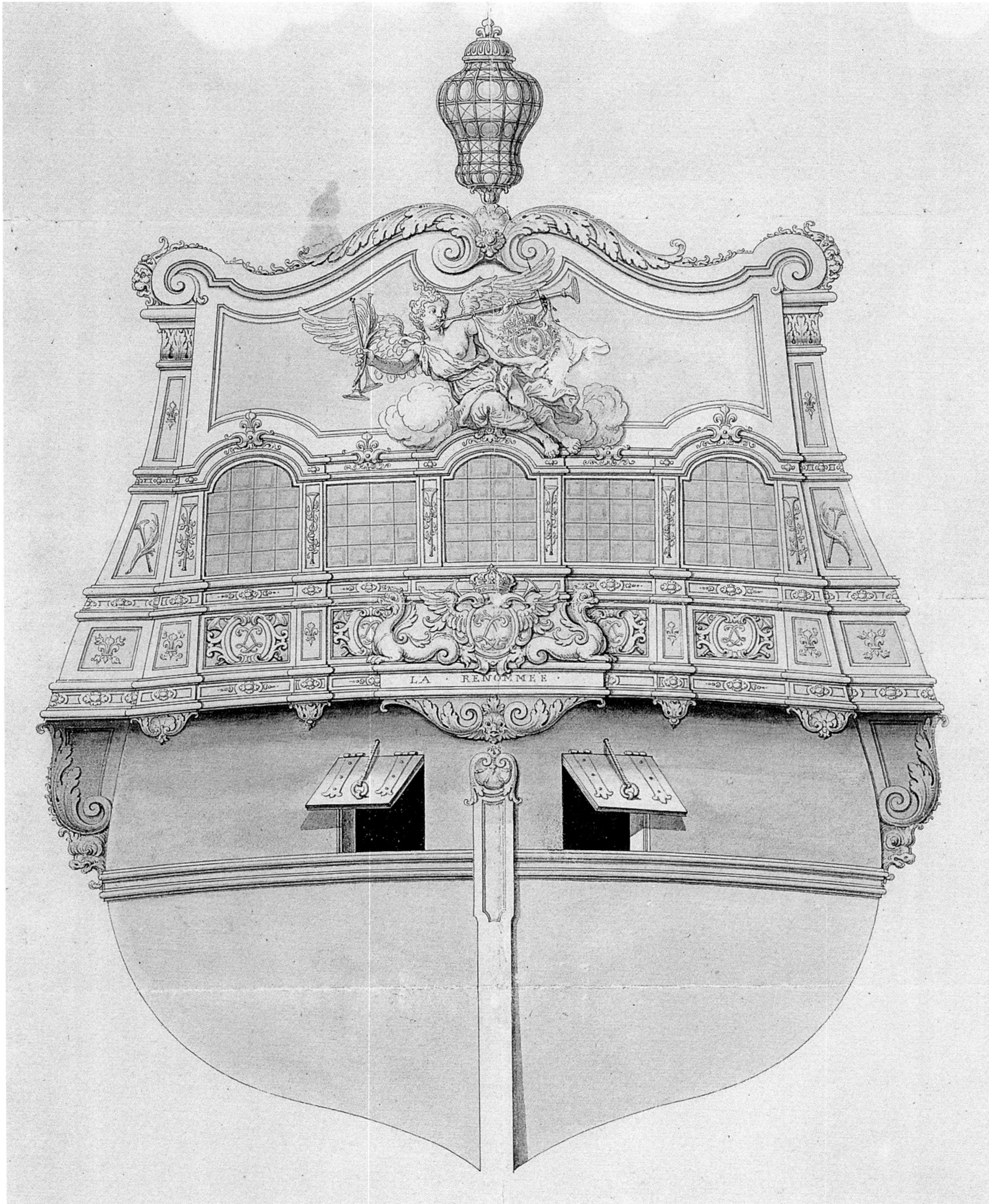
LA · RENOMMÉE ·

Anonymous

Attributed to the sculpture workshop at the Rochefort dockyard

Woman carrying a basket of fish and shellfish

Model for a figurehead . First half of 19th century . Red wax, painted wood . 48 x 16.7 x 46 cm . Entered museum collections 1950 . MnM 41 OA 289

In order to identify a wax model it must be compared to the preparatory drawing that preceded it. In the case of this figure executed at the sculpture workshop at the Rochefort dockyard, no known drawing has enabled the model's identification. It is nonetheless a remarkable example of the art of ceroplasty (wax modelling) as applied to naval sculpture, a tradition dating back to the late 17th century. M. M.

Attributed to Jacques Étienne Collet (1721–1808)

After Charles Philippe Caffieri (1695–1766)

Sculpture workshop at the Brest dockyard

Proteus

Project for a figurehead for the ship *Le Protée*, 1748 . Red wax, painted wood . 43.5 x 15.5 x 34.5 cm . Entered museum collections 1950 . MnM 41 OA 316

Following the preparatory drawing, the wax model was the second phase of the artistic creation. It provided the artist with a three-dimensional view of the work to be sculpted. The oldest preserved wax figures – of which there are around ten – are attributed to the Brest artist Jacques Étienne Collet. These models, particularly rare and fragile, are representative of naval decoration in the mid-18th century, while the finished figures, sculpted in the same period, have all disappeared. M. M.

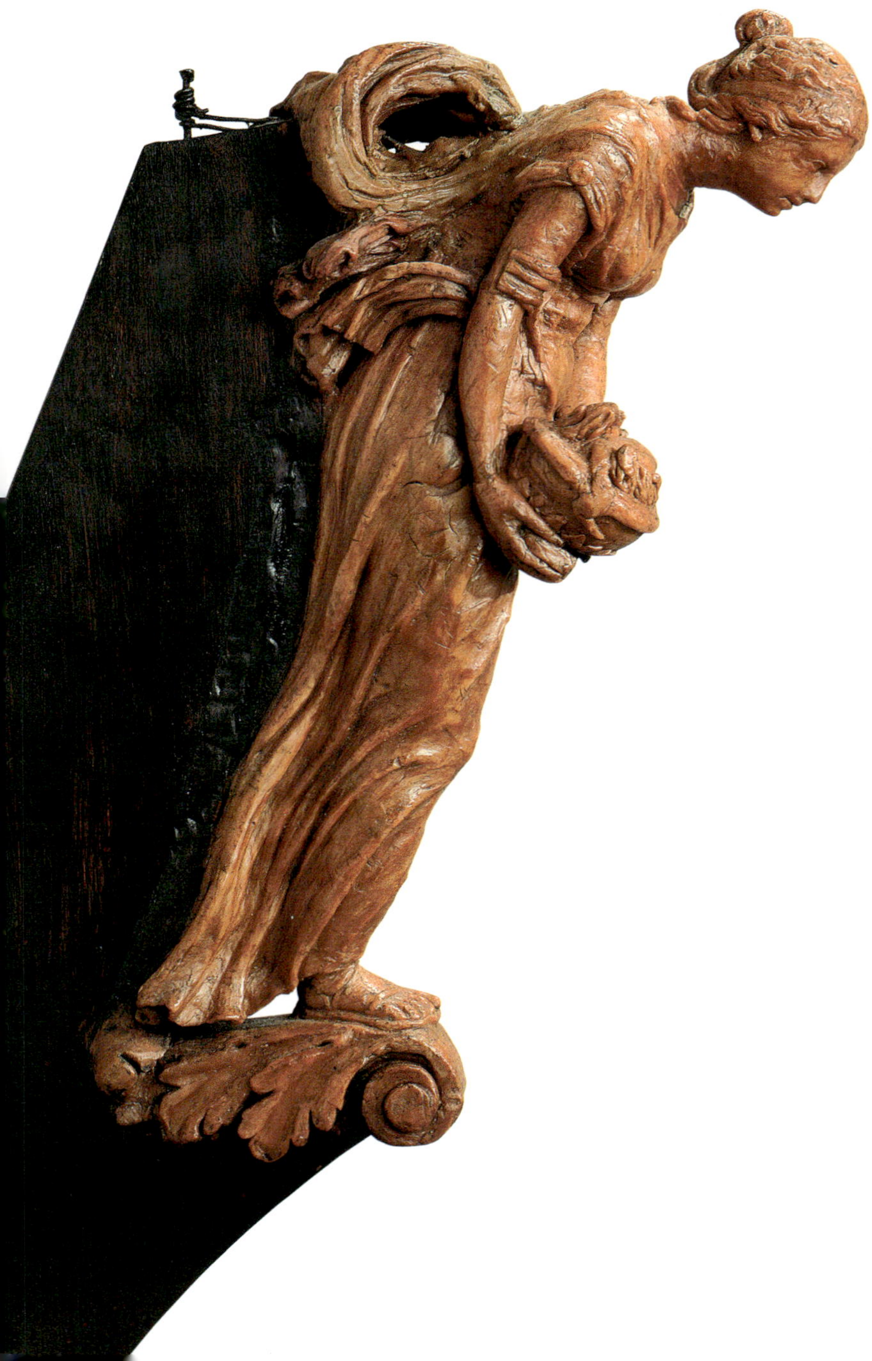

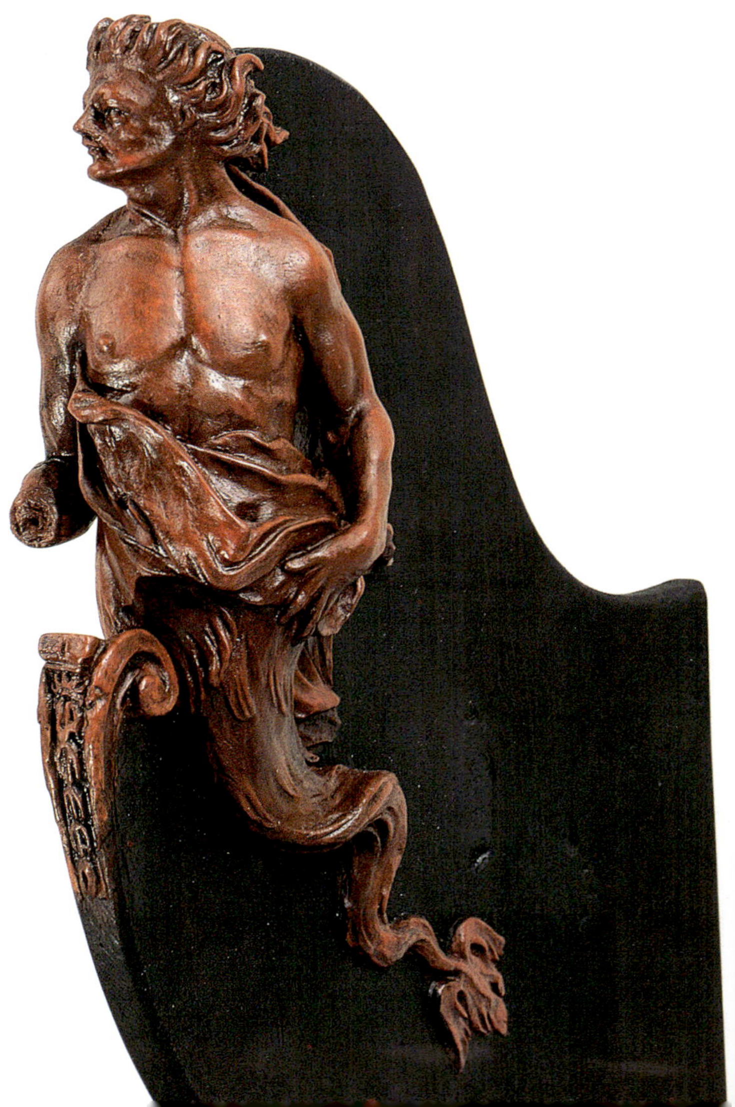

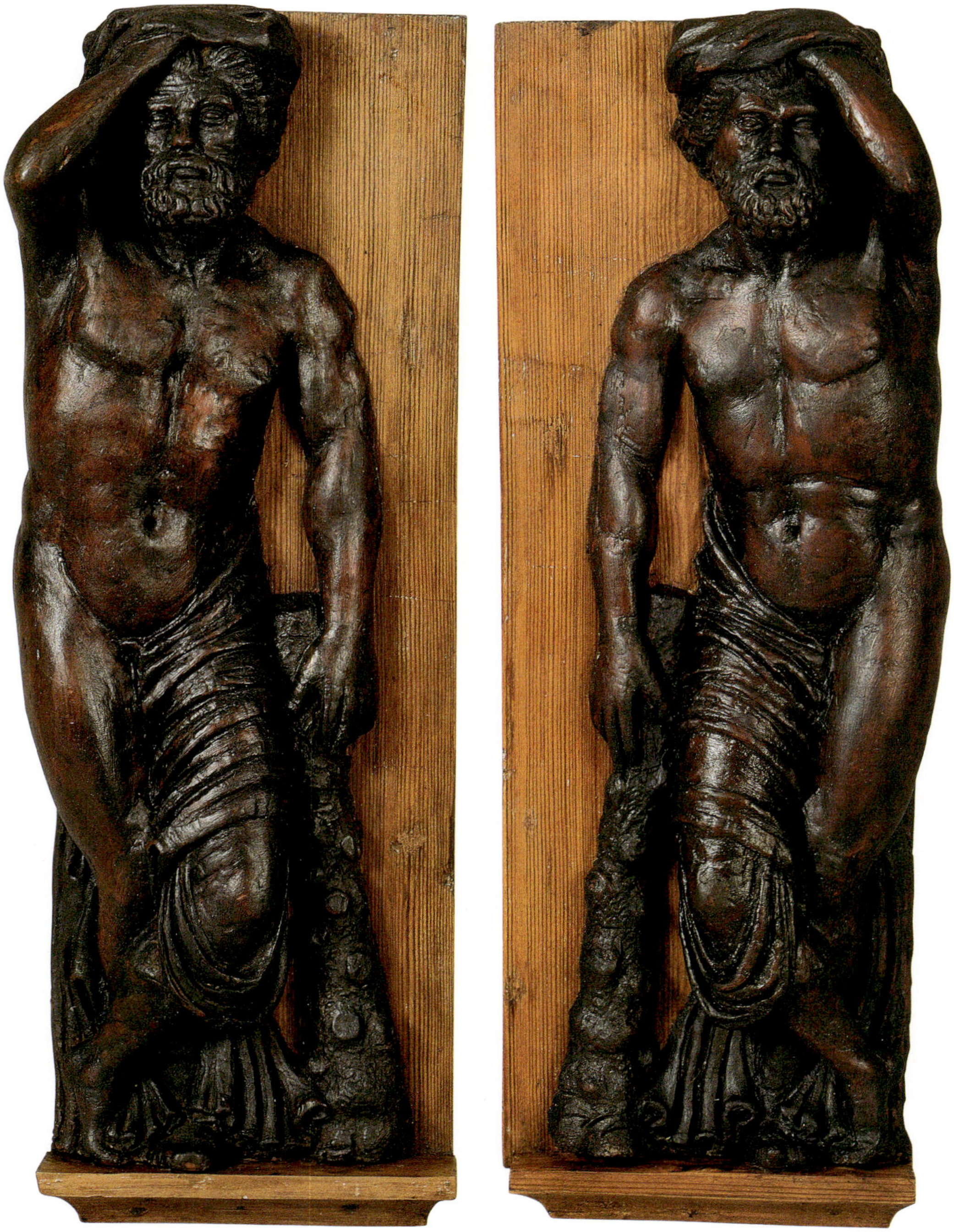

Anonymous
Sculpture workshop at the Rochefort dockyard

Two atlantes respresenting Hercules

Models for a pair of stern atlantes . First half of 19th century . Brown wax, painted wood . 33.5 x 12.5 x 7 cm each . Entered museum collections 1947 . MnM 41 OA 298, 299

These two atlantes are unique pieces. They are the only wax models for the ornamentation of a ship's stern to have come down to us. The wax was bulk-coloured a rather unusual brown colour. As in figureheads, the base was an integral part of the work, the artist using it as a framework to model the subject in the required position. M. M.

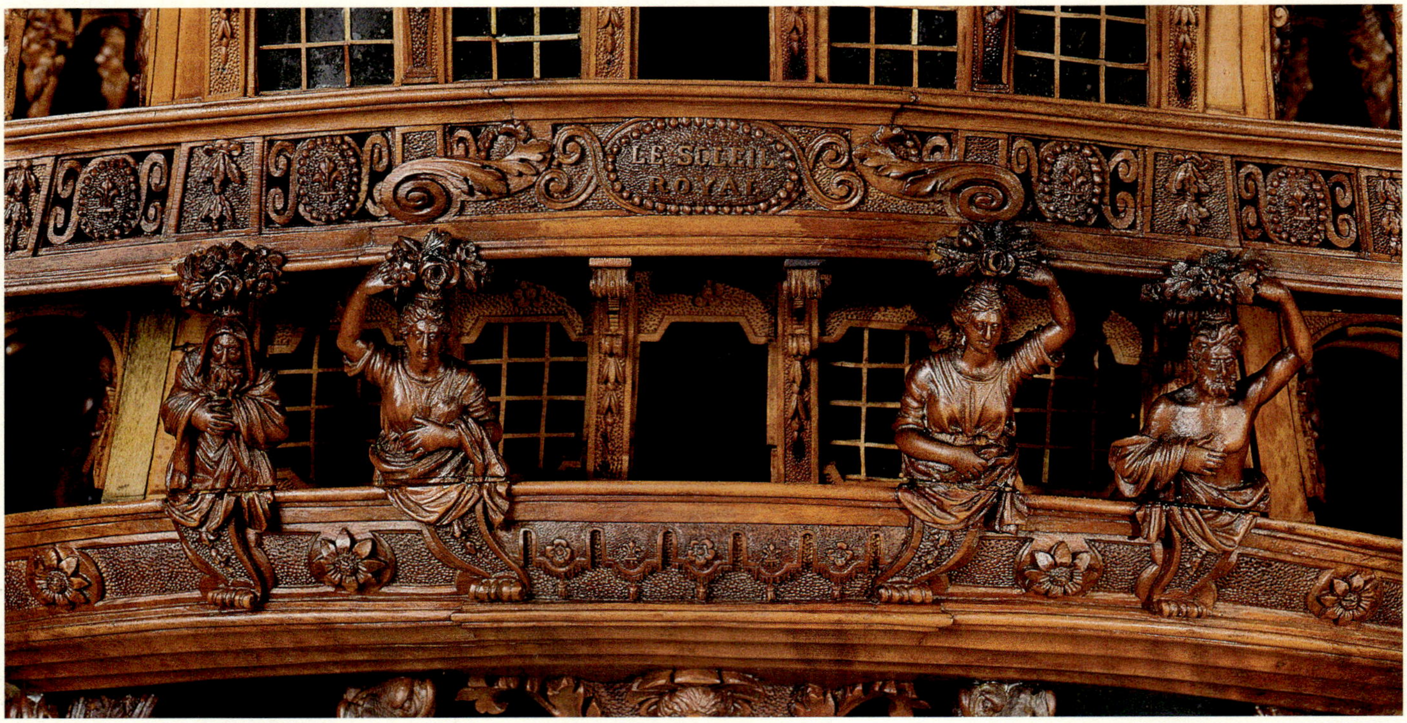

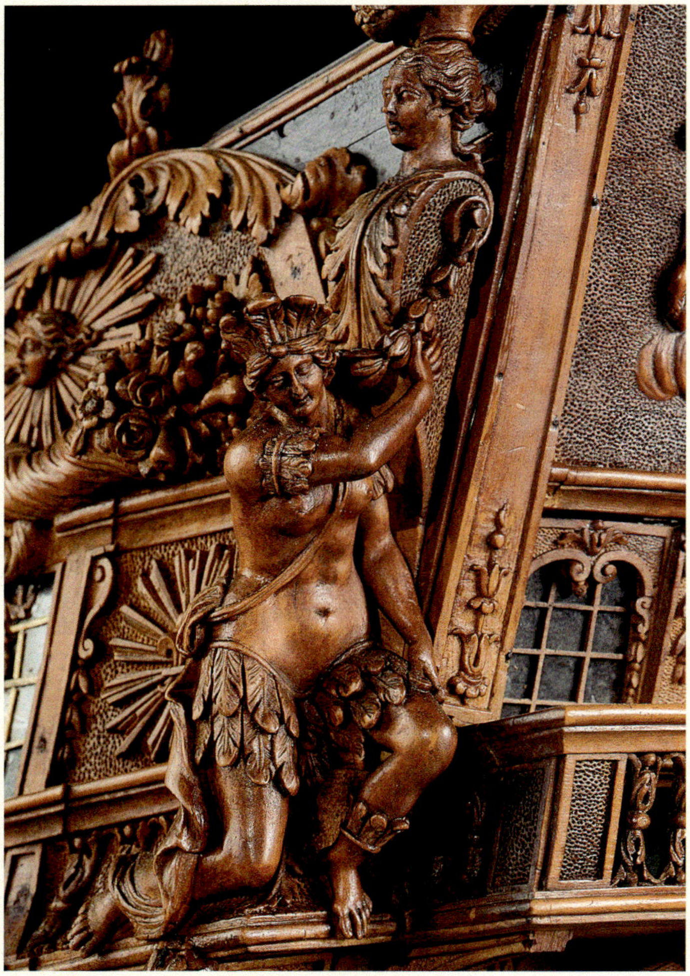

Le Soleil Royal

Unrigged model of a 100-gun ship, 1:40 scale . Constructed by Jean-Baptiste Tanneron (1807–1852) . 1839 . Walnut (planking and deck), boxwood (sculptures), ebony (gunwale and ribbands) . 69 x 173.5 x 45 cm . Entered museum collections 1939 . MnM 7 MG 3

A sculptor at the Toulon naval dockyard, Jean-Baptiste Tanneron was called to Paris in 1833 to work as a model maker at the Musée de la Marine. He was asked to construct a model of the *Soleil Royal*, a name borne successively by two prestigious ships of Louis XIV's fleet. Tanneron based his carved ornamentation on designs proposed at the time by Jean Bérain. The extremely delicate work of his miniature sculpting, notably in the decoration of the stern and roundhouses, makes this model one of the masterpieces of the collection. M. M.

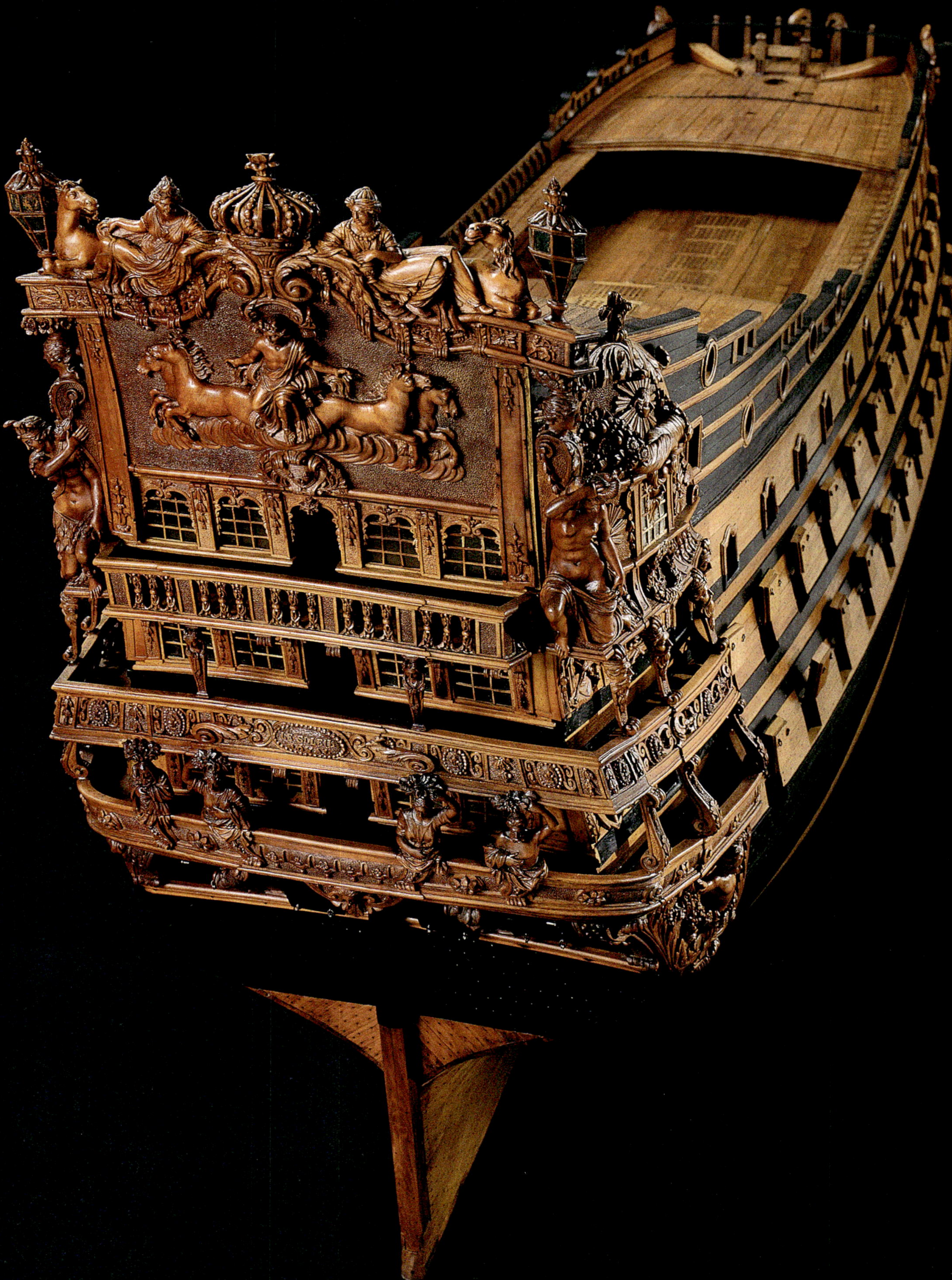

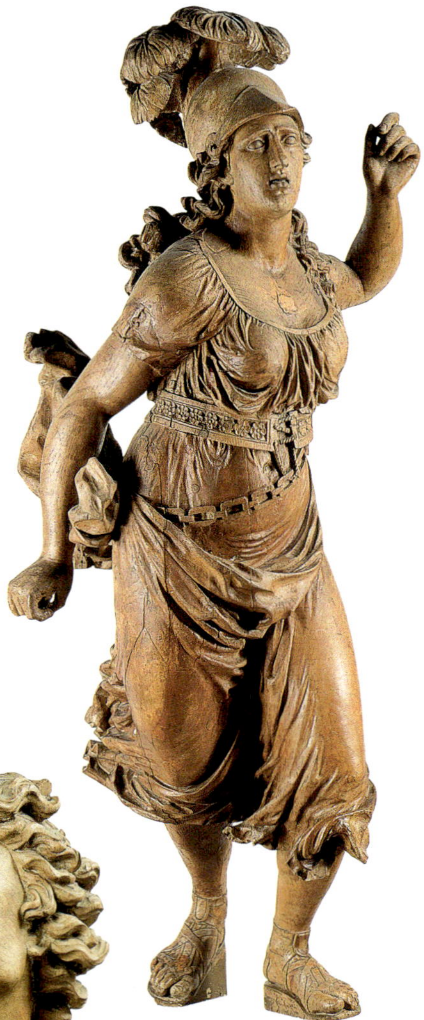

Jean Elshoecht (1762–?) and Benjamin Tellier (circa 1766–?)
Sculpture workshop at the Dunkirk dockyard

Female figure in the antique style

Figurehead of the frigate *La Poursuivante* . 1796 . Sculpture in the round, stripped elm . 220 x 92 x 110 cm . Entered museum collections 1947 . MnM 39 OA 24

Of the thirty figureheads of military ships in the collections of the Musée National de la Marine, *La Poursuivante* is the oldest, the only one dating from the 18th century. Although made in Dunkirk, this expressive full-size figure comes from the Rochefort naval dockyard, where the frigate it graced was decommissioned in 1806. The sculpture was kept in the sculpture workshop, which was converted into a storehouse after it ceased activity in 1891. M. M.

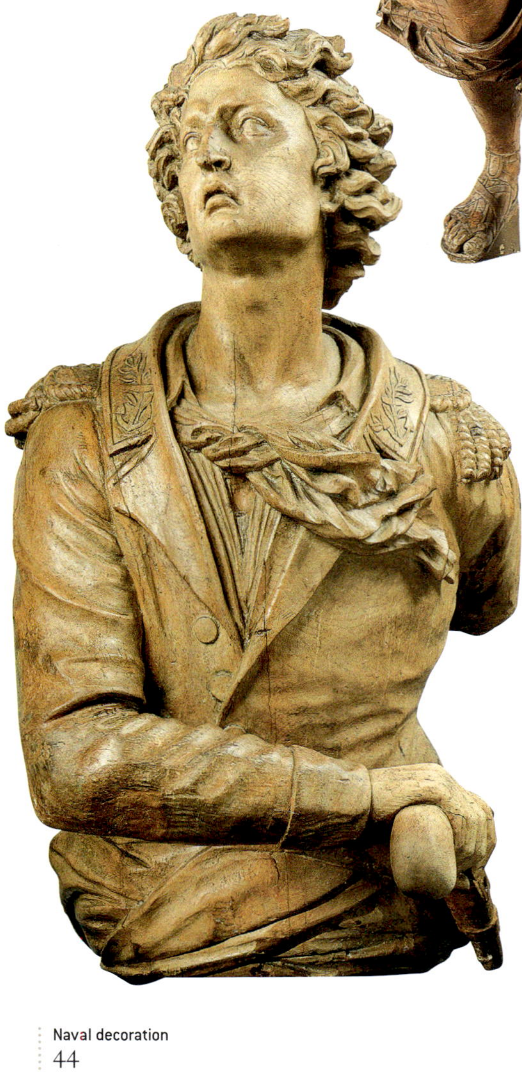

Anonymous
Sculpture workshop at the Brest dockyard

Bust of a naval officer

Figurehead of the corvette *La Bayonnaise* . 1846 . Sculpture in the round, stripped cembro pine . 132 x 70 x 65 cm . Entered museum collections 1894 . MnM 5 SO 9

This figurehead was sculpted at Brest for the corvette *La Bayonnaise*, built in Cherbourg in 1845–1846. The figure – no longer full-size but in bust format, as stipulated by ministerial order in 1829 – represents an officer boarding a ship. This pictorial theme was probably chosen to commemorate the famous exploit of a former corvette of the same name, which attacked the British frigate *Ambuscade* in 1798. M. M.

Attributed to Félix Brun (1763–1831)
Sculpture workshop at the Toulon dockyard

Hercules bringing down the Nemean lion

Stern figure of the ship *Le Montebello* . Circa 1817 . Sculpture in the round, stripped lime (with traces of gilding) . 240 x 80 x 95 cm . Entered museum collections 1949 . MnM 41 OA 79

Attributed to Félix Brun
Sculpture workshop at the Toulon dockyard

Hercules bringing down the Erymanthian boar

Stern figure of the ship *Le Montebello* . Circa 1817 . Sculpture in the round, stripped lime (with traces of gilding) . 230 x 72 x 90 cm . Entered museum collections 1949 . MnM 41 OA 80

The mythical figure of Hercules, very popular in ship carvings, is here shown with the wild beasts he vanquished in the twelve tasks set him by Eurystheus. Hercules is traditionally associated with the Nemean lion, but much more rarely with the Eryanthian boar. The two sculptures, originally gilded, adorned each side of the stern of the *Montebello*, one of the last large three-deck sailing ships. The ship, nicknamed 'the new floating Louvre', ended its long career in Toulon in 1889. M. M.

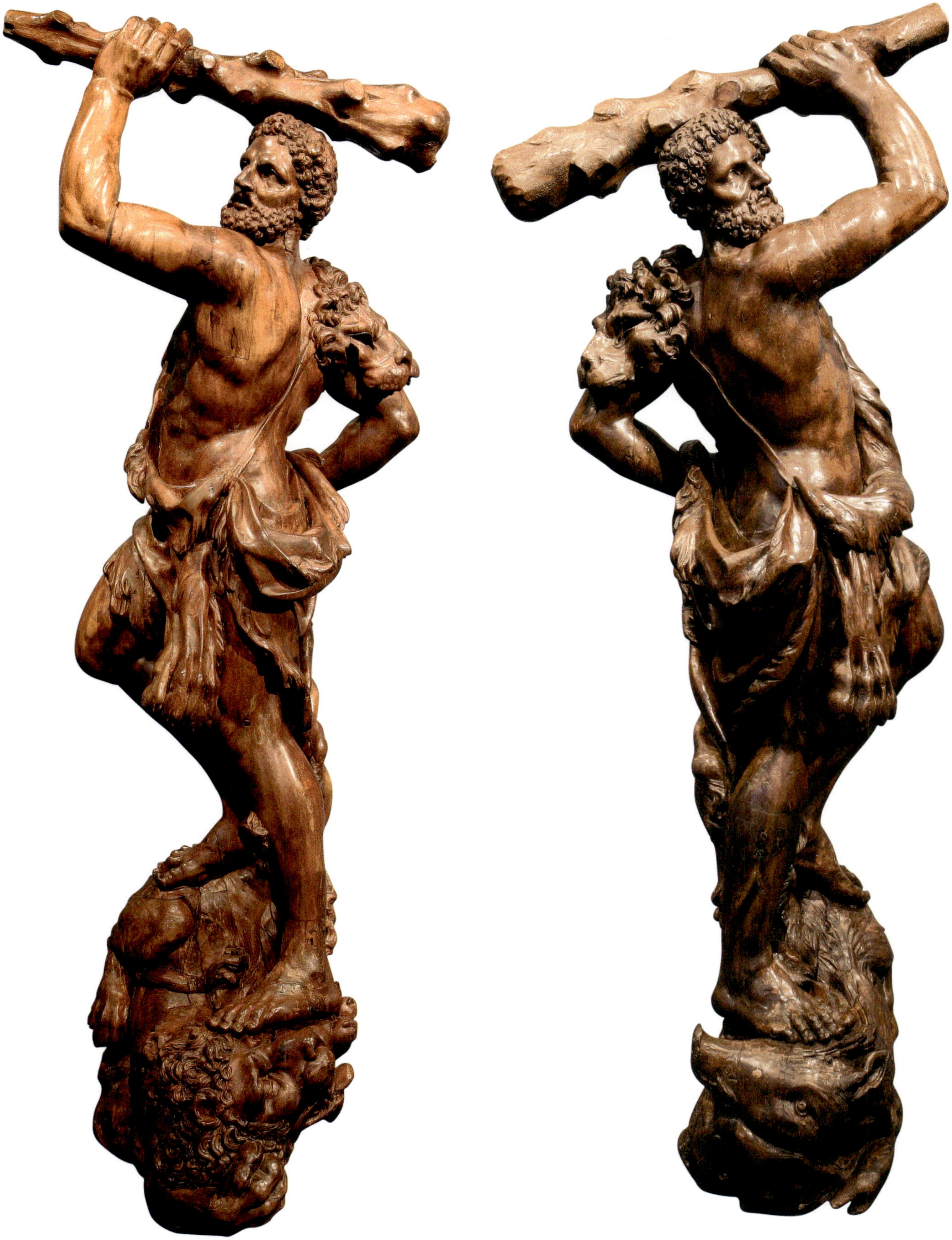

Naval battles

Unlike their Dutch and English counterparts, few French painters treated the subject of naval battles, despite the fact that it was one that belonged to the category of history painting, the 'grand genre' in academic tradition. However, in the late 18th century, with Louis XVI's modernisation of the navy, the victories of the American War of Independence and, on a pictorial level, the influence of Joseph Vernet, the genre blossomed. It was present at the Salon under the Revolution and the Empire, and promoted by Louis-Philippe with the creation of the Musée des Gloires de la France at Versailles.
Beyond the apparent simplicity of the pictorial scheme – the depiction of ships in action – a host of questions had to be addressed by the artist. The painter had first to choose a point of view. He often opted for the wide angle, in which naval squadrons were depicted all over the surface of the canvas in a clear, even didactic composition. In these works, the power of the ships is exalted and the line of battle idealised, but there is no trace of man. More rarely adopted was the close-up angle, drawing the viewer into the heart of the action. In Louis Philippe Crépin's *Battle of 'La Bayonnaise',* the human figures are visible, conveying the extreme violence of the boarding.
A battle painting was usually an officially commissioned work. As for all historical subjects, the painter had to gather information on his subject. He would sometimes use models of ships to prepare the composition. He would base his picture on accounts, if the event was recent, or else build up his own reconstruction of the event.
It was also a subject requiring specific knowledge. To achieve a realistic representation of a naval battle, the painter needed a minimum amount of experience in the art of navigation and strategy. The debate raged at the time: should the artist be a sailor first, or a painter? What is most important? The light in the sky, the reflections on the ocean's surface, or the precision with which the events are depicted? In marine painting, and particularly the representation of naval battles, an artist must be able to reconcile numerous demands, beyond those of his own painting technique.

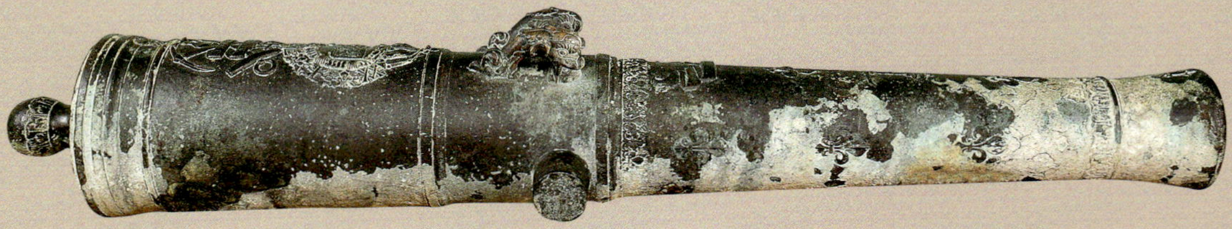

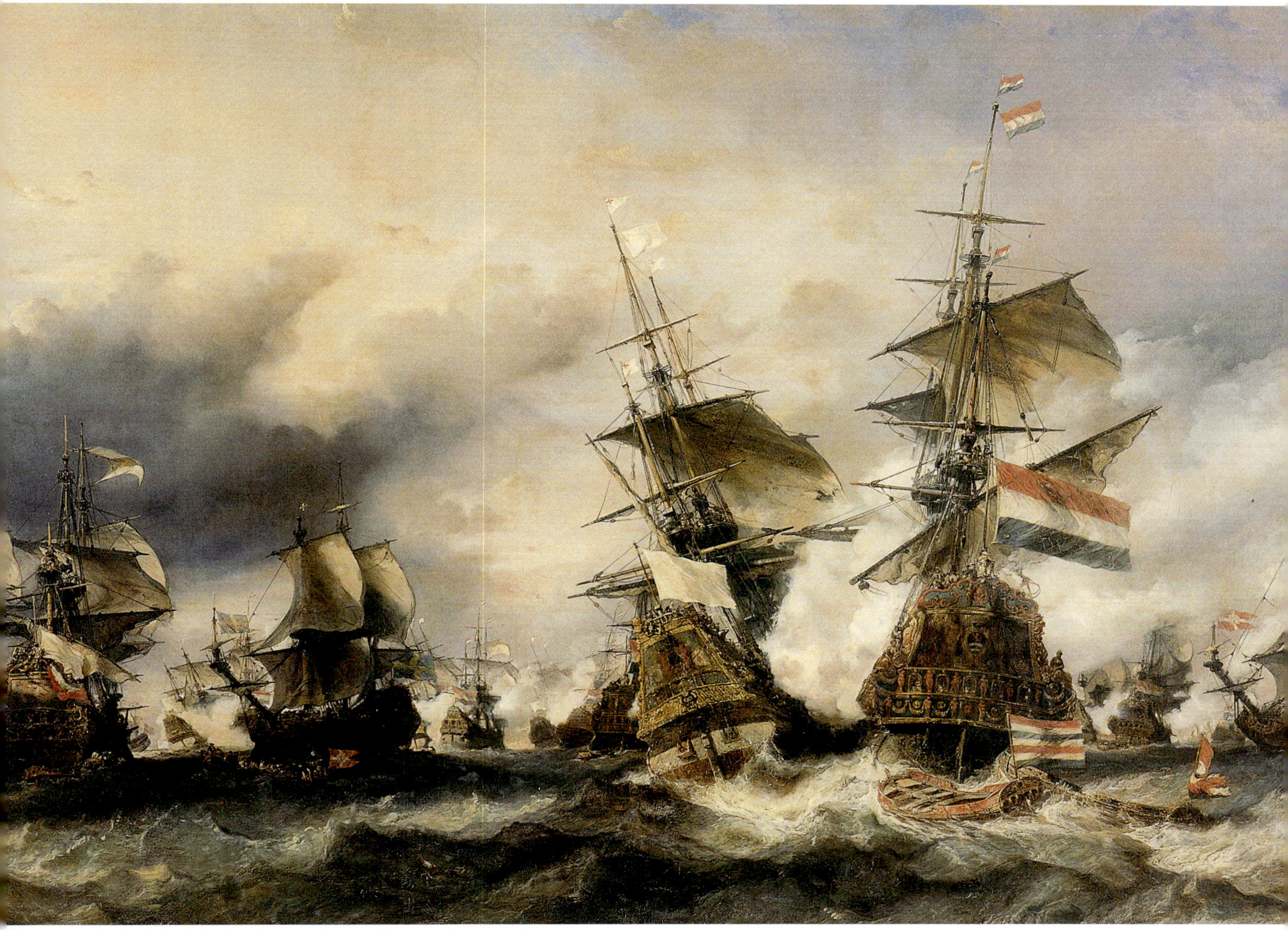

Le Duc de Beaufort

24-pound canon . Circa 1666 . Bronze . 318 cm . Entered museum collections 1963 . MnM 5 AR 76

This large-calibre canon came from the remains of the ships *L'Assuré* and *Le Sage*, wrecked in 1692 near Ceuta. Richly decorated, it bears the arms of François de Vendôme, Duc de Beaufort (1616–1669). Grandson of Henri IV and Gabrielle d'Estrées, the duke was the last person to hold the office of Grand Maître de la Navigation, from 1651 to 1669.

The use of bronze artillery, which would disappear in the course of the 18th century, was at the time a mark of distinction. The calibre, 24, indicates that the cannonballs weighed 24 pounds. F. C.

Eugène Isabey (1803–1886)

Combat du Texel, 29 juin 1694

1839 . Oil on canvas . 250 x 358.5 cm . Signed on lower left . On loan from the Museum and National Estate of Versailles, 1935 (MV 1407) . MnM 9 OA 1 D

The legendary naval engagement that took place near Texel on 29 June 1694 during the reign of Louis XIV alone symbolises the activities of the king's privateers. The most famous of these, Jean Bart from Dunkirk, seized a fleet of Dutch ships carrying grain so as to send it to the starving French. One and a half centuries later, Eugène Isabey painted this retrospective view of the event. Commissioned for Versailles in 1836, the painting was presented at the 1839 Salon, where critics unanimously praised these ships from another era, 'drawn with a master's touch'. M. M.

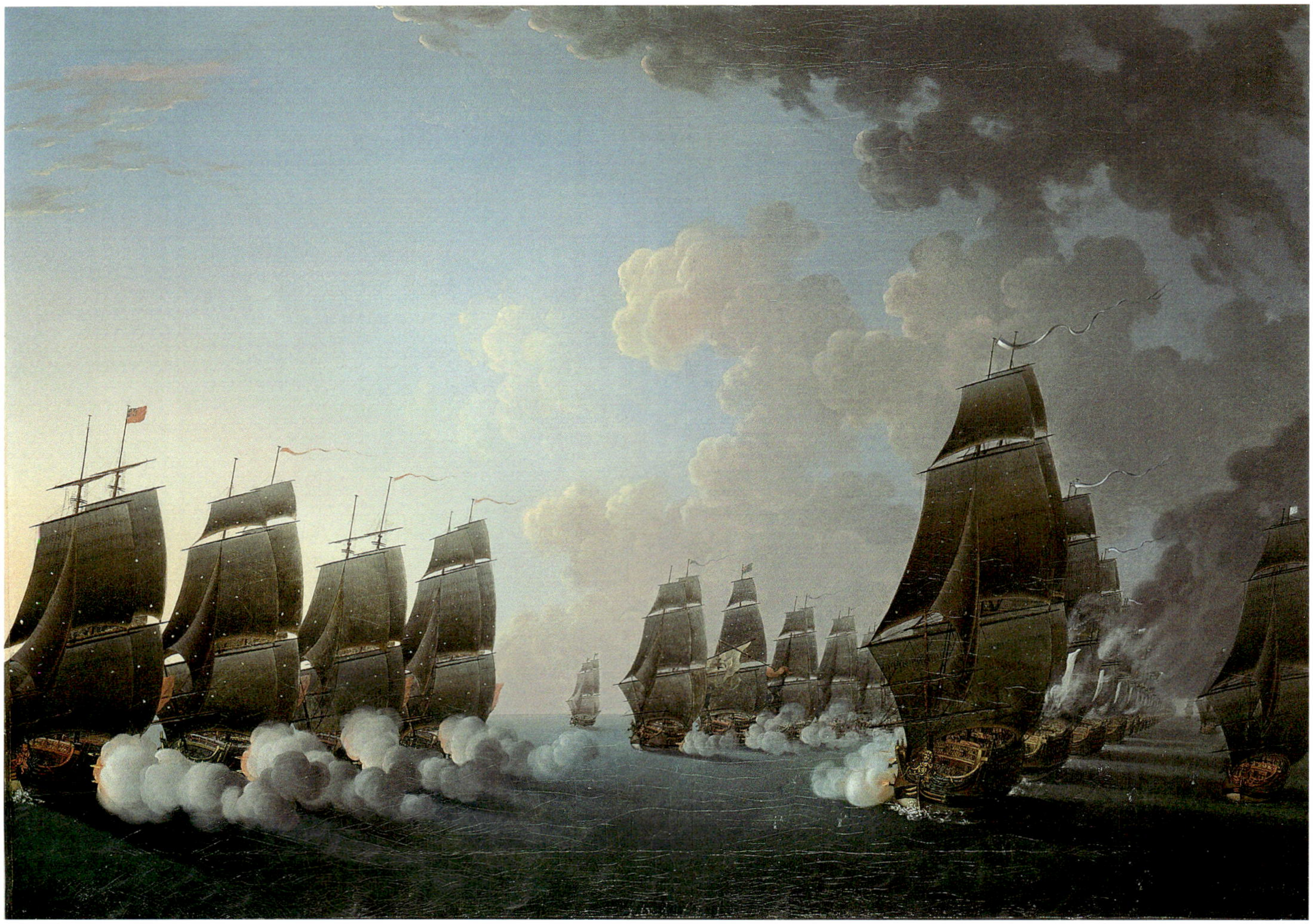

Auguste Louis de Rossel de Cercy (1736–1804)

Battle of Dominica, 17 April 1780

1789 . Oil on canvas . 112.5 x 163 cm . Signed and dated on lower right . Entered museum collections in 1945 . MnM 3 OA 11

The *Battle of Dominica* is one of the sixteen paintings executed by Rossel between 1786 and 1790 for an official commission, the purpose of which was to record the principal naval victories of the French navy during the American War of Independence. These paintings, which were to adorn the classrooms of the naval schools in Brest, Rochefort and Toulon, were each made in two copies, one of which was given to the naval minister and the other to the French officer who won the battle shown. Whether painting squadron battles or isolated engagements, Rossel, first and foremost a naval officer, depicted with precision these deadly clashes in American and European waters and in the West Indies. M. M.

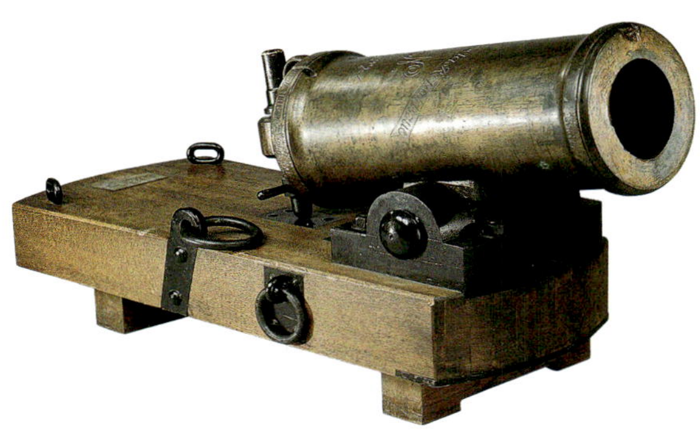

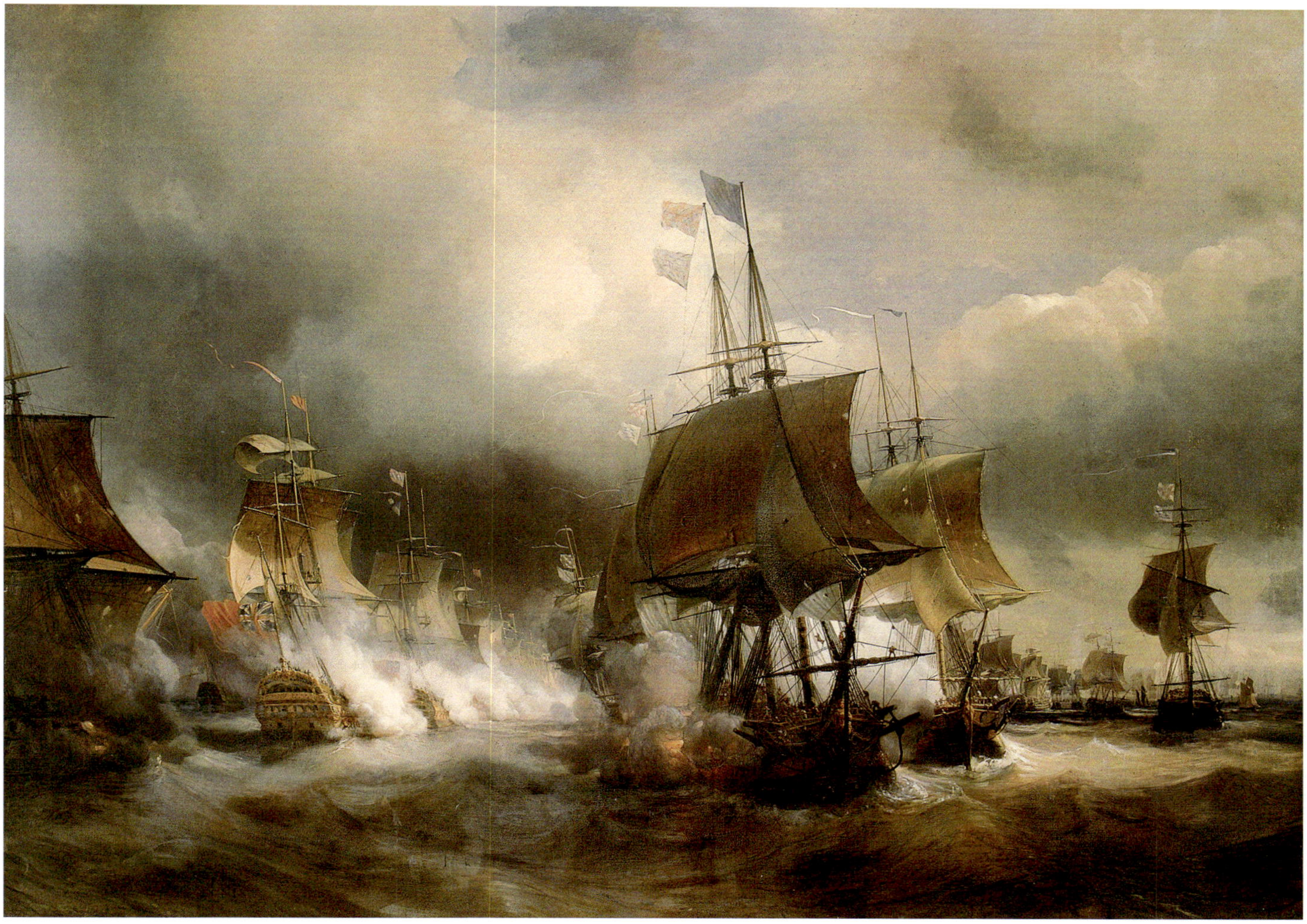

Théodore Gudin (1802–1880)

Battle of Ouessant, 23 July 1778

1848 . Oil on canvas . 248 x 349 cm . On loan from the Museum and National Estate of Versailles, 1935 (MV 1425) . MnM 9 OA 31 D

The Battle of Ouessant, marking France's entrance into the American War of Independence, was also the largest naval engagement of this war, with over 60 ships involved and the participation of most of the French navy's squadron commanders. A historical reconstruction of the event was commissioned from Théodore Gudin in 1839, to feature among the great glories of France that Louis-Philippe wished to honour in the new museum at Versailles. A far cry from the romantic genre, the artist's style here reflects his role as official painter attached to the navy ministry. His work is a monumental, scrupulous description of a 'line' battle, which was presented at the 1848 Salon. M. M.

Howitzer 36, 1787 model

Nantes foundry . 1794 . Bronze . 91.5 x 31.5 cm . On loan from the Département des Recherches Archéologiques Subaquatiques et Sous-Marines, 1985 . MnM D 2241.222

This ship's howitzer came from the wreck of *Golymin*, a ship built in Lorient in 1804 and wrecked at Brest in 1814. Howitzers had considerable fire power but a short range, and so were placed on ships' forecastles. They were replaced by carronades in the early 19th century. Often loaded with grapeshot or canister, they could inflict heavy damage to the adversary. F. C.

Louis-Philippe Crépin (1772–1851)

Battle of the French corvette 'La Bayonnaise' and the English frigate 'Ambuscade', 14 December 1798

1801 . Oil on canvas . 246 x 345 cm . On loan from the Museum and National Estate of Versailles, 1935 (MV 1437) . MnM 9 OA 17 D

The battle of 14 December 1798 was one of the fiercest episodes of the Franco-British conflict. When the French corvette *La Bayonnaise* was overwhelmed by the vastly superior firepower of the English, its captain ordered the boarding of the British ship; the French sailors were victorious in hand-to-hand combat. This remarkable confrontation caused a tremendous stir among the French public. Exceptionally, the Musée National de la Marine collections include not only the final painting presented by Louis-Philippe Crépin at the 1801 Salon, but also the preparatory drawing for the 1799 sketch. **M. M.**

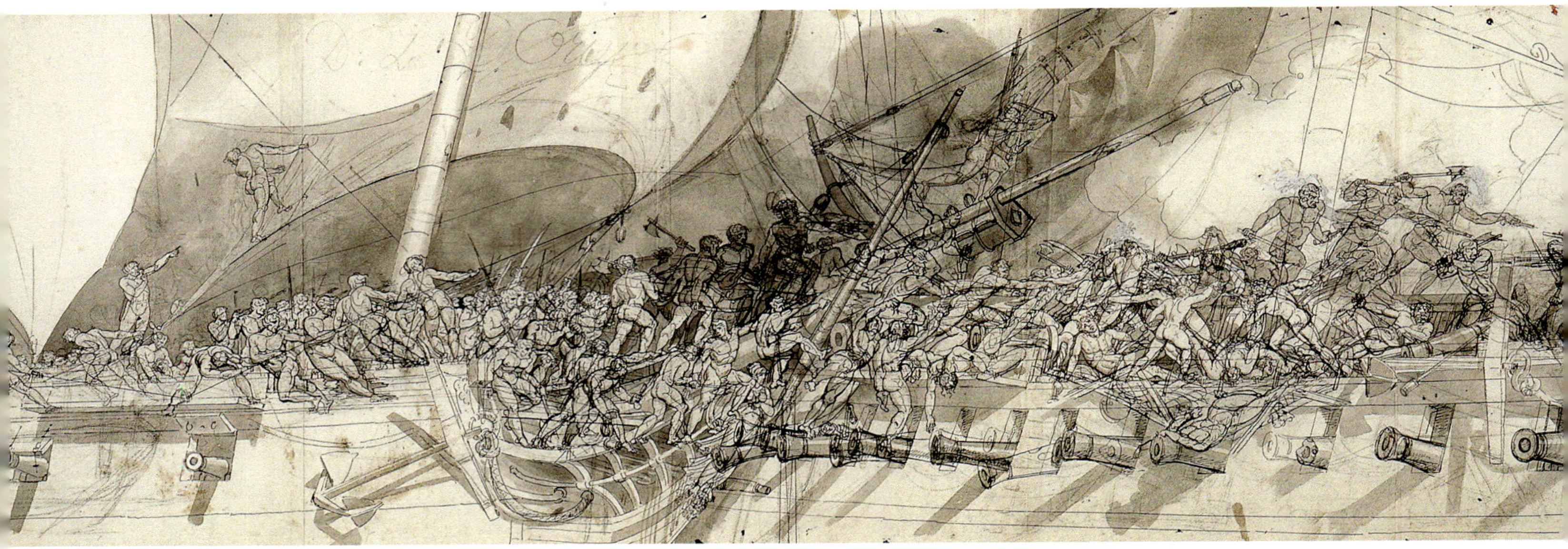

Louis-Philippe Crépin (1772–1851)

Battle of the French corvette 'La Bayonnaise' and the English frigate 'Ambuscade', 14 December 1798

1799 . Preparatory drawing . Black ink, black chalk, grey wash and white heightening on paper . 43.5 x 228.5 cm . Entered museum collections 1992 . MnM 27 OA 122

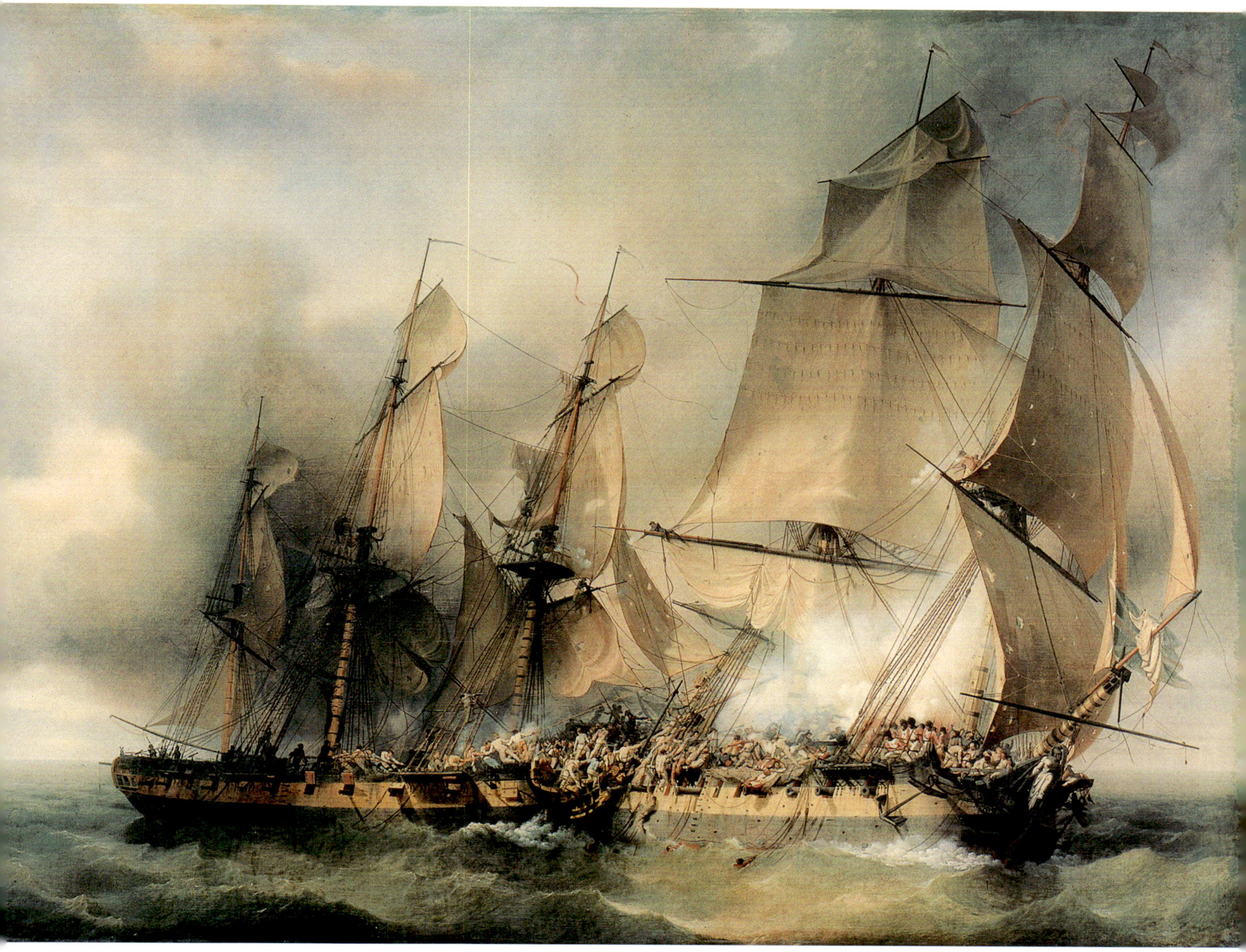

Images of ports

In Louis XV's 'register of decisions', under the date 27 September 1753, it is recorded that 'Vernet shall paint all the ports of France'. This unprecedented commission led the artist from town to town over a period of twelve years, from 1753 to 1765, during which he executed fifteen large-format canvases out of the twenty-four originally planned, for the greater glory of the king. He thus accomplished his mission, even though, tired of travelling around the country and of complying with strict instructions, he did not complete the entire original commission.

A well-regarded painter, Joseph Vernet became a celebrity with his 'Views of France's Ports'. When they were shown at the Salon, every picture met with an enthusiastic response. Other artists before him had painted works in the genre, but Vernet had created his own style. His ports were real-life places, devoid of mythological and allegorical content, and his great talent enabled him to go beyond banal depictions of urban landscapes. His paintings are a perfectly balanced combination of documentary accuracy and artistic quality.

What did his admirers, who included Diderot, say about them? Beyond Vernet's refined use of colour and clarity of composition, all recognised in his work an astonishing realism. He succeeded in capturing the spirit of each place without resorting to the picturesque. From the late 18th century on, his 'Views of France's Ports' were engraved and prints of them widely distributed in France and Europe. The master was an inspiration to other painters, such as Jean-François Hue and Antoine Léon Morel-Fatio.

Different picture formats call for different artistic choices: in its linear composition, the panorama emphasises the wide expanse of the port, depicting a succession of architectural structures and activities. For centuries, painters and draughtsmen worked in this difficult genre, which sought to capture reality. But with the advent of photography, instantaneous and objective representation of places gradually supplanted painted records.

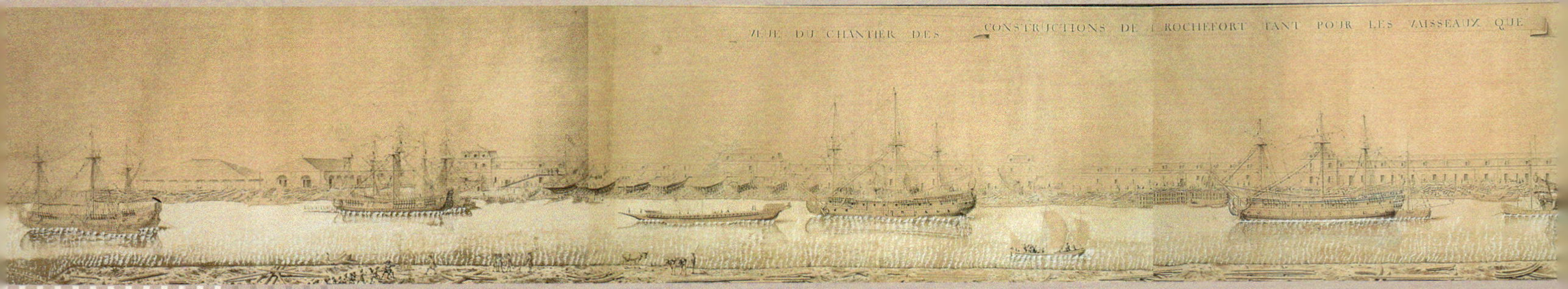

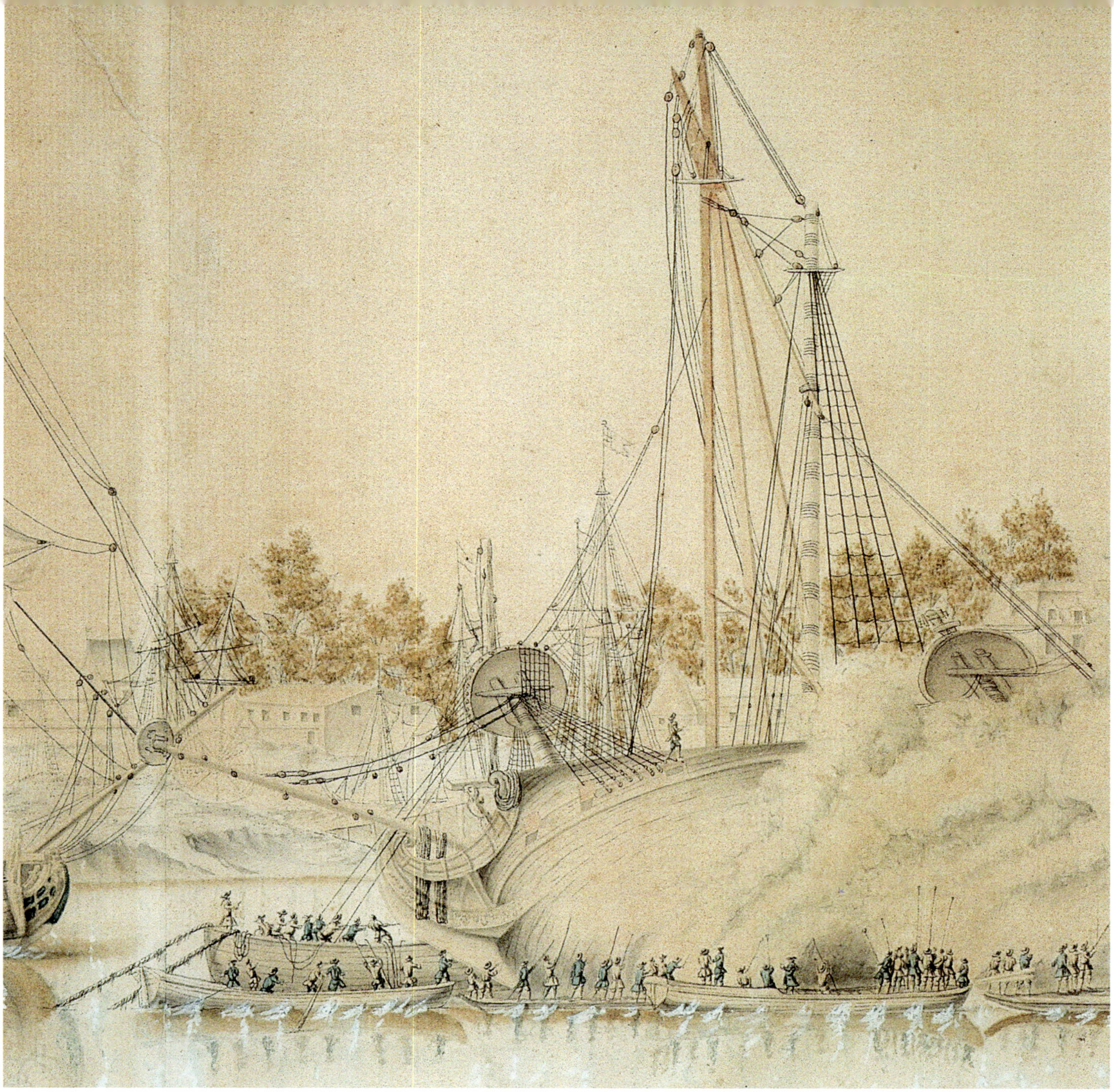

Nicolas Berquin (?–1706)

View of the ship and galley dockyards at Rochefort in 1690 (overall view and detail)

Late 17th century . Crayon, brown ink, watercolour and gouache on laid paper . 47 x 353 cm . Entered museum collections in 1998 . MnM 25 OA 142

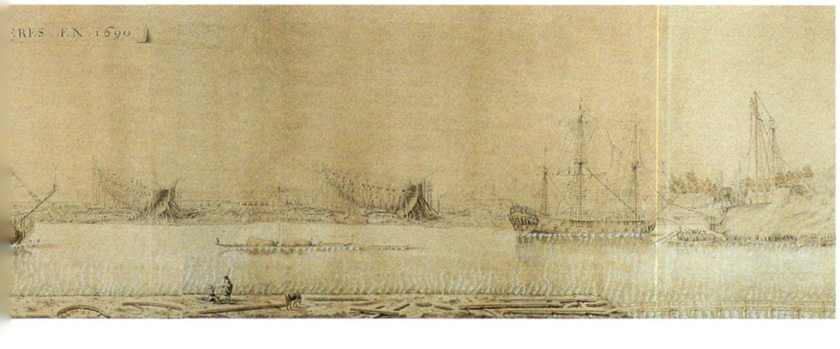

Between 1689 and 1690, the Rochefort dockyard played a central role in Louis XIV's naval policy. The king wanted to built a fleet of fifteen galleys, while neither the facilities, nor the specialised workers, nor even the raw materials were present on the spot. Thanks to the determination of Chevalier de Viviers, who directed the operations, and to the support of Seignelay, navy minister, men and material were transferred to Marseilles in time.
Berquin's striking panorama shows these fifteen galleys in different stages of construction. **A. M.-V.**

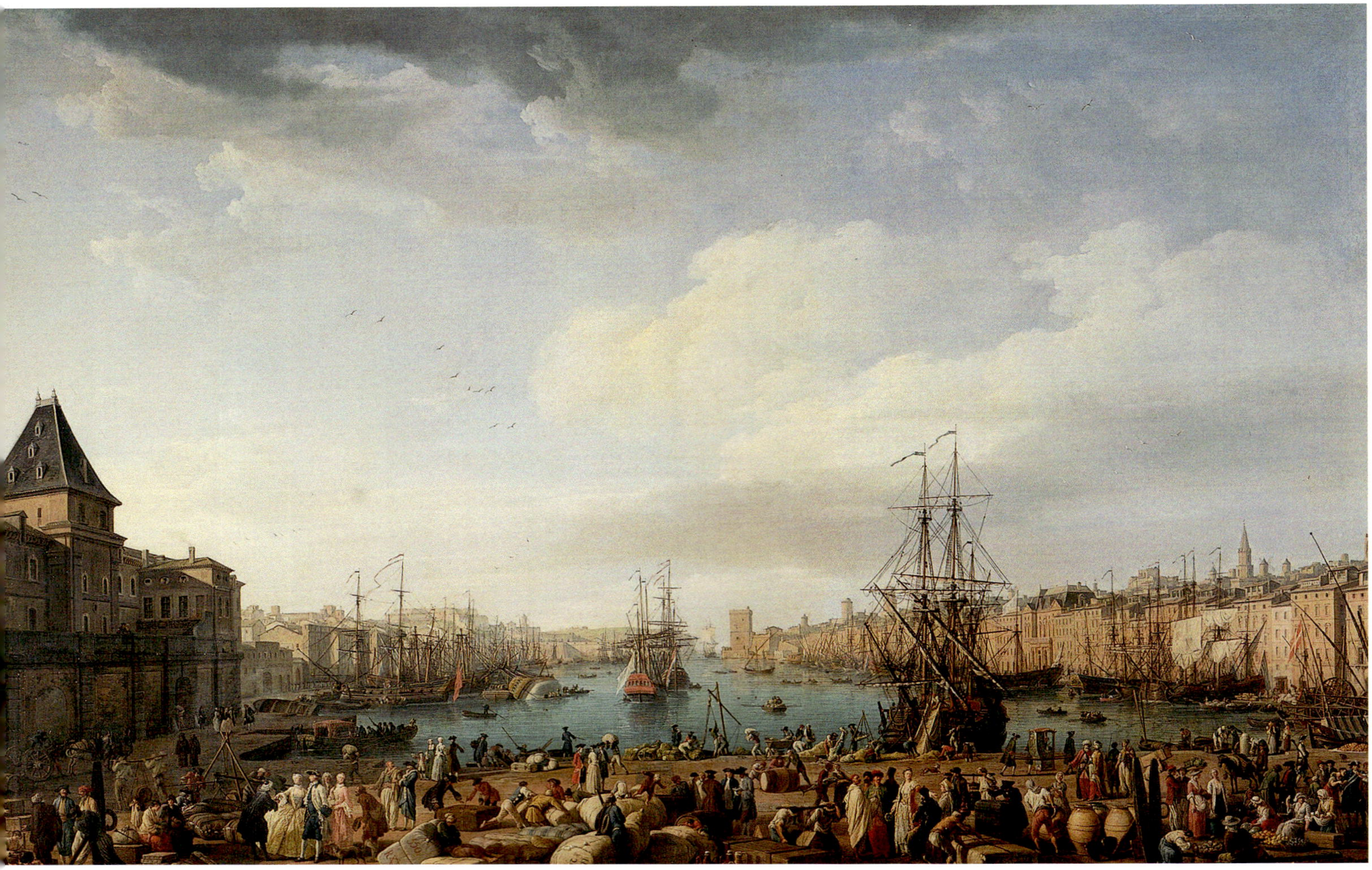

Joseph Vernet (1714–1789)

In the port of Marseilles,
seen from the Pavillon de l'Horloge in the Park

1754 . Oil on canvas . 165 x 263 cm . Signed and dated bottom centre . On loan from the Department of Paintings, Musée du Louvre, 1943 (inv. 8294) . MnM 5 OA 3 D

This view of the port of Marseilles, the first canvas commissioned by Louis XV from Joseph Vernet, shows the cosmopolitan crowd in a port of trade. Along the wharf are Turks in richly coloured costumes, elegant ladies in flowing dresses, and small fruit sellers. Each group, treated as a little individual genre scene, succeeds in contributing to an overall composition of exceptional virtuosity.

In the dock, fat-bellied Dutch ships lie next to Mediterranean tartans and narrow British ships. This international presence highlights the importance of the port of Marseilles in the mid-18th century. **A. M.-V.**

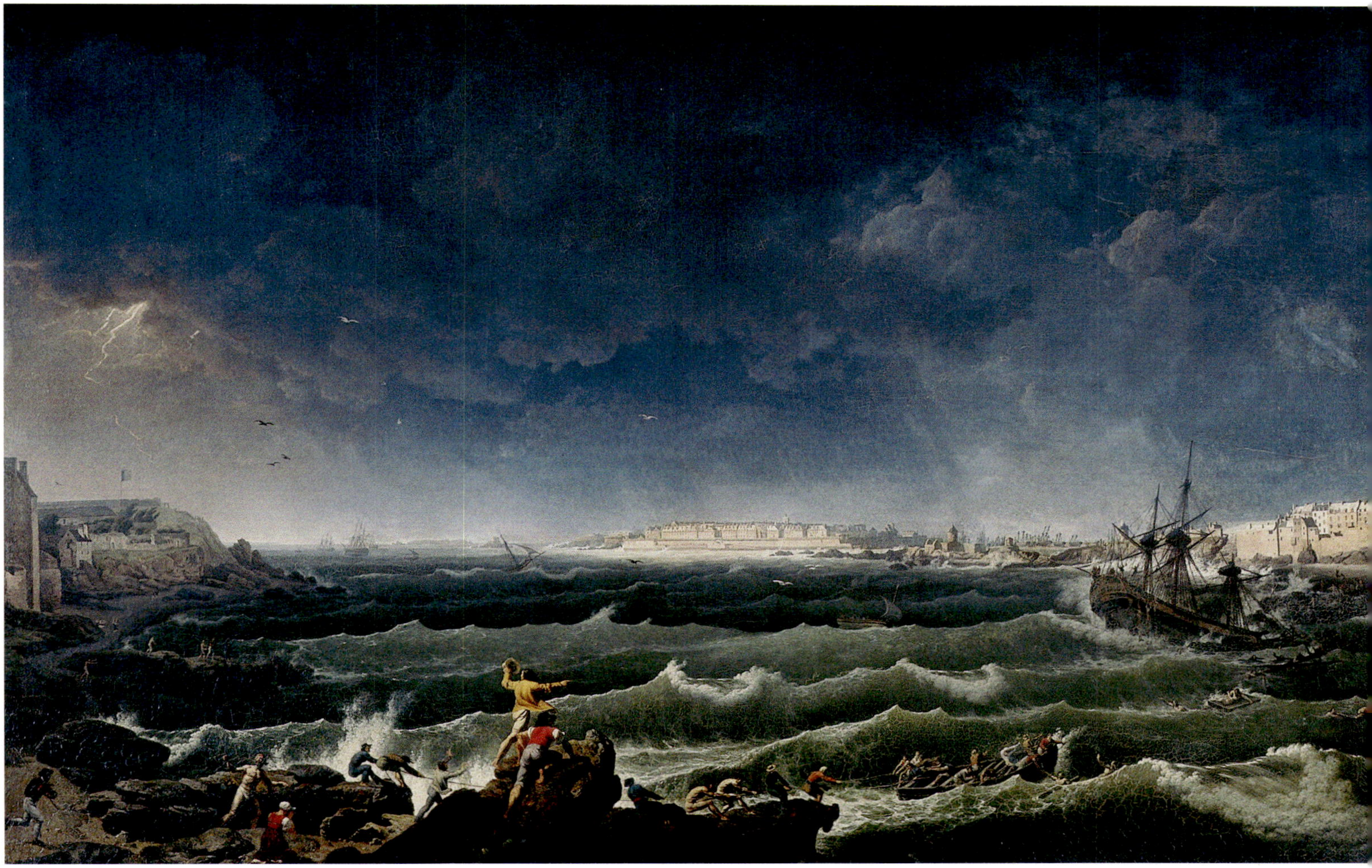

Jean-François Hue (1751–1823)

View of Saint-Malo

Second half of 18th century . Oil on canvas . 165 x 260 cm . Signed on lower left . On loan from the Department of Paintings, Musée du Louvre (inv. 5399) . MnM 7 OA 3 D

Scenes in which man struggles against the elements were in vogue in the late 18th century. In Hue's painting, where minuscule figures set in an immense landscape desperately try to fight the fury of the waves, the artist gives a metaphysical dimension to the scene; he shows not only a storm in the bay of Saint-Malo, but man's eternal struggle against hostile nature. A. M.-V.

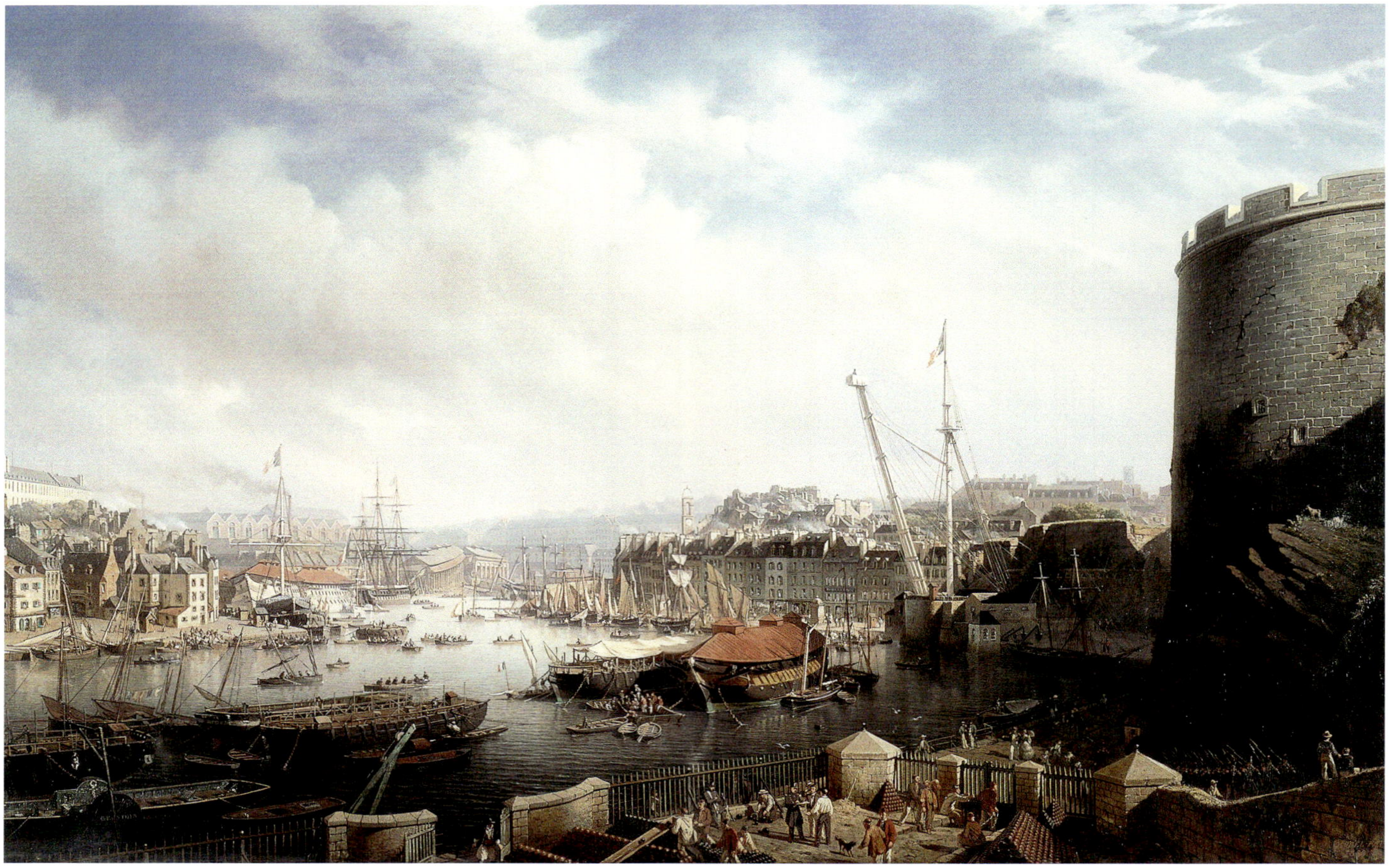

Antoine Léon Morel-Fatio (1810–1871)

The port of Brest

1854 . Oil on canvas . 163 x 260 cm . Signed and dated on lower right . Entered museum collections 1939 . MnM Paris 9 OA 11

When Morel-Fatio painted the Penfeld River packed with fishing boats and naval ships, Brest was on the verge of transformation. The painter shows the last convicts in the cannonball park, just before the penal colony was transferred to Guyana, as decreed by the law of 1854. The construction of the swing bridge began in 1856.
This painting was executed when Antoine Morel-Fatio was deputy curator of the Musée de Marine, the year of his appointment as official painter to the navy. A. M.-V.

Anonymous

Swing bridge in Recouvrance, Brest

Panorama in three parts . July 1861 . Print on albumen paper . 26 x 89.2 cm . Entered museum collections 1913 . MnM Photographs collection

Anonymous

Port of Brest

Panorama in three parts . 6 August 1861 . Print on albumen paper . 25.9 x 88 cm . Entered museum collections 1913 . MnM Photographs collection

Anonymous

Entrance to the port of Brest, view taken from the royal battery

Panorama in four parts . 1861 . Print on albumen paper . 48.5 x 91 cm . Entered museum collections 1913 . MnM Photographs collection

The imperial bridge – a metal swing bridge over the Penfeld River – was opened on 23 June 1861. These three views of the Brest dockyard were taken shortly afterwards by a photographer sent by the navy to document the modernity of France's leading naval port. Arranged in panoramas, these admirably preserved prints also serve as records of a lost architectural structure, designed in the 18th century by Choquet de Lindu and destroyed in 1944. Because of the very long exposure time, hundreds of workers busy on the construction and maintenance of ships were not captured on the negative. A. M.

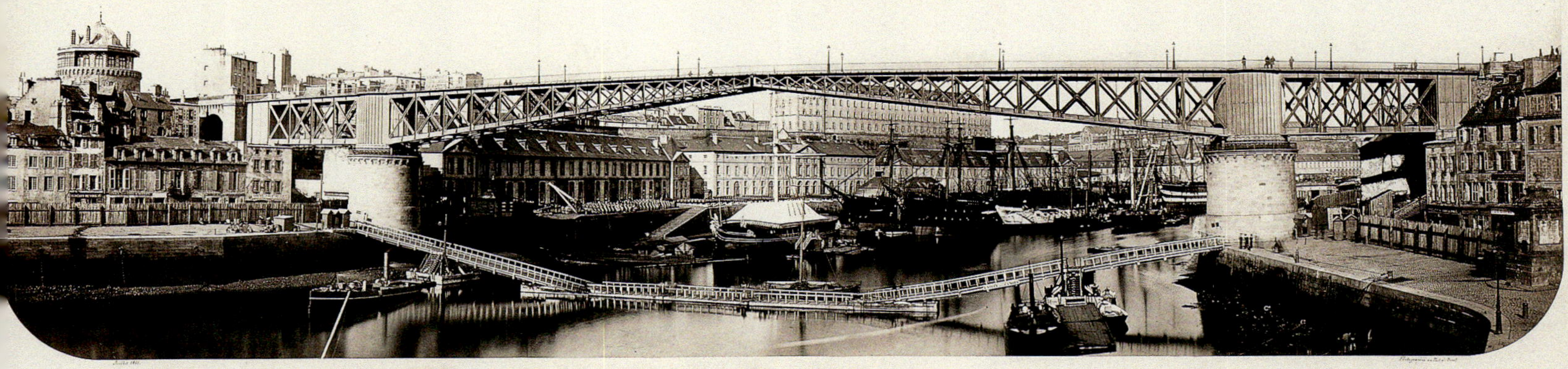

Pont tournant de Brest à Recouvrance.

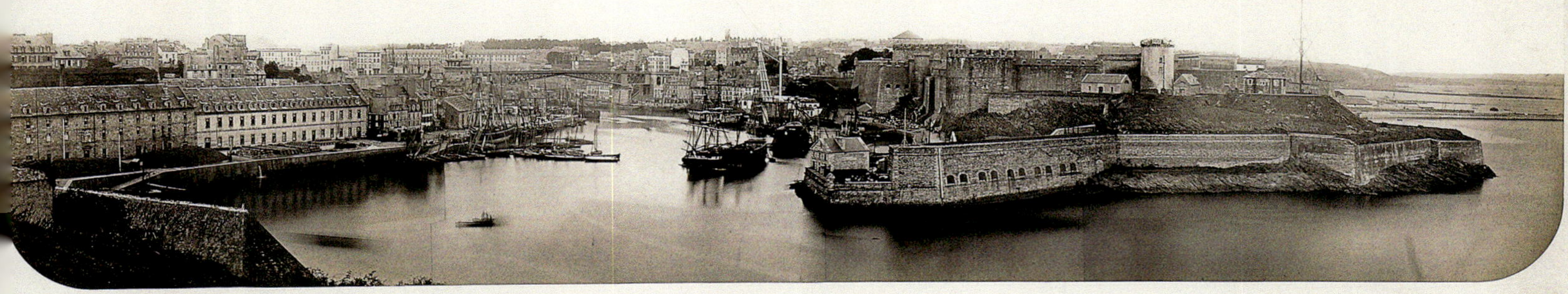

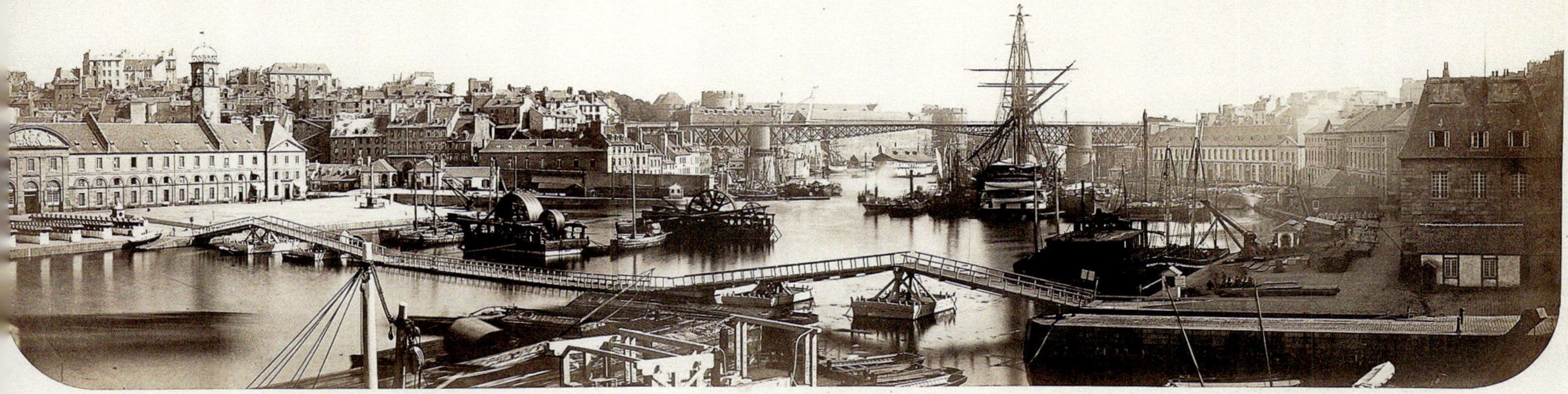

Port de Brest

Brest, 6 Août 1861

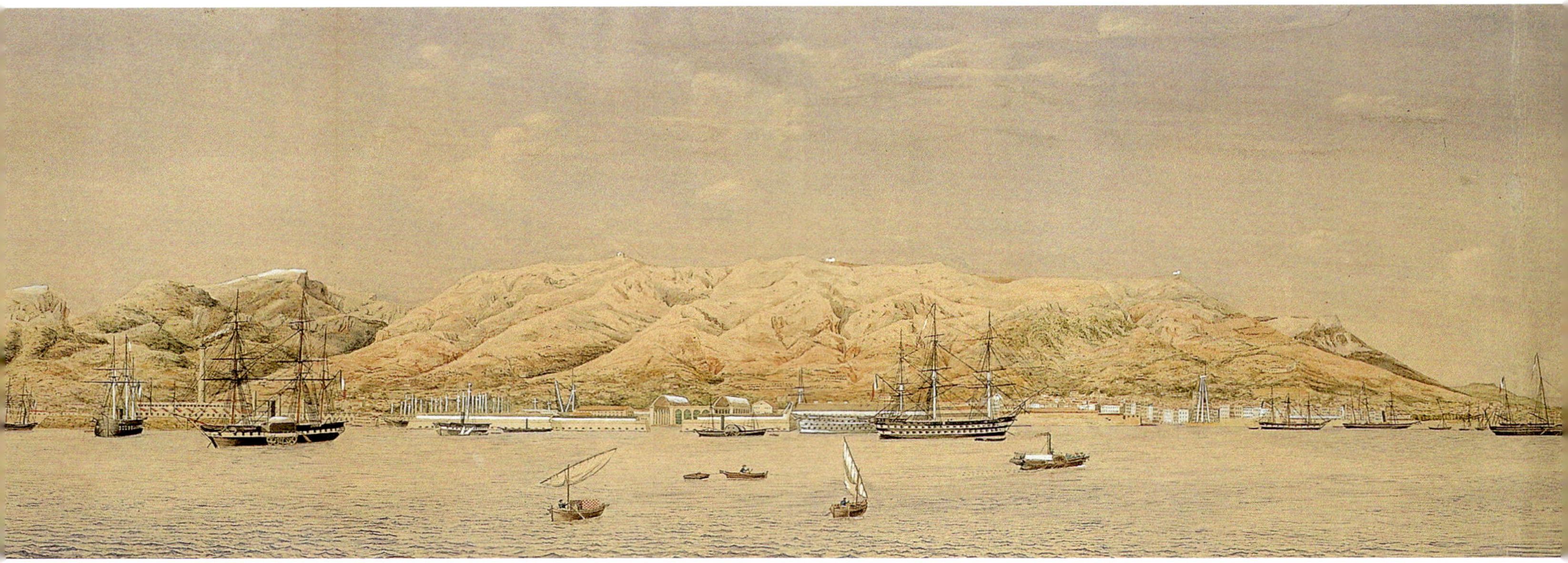

François Edmond Pâris (1806–1893)

Toulon, wide-angle view of the harbour (overall view and detail)

Circa 1856 . Watercolour, white gouache and crayon on vellum paper . 63.7 x 698 cm . Entered museum collections 1907 . MnM 15 OA 78

Curator of the Musée de la Marine from 1871 to 1893, Amiral Pâris devoted much of his life to preserving the maritime heritage of his century. This picture is a snapshot of the ships used in the Mediterranean in the mid-19th century, from fishing boats to naval ships, both sail- and motor-powered.

The admiral executed a number of watercolours in unusual formats. Six panoramas representing the Bay of Rio, the Suez Canal and Port Said are kept in the museum. A. M.-V.

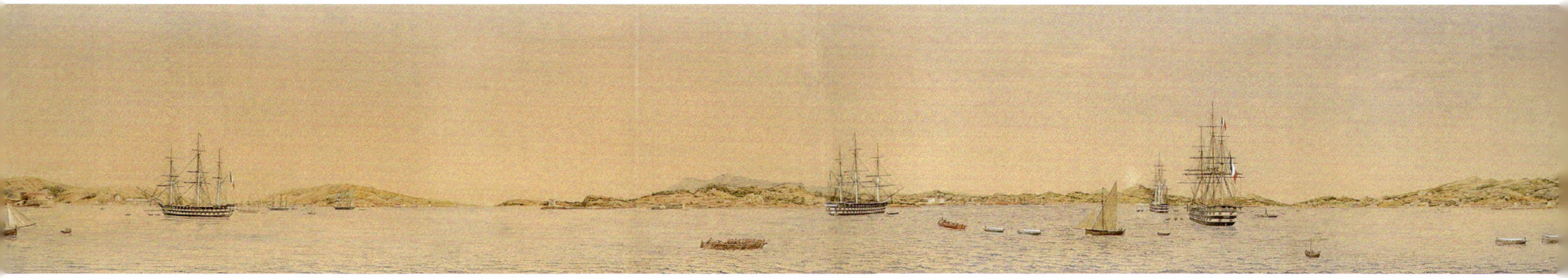

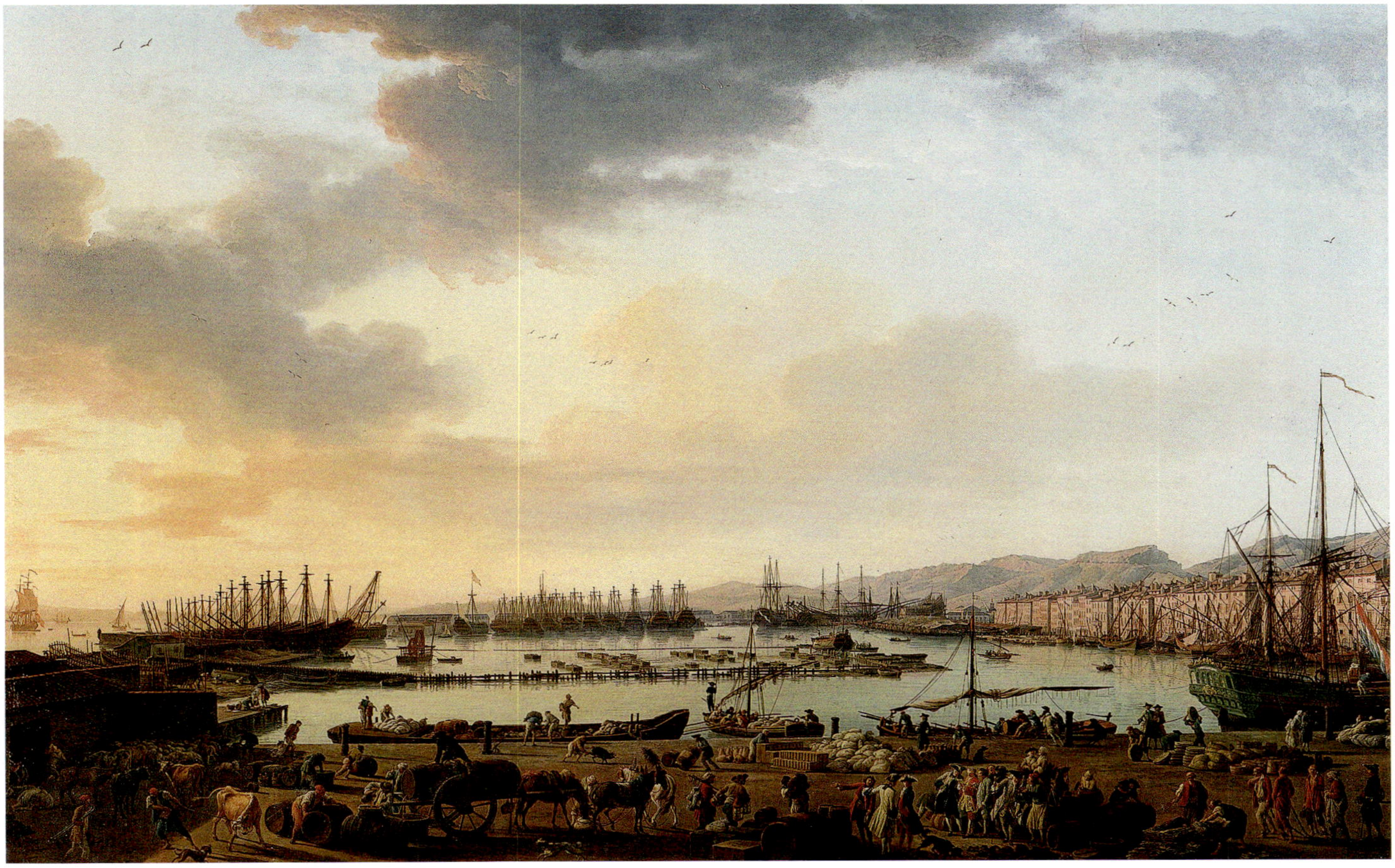

Joseph Vernet (1714–1789)

The old port of Toulon. View taken from the provisions stores

1756 . Oil on canvas . 165 x 263 cm . On loan from the Department of Paintings, Musée du Louvre, 1943 (inv. 8298) . MnM 5 OA 1 D

In this sixth painting in the 'Views of France's Ports' series, Vernet depicts a range of Mediterranean ships of the time: xebecs, a lateen-rigged boat and galleys lie side by side. In a play of golden light and shade at sunset, the painter contrasts the silhouetted ships on the left with the light row of houses on the right. In the foreground are piles of sacks of biscuits, barrels of wine and dried fish, ready to be loaded on the ship in the background. A. M.-V.

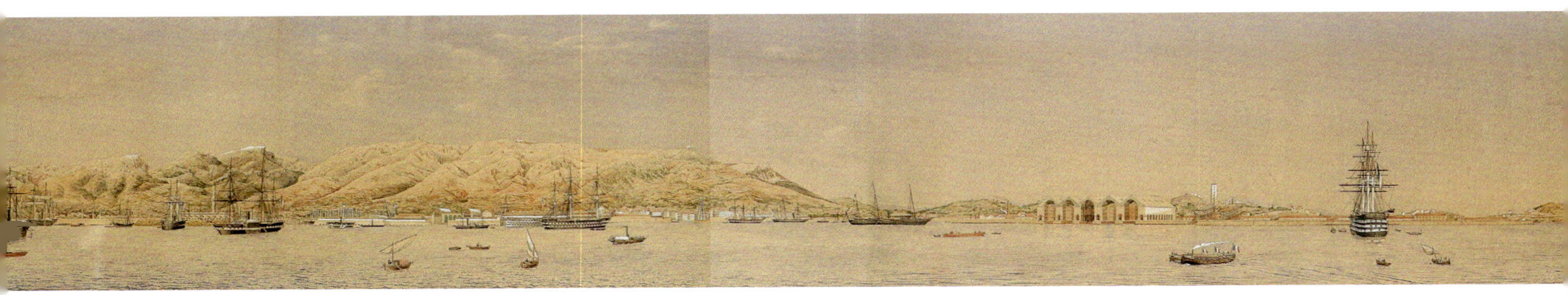

Official visits

Whether military or commercial, sea ports regularly served as the settings for official ceremonies. Following a protocol dating largely from the Ancien Régime, the sovereign or head of state or government would come to inspect the military or economic facilities he had ordered to be developed. A naval revue usually constituted the high point of these visits. Each major port had a lavishly decorated ceremonial barge that was used for these grand occasions. It served to tour the dockyard, sail out to the flagship anchored in the harbour, and to entertain illustrious visitors aboard. One of the finest preserved specimens is housed in the Musée National de la Marine.

Moreover, at a time when any distant journey was made by sea, entry into the harbour during state visits also entailed a diplomatic ritual. Beyond the protocol, this arrival of a foreign monarch or head of state was sometimes a political event in its own right: Napoleon III's welcoming of Queen Victoria at Cherbourg in 1858 symbolised Franco-British reconciliation. Little would remain of these grandiose ceremonies were it not for official paintings, which captured them for posterity on great canvases, and for diplomatic gifts, a number of which have been preserved in national collections.

It was in this period in the mid-19th century that the first great state yachts were built. In a Europe of monarchies, these prestigious vessels naturally served to represent France, but they were also used for leisure purposes, at a time when a taste for sailing cruises was developing. However, this decorum, deemed extravagant, was hard to reconcile with Republican values: After the fall of the Empire, Napoleon III's imperial yacht *L'Aigle* was transferred to the navy and converted into a corvette with paddle wheels under the name *Rapide*.

The Emperor's Barge

Ceremonial barge built for Napoleon I . After drawings by the engineer Guillemard (fl. 19th century) . 1810 . Painted wood, gilded wood (sculptures), metal . 18.80 x 5.45 x 3.80 cm . Entered museum collections 1943 . MnM 7 SO 2

Ceremonial barges were small oar-powered boats, sometimes rigged, more or less lavishly decorated, traditionally used in naval dockyards until the mid-20th century for official visits by royalty and heads of state. The only complete specimen preserved in France is the one built for Napoleon I's visit to the Antwerp dockyard in 1810. Transferred in 1814 to Brest, where its decoration underwent a series of alterations, it remained the only ceremonial barge in use in France for over a century. Its transfer to Paris in 1943 saved it from the bombing of Brest at the end of World War II. M. M.

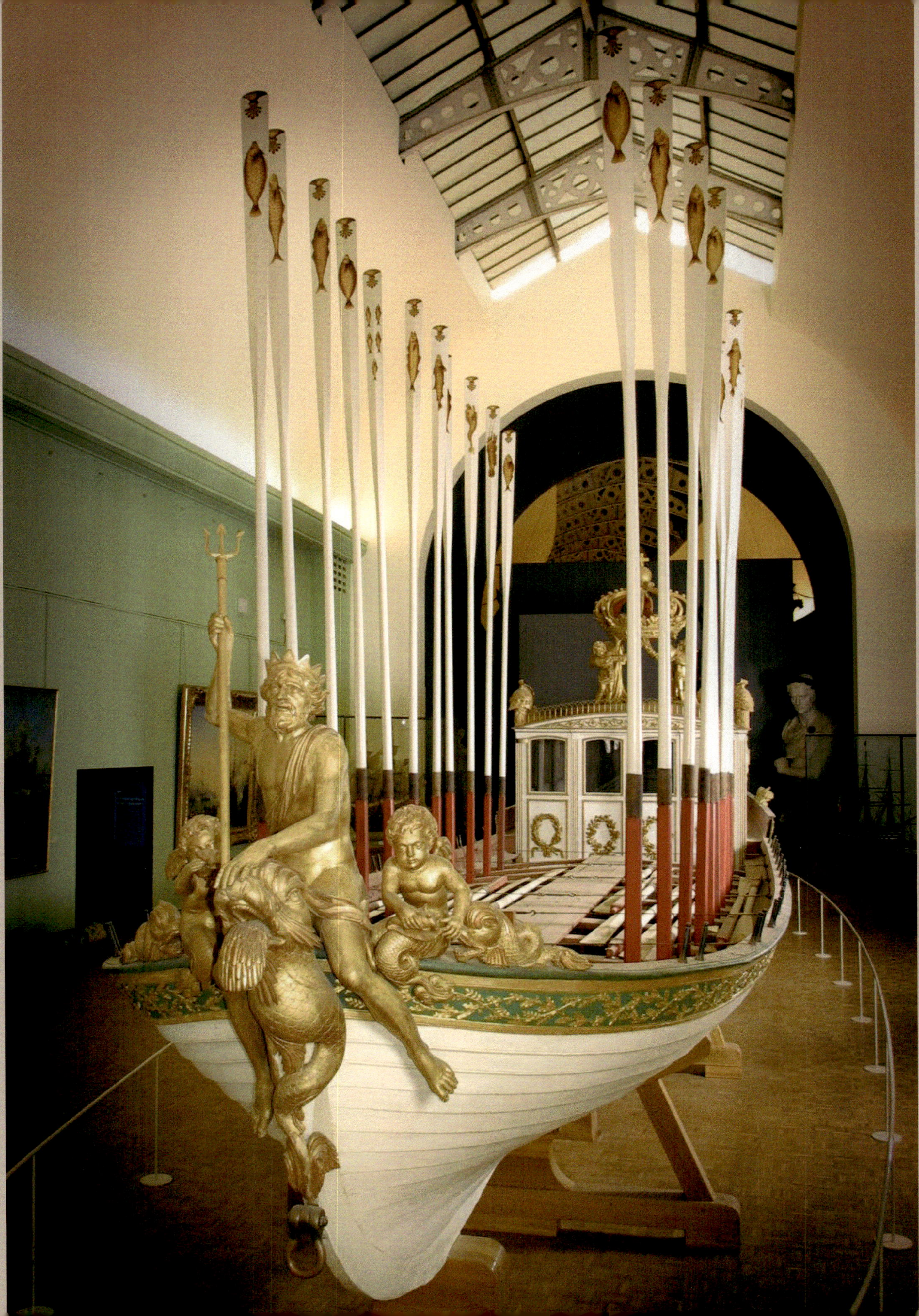

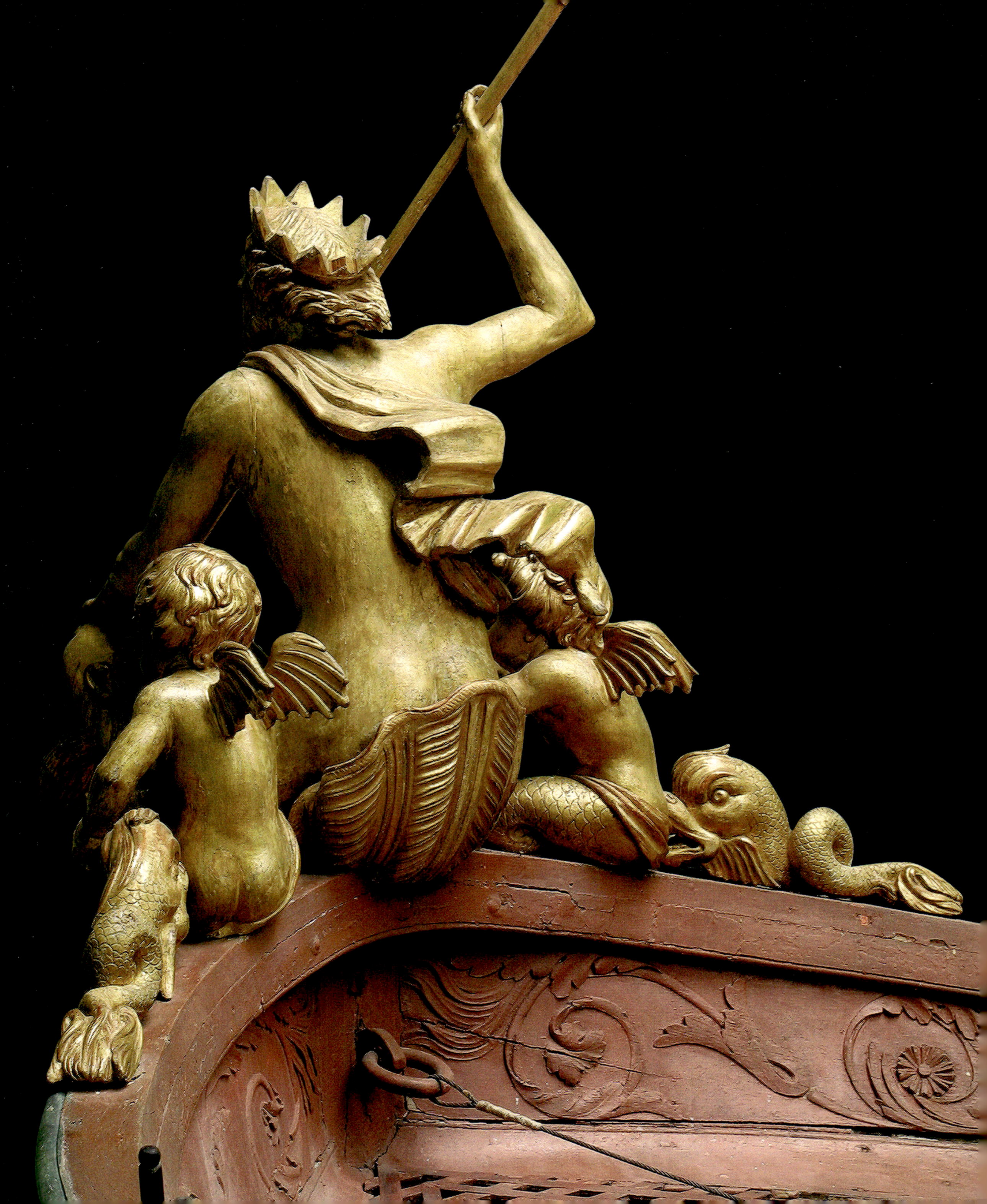

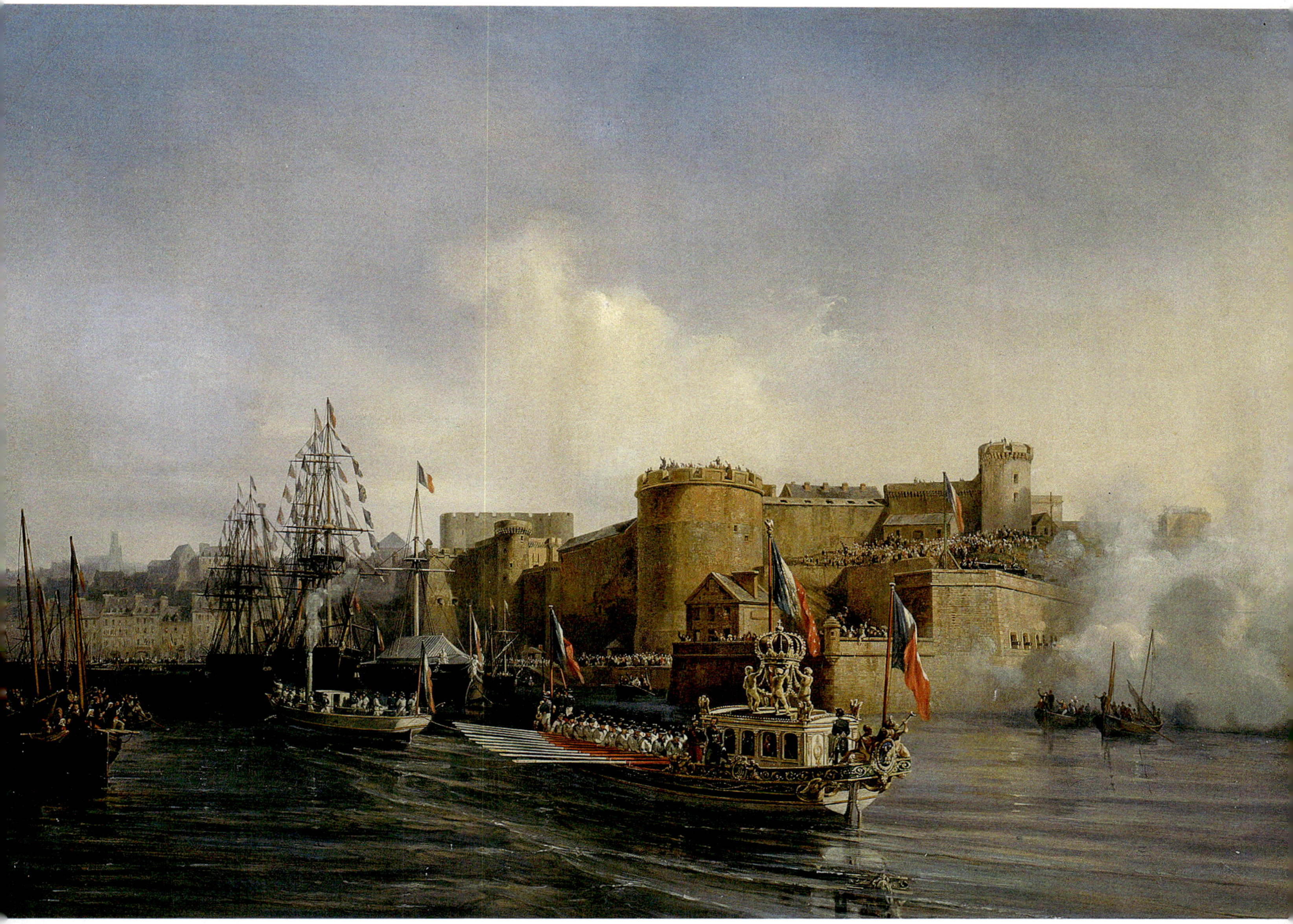

Detail of the figurehead of the Emperor's Barge, seen from behind

Neptune riding a sea monster accompanied by Tritons and dolphins

Sculpture in the round, gilded wood . MnM SO 2

Auguste Mayer (1805–1890)

Napoleon III's visit to Brest, 11 August 1858

1859 . Oil on canvas . 64 x 96.5 cm . Entered museum collections 1939 . MnM 9 OA 14

Once royal, the old Brest barge became imperial once again for the official visit of Napoleon III in August 1858. In the course of the events organised in honour of the British sovereigns' visit to France, the emperor made a tour of the Penfeld River aboard his barge. Auguste Mayer captured the moment when the boat, towed by a steamer, passes before the castle. A masterly illustrator, Mayer reproduced in detail all the carvings making up the sumptuous decoration of the barge; they remain, with a few small exceptions, those we can admire today. M. M.

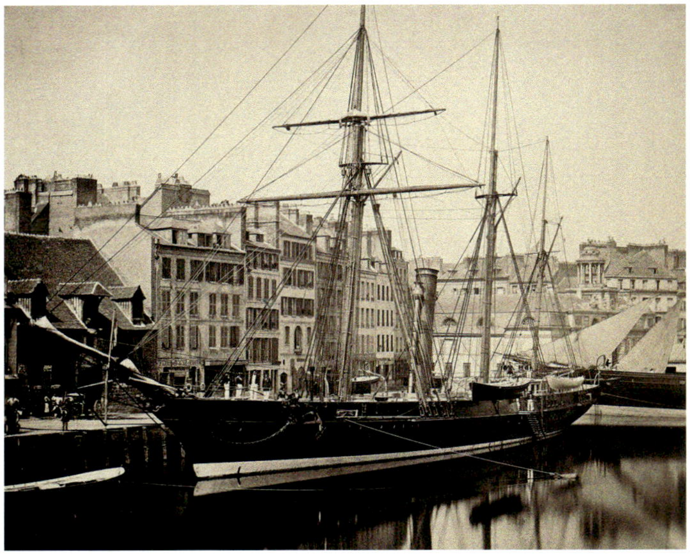

Gustave Le Gray (1820–1884)

The imperial yacht 'Reine-Hortense' in Le Havre harbour

1856 . Albumen print after glass negative . 30.4 x 36.2 cm . Entered museum collections 1913 . MnM Photographs collection

The *Reine-Hortense*, the imperial family yacht from 1853 to 1867, is here photographed docked at Le Havre. An excellent photographer, inventor and author of photography treatises, Gustave Le Gray was one of the most prolific official photographers of the Second Empire. He executed this remarkable portrait of a boat in subtle tones just before its departure for Spitsbergen. The official yacht's participation in a scientific expedition was due to Prince Napoleon's (cousin of the emperor) keen interest in science. The people on the deck stand immobile, turned towards the photographer, suggesting that Le Gray, positioned on one of the escort vessels, had asked them to strike the pose. **A. M.**

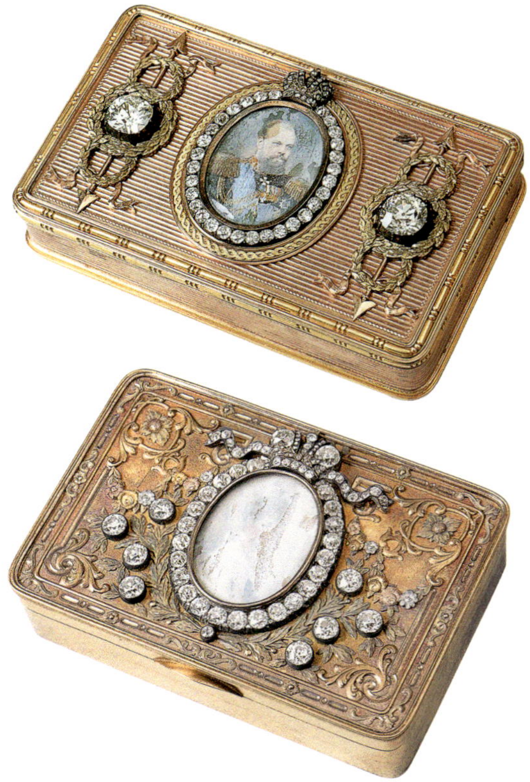

Mikhail Evlampievich Perkhin (1860–1903)
Carl Fabergé workshop in St Petersburg

Boxes with portraits of Alexander III and Maria Feodorovna

1891 . Gold, diamonds (boxes); miniatures on ivory . 2.5 x 10.2 x 6.3 cm; 2.5 x 9.5 x 6.2 cm . Entered museum collections 1922 . MnM 7 SO 32, 33

These two gold boxes studded with diamonds are decorated with miniatures of Emperor Alexander III of Russia and his consort Maria Feodorovna. They are among the rarest gifts exchanged in the context of the Franco-Russian Alliance and were presented to Amiral Gervais in 1891. Each bears the hallmarks of the Fabergé workshop in St Petersburg, as well as the initials of Mikhail Evlampievich Perkhin, head workmaster to Carl Fabergé since 1886. It was during this period that the Fabergé house produced its collection of objets d'art, particularly the famous Easter eggs, and became official supplier to the Russian court. **M. M.**

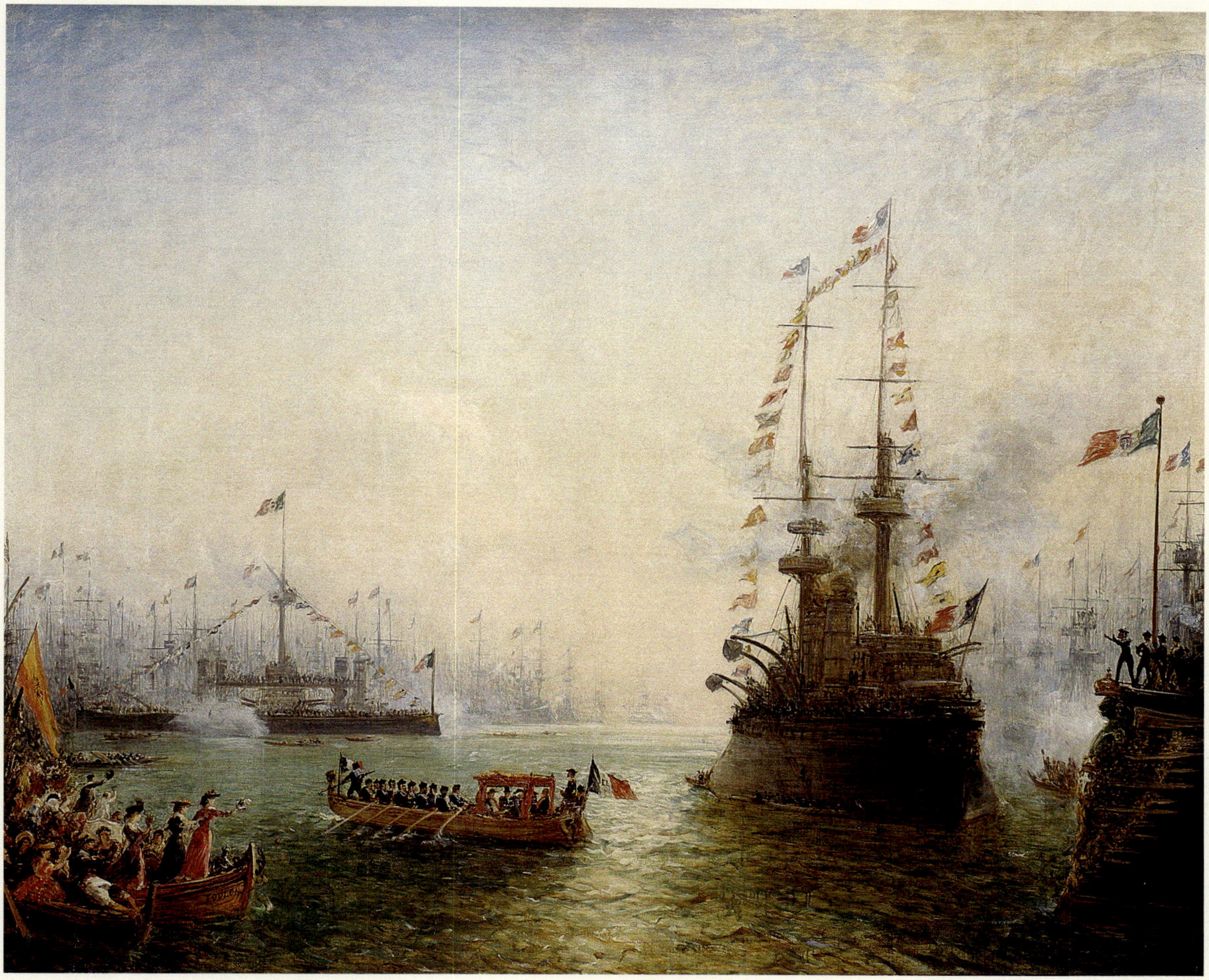

Félix Ziem (1821–1911)

Toulon, visit of President Loubet to the French and Italian squadrons, 10 April 1901

1901 . Oil on canvas . 200 x 250 cm . Signed and dated lower left . Entered museum collections 1943 . MnM 11 OA 139

When Félix Ziem was commissioned to paint this picture – a few days before the festivities held in Toulon for the official visit of the Duke of Genoa, admiral of the Italian fleet – the navy minister informed him that he was free to choose its subject. The painter chose the scene when President Loubet has just left the battleship *Saint-Louis*. The composition is centred on the traditional ceremonial barge, which the authorities have boarded to cross the harbour, and which appears rather fragile amongst the battleships of the two squadrons. This work, the largest of Ziem's pictures known to us to date, established the artist's appointment as official painter to the French navy. M. M.

The wooden shipbuilding industry

The 18th-century harbour-dockyard, the first state-owned industrial structure in the Western world, was the seat of naval shipbuilding and technological experimentation. The large sailing ships built there were probably the most complex machines made by man at the time.

The shipbuilders' lack of scientific training was a weakness that did not escape the attention of the French navy's general inspector Duhamel du Monceau when he visited the shipyards. A man of the Enlightenment, a staunch advocate of progress, encyclopaedist and member of the Académie des Sciences, in 1741 Duhamel du Monceau proposed the establishment of a naval school where trainee shipwrights would learn mathematics, physics and the best methods of calculation for ship drawings. To complete the students' training, Duhamel du Monceau gave the king his collection of models of ships and dockyard facilities, the largest of the time, on condition that it be installed in the old Louvre palace, next to the school. In the Salle de Marine, opened for this purpose in 1748, rope-making and mast-raising machines, bucket dredges, dioramas of careened ships and so on were used in the students' practical work. The collection demonstrated how these machines worked and gave students a better understanding of the production capacities of a shipyard. Until its closure in 1793, the Salle de Marine reflected the diversity and wealth of the history of shipbuilding and associated techniques.

The enthusiasm of high society for scientific and technical culture and the great voyages of discovery gave rise to other collections of maritime objects, such as those of the Duke of Orleans and the Académie de Marine in Brest, for which the remarkable 'Coque de Pic' (Pic's hull) was originally made. But owing to its richness, and because its donator considered it to be of more use to the Nation than to himself, it was the Duhamel du Monceau collection that laid down the cultural and institutional bases of a national maritime museum.

Mast-raising vessel

Model of the floating machine in Toulon harbour . Anonymous . Early 18th century . Wood, metal, cotton . 100 x 105 x 55 cm . Entered museum collections 1829, former Salle de Marine Collection . MnM 13 PA 11

Masting machines, which could be floating or on shore, were used to install lower masts on ships that were near completion. The lifting system was operated by capstans or wheels driven by workhands. In 1722, Toulon harbour received a masting machine built out of an old 50-gun ship, *L'Entreprenant*, launched in 1679 and decommissioned in 1720. A. N.

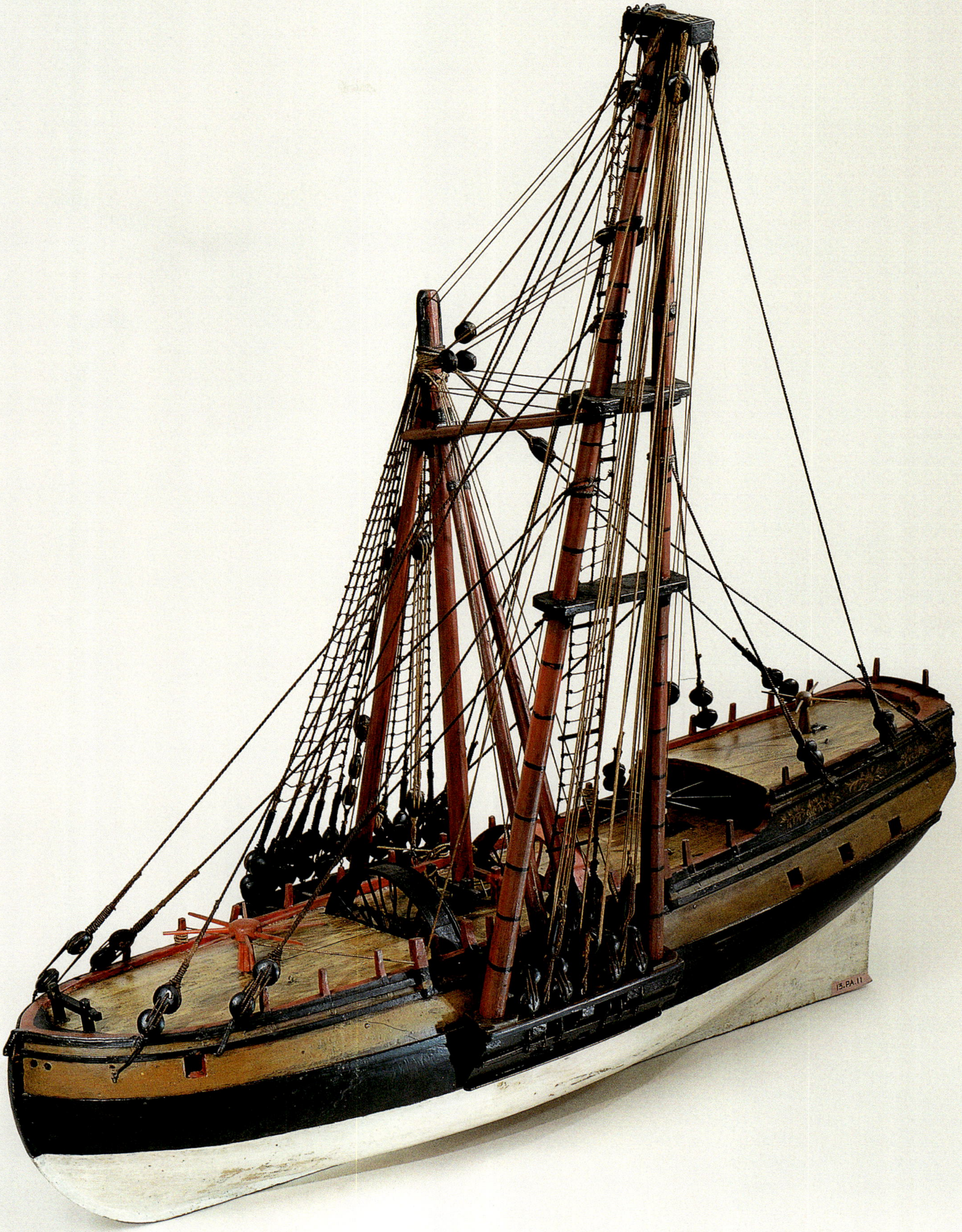
13.PA.11

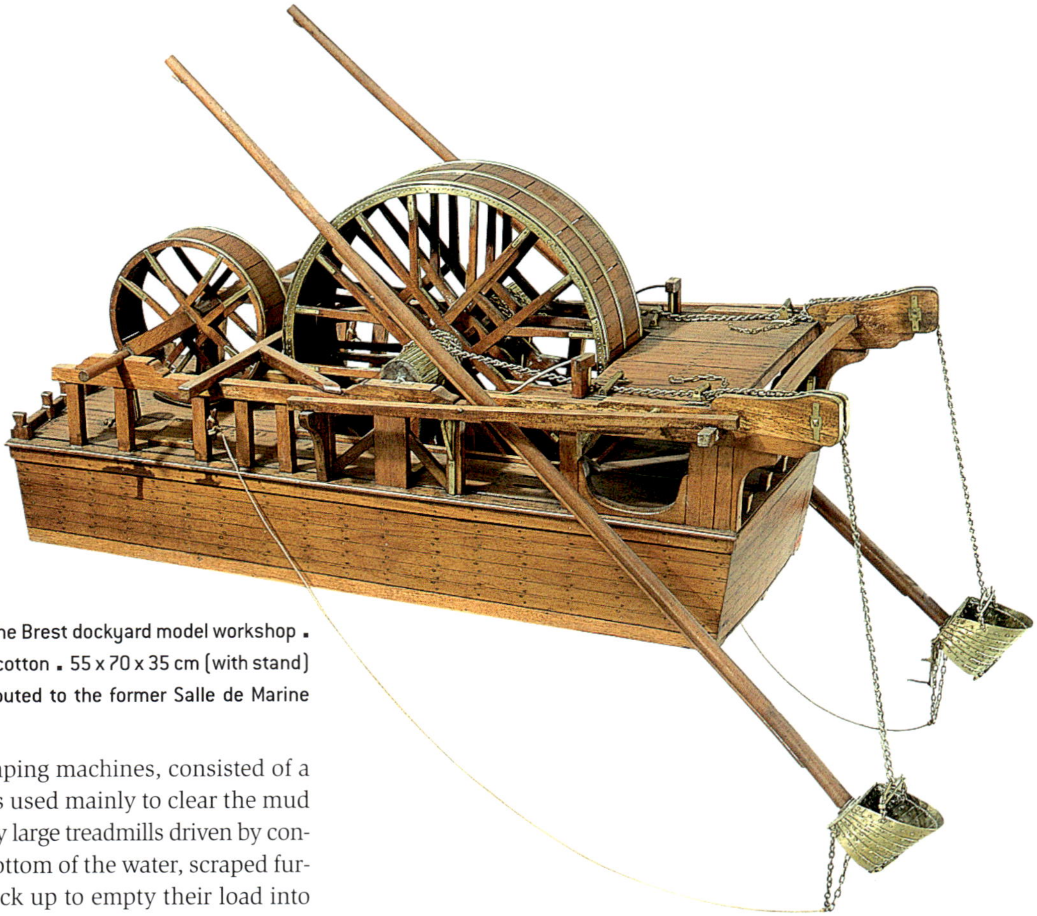

Dredge

Model of harbour dredge ▪ Constructed by the Brest dockyard model workshop ▪ Second half of 18th century ▪ Wood, metal, cotton ▪ 55 x 70 x 35 cm (with stand) ▪ Entered museum collections 1829, attributed to the former Salle de Marine Collection ▪ MnM 15 PA 4

In the 18th century, dredges, or scraping machines, consisted of a pontoon equipped with huge scoops used mainly to clear the mud off the bed of the harbour. Powered by large treadmills driven by convicts, the scoops descended to the bottom of the water, scraped furrows out of the sea bed and rose back up to empty their load into 'flap' dumb-barges. A. N.

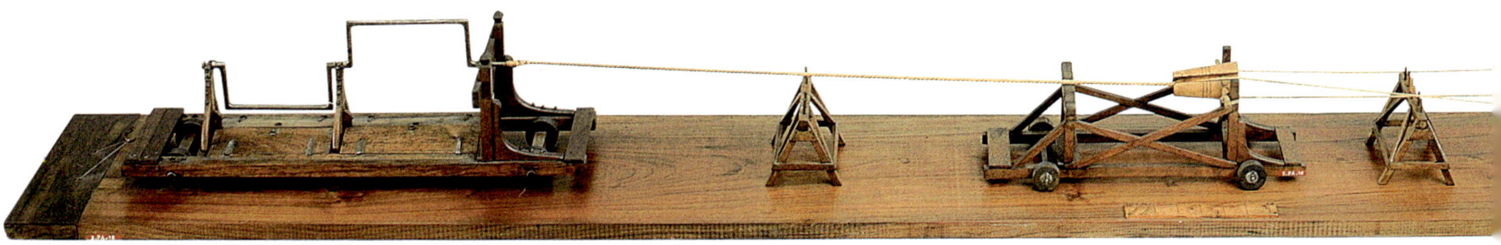

Rope-walk

Model of a rope-making machine, 1:12 scale ▪ Attributed to the Toulon dockyard model workshop ▪ Second half of 18th century ▪ Wood, iron ▪ 23 x 236 x 31 cm ▪ Entered museum collections 1949 ▪ MnM 3 PA 16

The operation shown on this rope-making machine, or rope-walk, installed in every major naval port in the 18th century, illustrates the 'laying up' or twisting together of three strands into a hawser (anchor cable). To provide a clearer overall picture of the system, the distances between the various elements (fixed and mobile frames, trestles, truck and strand separator) have been reduced to scale (anchor cables were almost 195 meters long). A. N.

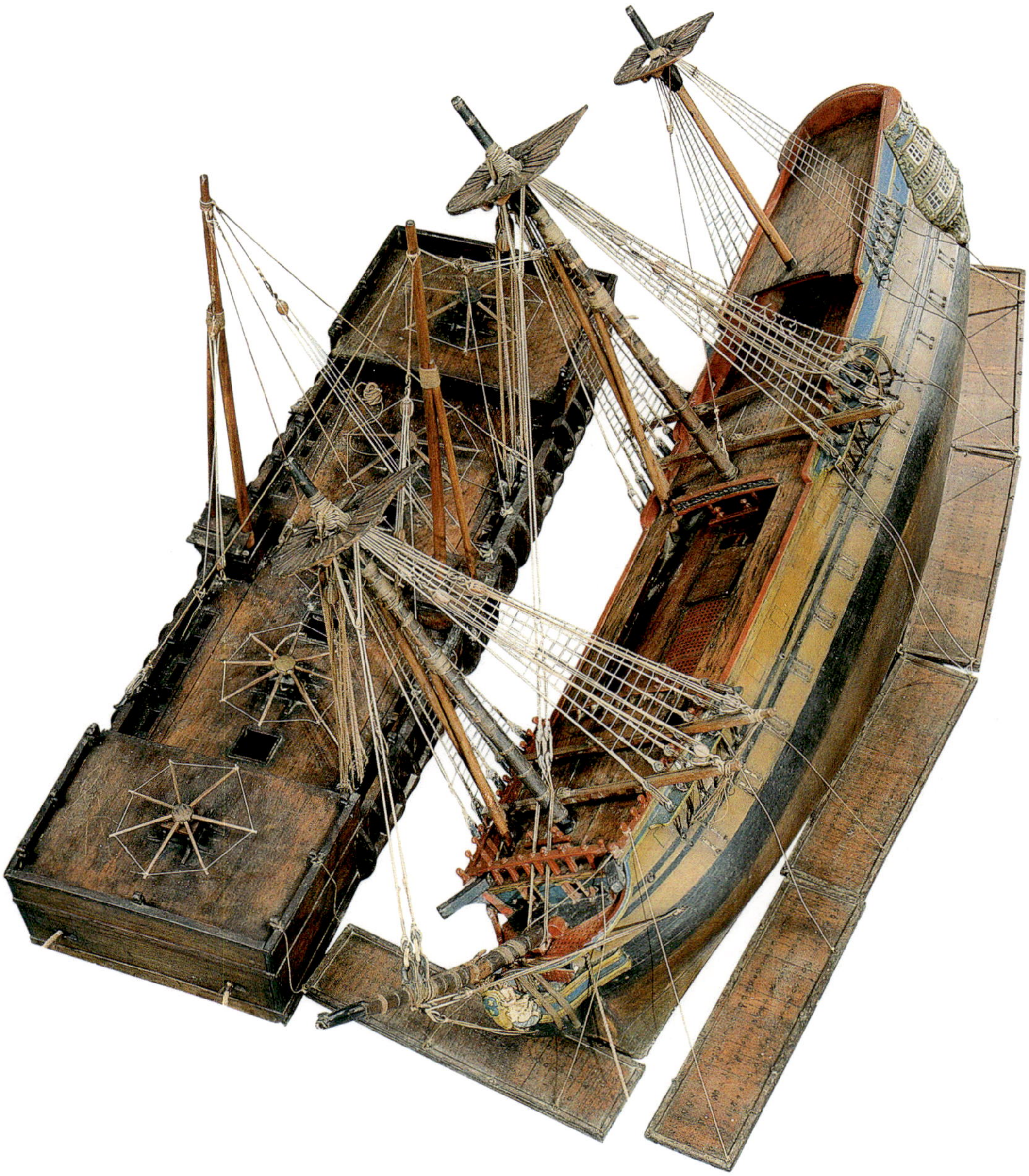

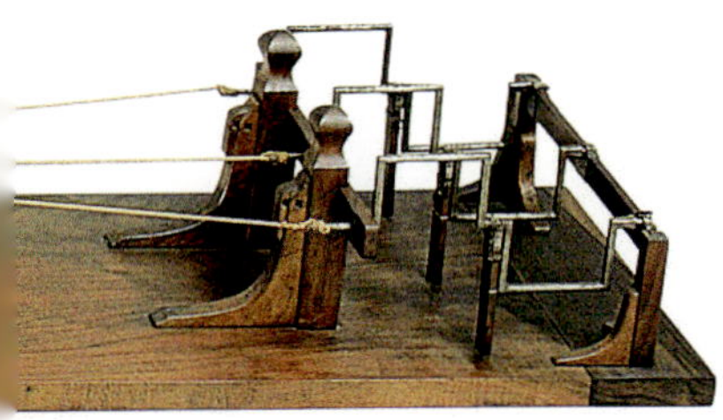

The *Brillant* careened

Model of the ship *Le Brillant* careened, 1:72 scale ▪ Anonymous ▪ Second half of 18th century ▪ Wood, cotton ▪ 49 x 107 x 64.5 cm ▪ Entered museum collections before 1829, former Salle de Marine Collection ▪ MnM 13 PA 28

Careening was the method employed in the 18th and 19th centuries to carry out maintenance and repairs of hulls of sailing ships when there was no dry dock available. The operation consisted in heeling the ship to one side, at sea or on land, in order to access that part of the hull that was normally underwater. It was generally done using hoists, capstans and heavy-load derricks, the careening itself being carried out on floating pontoons. A. N.

The Amphidrome

Model of an 'amphidrome corvette' ▪ Anonymous, after drawings by Amiral Willaumez (1761–1845) ▪ Circa 1830 ▪ Wood, iron, brass, cotton ▪ 105 x 105 x 53 cm ▪ Entered museum collections 1977 ▪ MnM 21 MG 64

This corvette identical at each extremity and equipped with 180° mobile yards could, in theory, change course without tacking (i.e. without bringing the wind on the opposite side). To compensate for the absence of wind, the ship could also be propelled with a system of wheels connected to the large capstan. This project was of course never built. *L'Amphidrome* belongs to a series of ten model ships designed or modified by the admiral Willaumez. On loan to the Musée de la Marine at the Louvre in 1837 and withdrawn in 1839, these models disappeared in the 19th century. The model of *L'Amphidrome* was rediscovered in the United States in the mid-20th century and was given to the Musée de la Marine by the New Bedford Whaling Museum (Massachusetts). A. N.

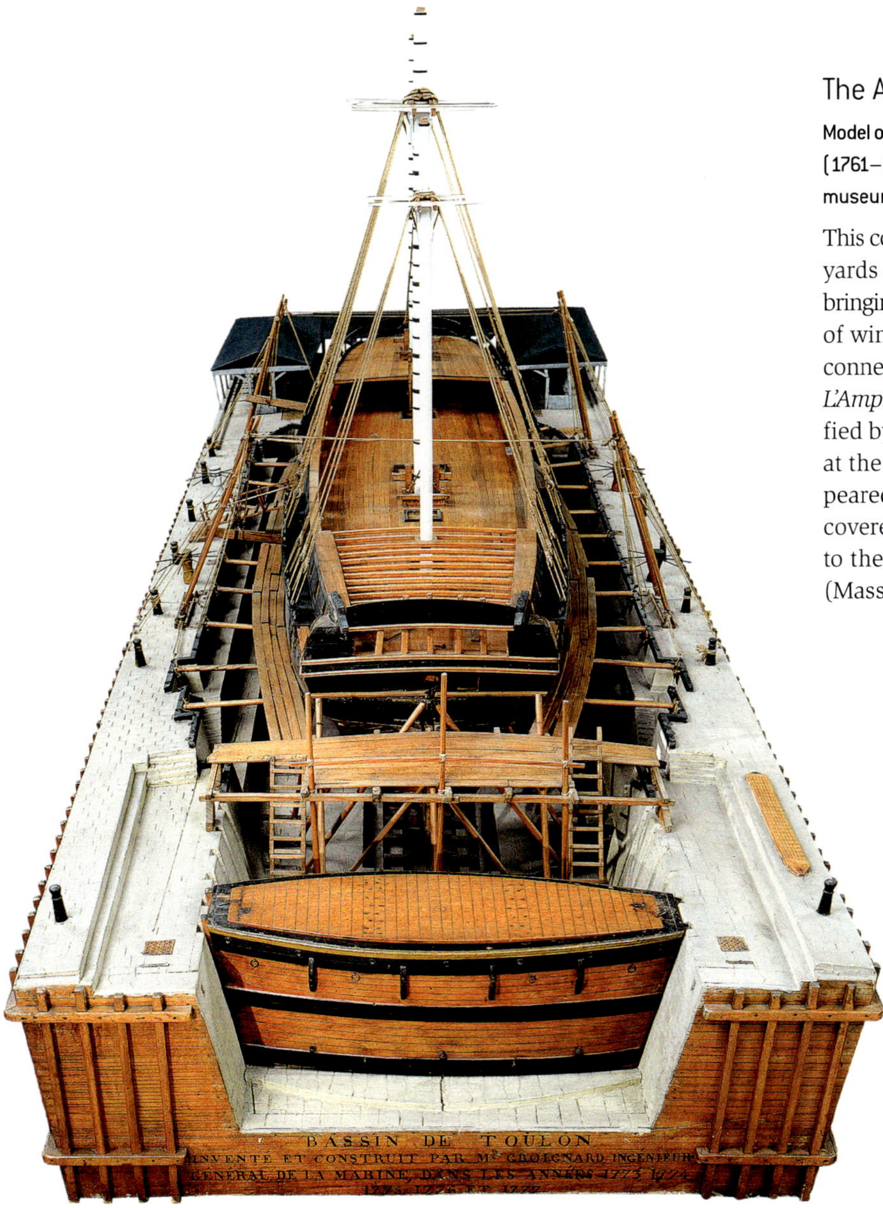

Toulon dry dock

Model of the No. 1 dry dock at Toulon, 1:48 scale ▪ Anonymous, after drawings by Antoine Groignard (1727–1799) ▪ Circa 1778 ▪ Wood, metal ▪ 36 x 218 x 75 cm ▪ Entered museum collections 1829, former Salle de Marine Collection ▪ MnM 1 PA 7.1

In 1774, the Académie des Sciences commended a project to construct a dry dock for ship maintenance at Toulon designed by the naval construction engineer Groignard. Built between 1774 and 1778 using an ingenious submerged coffering system that enabled masonry to be laid below sea level, the No. 1 dock at Toulon is still in activity to this day. A later model, that of the frigate *La Guerrière*, was added in the late 19th century. A. N.

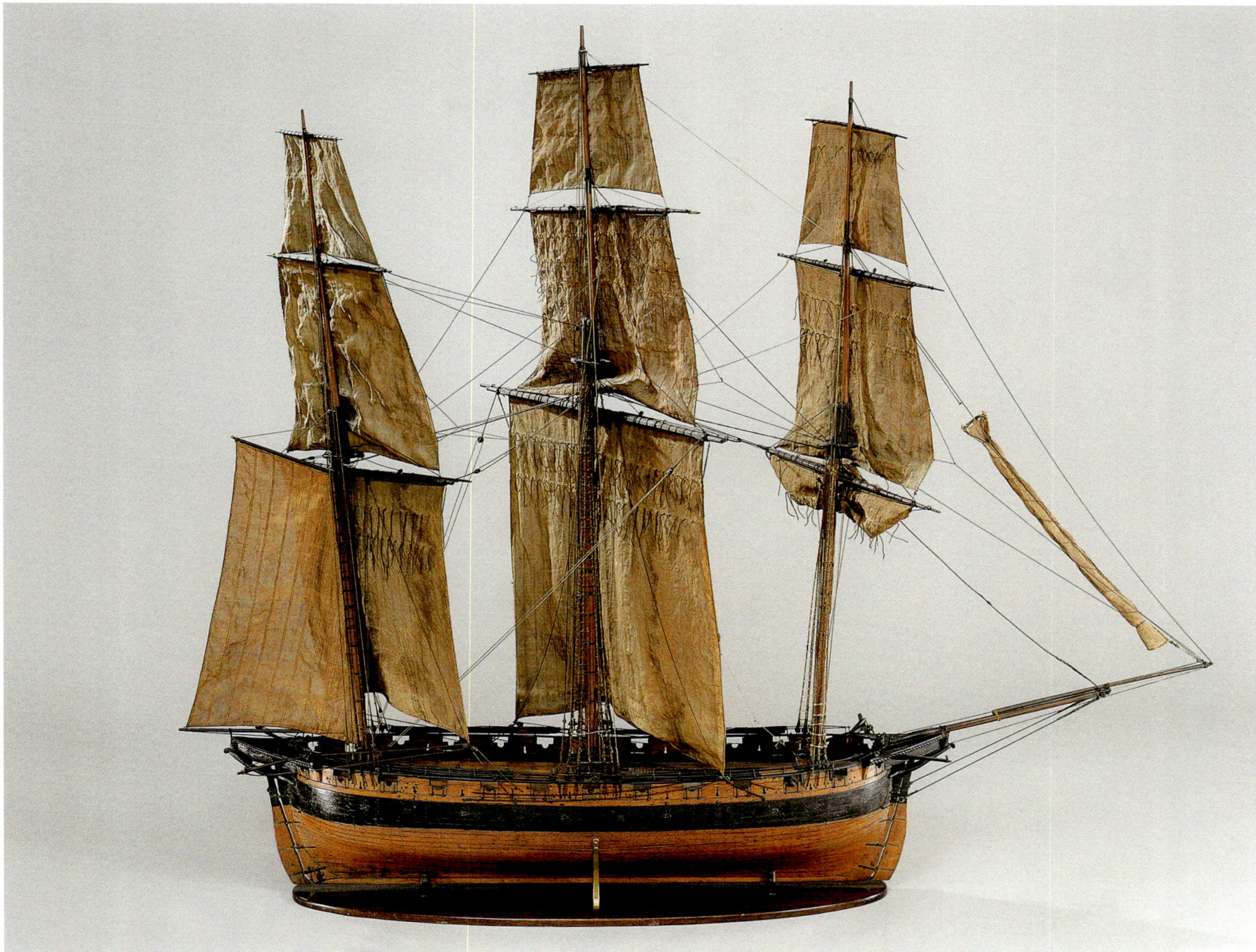

Frédéric Roux (1805–1870)

L'Amphidrome (three-masted corvette)

Watercolour from family album no. 1: ***Vie maritime et militaire de M. le comte Philibert Willaumez, né le 7 août 1763 à Belle-Isle-en-Mer et mort vice-amiral le dix-sept mai 1845, folio 39*** **. 1827–1828 . 40 watercolours on paper, 1 map, 1 portrait, with 2 manuscript letters . 27 x 32.5 cm . Entered museum collections circa 1948 . MnM J1102**

This album, combining the talents of watercolourist Frédéric Roux and the technical know-how of Amiral Willaumez, constitutes an exceptional artistic ensemble. It traces the career of this great mariner through portraits of ships on which he sailed and models he had built to improve their performances, providing us with a view of the ships in use over a period of half a century. M.-P. D.

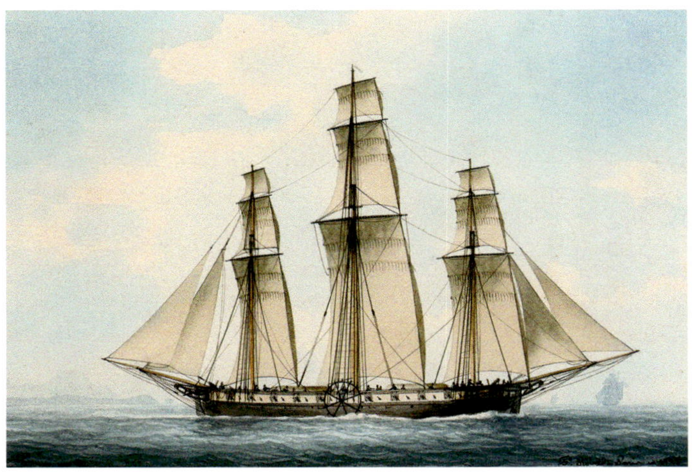

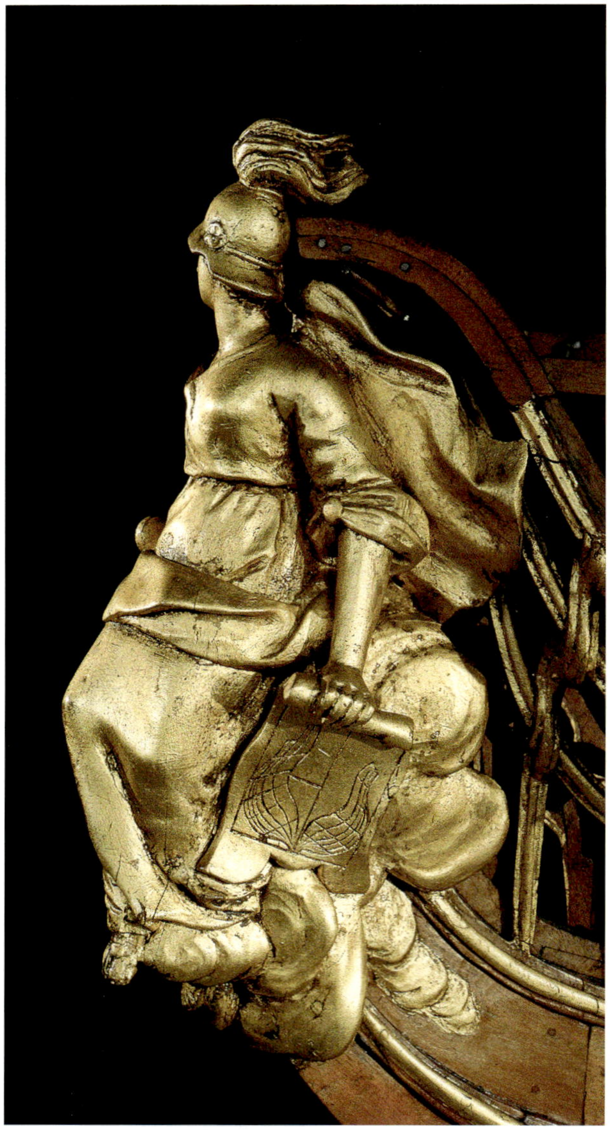

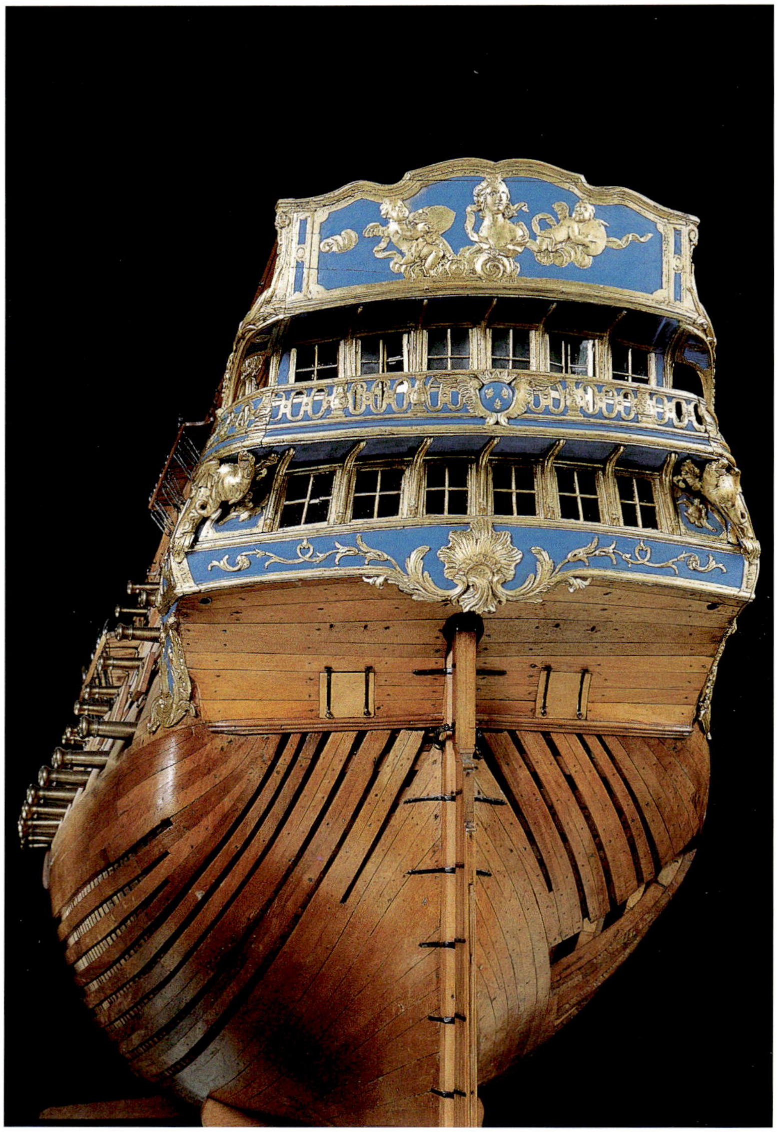

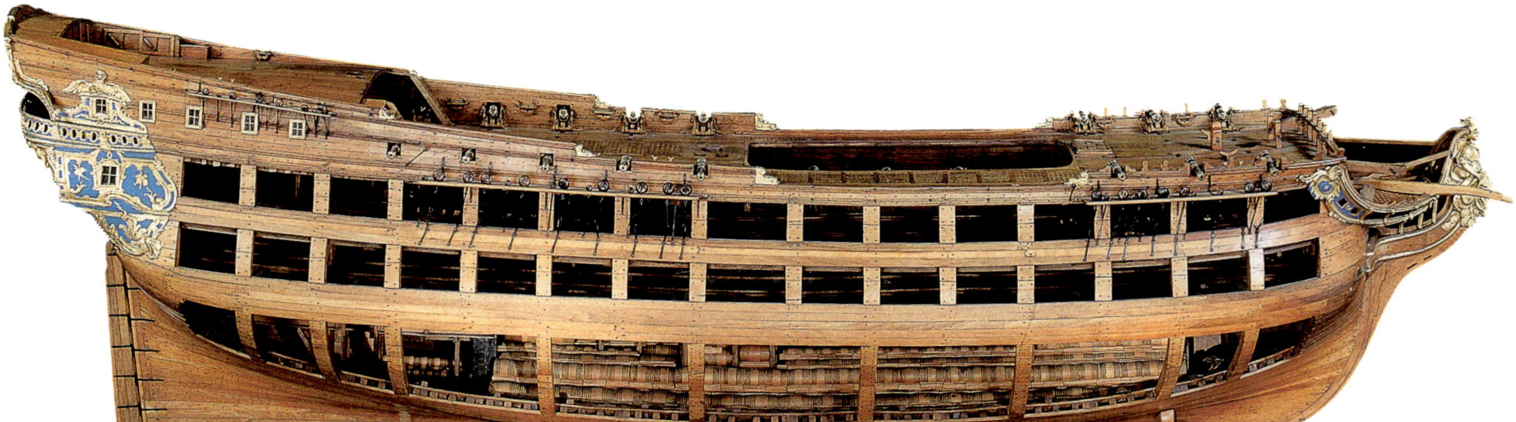

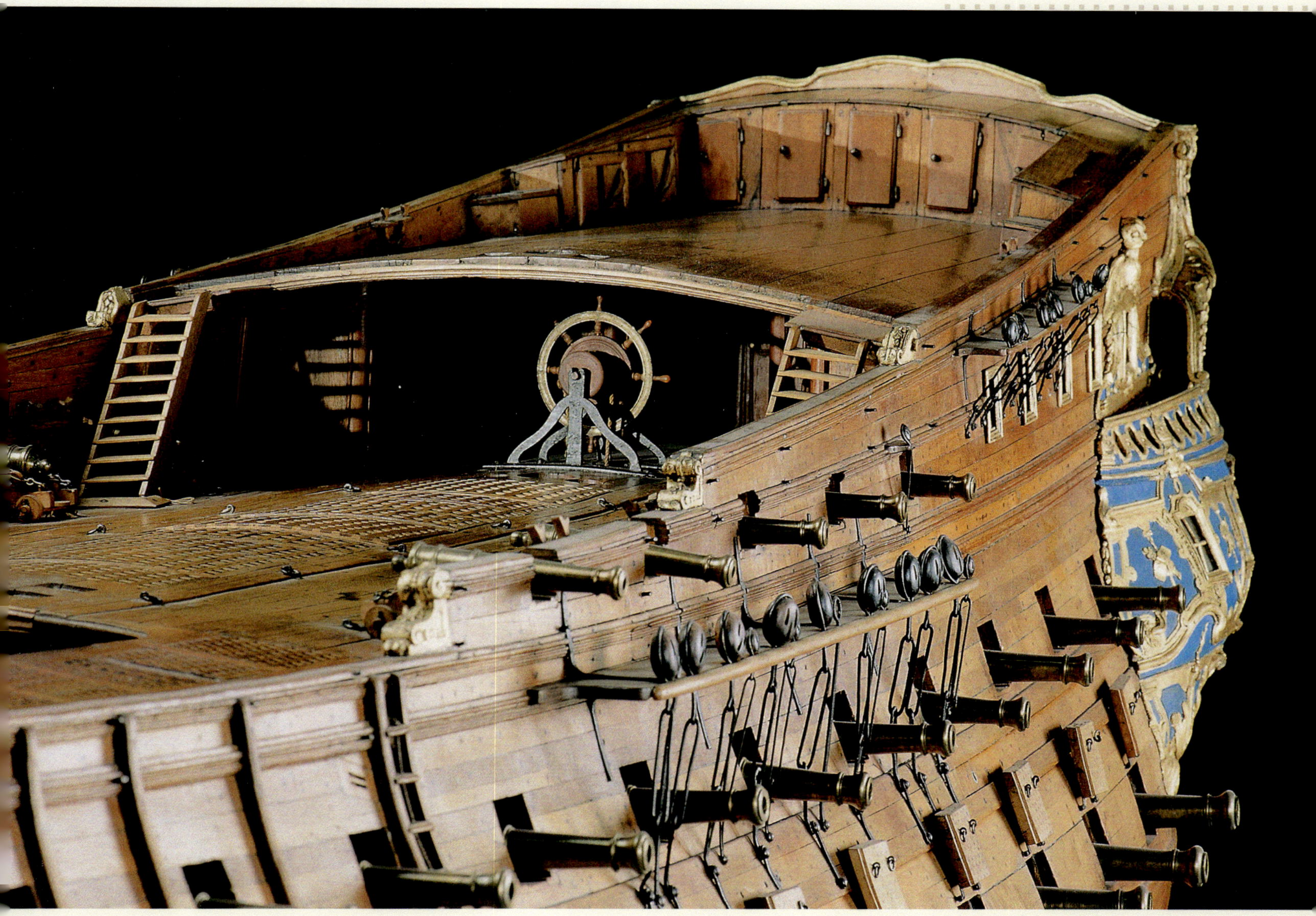

Hull of a 74-gun ship, known as the 'Coque de Pic'

Model of ship, 1:24 scale ▪ Constructed by Augustin Pic (1722–after 1780) ▪ 1755–1756 ▪ Walnut, pearwood, gilt wood, brass ▪ 85 x 268 x 64 cm ▪ Entered museum collections 1829, former Salle de Marine Collection ▪ MnM 11 MG 3

On the prow of this exceptionally crafted model, engraved on a silver plaque, is the signature of Augustin Pic, at the time deputy shipwright at the Rochefort shipyard. Designed for educational purposes, the model is open on the starboard side to reveal all the fittings, but was never rigged. According to its constructor, the model was made for the Académie de Marine room at Brest, and it is recorded in around 1780 as part of the Salle de Marine collections at the Louvre. A. N.

Mechanical propulsion

The sailor's dream of being able choose his route without being dependent on capricious winds was fulfilled in the 19th century with the Industrial Revolution. The invention of the steam engine paved the way for the extraordinary transformation of maritime transportation: for the first time, man was able to produce a driving force independent of natural phenomena. The history of this period of profuse research and metamorphosis is traced through the museum's collection of full-size objects and models.

These objects, which hail from shipyard workshops or result from private initiatives, reflect the scientific and technical dimension of the museum. Certain scale models in working order were made for the training of shipwrights at naval dockyards. Others were prototypes, such as Frédéric Sauvage's propeller, which served for his research work but failed on a technical level. Seemingly promising projects did not always lead to industrial applications. One of these was Jouffroy d'Abbans' steamship, the victim of a conspiracy; only the model remains, built to obtain a patent. Among the major pieces in this technical heritage is the steam engine of *La Persistante*.

These remarkable objects are also highly evocative. Mixed sail- and engine-powered models conjure up the confrontation between the advocates and adversaries of steam, and the strong resistance encountered by inventors to this new system of propulsion. Amid nostalgia for sail-powered navigation, a modern myth emerged: that of the machine. With its banks of indicators and controls, the instrument panel of the *Clemenceau* is symbolic of the deep and irreversible transformation of the sailor's profession. On display in the museum, it has today, like other objects of its kind, taken on a new aesthetic dimension.

Steam engine of the *Sphinx*

Model, scale 1:10 . Constructed by Marcelot, Rochefort dockyard model workshop . 1837 . Waxed mahogany, ebony, bronze, brass, steel . 97 x 148 x 122 cm . Entered museum collections 1837 . MnM 17 CN 3

Built by Fawcett at Liverpool, *the Sphinx*'s low-pressure double-acting steam engine could generate a power of 160 h.p. and weighed 135 tons. Its cylinders were 1.22 meters in diameter. F. C.

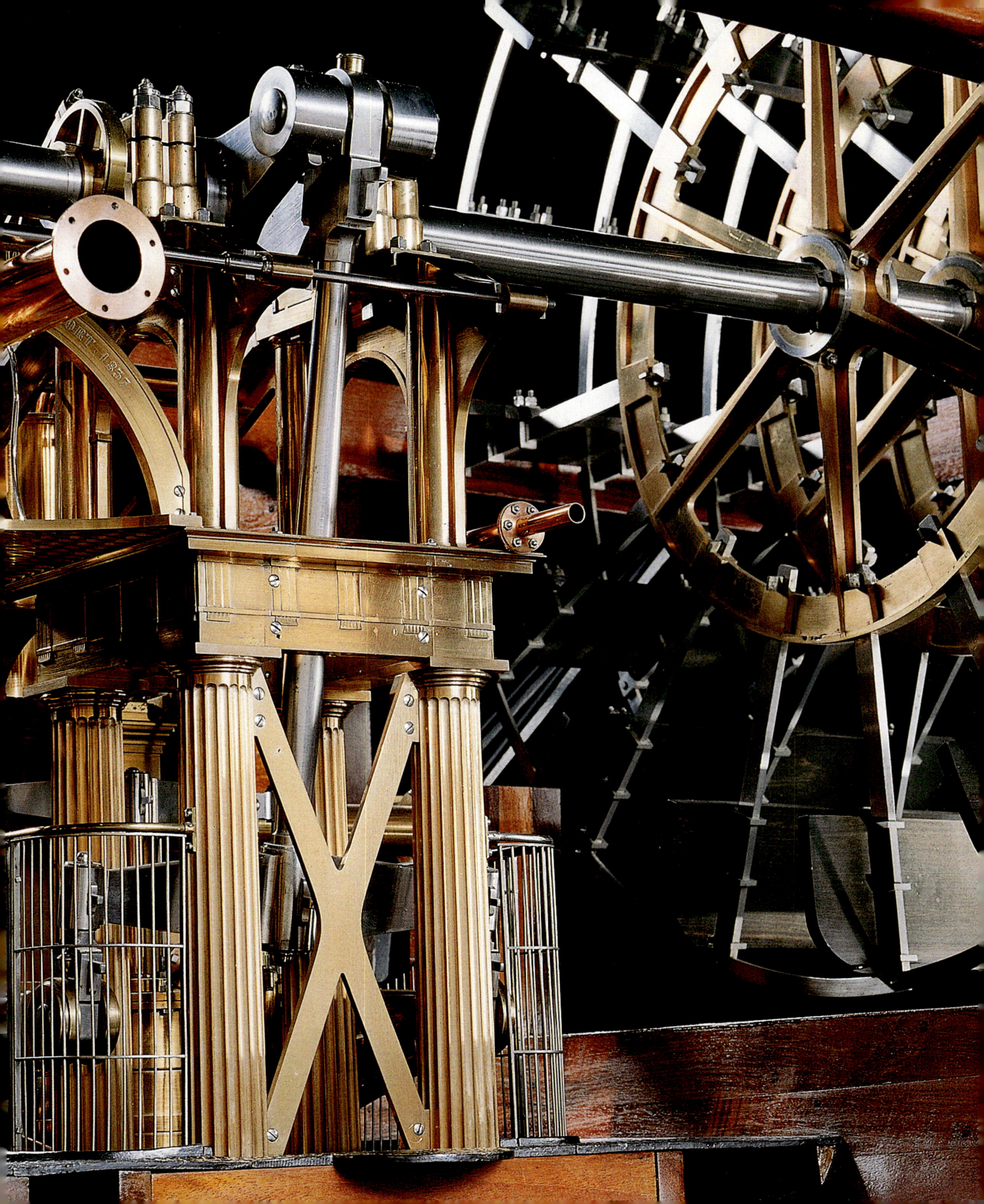

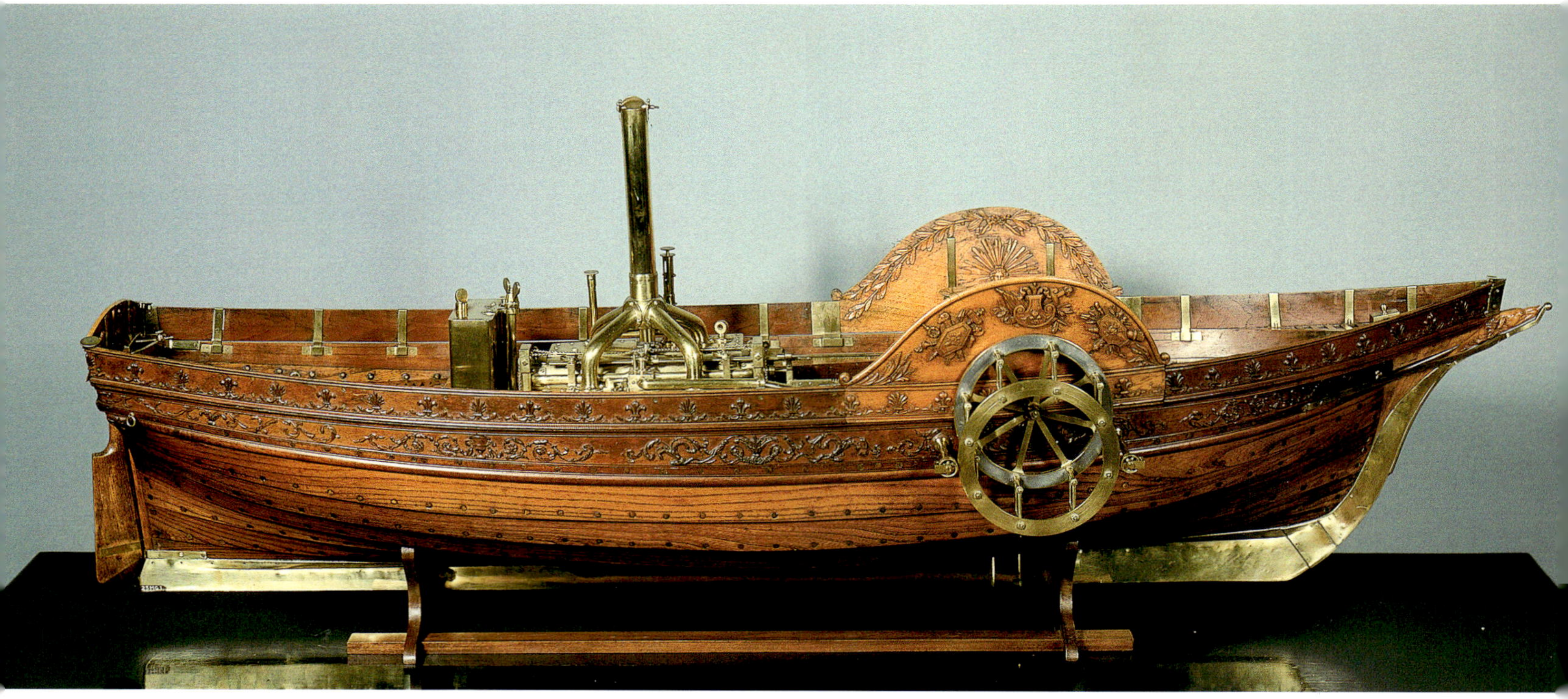

Steamship by Jouffroy d'Abbans

Machine model . Claude François de Jouffroy d'Abbans (1751-1832), inventor . Early 19th century . Oak, ash, teak, boxwood, brass . 62 x 182 x 60 cm . Entered museum collections 1829 . MnM 23 MG 1

Jouffroy d'Abbans can be considered as the inventor of the first steamship. In 1783, his ship the *Pyroscaphe*, driven by a system of paddle wheels with rack and pinion transmission, performed highly satisfactory trials on the Saône near Lyon. The Académie des Sciences did not appreciate the importance of his invention, however. Bankrupt, Jouffroy d'Abbans emigrated during the Revolution, returned to France under the Empire, and resumed his research without resources.

This model is not that of the *Pyroscaphe* but that of a later prototype built by Jouffroy d'Abbans on a different hull, in view of obtaining a patent. F. C.

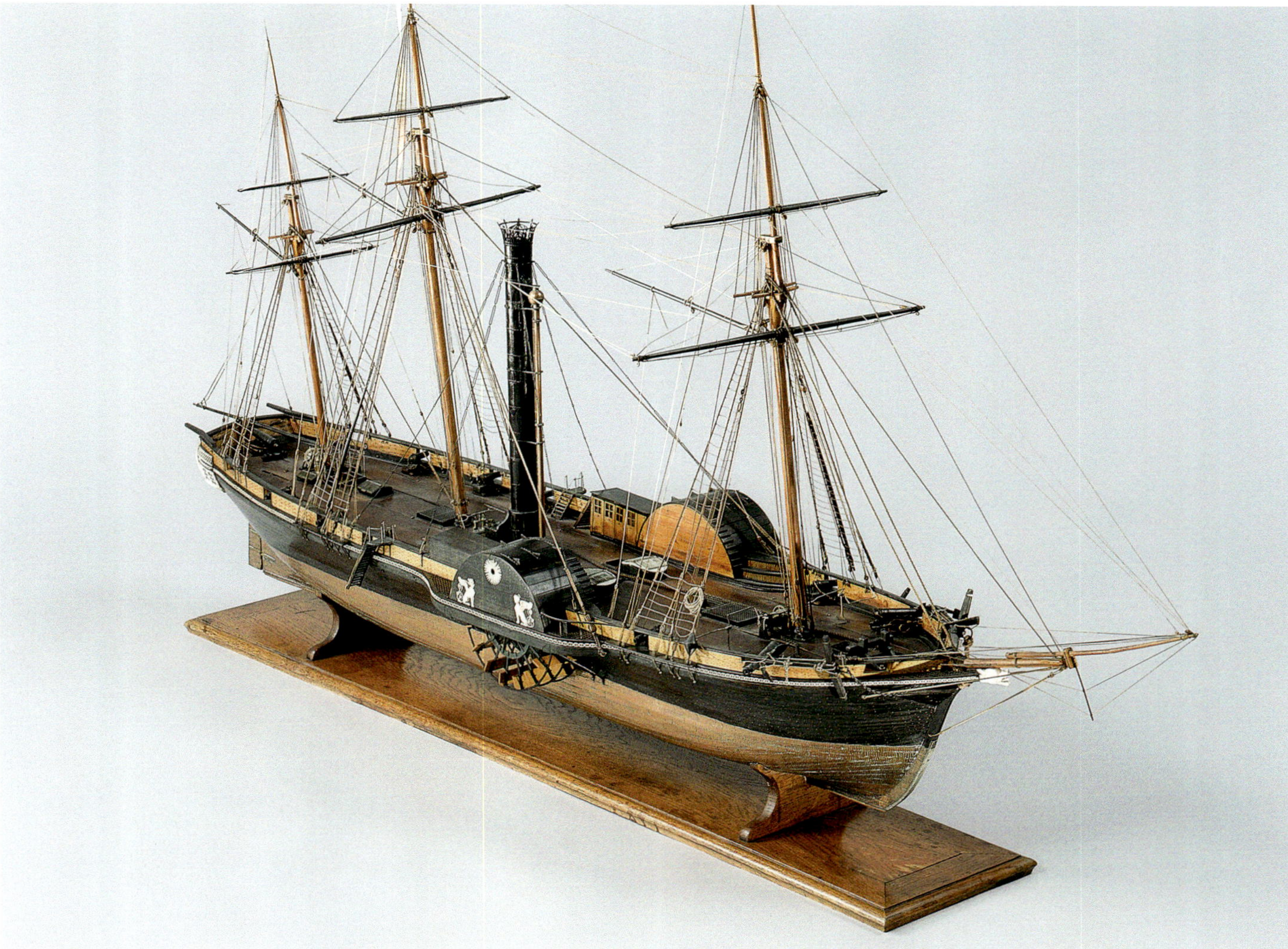

The *Sphinx*

Model of a six-gun side-wheel dispatch boat launched in Rochefort in 1829, 1:40 scale . Constructed by the Rochefort dockyard model workshop . Circa 1829 . Stained wood, ebony, ivory, bone, plant fibres, brass, copper, iron . 96 x 167 x 42 cm . Entered museum collections 1836 . MnM 23 MG 2

In the French navy, steam power was introduced on a trial basis on small service boats, coastal or river tugboats. The first steam-powered armed warship was the *Sphinx*. Its 160-h.p. double-acting steam engine drove side paddle wheels 5.94 meters in diameter, enabling it to reach a speed of seven knots. In 1833, it towed the lighter *Louxor* that carried the obelisk for the Place de la Concorde in Paris along the Nile and all the way to Le Havre. The *Sphinx* served as a model for a whole series of dispatch boats. F. C.

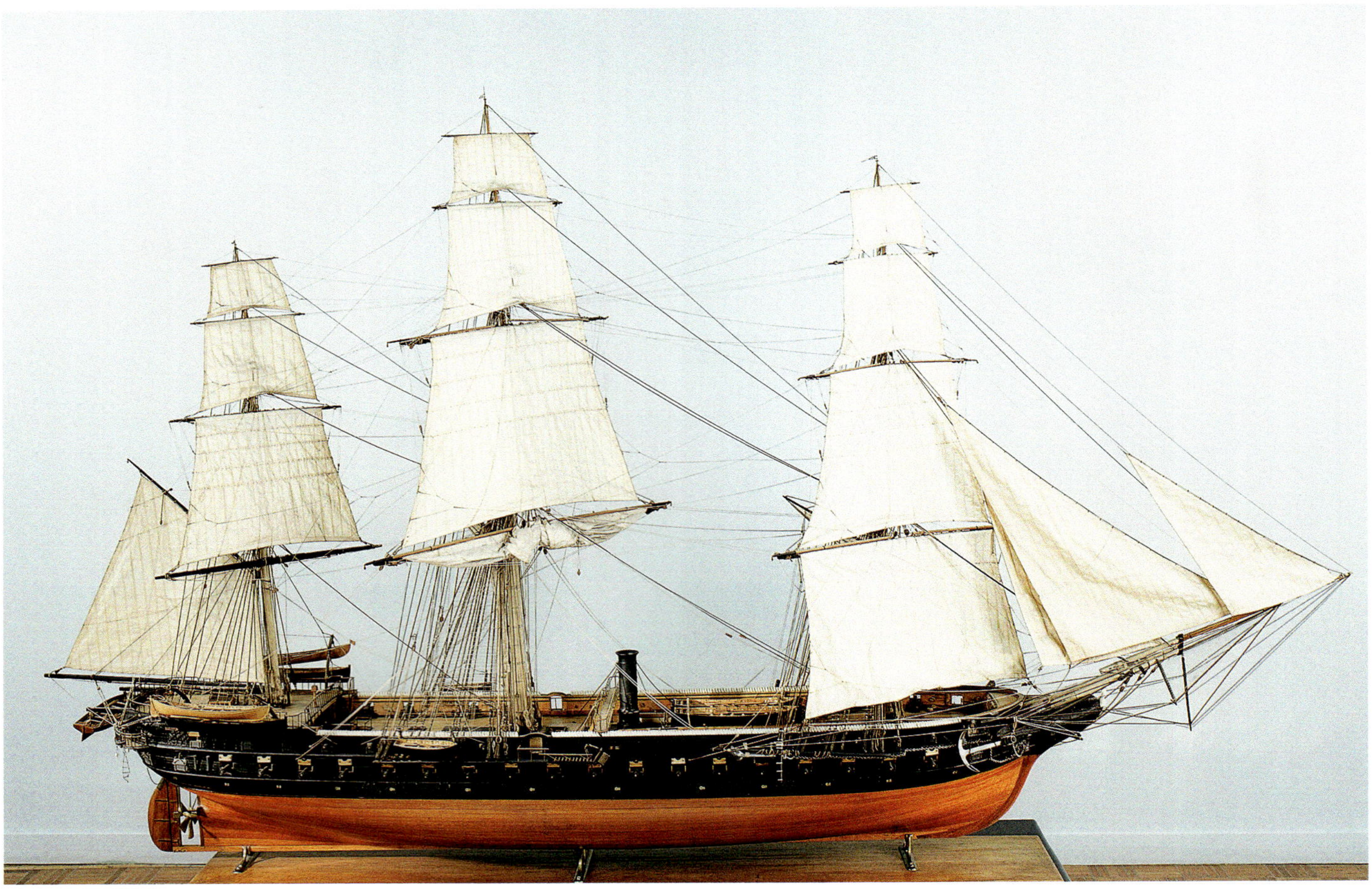

L'Audacieuse

Model of the frigate launched at Brest in 1856, 1:33 scale ▪ Anonymous ▪ Circa 1876 ▪ Wood, steel, iron, brass, cotton ▪ 185 x 301 x 64 cm ▪ Entered museum collections 1876 ▪ MnM 23 MG 10

Launched in 1856, *L'Audacieuse* was a 800-h.p.sail- and propeller-powered frigate, built after drawings by Dupuy de Lôme. Unlike the first generation of propeller warships – sailing ships to which a propelling engine had been added – the six long, fast frigates of the *L'Audacieuse* type were the first designed to sail primarily under steam. They nevertheless retained the rigging of a third-rate frigate. A. N.

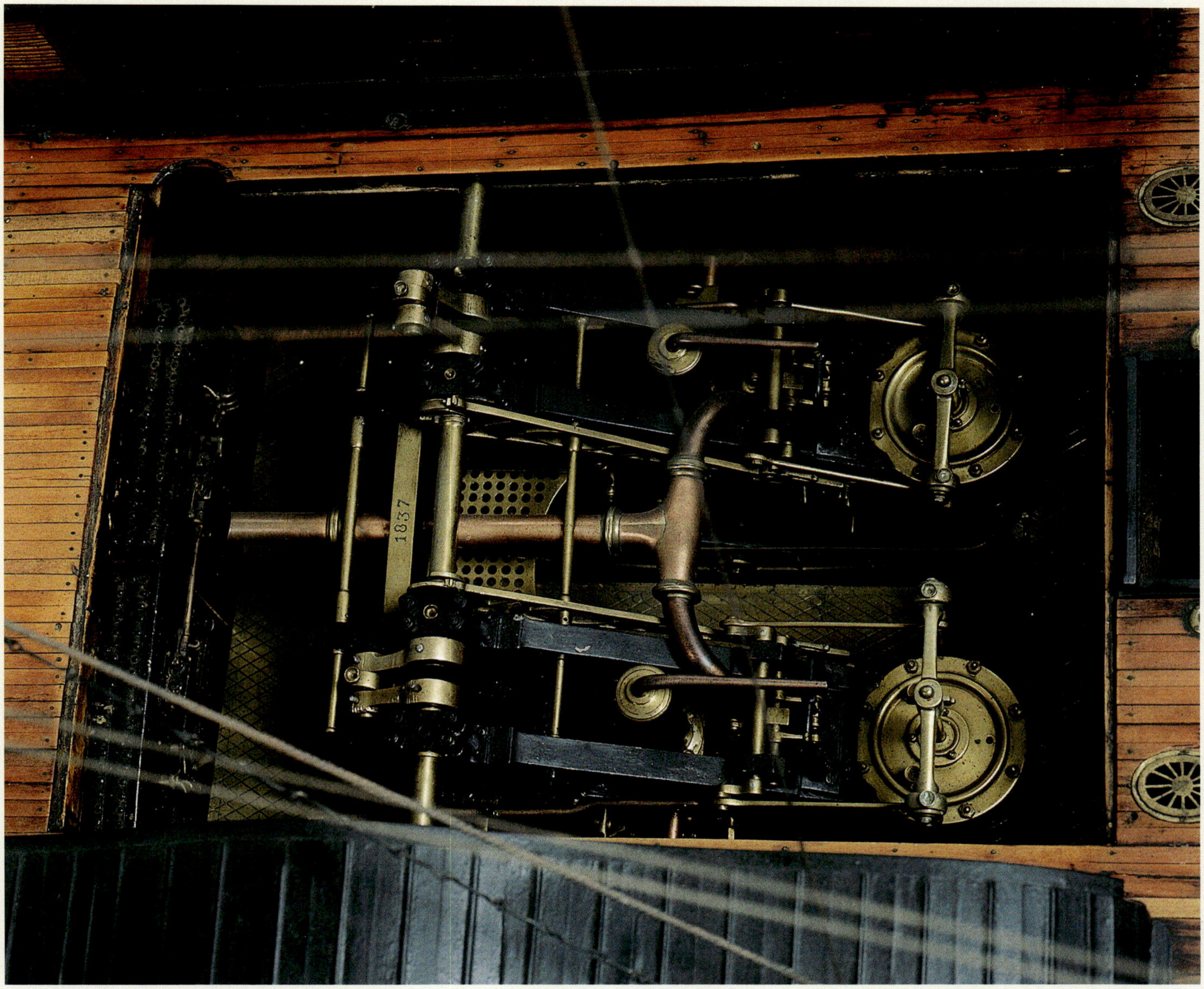

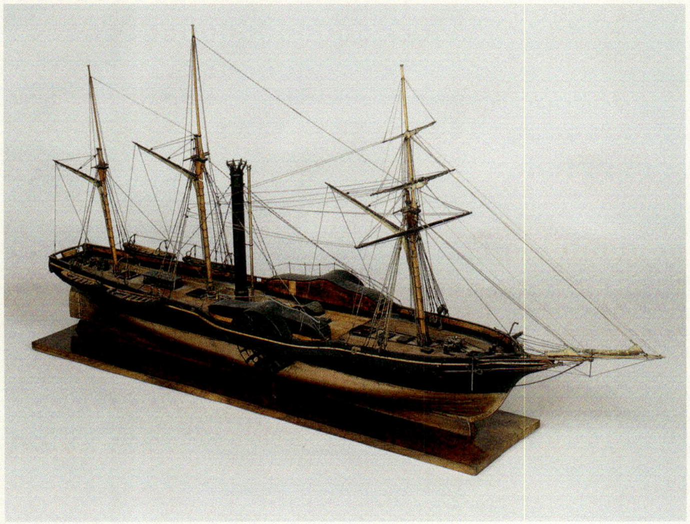

The *Sésostris*

Model and engine of the side-wheel dispatch boat launched at Cherbourg in 1836, 1:40 scale, and detail of its engine ▪ Constructed by the Cherbourg dockyard model workshop ▪ Circa 1836 ▪ Wood, iron, steel, copper, brass, cotton ▪ 86 x 173 x 40 cm ▪ Entered museum collections 1933 ▪ MnM 23 MG 3.1, 3.2

Following the French law of 10 July 1835 instituting the postal service of the Levant, ten postal liners were built and equipped by the French navy. Only two of them were fitted with a French engine, including the *Sésostris*, powered with a Hallette. This model shows all the details of this machine. A. N.

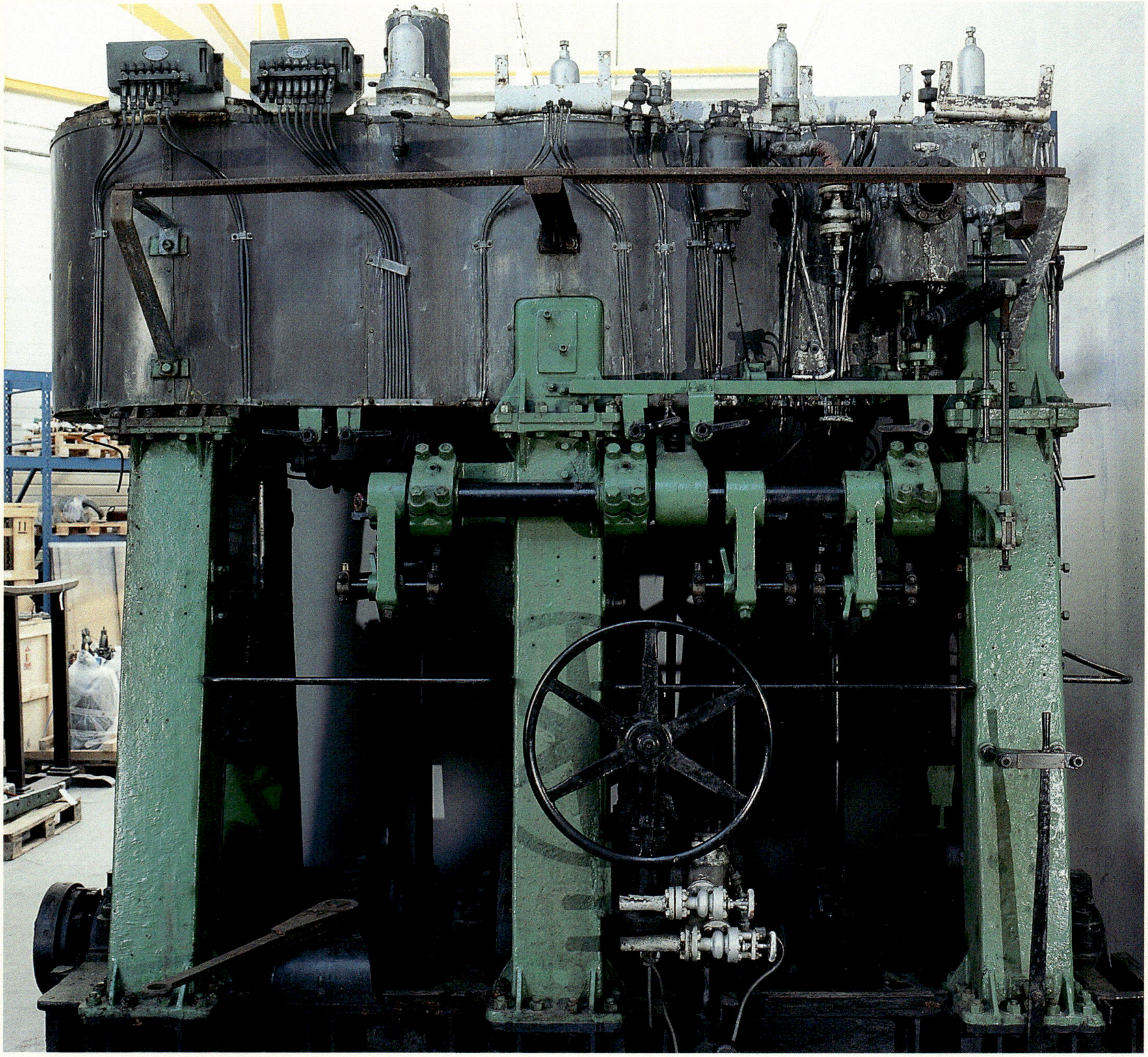

Steam engine

Alternating triple expansion 500-h.p. steam engine of the dumb barge *La Persistante* (1938–1976) . Société Provençale de Constructions Navales (La Ciotat) . 1932 . Steel, cast iron, brass, bronze, aluminium . 3.60 x 3.70 x 1.70 cm; 16 tons . Entered museum collections 2005 . MnM 2005.20.1

La Persistante's engine, built in 1932 but whose principle had been applied since the late 19th century, shows the progress of the marine steam engine. It has a condenser, cooled with seawater, which enabled spent steam to be reused. Moreover, its structure, based on three cylinders at different pressures, known as the 'triple-expansion compound system', was highly efficient. This engine is probably the last of this type and size conserved in France. A. N.

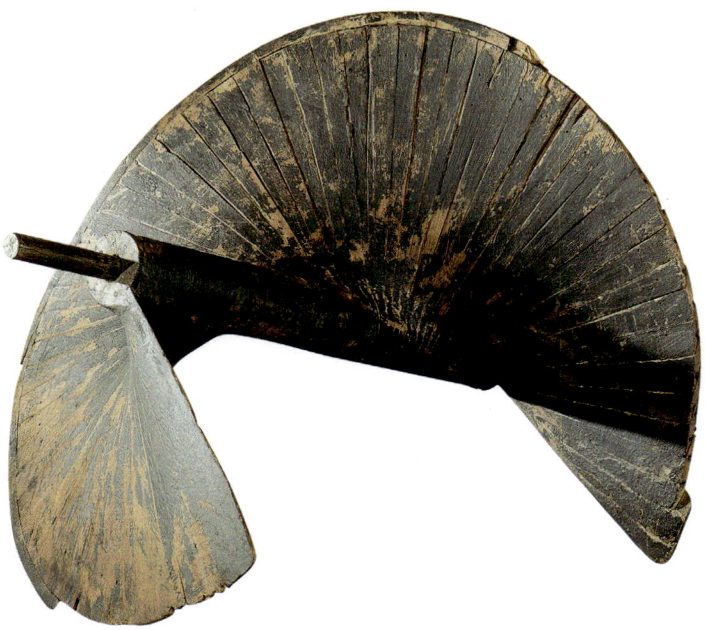

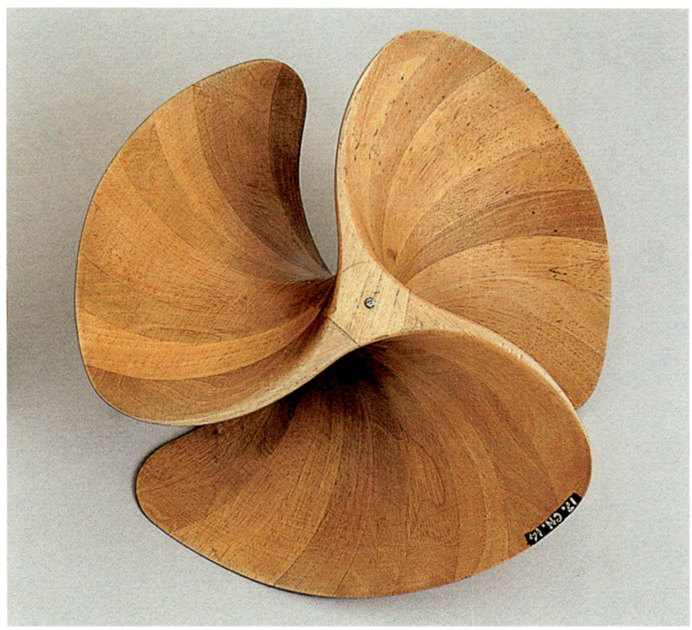

Model for a propeller

Frédéric Sauvage (1786–1857), designer . Wood . 49 x 54 x 45 cm . Entered museum collections 1894 . MnM 7 SO 9

Frédéric Sauvage made this model to support his research and experiments to invent a device that would replace the paddle wheels of steamships. In his research he collaborated with the shipbuilder Augustin Normand. Unfortunately, his full-spiral, single-screw propeller wasted engine power. Normand had the idea of dividing the propeller into three blades, which was a complete success. Sauvage refused to accept this modification; debt-ridden, he went mad and ended his days in a psychiatric hospital. F. C.

Model for a propeller

Model . Augustin Normand (1792–1871), inventor . 1843 . Wood, iron . 24 x 24 x 11 cm . Entered museum collections 1947 . MnM 17 CN 14

This is a scale model of one of the propellers developed by Augustin Normand that were tested on the dispatch boat *Napoléon*. The trials were conclusive and the technical solution – a propeller with a short pitch – was retained at the expense of the full-spiral single-screw propeller recommended by Frédéric Sauvage. F. C.

Instrument panel of the *Clemenceau*

Aft engine instrument panel of the aircraft carrier *Clemenceau* (1961–1997) . Built by the Chantiers de l'Atlantique, Saint Nazaire . 1955 . Steel, brass, glass . 250 x 430 x 88 cm . Entered museum collections 1999 . MnM 17 CN 50

This engine-control and instrument panel with its host of gauges and indicators is the only one of its kind to have been preserved since the computerisation of engine control systems. It enabled the operator to adjust parameters of the propulsion system (ahead and astern, steam pressure, propeller rpm etc.) while monitoring their correct functioning. The large central wheel controlled the flow of steam into the turbines. A. N.

Two models of the submarine known as *Le Plongeur*

Two models of the submarine *Le Plongeur*, 1:33 scale . Constructed at the Rochefort dockyard model workshop . Circa 1863 . Iron, copper . 26 x 160 x 40 cm (base included) . Entered museum collections 1867 . MnM 31 MG 1.1, 1.2

Designed by the ship's captain Bourgeois and engineer Brun, and launched at Rochefort in 1863, *Le Plongeur* was the first experimental submarine of the French navy and the first mechanically propelled submarine in the world. Powered with compressed air, it had a torpedo-carrying ram and an inbuilt lifeboat. Unstable when diving, it was laid up after four years of unsatisfactory trials. These two models were shown at the 1867 Paris World's Fair. A. N.

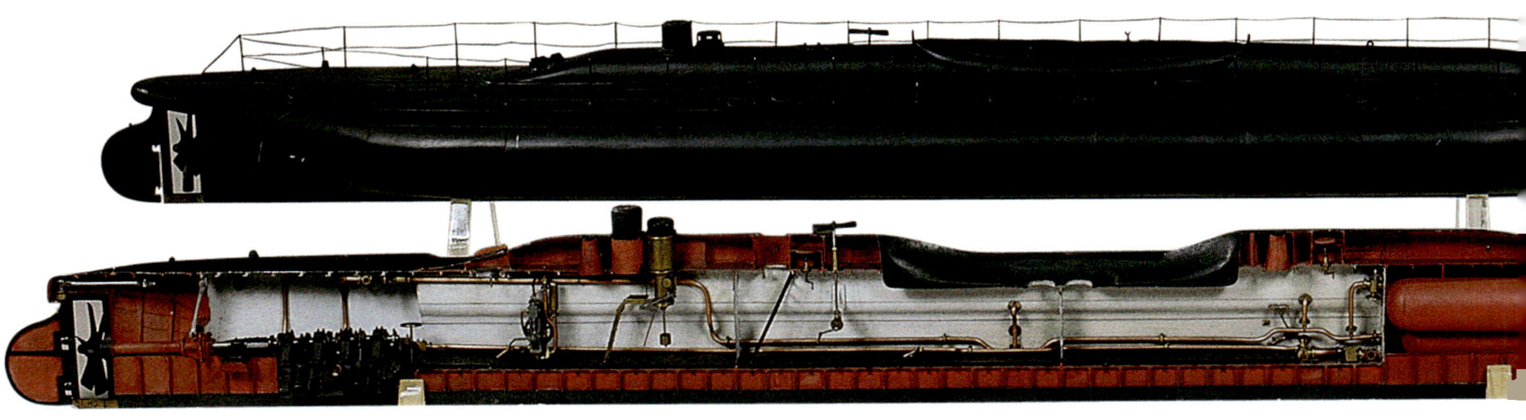

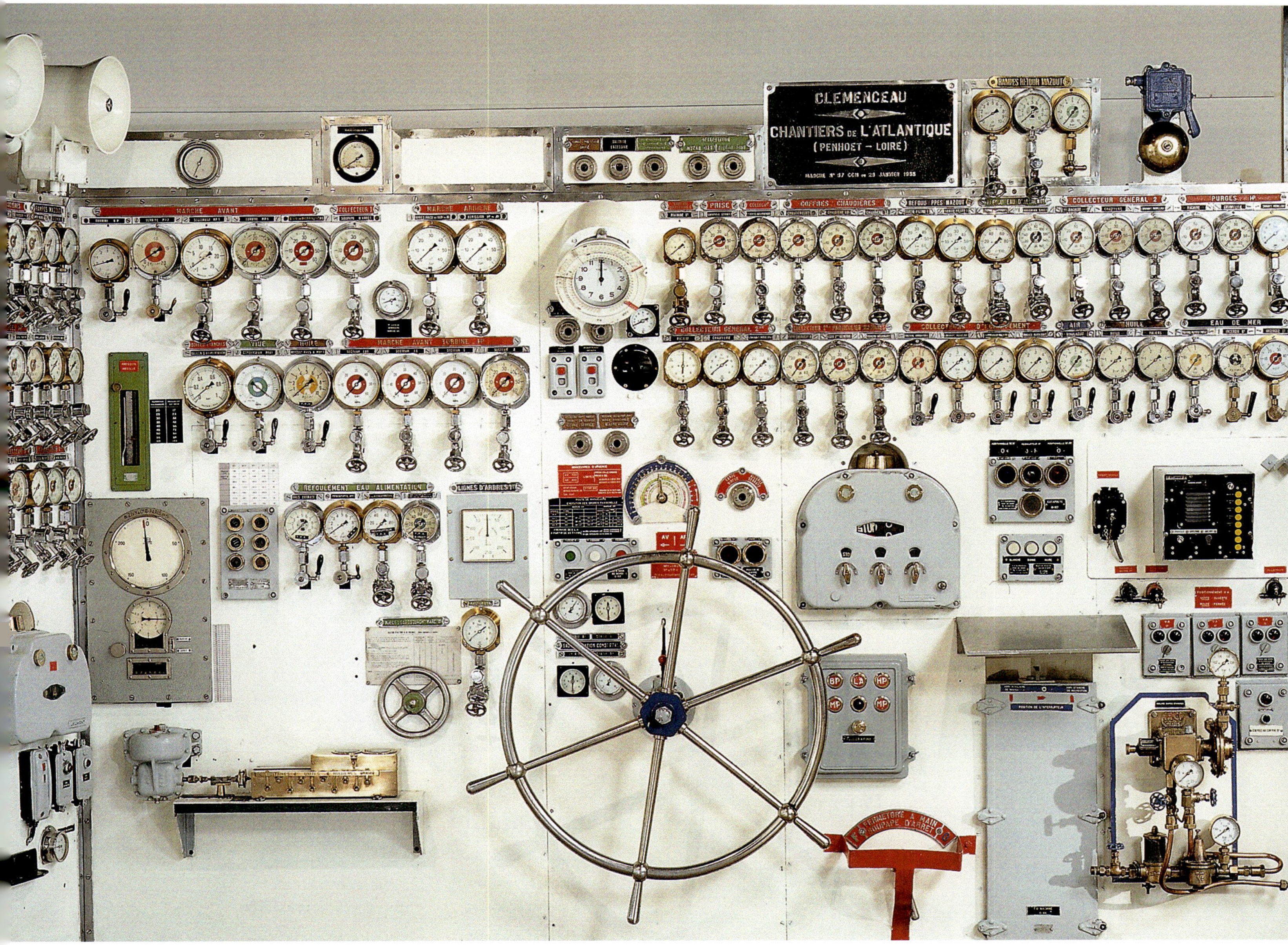
CLEMENCEAU
CHANTIERS DE L'ATLANTIQUE
(PENHOET – LOIRE)
MARCHE AVANT
MARCHE ARRIERE
REFOULEMENT EAU ALIMENTATION
COLLECTEUR GENERAL 2
EAU DE MER

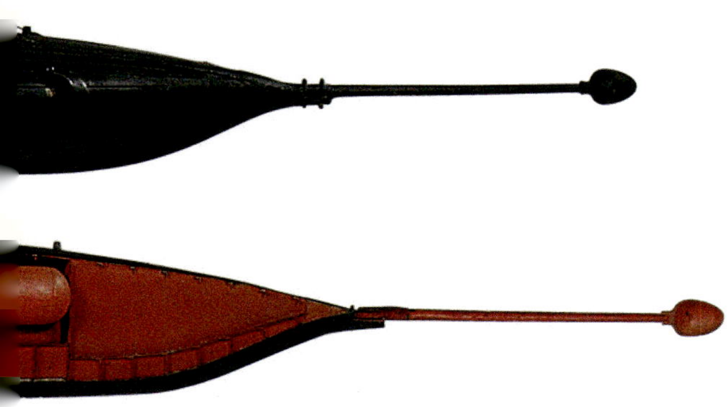

Traditional craft

The man at the origin of the museum's collection of traditional boats is Amiral François Edmond Pâris, whose work was decisive in promoting the idea of a maritime heritage.
The maritime and scientific career of Amiral Pâris fostered his interest in modern and traditional craft. In the course of his travels around the world in the 1820s and 1830s, he studied the boats of populations living on the shores of warm seas. In plans, notes and precise records, he described and analysed the construction methods and propulsion systems of these vessels, which would disappear with the Industrial Revolution. In his more freely executed watercolours, he depicts the navigational context, showing the relationship between a boat and its environment. In so doing, he laid the foundations of nautical ethnography. The drawings of Amiral Pâris reflect his scientific and technical knowledge, as well as his artistic sensibility. Wishing to disseminate his work, he published this valuable documentation in two publications, *Essai sur la construction navale des peuples extra-européens and Souvenirs de marine conservés*, six volumes published between 1882 and 1906.
After his appointment as curator of the Musée de la Marine in 1871, Amiral Pâris pursued his conservation work and ordered the construction of around 230 models of traditional European and non-European boats. They were made by craftsmen at the museum's model workshop, on the basis of his records and those compiled by his son Armand and his correspondents. This documentary ensemble, along with the drawings, watercolours, and models, constitute a source of information that is unique in the world.
The museum also houses other models of traditional boats that were built by native populations for a European clientele, and which complete Pâris's survey. In the course of its history, the museum has received exceptional donations of full-size traditional boats, valuable sources of information on bygone building techniques.

François Edmond Pâris (1806–1893)

Chile. Valparaiso. No. 1 Horizontal view of a balsa. No. 2 View from the side. No. 3 Paddle (A)

Pl. 112, from the album *Voyage de la corvette La Favorite en 1830, 1831, 1832* ▪ 1831 ▪ Ink and watercolour on paper ▪ 32.7 x 21.7 cm ▪ Entered museum collections 1913 ▪ MnM B178

François Edmond Pâris

Balsa of the Intermedios, Chile (B)

Plan, 1:10 scale ▪ Black and red ink on paper ▪ 60.5 x 42 cm ▪ Entered museum collections 1913 ▪ MnM Plan-8189

Balsa raft of the Intermedios, Chile (C)

Model, 1:10 scale ▪ Made by François Yves Couadoux junior (1831–?) after records by François Edmond Pâris ▪ 1873 ▪ Animal hide and wood ▪ 8.5 x 35.5 x 17 cm ▪ Entered museum collections 1873 ▪ MnM 37 EX 14

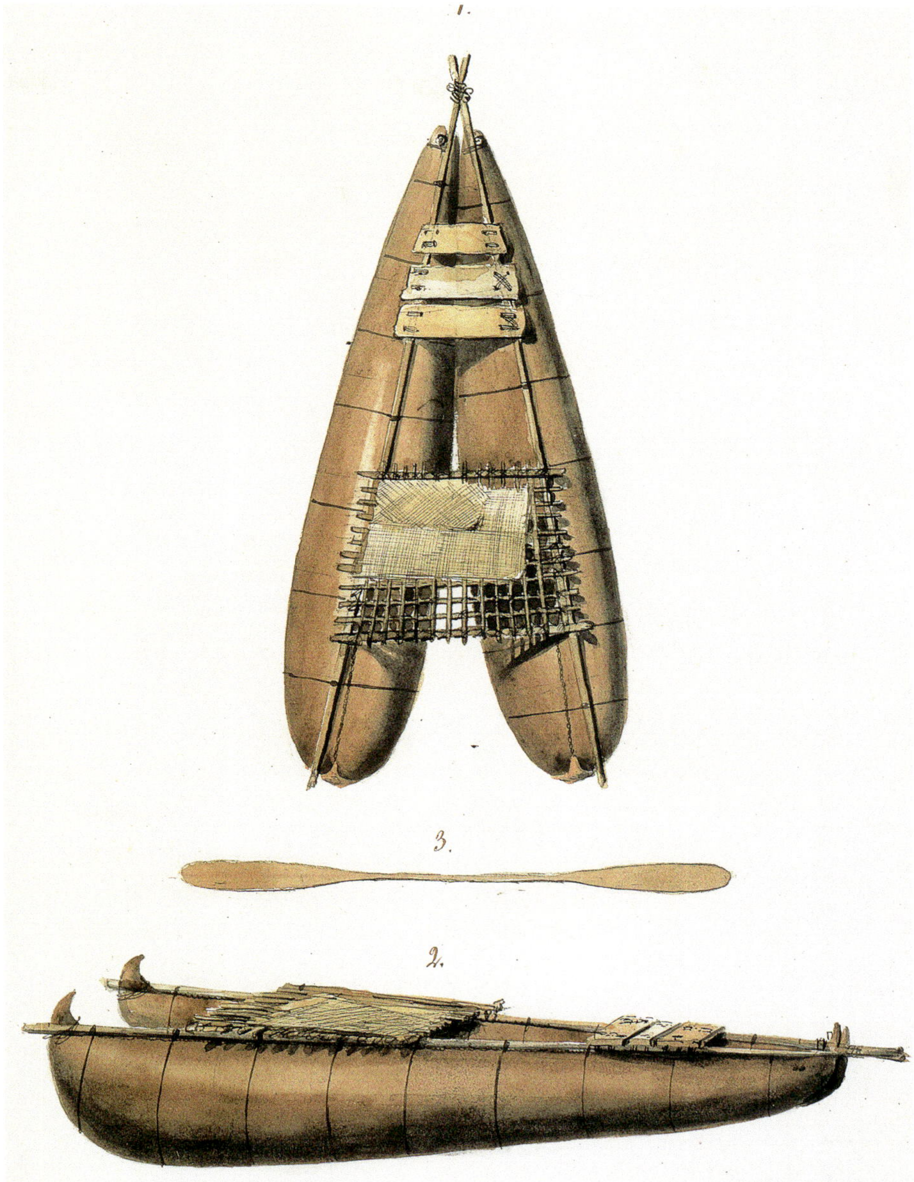

A

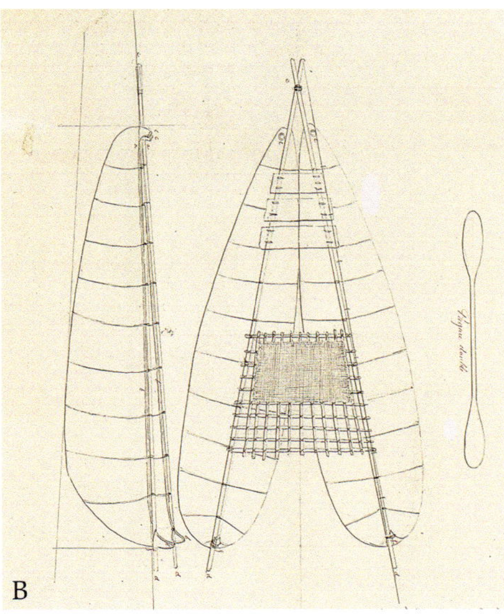
B

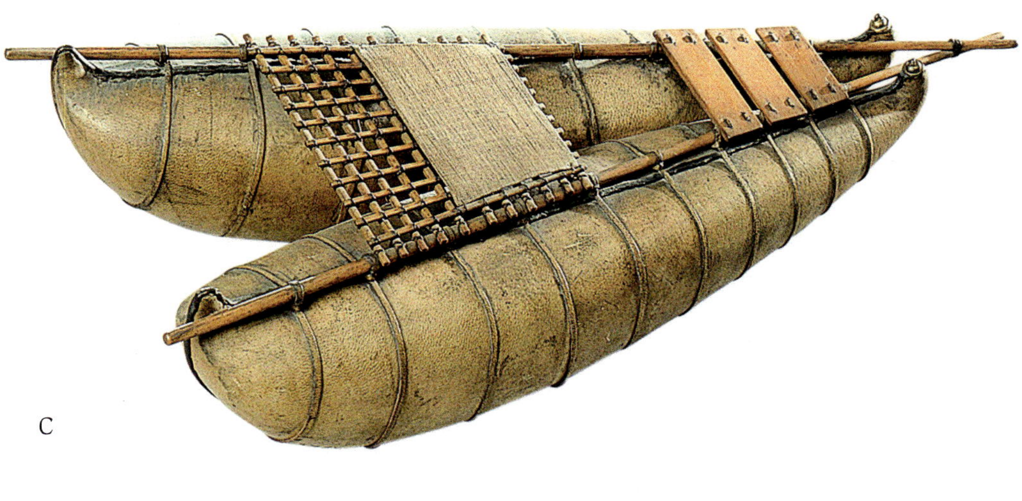
C

From the two-dimensional view (A) sketched during his voyage on *La Favorite* to the model (C) constructed after a precisely annotated drawing (B), Pâris's approach to conservation was a rigorous one. This balsa (a traditional Chilean boat) is a fine example of the workmanship of the model makers he engaged, who were able to draw on precise documentation. François Couadoux used materials that were unusual in France to execute this detailed reconstruction of a boat he had never seen himself. **H. T.**

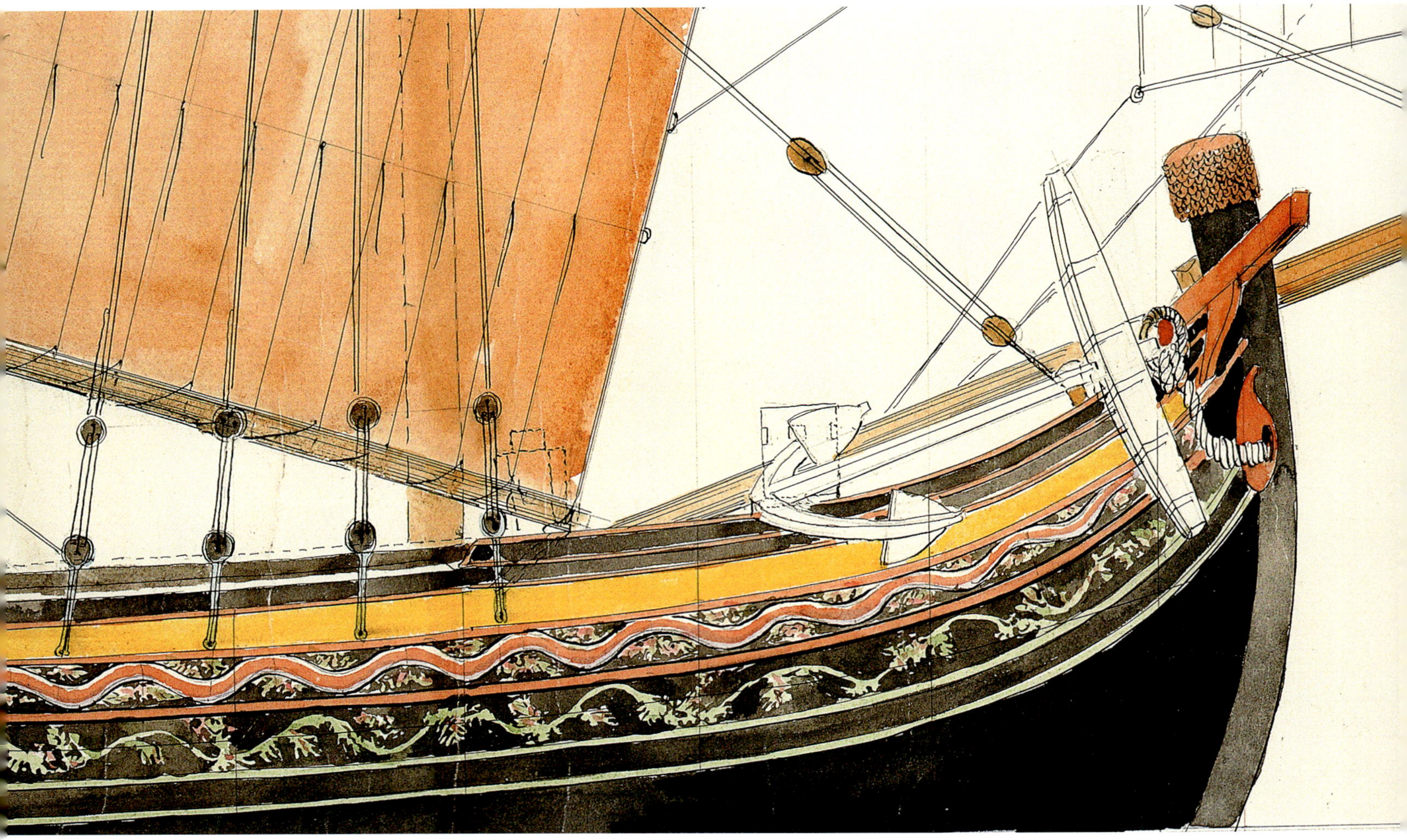

François Edmond Pâris, after records by Admiral Acton and Admiral Fincati

Adriatic Sea. Trabacolo. 1882 (detail)

Black ink and watercolour on paper . 150 x 150 cm . Entered museum collections 1913 . MnM Plan-8080

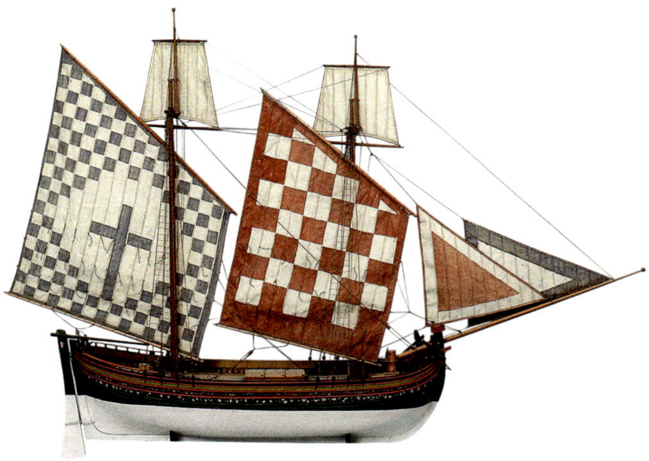

Trabacolo, Adriatic coaster, 1882

Model, 1:25 scale . Constructed by Charles Hamelin at the Musée de la Marine model workshop after records compiled by Admirals Acton and Fincati . 1883 . Wood, plant fibres, metal . 88.5 x 118.5 x 26 cm . Entered museum collections 1881 (date of commission) . MnM 13 CP 5

Amiral Pâris was particularly interested in working boats used along the coasts of Europe. It was the late 19th century, and he knew that these vessels were doomed to disappear. Not only did he publish the drawings and records compiled for him by his correspondents, but he ordered the construction of a model for each boat, which would leave a trace of its shape and structure and enable it to be shown to the public. This model of a fishing coaster from the Venice region accurately reproduces every detail of construction and decor indicated in the records. H. T.

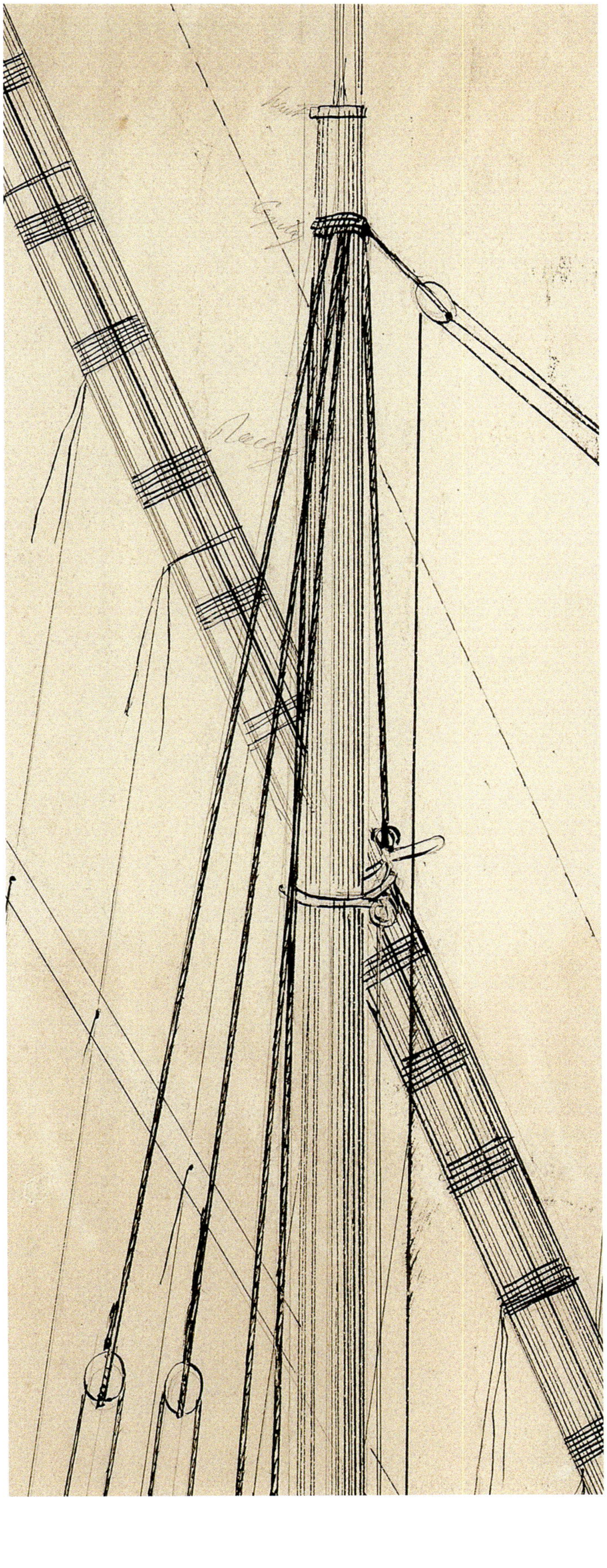

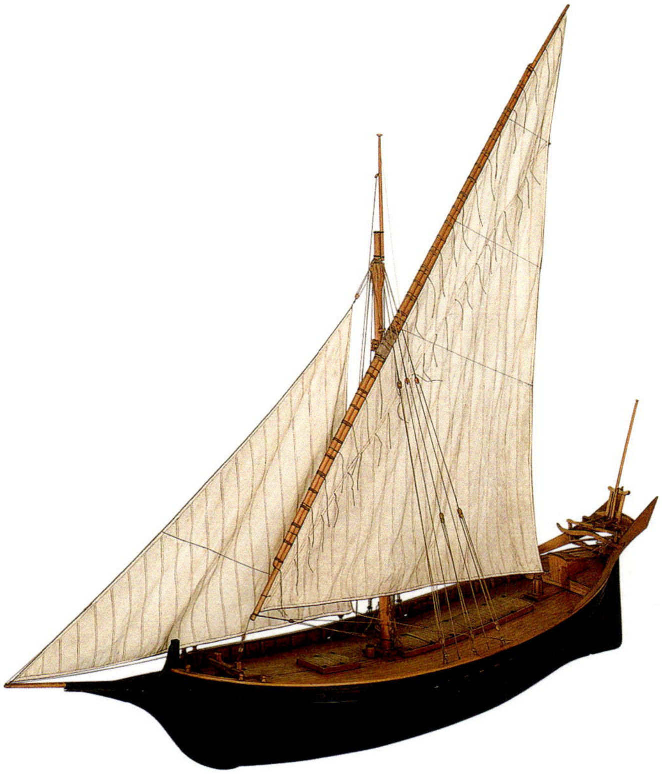

Large lighter from Arles

Model, 1:25 scale . Constructed by Charles Hamelin at the Musée de la Marine model workshop after drawings by shipwright Victor Jouvin . 1881 . Wood, plant fibres, metal . 123 x 127 x 29.5 cm . Entered museum collections 1881 . MnM 5 CP 1

Victor Jouvin (fl. 19th century)

Arles lighter 1840 (detail)

1840 . Black ink on paper . 170 x 150 cm . Entered museum collections 1913 . MnM Plan-8053

This model is of a type of boat that had already disappeared when Amiral Pâris ordered its construction. It was built after a drawing made in 1840 and passed on to the Musée de la Marine by the painter François Roux. These lighters, flat-bottomed lateen-rigged cargo vessels, were in common use on the Rhône and along the Mediterranean coast until the arrival of the railway. **H. T.**

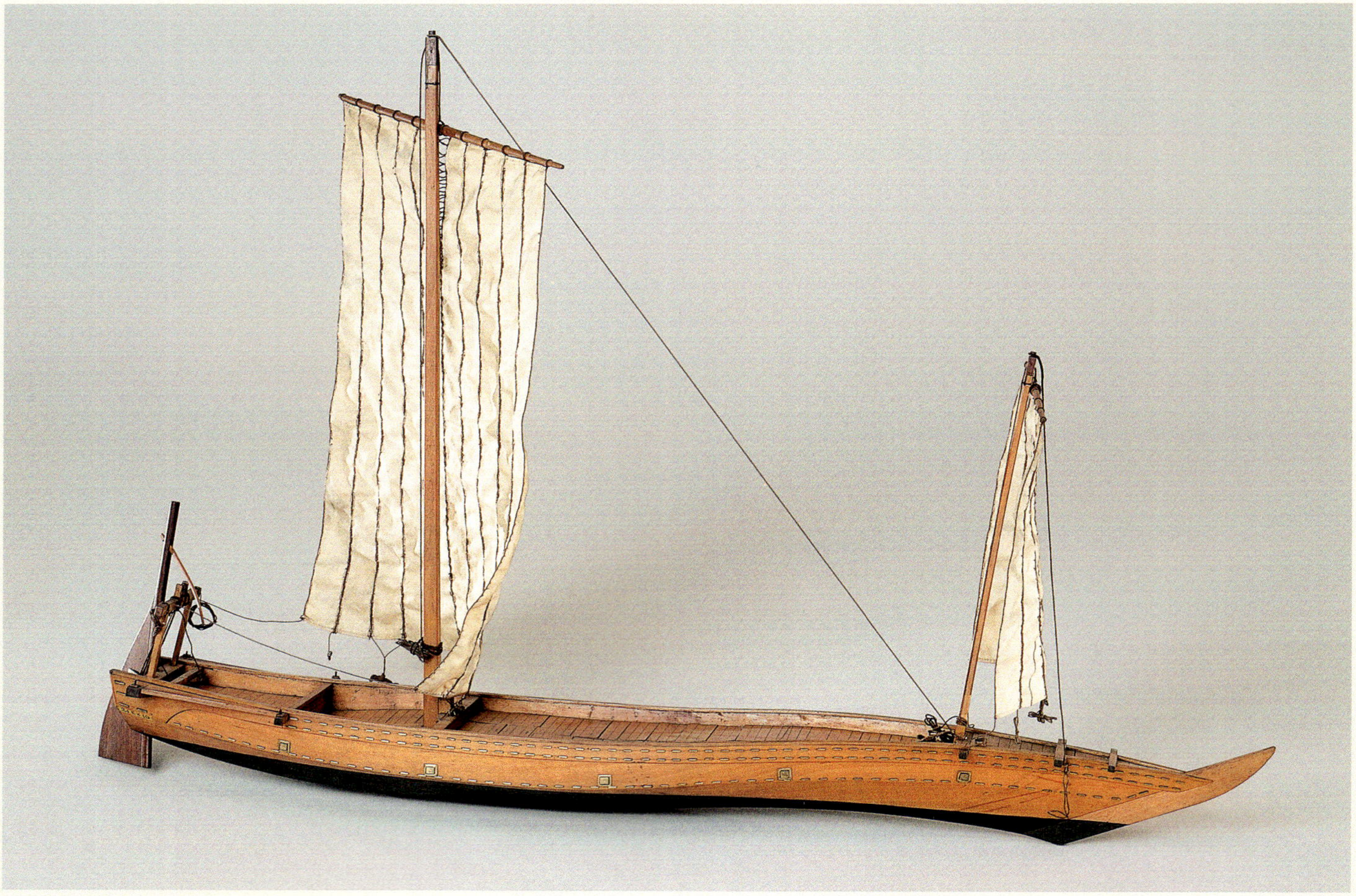

François Edmond Pâris (1806–1893)

Coasters from the Tonkin coast, close-hauled on the port tack

Pl. 85, from the album *Voyage de la corvette La Favorite en 1830, 1831, 1832* . 1831 . Ink and watercolour on paper . 21.4 x 32.7 cm . Entered museum collections 1913 . MnM B178

Fishing boat with curved keel from Jedo Bay

Model, 1:25 scale . Constructed by François Couadoux junior after records compiled by Armand Pâris . 1872 . Wood, plant fibre . 46 x 73 x 14 cm . Entered museum collections 1873 . MnM 21 EX 10

Armand Pâris was the son of François Edmond Pâris. His career as a naval officer enabled him to pursue and complete the work of his father, notably during his voyage to Japan on board the corvette *Dupleix*. There, in 1868, he took measurements of fishing boats, merchantmen and fighting ships which could be used later for modelling in France. His work gave rise to an exceptional collection of Japanese boats. This model highlights a particularity of certain fishing boats of the Far East: the curved keel. **H. T.**

Coaster from the Gulf of Tonkin

Model, 1:20 scale . Constructed by François Baude at the Musée de la Marine model workshop after records compiled by François Edmond Pâris . 1875 . Wood, plant fibres . 62.5 x 107 x 27 cm . Entered museum collections 1875 . MnM 17 EX 11

Most of the watercolours in Amiral Pâris's album showed the boats in context. The purely architectural as well as functional aspects of the vessel are rendered with technical rigour, and given movement. They provide a further source of information about these 'extra-European' boats. Few of the drawings made during *La Favorite*'s call in Cochin-China were used to build a model. This modest cargo coaster was certainly selected for its beautiful, wide ribbed sails. **M.-P. D.**

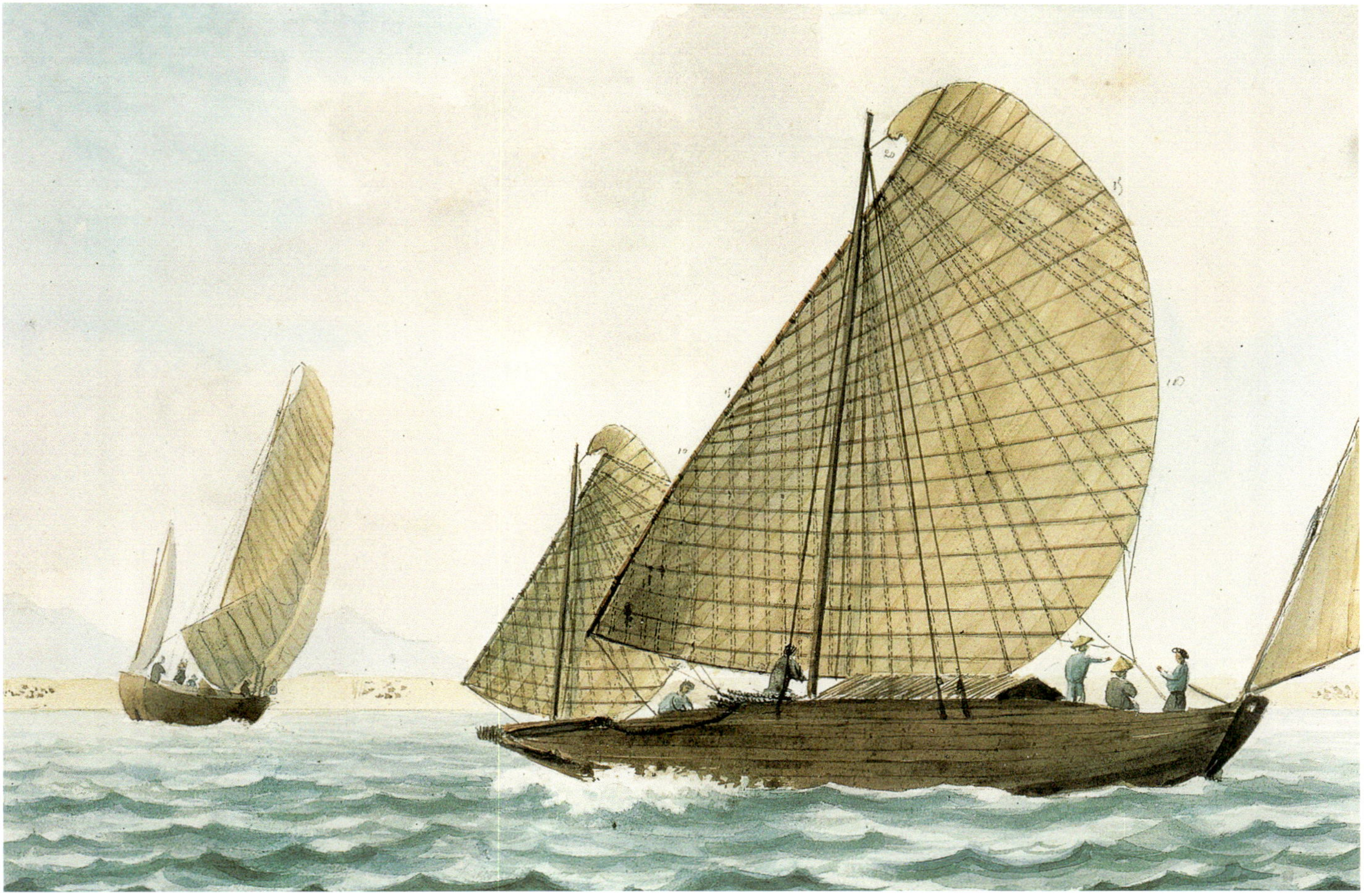

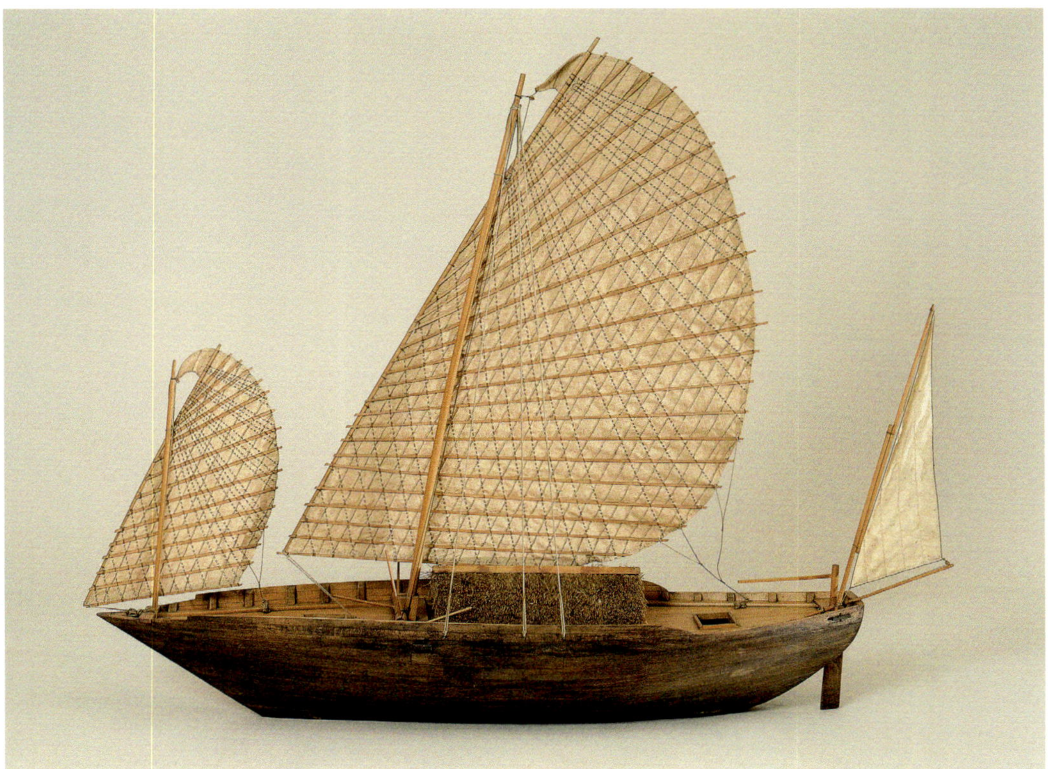

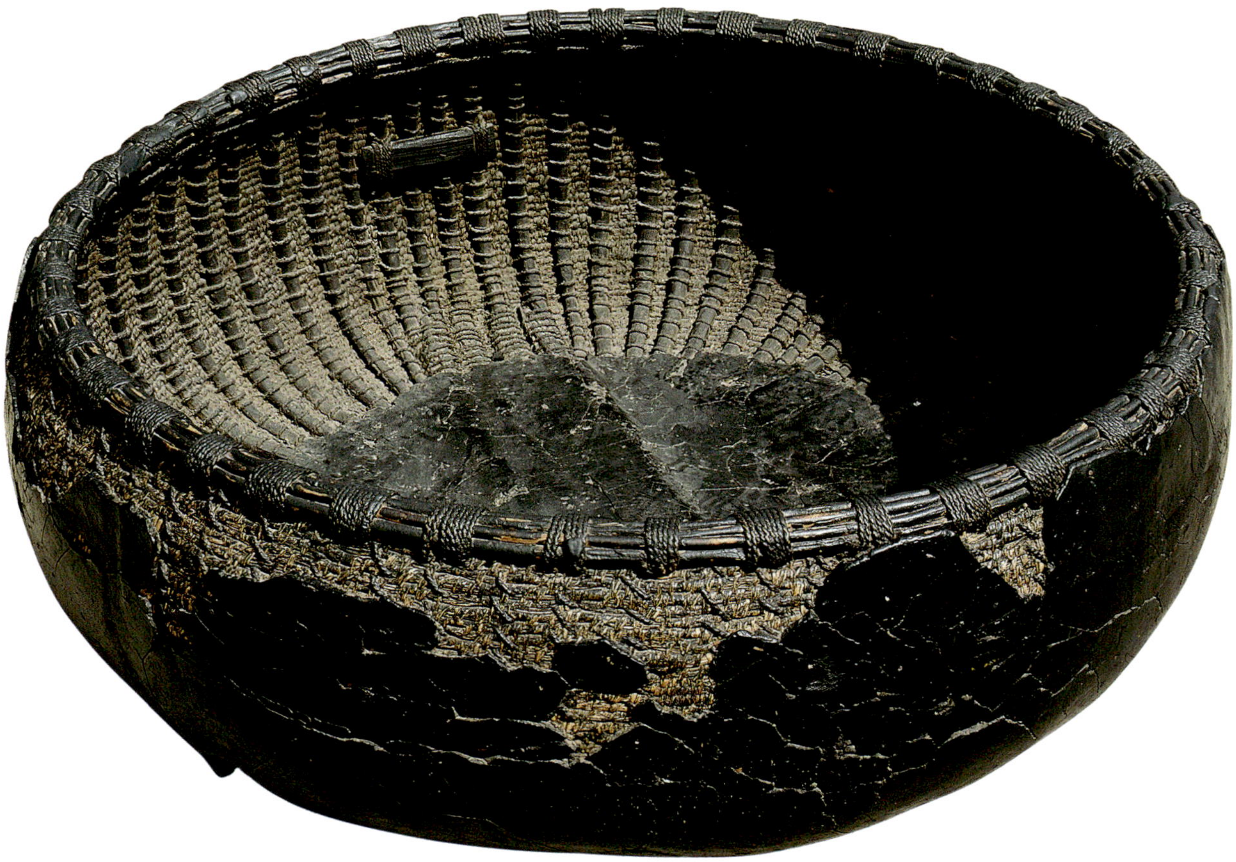

Quffah, basket-boat from the Tigris

19th century, Baghdad, Iraq . Wood, palm, plant fibres, bitumen . H. 58 cm x Ø 163 cm . Entered museum collections 1901 . MnM 3 EX 9

Paddle-propelled basket-boats, which served to transport people and goods, were used from the 9th century BC to the 20th century on the Tigris in the Baghdad and Basra regions. This specimen, donated by the French mission in Baghdad, is an exceptional full-size example of a rare boat-building technique: the palm wickerwork was waterproofed with a coating of bitumen, a natural resource found in the Near East. Basket-boats are used to this day in Vietnam. H. T.

Canoe used by the Naas Indians

Model attributed to the Naas Indians, Northwestern America . Early 19th century . Wood . 21 x 111 x 19 cm . Entered museum collections 1843 . MnM 37 EX 2

Canoe used by the Micmac Indians

Model attributed to the Micmac Indians, Eastern Canada . Early 19th century . White-birch bark, spines of the North American porcupine (*Erethizon dorsatum*) . 14.5 x 83 x 14.5 cm . Entered museum collections 1843 . MnM 37 EX 5

Since the 17th century, many models of canoes from North America have been brought to Europe. A dozen of these models, which were acquired by the Musée de la Marine in the 19th century, are still kept there. They are of significant interest because they were made by the Indians themselves using the specific materials and construction and decoration techniques of each of their cultures. The Micmac canoe, made of white-birch bark, is decorated with motifs embroidered with porcupine spines, such as an eight-arm starfish that was an emblem of this tribe. The model of the Naas Indian canoe has a hollowed-out wooden hull and its painted decor distinguishes it from canoes used in other regions, to the extent that it was once identified as Chinese. H. T.

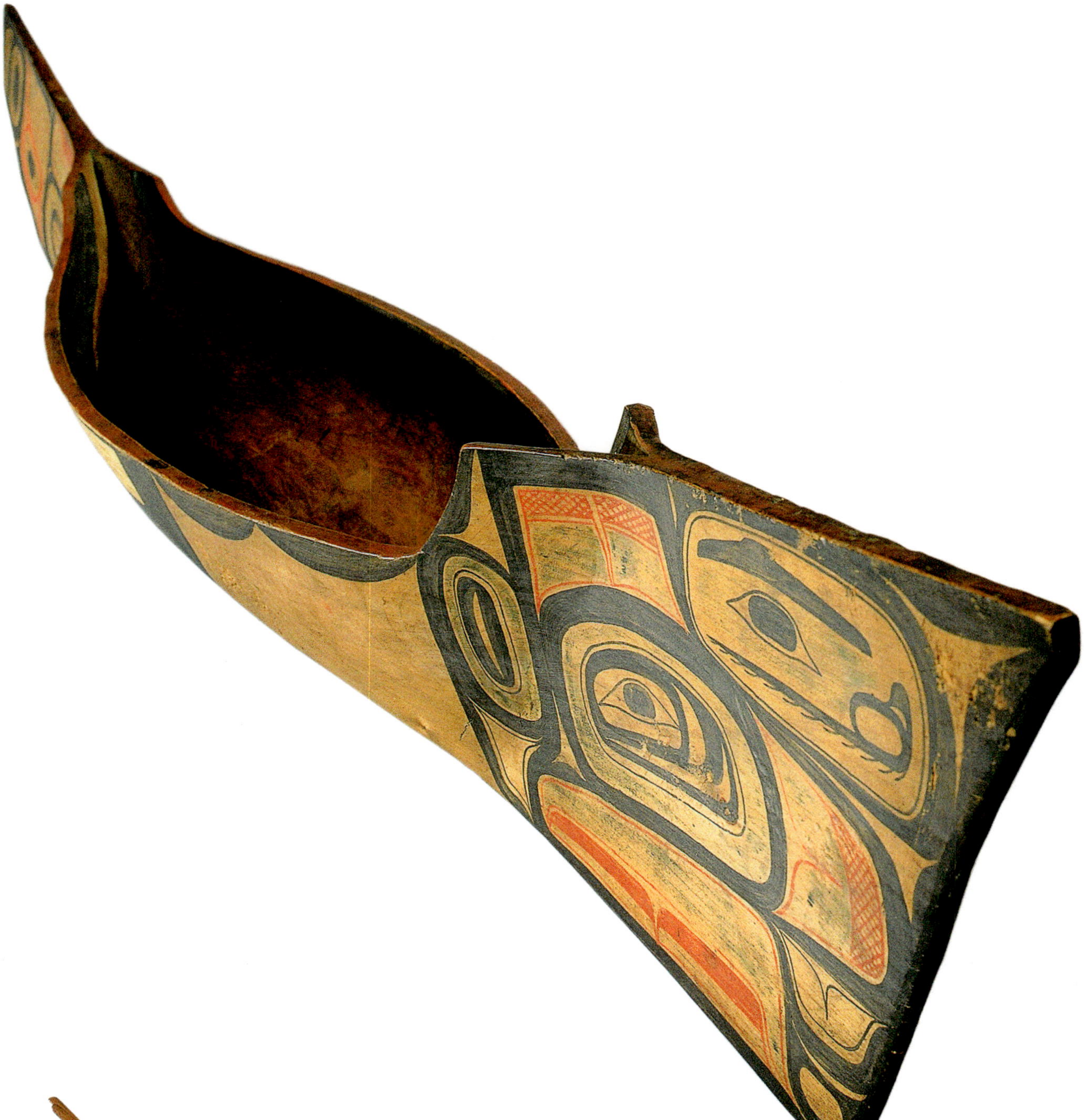
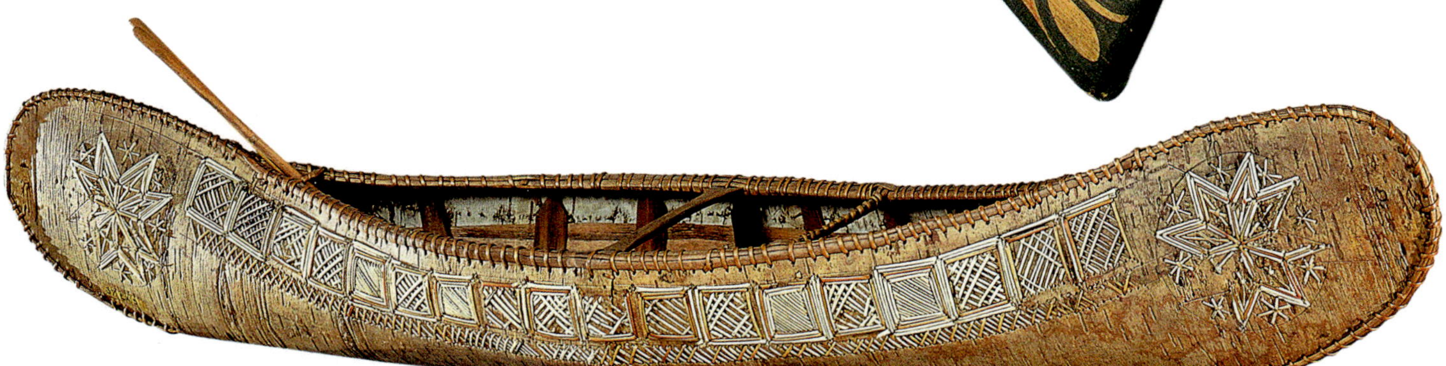

Navigational instruments

The use of navigational instruments developed out of the long-distance exploratory voyages and large-scale trade with the East and West Indies. Navigation on the high seas required a greater degree of geographical precision. Astronomical observations played a major role. It was relatively easy to calculate latitude but there was a problem with longitude. Traditional pendulum-regulated clocks did not keep time in a rolling and pitching ship. The invention in France and in England in the late 18th century of the first marine clocks, which could keep home time for comparison to local time, provided the long-awaited solution.

Devices such as the cross-staff and astrolabe, followed by the Davis Quadrant, octants and sextants, enabled the calculation of a ship's latitude by measuring the height of the stars. All these scientific instruments were made with selected materials that heightened their design and aesthetic appeal. The museum has twelve exceptional pieces from the Académie de Marine, including Baradelle's octant and a compass after Bouguer. Founded in Brest in 1752 by a group of officers, the Académie de Marine sought to 'support the practice of navigation by subjecting it to rigorous theory'. The academy's work emanated from a spirit of intellectual and scientific emulation that was characteristic of the Enlightenment.

Measuring instruments may have helped to calculate longitude, but for many years sailors came up against their unreliability. Traditional clocks could not withstand humidity, temperature changes, or the movement of a ship. Until Ferdinand Berthoud and his invention of a watch-chronometer in 1760, sandglasses were the only way to keep track of time on board. These were only as reliable as the person in charge of turning them over; a lazy helmsman would sometimes 'flog the glass' (*manger du sable* – 'eat sand' – in French), i.e. turn over the sandglass slightly ahead of time so as to shorten his watch.

Vesconte de Maggiolo (?–1551)

Map of the Mediterranean Sea and the Eastern section of the Atlantic Ocean

1537 . Illuminated manuscript on parchment . 70.5 x 102 cm . Signed and date halfway up on the left . Entered museum collections 1944 . MnM 9 NA 24

A fine specimen of 16th-century Genoese cartography, this portolan chart is the work of Vesconte de Maggiolo, appointed *magister cartarum pro navigando* of the Republic of Genoa in 1519. Only fifteen or so maps signed by him have come down to us. This one covers the whole of the central section of the Mediterranean. It extends in the east to the Black Sea in the north and the Red Sea in the south, while the western section shows the Atlantic Ocean, from Senegal to Norway. M. M.

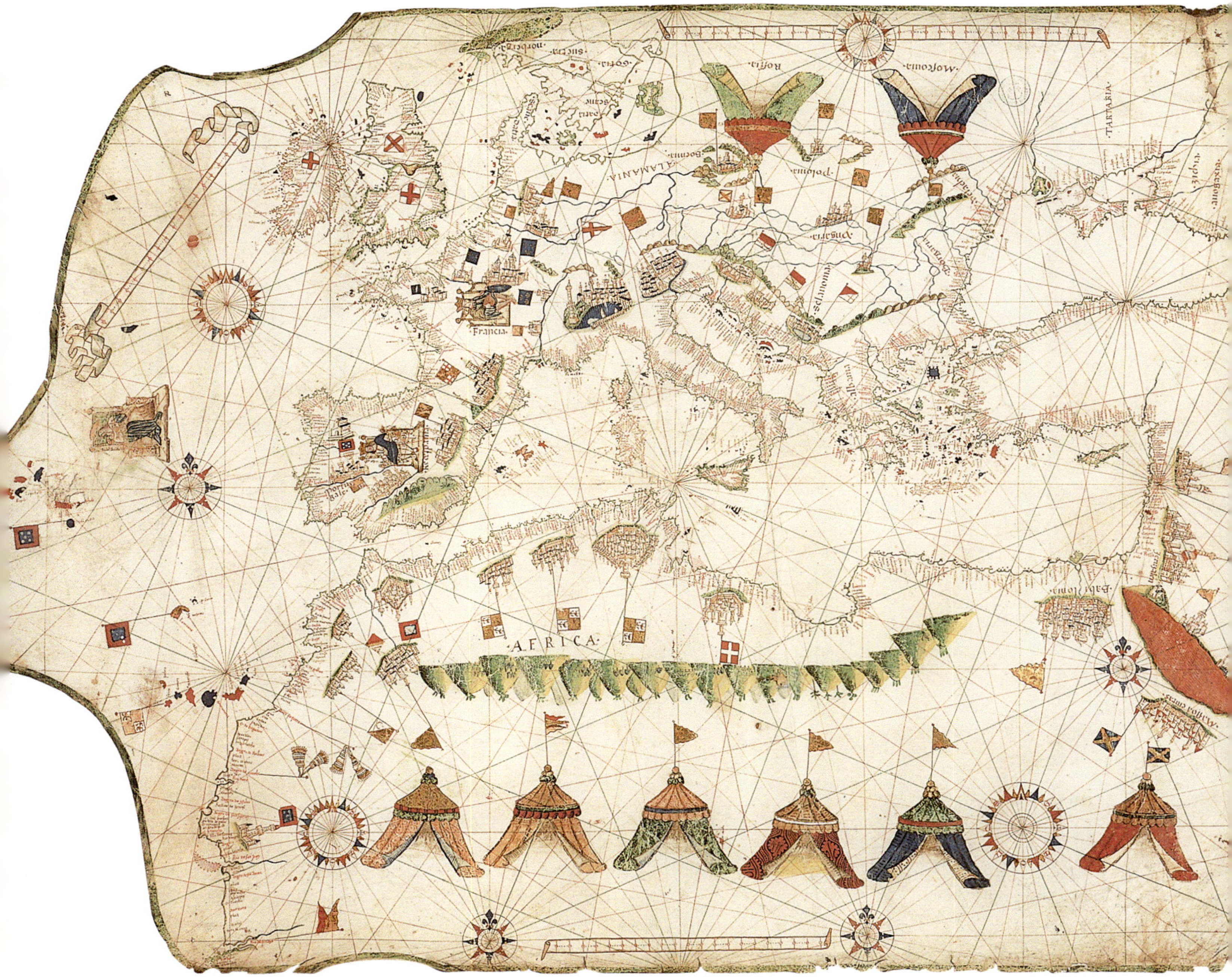

Francia
AFRICA

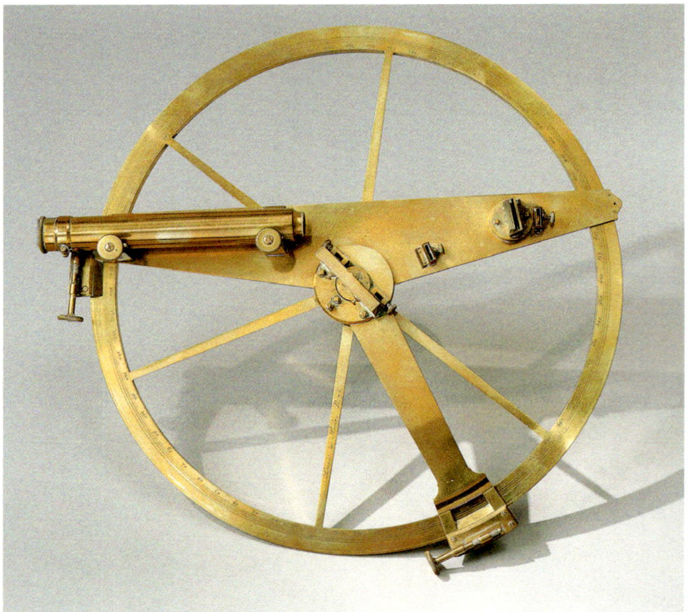

Reflecting circle or Borda circle

Jean-Charles de Borda (1733–1799), inventor . Étienne Lenoir (1744–1832), maker . Circa 1786 . Brass, glass, steel . Ø 30 cm . Entered museum collections 1830 . MnM 11 NA 21

Designed by the sailor and scientist Jean-Charles de Borda after an improved principle of the circle invented by Tobias Mayer (1765), the Borda circle was developed by the Lenoir workshop in Paris from 1772 to 1777 and finished in 1784. Originally used to calculated longitude from lunar distances, by repeated measurements of observations on the circular limb of the moon, it later became, under the name 'hydrographical circle', the principle instrument used to draw maps. F. C.

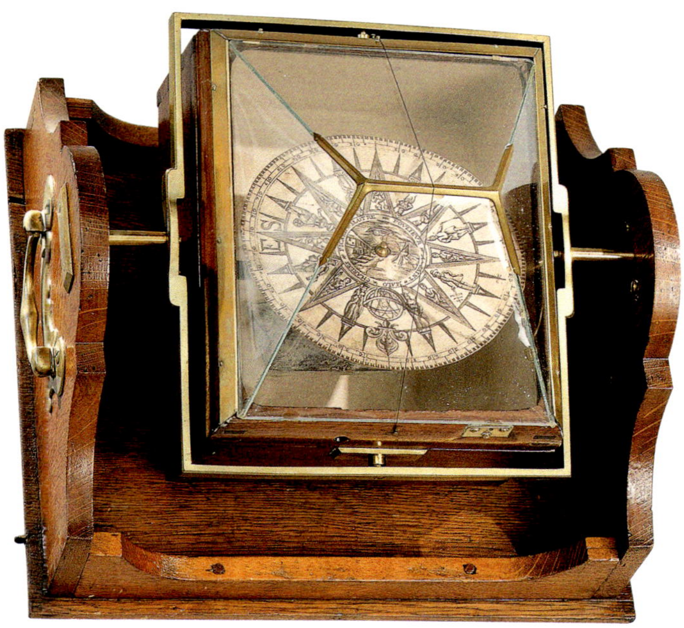

Variation compass

Pierre Bouguer (1698–1758), designer . Compass rose signed by Charles Picard, master pulley maker at Saint-Malo . Before 1756 . Wood, brass, paper, iron, glass, plant fibres . 21 x 38.5 x 31 cm . Entered museum collections 1895, former Académie de Marine collection . MnM 1 NA 11

An improvement on the bearing compass, the variation compass enabled magnetic deviation to be measured by comparison of the north-south axis with the shade cast by the sun overhead, thanks to a wire stretched over the binnacle. This compass corresponds to the description of a new variation compass proposed by the mathematician and hydrographer Pierre Bouguer in his *Traité de navigation* published in 1753. It was purchased in 1756 in Paris on behalf of the Académie de Marine, whose aim was to encourage progress in naval sciences. F. C.

Octant

Jacques Baradelle (1725–1794), inventor and maker ▪ Before 1752 ▪ Mahogany, brass, glass ▪ 55 x 50 x 53 cm ▪ Entered museum collections 1830, former Académie de Marine collection ▪ MnM 11 NA 8

In 1731, the English astronomer John Hadley invented a revolutionary instrument, the octant, which permitted the measurement, by day or night, of the altitude of celestial bodies, by reading angles up to 90°, or 1/8 of a circle, to about one minute of arc. The octant invented by Baradelle after Hadley's model was presented at the Académie de Marine in 1752. It was one of the best instruments of its time for determining a vessel's position. F. C.

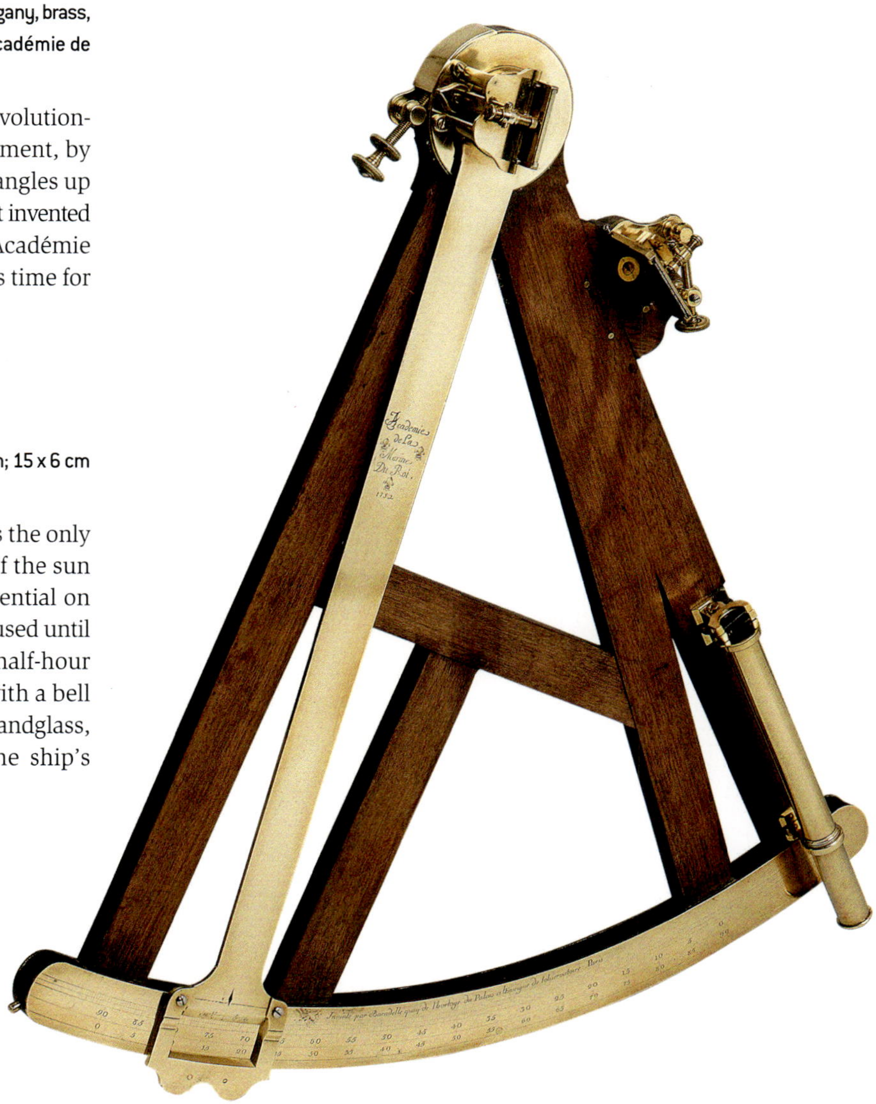

Set of sandglasses

18th century ▪ Pine, oak, glass, paper, eggshell ▪ 36 x 29 cm; 22 x 13 cm; 15 x 6 cm ▪ Entered museum collections 1949 ▪ MnM 5 NA 12, 10, 11

From the 15th to the 19th century, the ship's hourglass was the only means to measure time on board between each passage of the sun through the meridian. Three types of sandglass were essential on board: the four-hour *sablier de combat* ('battle' sandglass), used until the 19th century to keep track of time during battles; the half-hour *horloge* ('clock'), which marked daily routine on board, with a bell striking each time it was turned over; and the half-minute sandglass, or *ampoulette*, used for heaving the log (measuring the ship's speed using a trailing float). F. C.

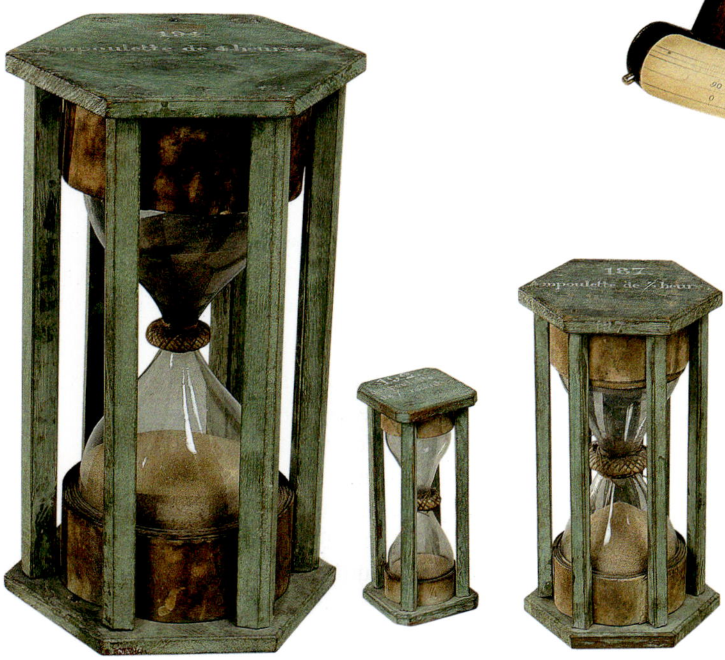

Modern warships

True to its origins as a naval museum, the Musée National de la Marine also pays tribute to the modern-day navy.
The launch of *La Gloire* in 1859 marked the beginning of a period of profound transformation. The naval fleet of wooden sailing ships evolved into one of steam- and propeller-powered armoured ships. New weapons called for new types of warships. The explosive shell gave rise to armour-plated battleships; the airship to aircraft carriers, helicopter carriers and anti-aircraft frigates; the torpedo to torpedo boats and submarines; the nuclear warhead missile to nuclear submarine missile launchers, and so forth. Over the decades, wood gave way to steel, then to lighter alloys, and warships' hulls were painted a uniform grey. Recent years saw the arrival of stealth ships whose armaments were concealed.
The collections include paintings, photographs, on-board equipment and technical objects, as well as numerous model ships built by the museum workshop or professional model makers; these models were donated by the Direction des Constructions Navales and the Délégation Générale pour l'Armement, or by private collectors, and constitute a unique ensemble. The models of the most recent ships of the French navy are particularly evocative.
Naval dockyards no longer have workshops dedicated to the ancient craft of model making. Today's models are made in the private sector. They play a promotional role in shipbuilding projects. A very few works have been especially built to the museum's precise specifications in view of their integration into the collections.

The *Gloire*

Model of the amour-plated frigate launched at Toulon in 1854, 1:33 scale . Constructed at the Toulon dockyard model workshop . Circa 1859 . Wood, iron, steel, copper, brass, cotton . 178 x 271 x 83 cm . Entered museum collections 1867 . MnM 25 MG 1

The first armour-plated warship in the world, the *Gloire*, was built after drawings by the naval engineer Dupuy de Lôme. Its armour plating, screwed onto the wooden hull, was made up of wrought-iron plates 10 to 12 cm thick that were welded together. This ship of revolutionary design, fast despite its weight, was copied by all the major naval powers. It was soon followed by a dozen similar frigates, which gave the French navy a technological lead of almost twenty years. This model was shown at the 1867 Paris World's Fair. A. N.

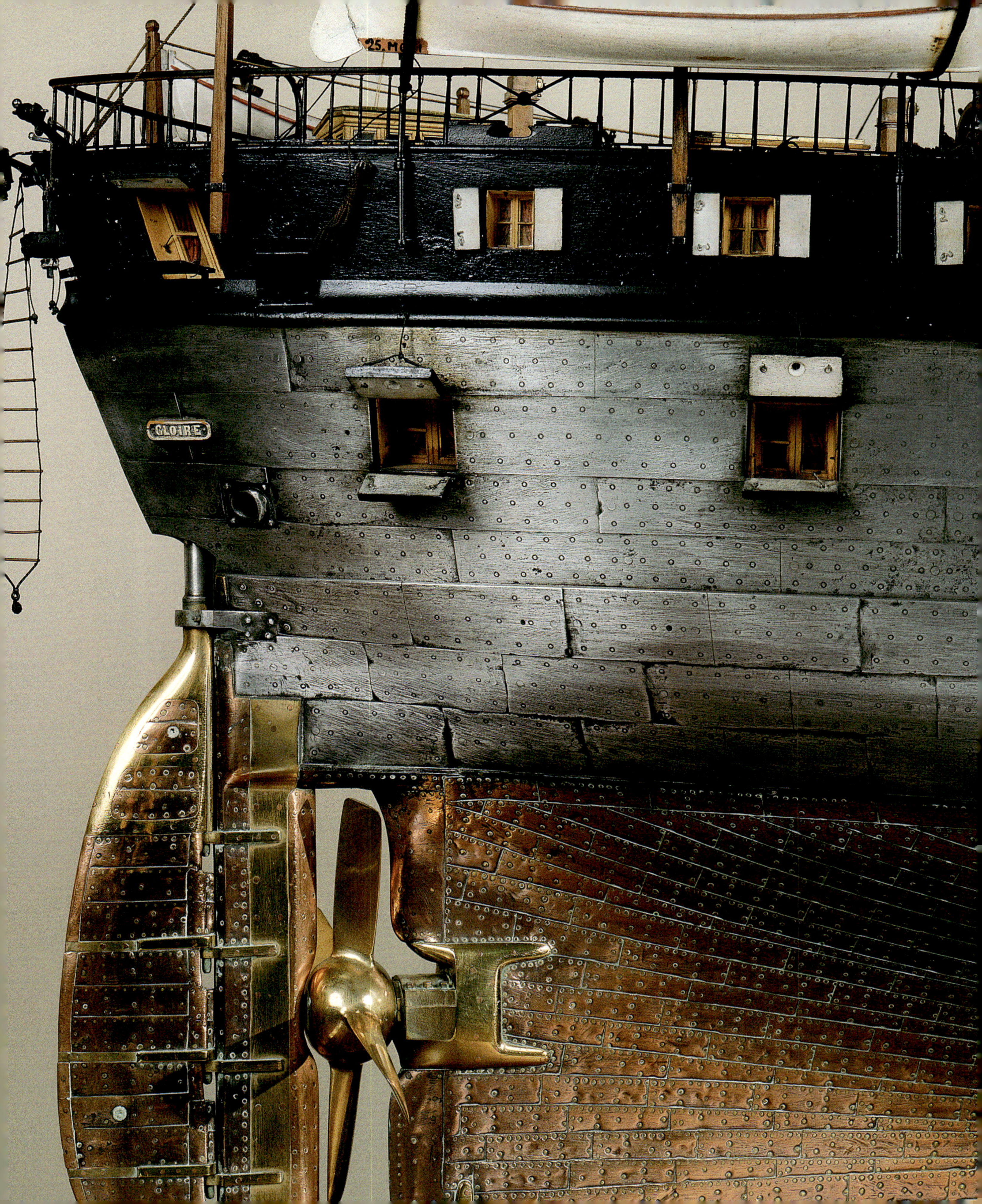
GLOIRE

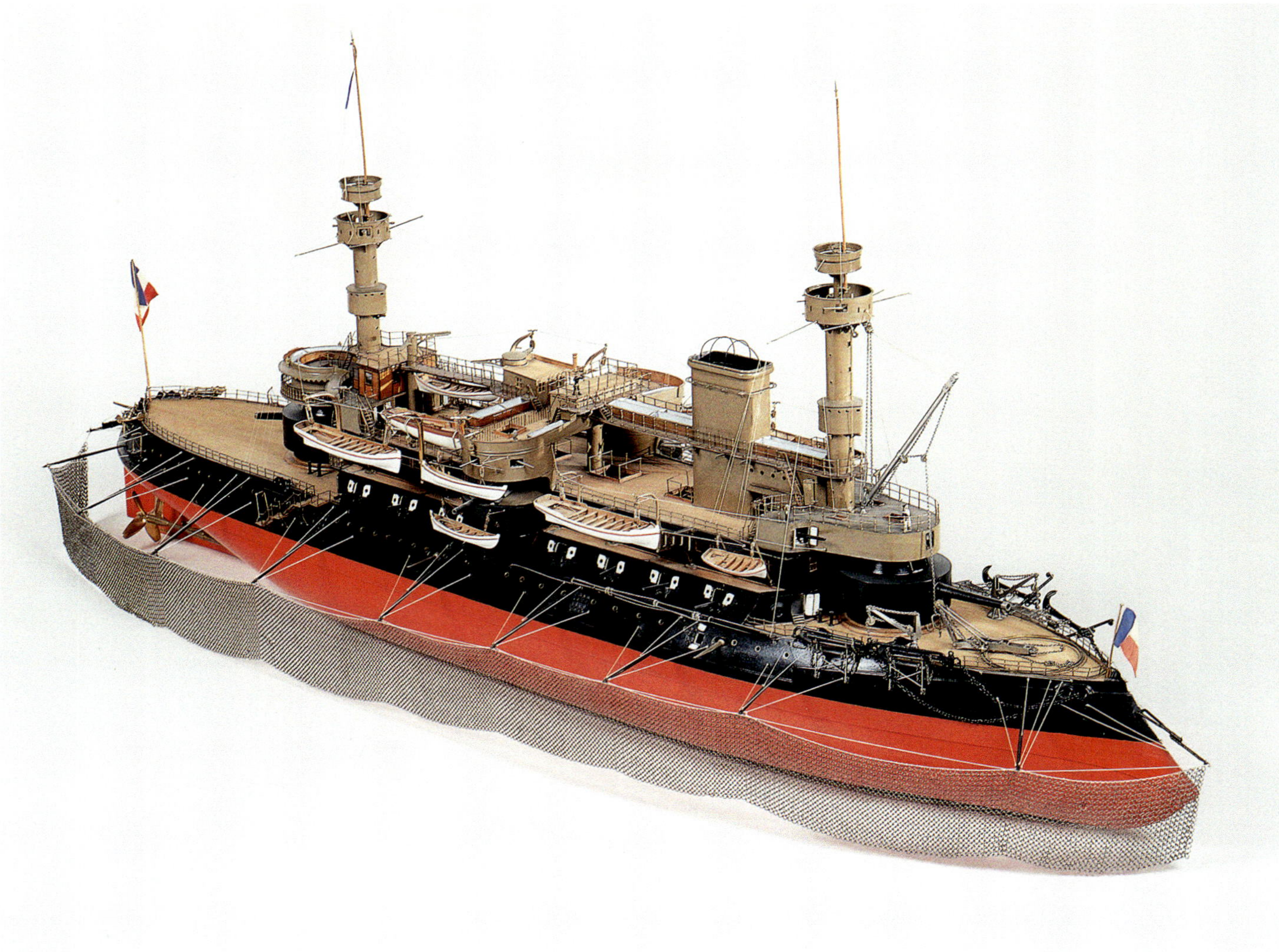

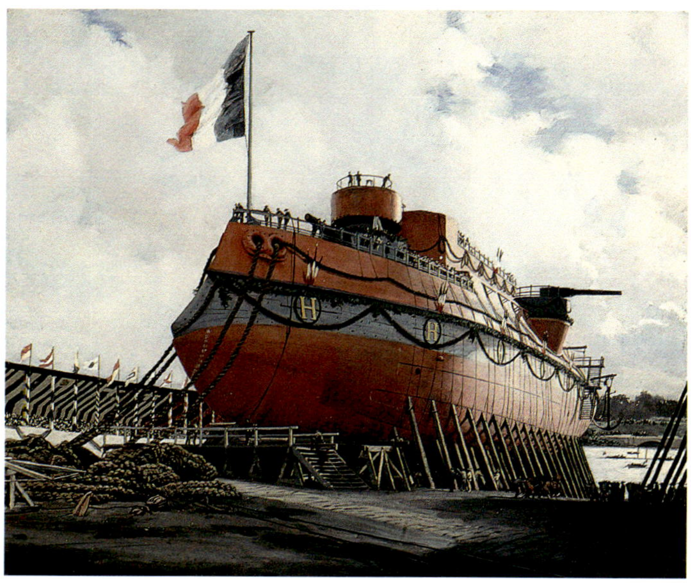

The *Hoche*

Model of the squadron battleship launched at Lorient in 1866, 1:66 scale . Constructed by the Lorient dockyards model workshop . Circa 1886 . Wood, steel, metal, brass, cotton . 76 x 172 x 46 cm . Entered museum collections 1896 . MnM 25 MG 16

The *Hoche* was the first French battleship with gun turrets. This rather heavy ship with massive superstructures was soon nicknamed 'the big hotel' by its crew, and 'the big target' by the German emperor. The model was equipped on starboard by anti-torpedo nets of the Bullivant type, used when the ship was at anchor as protection against attacks from torpedo boats. A. N.

Alexandre Brun (1853–1941)

Launch of the battleship 'Hoche' at Lorient in 1886

1886 . Oil on wood . 46 x 56 cm . Signed on lower left . Entered museum collections 1995 . MnM 9 OA 211

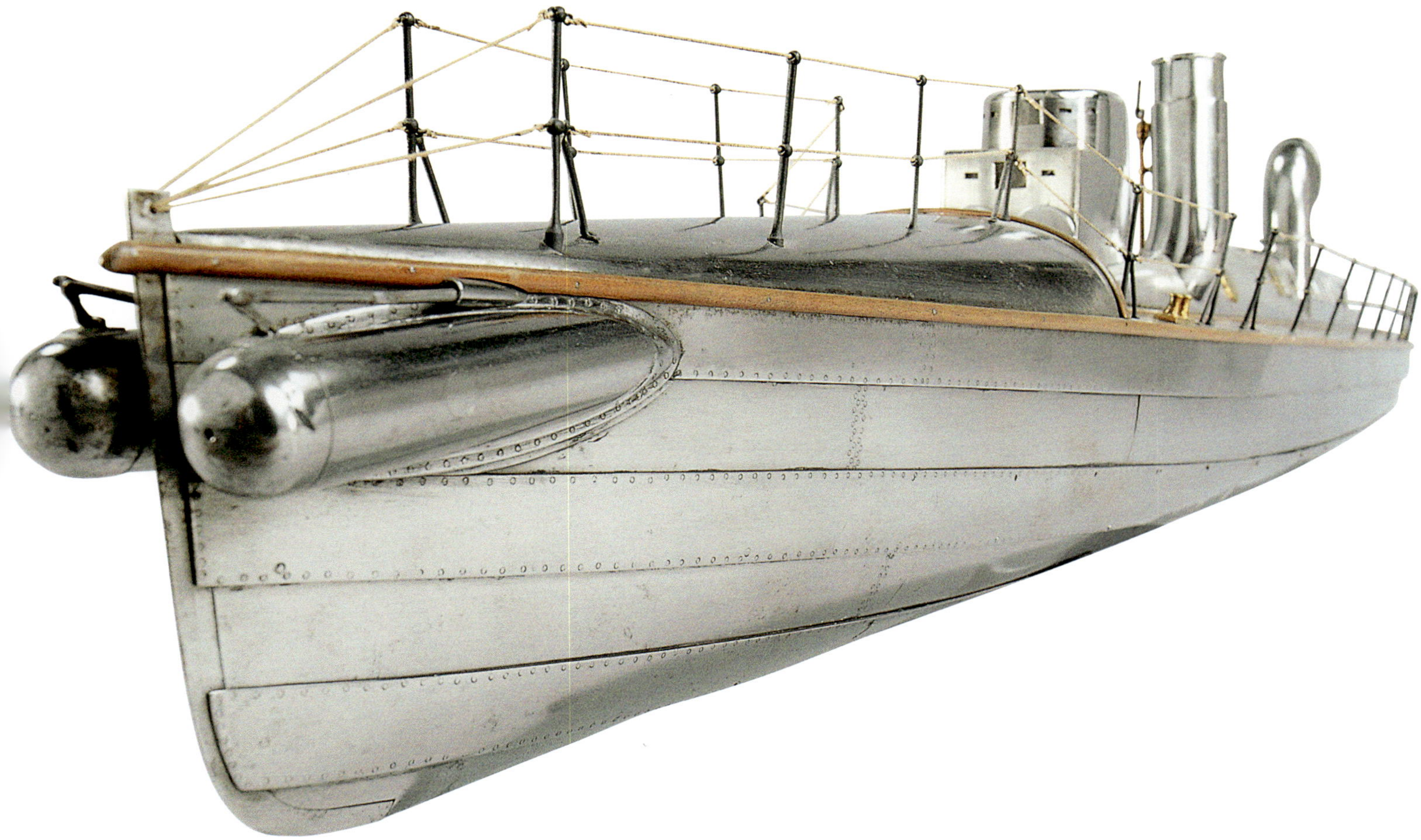

Torpedo boat n° 63

Model of a numbered torpedo boat, 1:20 scale . Constructed by Charles Hamelin (1831–after 1885) . 1882 . Wood, steel . 25 x 144 x 16 cm . Entered museum collections 1882 . MnM 29 MG 19

Built from 1875 on, torpedo boats seemed capable of overturning the logic of naval combat by opposing, as an expression of the time went, 'bugs to giants', i.e. torpedo boats to battleships. But their poor stability at sea checked the ambitions of their admirers, members of the 'Jeune École', a French naval school of thought. The No. 63 torpedo boat, built by the Augustin-Norman shipyard in 1881, was the first ship of its kind to cross the English Channel. A. N.

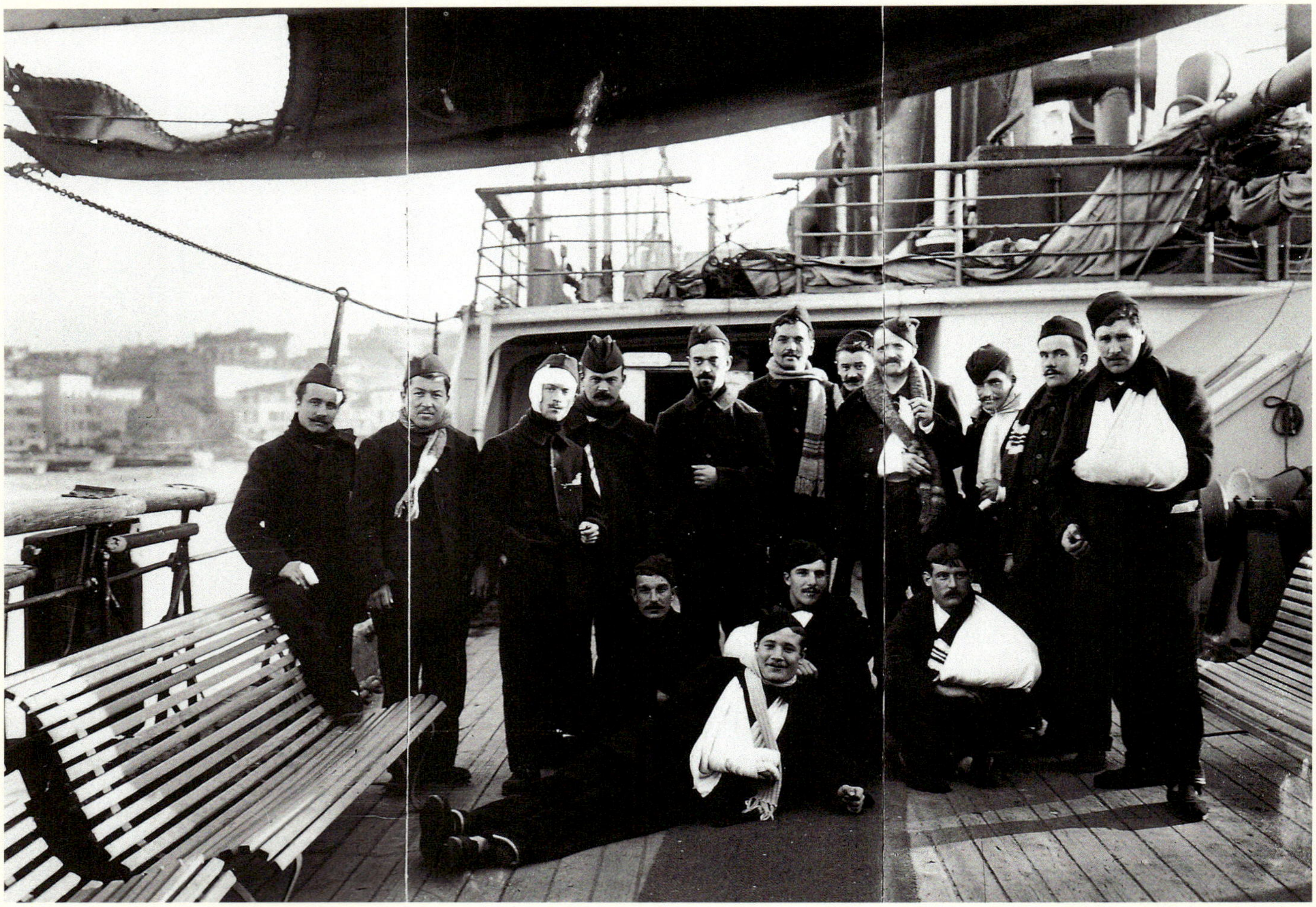

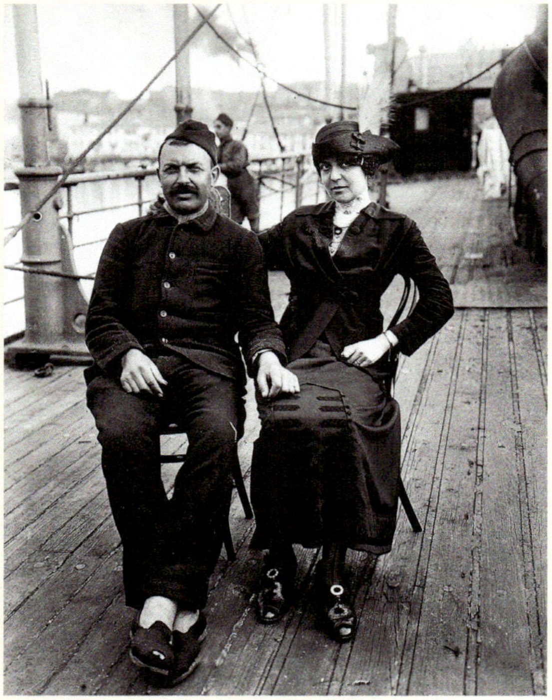

Claude Ropolo (1877–1967)

Soldiers aboard the hospital ship 'Aquitaine'
A couple aboard the hospital ship 'Aquitaine'

1914–1915 ■ Modern photographic prints from glass-plate negatives ■ 13 x 18 cm each ■ Plates entered museum collections 1994 ■ MnM Photographs collection

These photographs are part of a series of glass-plate photographs taken on board the *Aquitaine* during World War I. This merchantman, requisitioned in Toulon by the war ministry, was converted into a hospital. Shortly before he was called up, the skilled amateur photographer Claude Ropolo took some moving portraits of wounded soldiers that were quite unlike the official photographs and sensational images published by the newspapers. A. M.

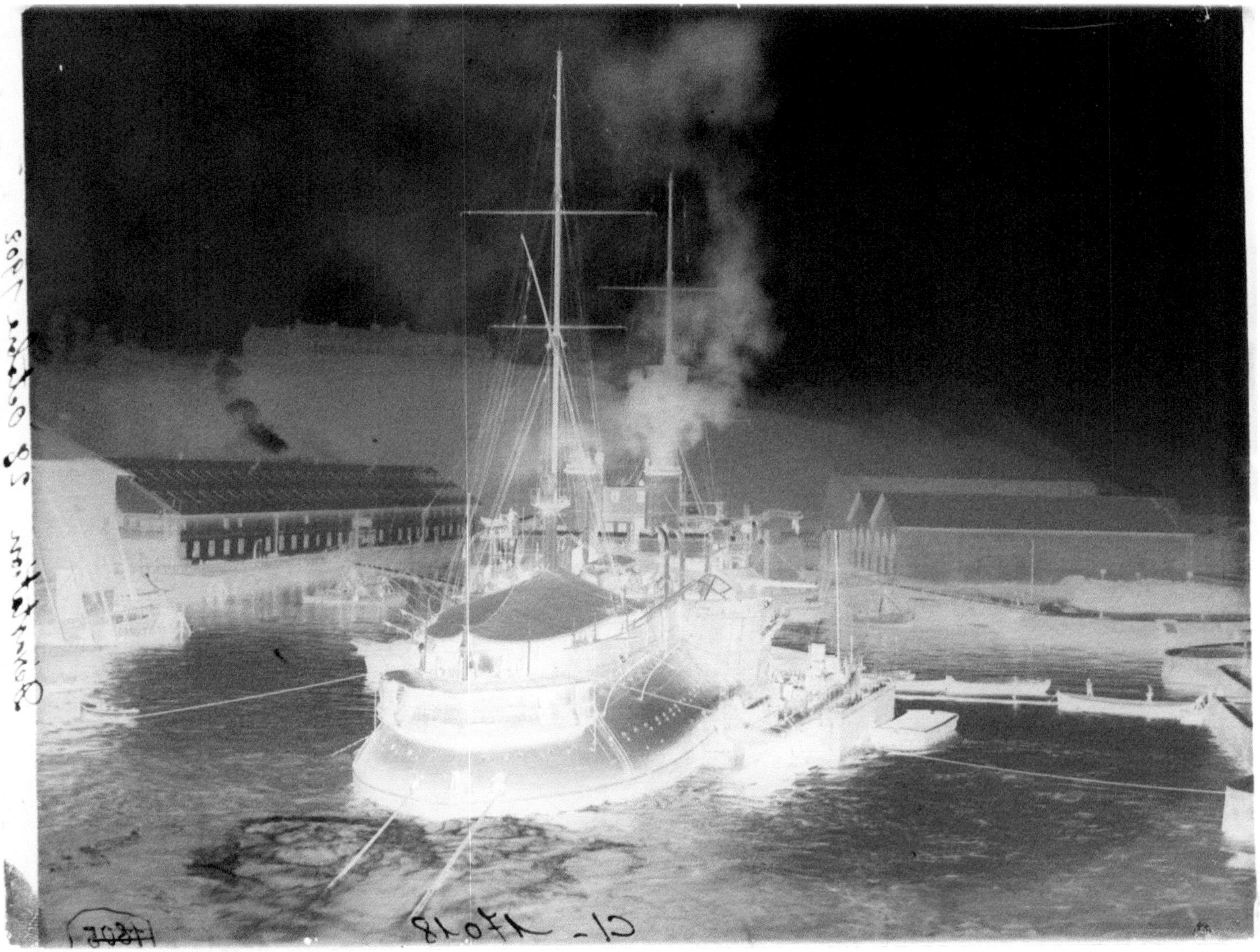

Anonymous

The squadron battleship 'Dévastation'

28 October1902 ▪ Glass-plate negative ▪ 18 x 24 cm ▪ Entered museum collections 1953 ▪ MnM Photographs collection

Built at Lorient in 1875, the *Dévastation* belonged to the first generation of battleships made almost entirely of steel. Given a powerfully suggestive name, the ship was one of the most modern of its times. In 1900 a major overhaul of the vessel was begun in order to replace part of the old armour-plating with a thinner armour and install more efficient engines. Here the ship is photographed at a standstill, having been made fast for heating trials. The Musée National de la Marine has several thousand glass-plate negatives including this one, a remarkable example of the photographic documentation of the Constructions Navales de la Marine. **A. M.**

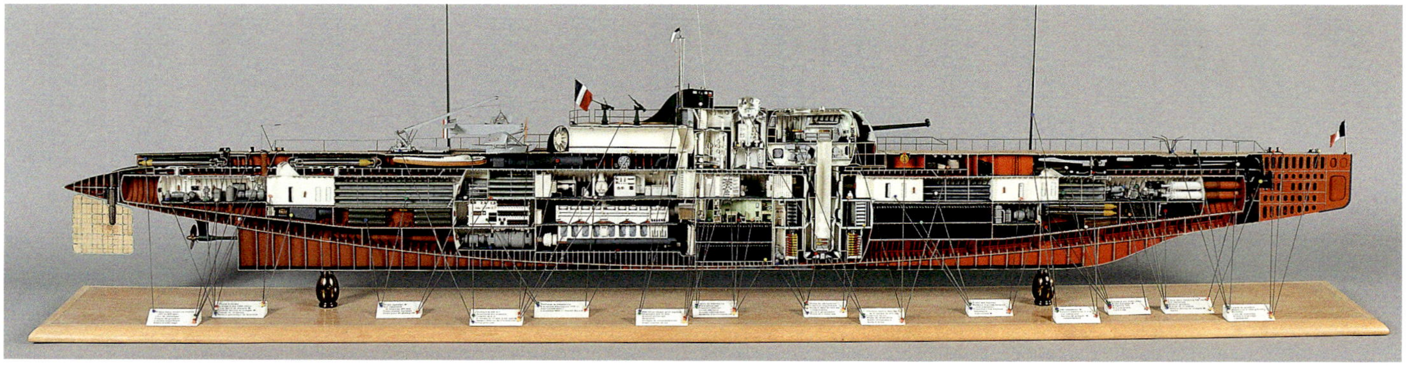

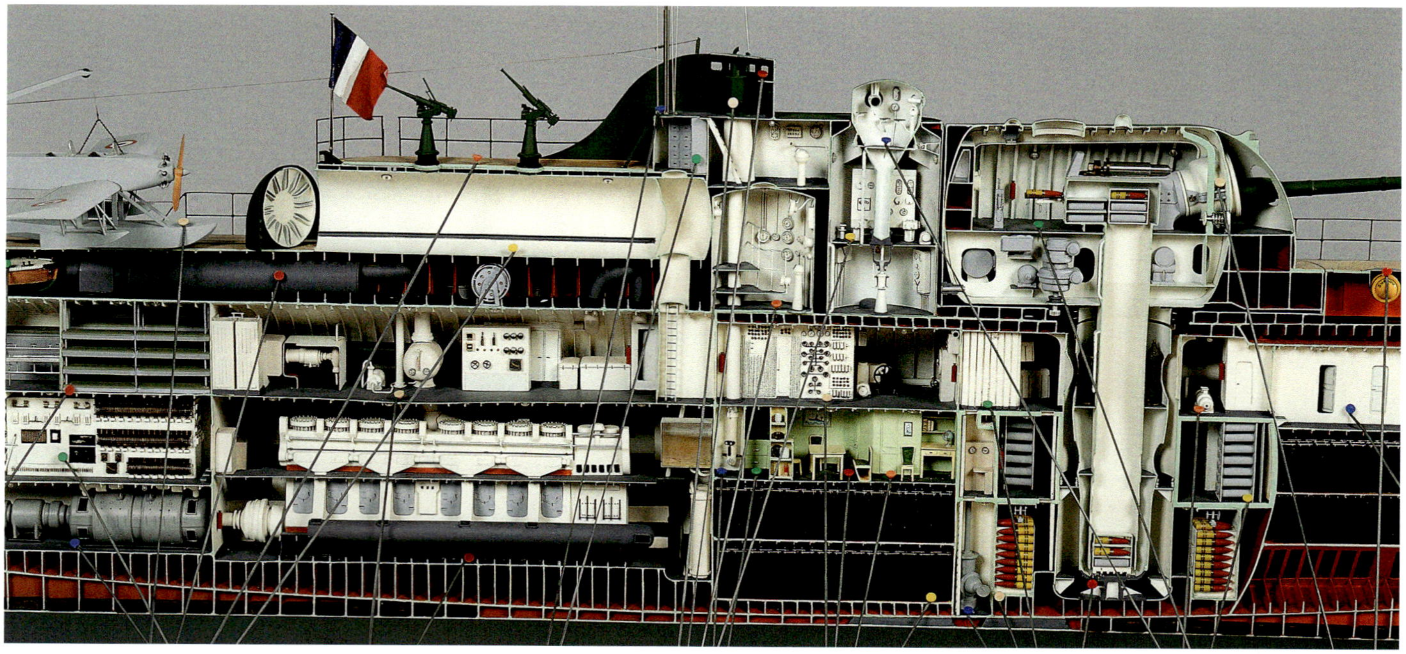

The *Surcouf*

Model of the long-range submarine launched at Cherbourg in 1929, 1:50 scale ▪ Constructed by the Musée de la Marine workshop ▪ 1954 ▪ Wood, brass, steel ▪ 65 x 226 x 30 cm ▪ Entered museum collections 1954 ▪ MnM 31 MG 16

The only one of its kind, the *Surcouf* was in its time the largest submarine in the world, and the one with the widest range. Designed as a privateer capable of attack far from its base, it was armed with two 203-mm guns and a seaplane with folding wings. It was transferred to the Free French Naval Forces during World War II, and sank following an accidental collision with an American cargo boat on 19 February 1942. **A. N.**

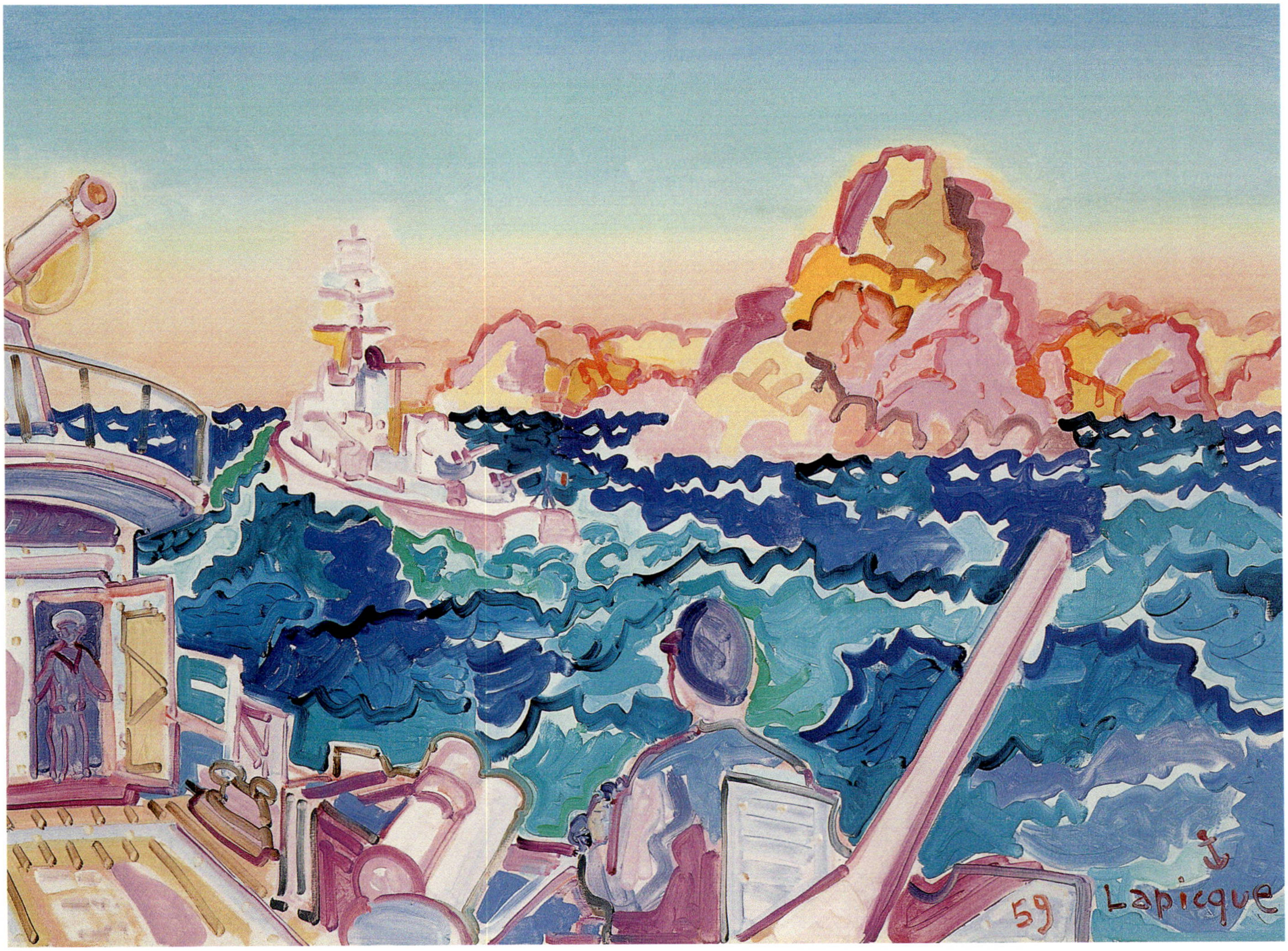

Charles Lapicque (1898–1987)

Manoeuvres off the coast of Brest

1959 . Oil on canvas . 65 x 91 cm . Signed and dated on lower right . Entered museum collections 1997 . MnM 11 OA 359

The sea was one of Charles Lapicque's principle sources of inspiration. In his capacity of official painter to the French navy from 1948 to 1966, he participated in naval manoeuvres in Brest and Toulon harbour. These voluntary outings gave him the opportunity to produce several series of paintings in which he could experiment with transparent effects and vibrant use of colour. Under Lapicque's brush, even the grey ships of the navy are a display of color. M. M.

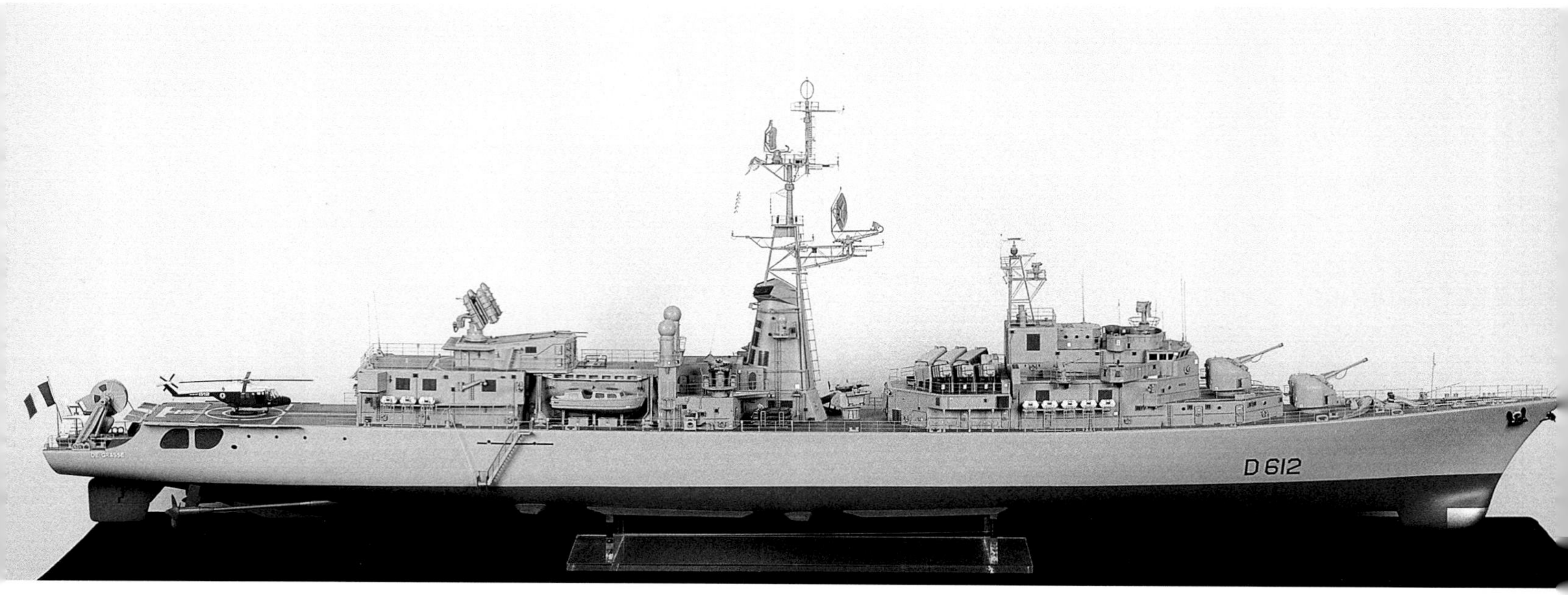

The frigate *De Grasse*

Model of the anti-submarine frigate D 612 launched at Lorient in 1974, 1:75 scale . Constructed by Claude Pittoreau (born 1938) . 1986–1991 . Wood, aluminium, metal . 64 x 210 x 27 cm . Entered museum collections 1992 . MnM 29 MG 74

Resulting from the French framework act of 1965–1970, the frigate *De Grasse* was an F 67-class ship, as were the frigates *Duguay-Trouin* and *Tourville*. The construction of this model, reproducing the superstructure in meticulous detail, took five years to complete. **A. N.**

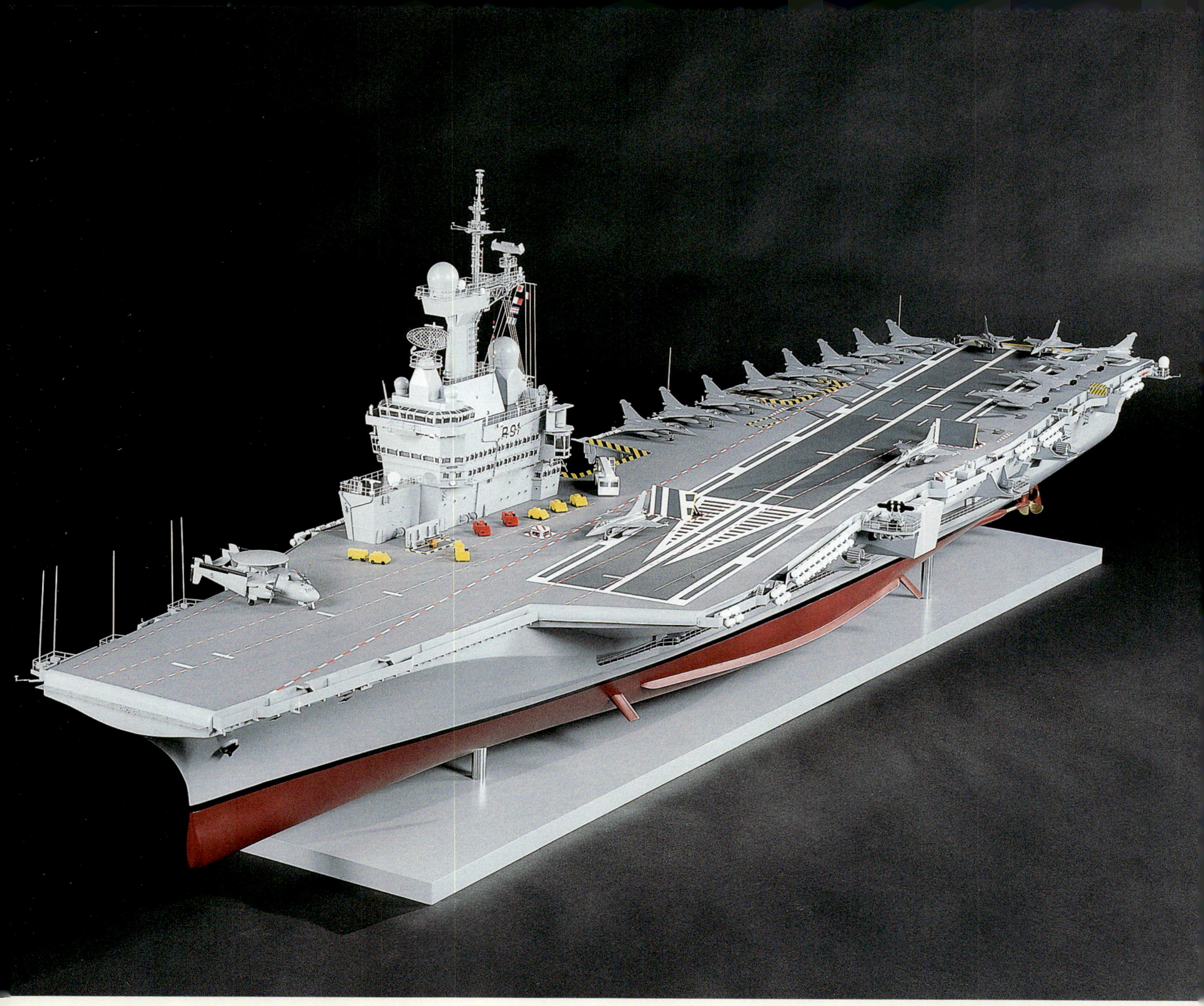

The aircraft carrier *Charles De Gaulle*

Model of the nuclear-powered aircraft carrier, 1:100 scale . 2004 . Built by the Maquettistes Réunis de Suresnes (MRS) . Synthetic materials, wood, metal . 76 x 266 x 69 cm . Entered museum collections 2004 (Délégation Générale pour l'Armement) . MnM 2004.17.1

Commissioned in 2001, the nuclear-powered aircraft carrier *Charles De Gaulle* is the spearhead of France evolving naval force. It is capable of both ground and sea attack, aerial cover of a theatre of operations and of nuclear deterrence. This large-scale model reproduces faithfully the relative size of armaments and other equipment carried by this giant ship, manned by a 1,950-strong crew. A. N.

Commerce and trade

The collection devoted to commercial shipping reflects the diversity of maritime commercial activity and trade and showcases some legendary and present-day vessels. Regularly enriched with new acquisitions and donations, it is offers visitors an invitation to voyage.

From the 17th century on, with the wealth of the trading posts acting as a powerful economic stimulant, France joined the fierce competition between nations for the conquest of new maritime routes. The cargoes of vessels hailing from distant lands were the stuff of dreams: silk, porcelain, spices, coffee, and the like. The collection of models is complemented by precious objects, vestiges of cargoes salvaged from the ocean depths including Chinese porcelain, and items of decorative arts such as a lacquer panel depicting the Dutch trading post at Deshima, Japan. The present-day equivalents of these long-range vessels – container ships and giant oil tankers, for example – are also represented.

But maritime trade can also be carried out nearer home. Exotic goods and financial gain can be found a day's sail away. Coastal navigation is illustrated by a rare model dating from the early 18th century, a Flemish-type galliot. But whether they plied the North Sea or the Mediterranean, the sailing ships of old – tartans, pinques, luggers, among others – were all eventually succeeded by mechanically-propelled cargo vessels.

The most emblematic commercial vessel was the ocean liner. These ships represented not only an economic activity in their own right but also a lifestyle and an aesthetic. The shipping companies that ran them commissioned well-known artists to attract customers. The most prestigious of them all, the sumptuously decorated transatlantic liner *Normandie*, was a true ambassador of the French decorative arts.

François Kollar (1904–1979)

The liner 'Normandie' a few hours before its launch

1932 . Baryta print . 22,6 x 16,6 cm . Stamp of photographer on back . Entered museum collections 1948 . MnM Photographs collection

During the journey he made for the extensive survey *La France travaille* commissioned by Éditions Horizons de France, François Kollar took this photograph of the majestic hull of the liner *Normandie* from waterline level. The slightly off-centre framing, abruptly cutting off the prow, overemphasises the proportions and silhouette of the ship, described in its time as a 'floating cathedral'.

Kollar's work in various styles, featuring powerful composed images and spare lines that transcend the documentary genre, reached its peak in the avant-garde aesthetic of the 1930s. **A. M.**

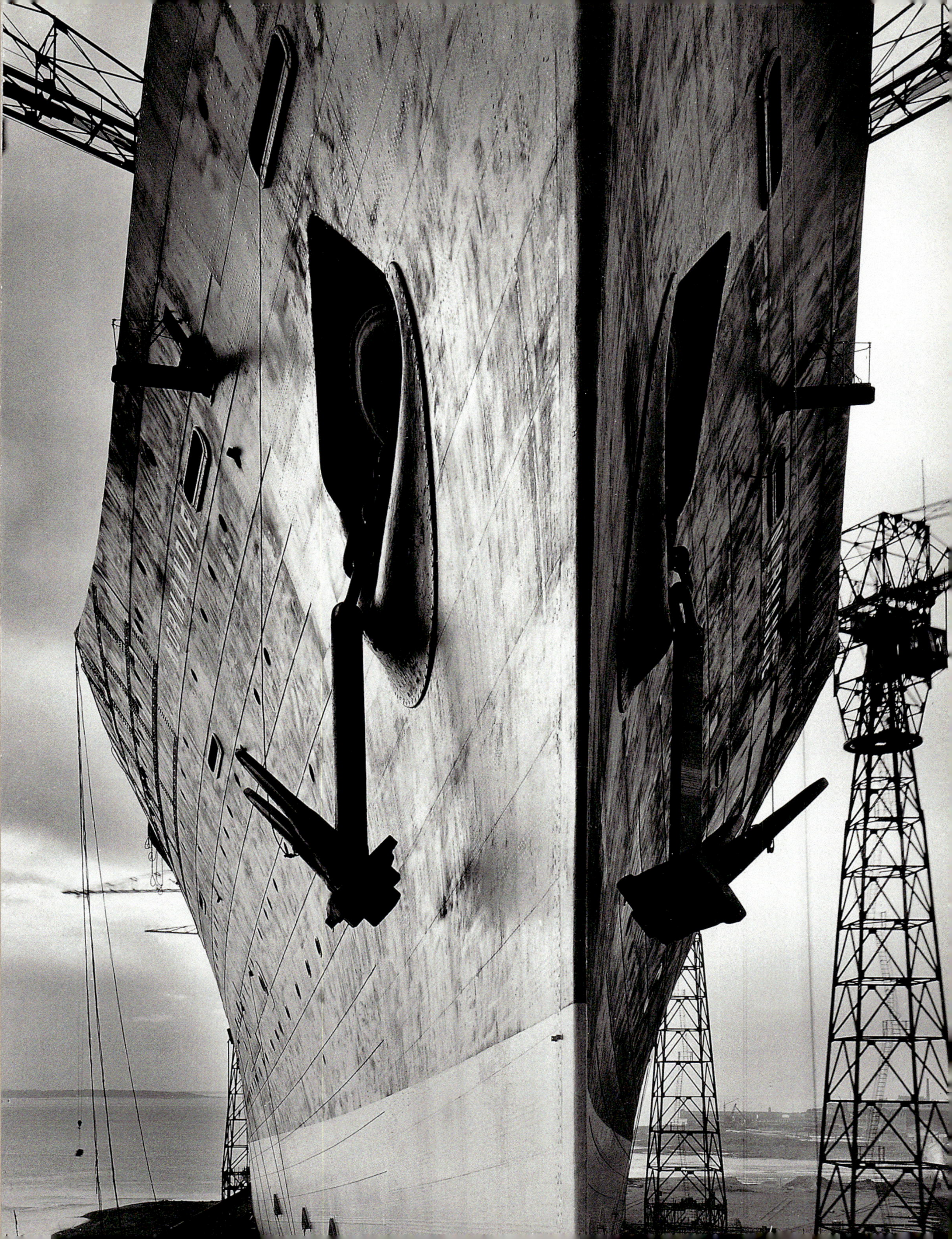

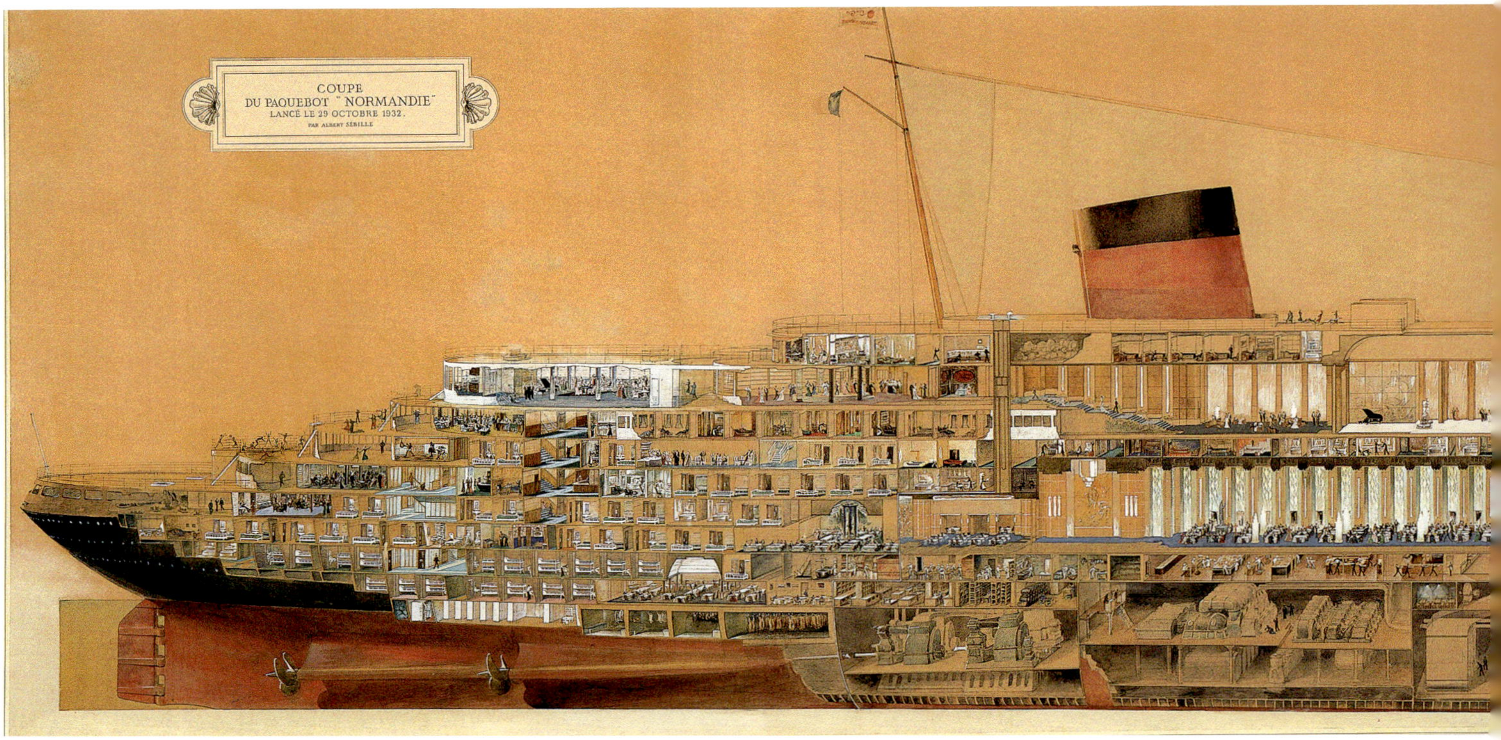

Albert Sébille (1874–1953)

Longitudinal section of the liner 'Normandie'

Circa 1934 . Gouache and watercolour on paper . 140 x 517 cm . Signed on lower right . Entered museum collections 1952 . MnM 23 OA 98

The *Normandie* is the liner worthy of every superlative: the most luxurious, the largest, the fastest, the most expensive too. On board, all is luxury and immoderation: the dining room is longer than the Galerie des Glaces at Versailles; a host of film-projection rooms, concert rooms, lounges and smoking rooms fill the floors. Fascinated as much by the liner's technical capabilities as by its luxuriousness, Albert Sébille sought to reproduce the engine rooms and ballrooms in equal detail. **A. M.-V.**

Jean Dupas (1882–1964) and Charles Champigneulle (1907–1955)

Mural panel, preparatory work

Circa 1935 . Fixed under glass, gold and silver heightening . 80 x 120 x 0.9 cm . Entered museum collections 1998 . MnM 49 OA 237

For the decoration of the liner *Normandie*, the Compagnie Générale Transatlantique employed the services of the greatest artists and craftsmen of the time. This piece was executed by the master glass-maker Charles Champigneulle after drawings by Jean Dupas.
This glass panel shows an element from Dupas' *Chariot of Thetis*, a detail from a 400-m^2-composition that was to adorn the Grand Salon in the first-class quarters of the ship. This panel, executed to obtain the company's approval of the whole project, was never installed on board. **A. M.-V.**

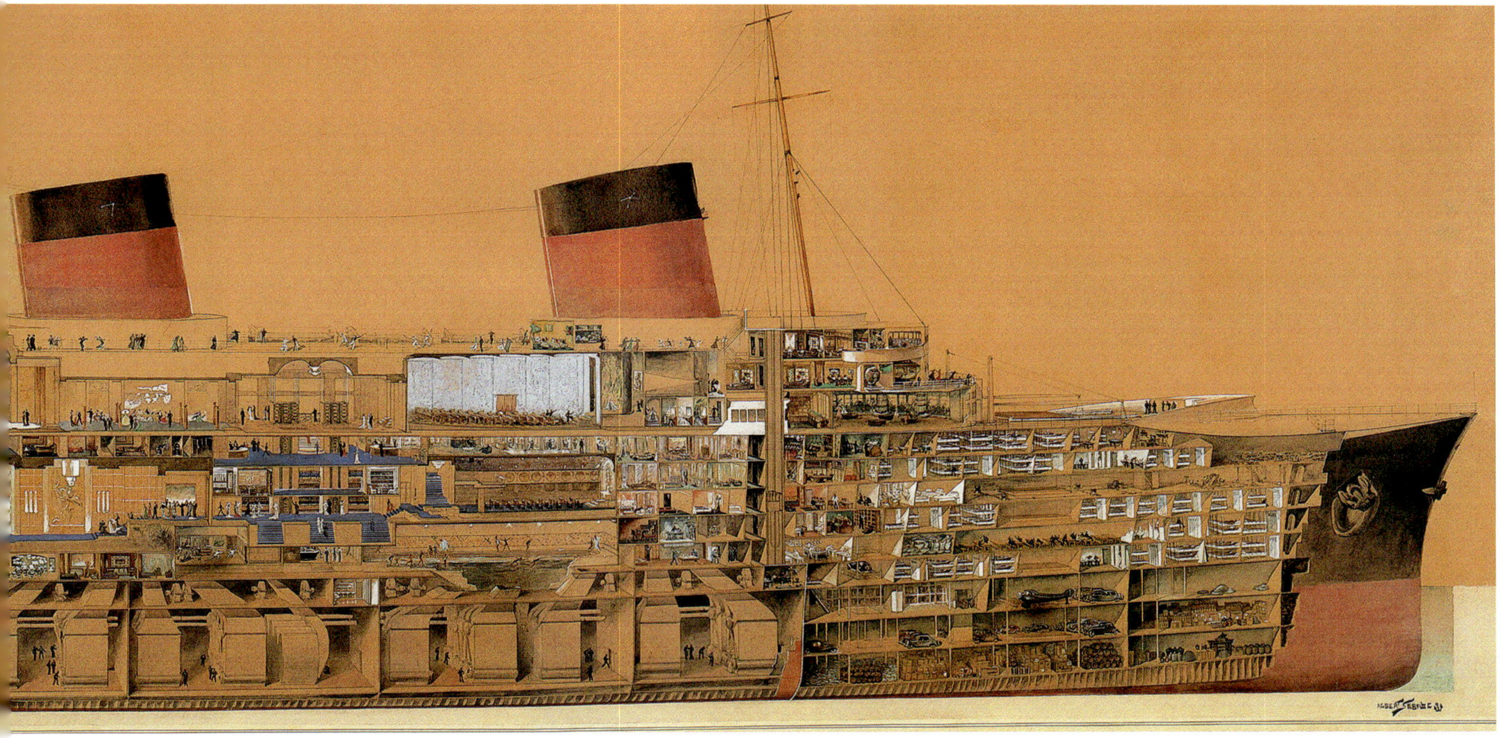

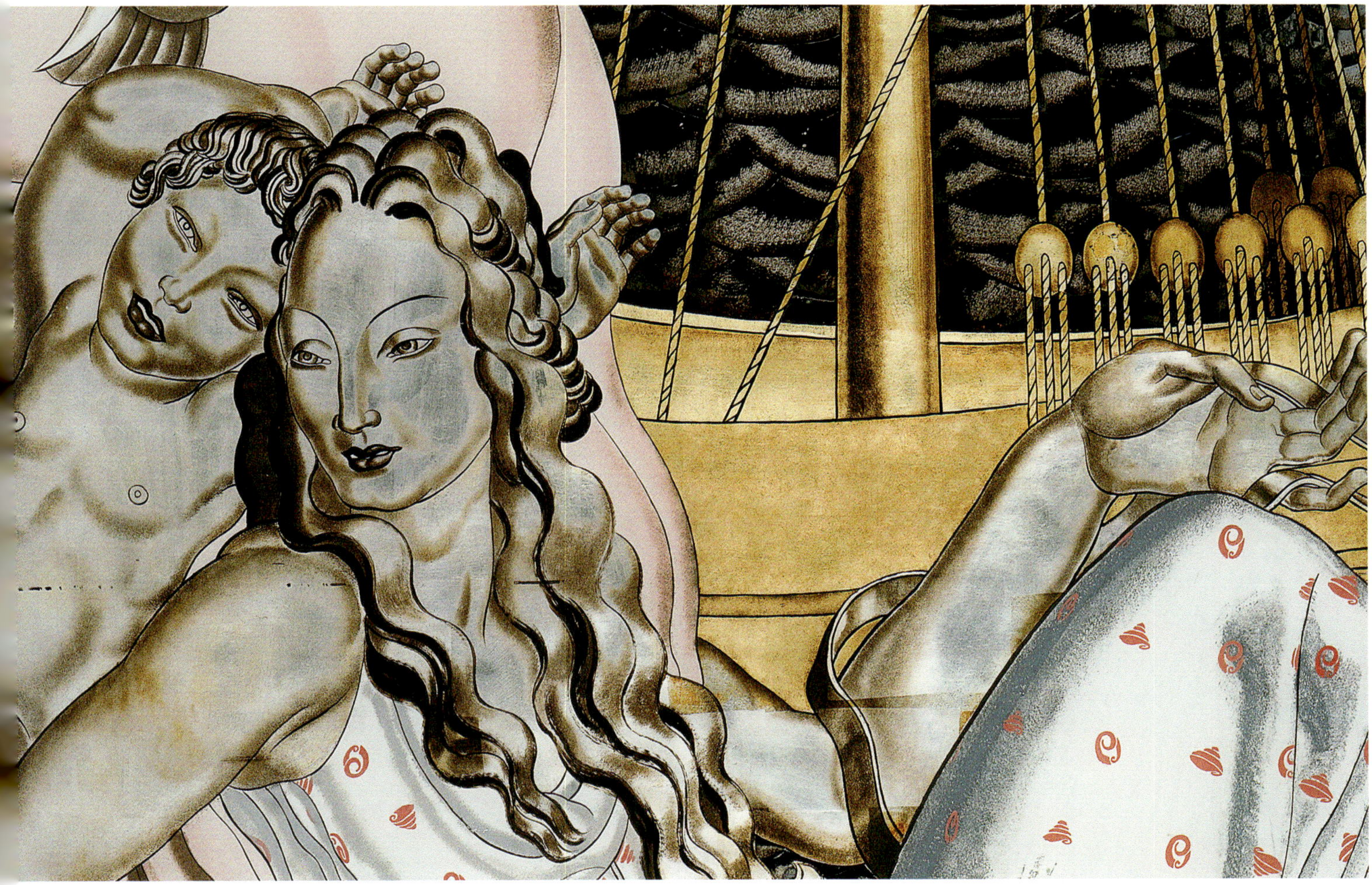

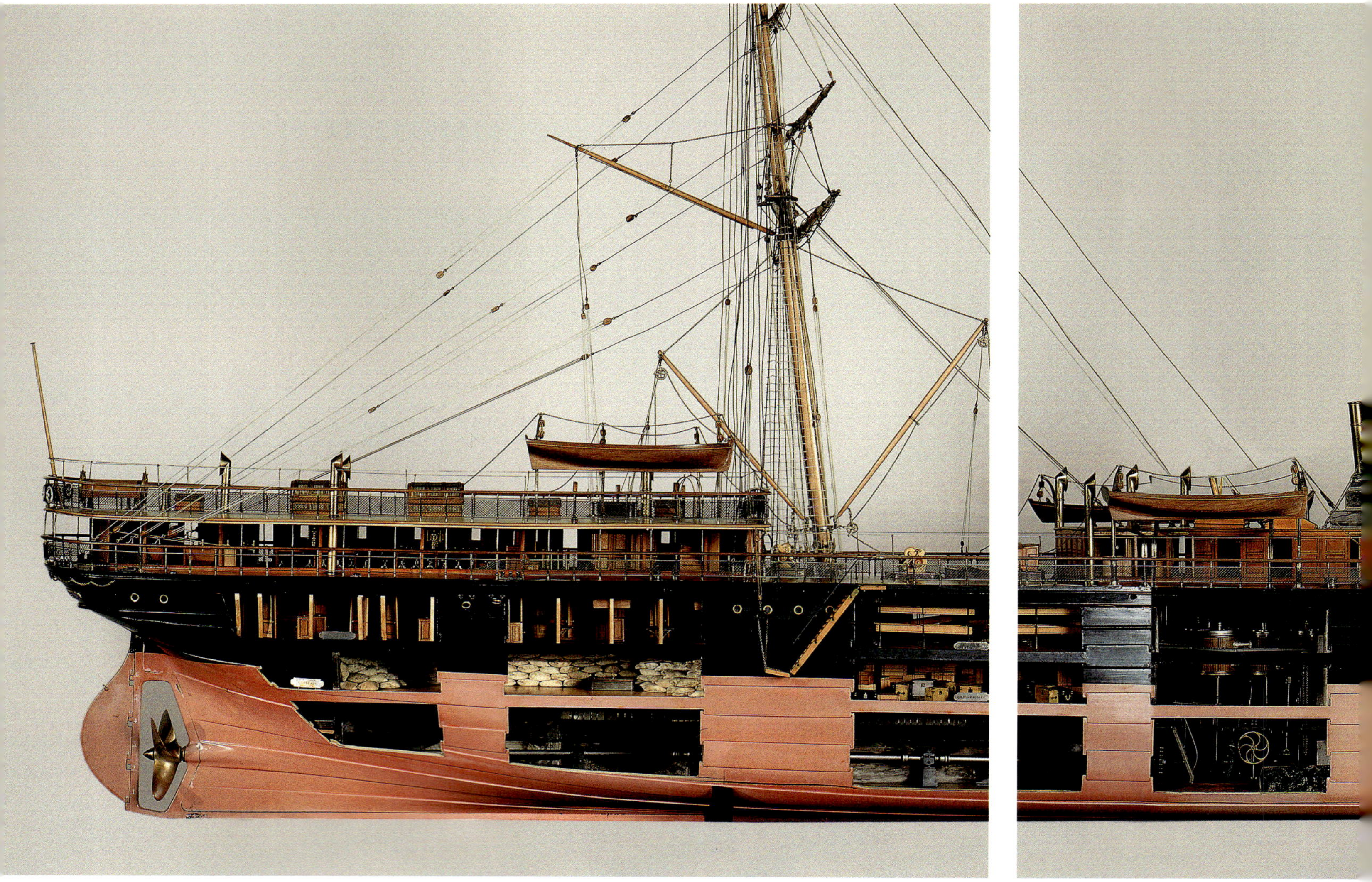

The *Paraguay*

Shipyard model of the liner launched at Saint-Nazaire in 1888, 1:40 scale ▪ Built by the Ateliers et Chantiers de la Loire, Saint-Nazaire ▪ Circa 1888 ▪ Wood, brass, iron, plant fibres ▪ 132 x 289 x 50 cm ▪ Entered museum collections 1889 ▪ MnM 7 MM 3

The cargo-passenger liner *Paraguay* was built for the Société des Chargeurs Réunis. Its steel hull was over 110 meters long. It was fitted with a triple expansion compound steam engine. Built to sail the South American route, it carried passengers and freight before operating the postal service on the west coast of Africa, and later the South Africa–Madagascar line. The hull of this model was left open to show the interior fittings. F. C.

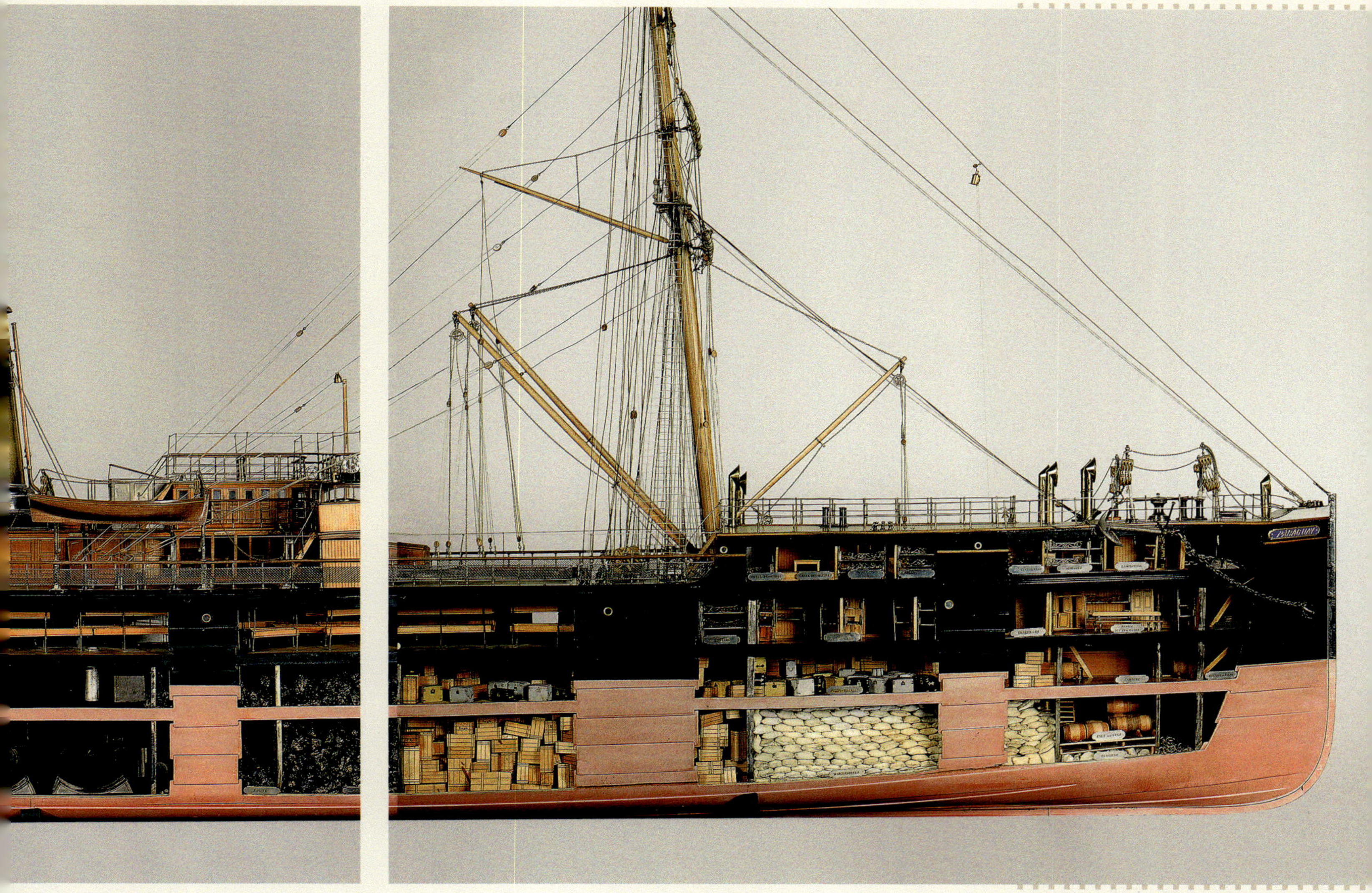

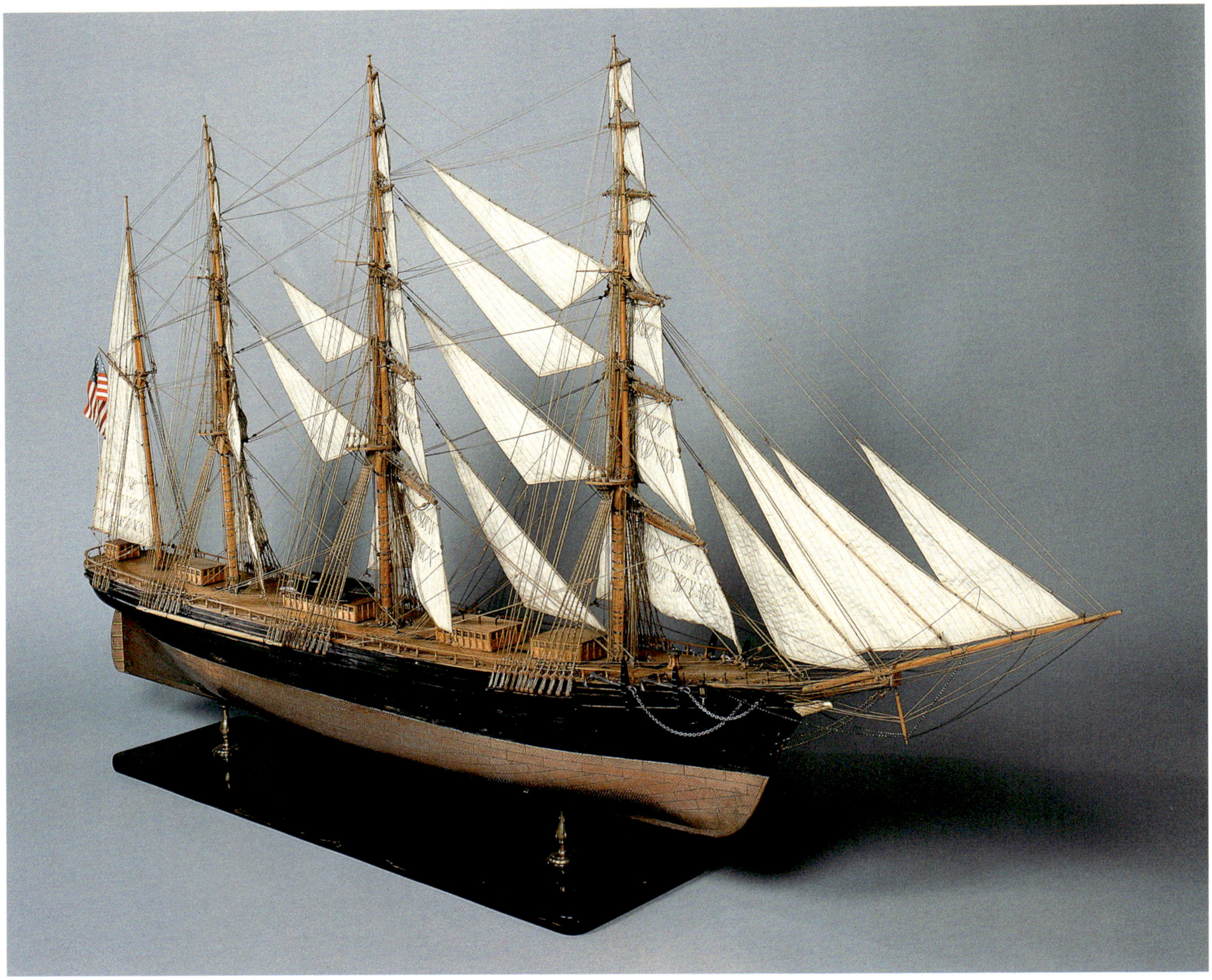

The *Great Republic*

Model of the clipper launched at Boston in 1853, 1:66,6 scale . Built by Charles Hamelin (1831–?) . 1885 . Wood, copper, cotton . 118 x 202 x 30 cm . Entered museum collections 1885 . MnM 5 MM 7

Built in Boston in 1853, the *Great Republic* was, at the time of its launch, the largest clipper in the world, and the first to have four masts. These 'greyhounds of the sea', with their streamlined hulls and oversized sails, were faster than steam-powered vessels over long distances until the late 19th century. This remarkably delicate model is one of the rare models of a foreign ship built by Charles Hamelin, the head of the Musée de la Marine workshop. **A. M.-V.**

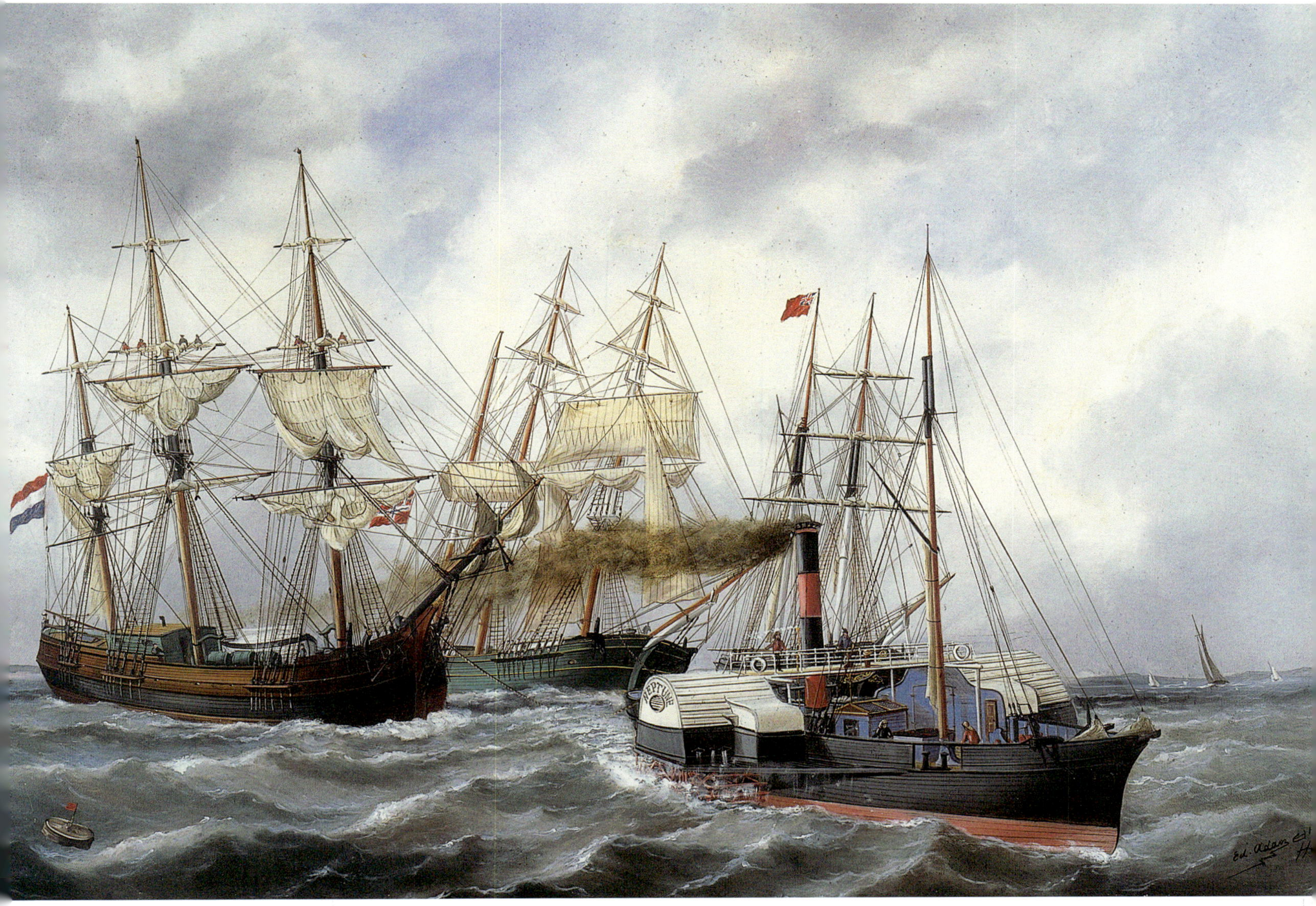

Édouard Marie Adam (1847–1929)

Ships entering Le Havre behind a tugboat

1882 . Oil on canvas . 57 x 80 cm . Signed and dated on lower right . Entered museum collections 1882 . MnM 21 OA 11

From 1882, Édouard Adam, official painter to the French navy and successor to François Roux (1811–1882), received many commissions from the Musée de la Marine. Eighteen of his paintings are kept in the museum collections, mostly in the 'ship portrait' category. These works illustrate the progression from sail-powered propulsion to steam power. A. M. V.

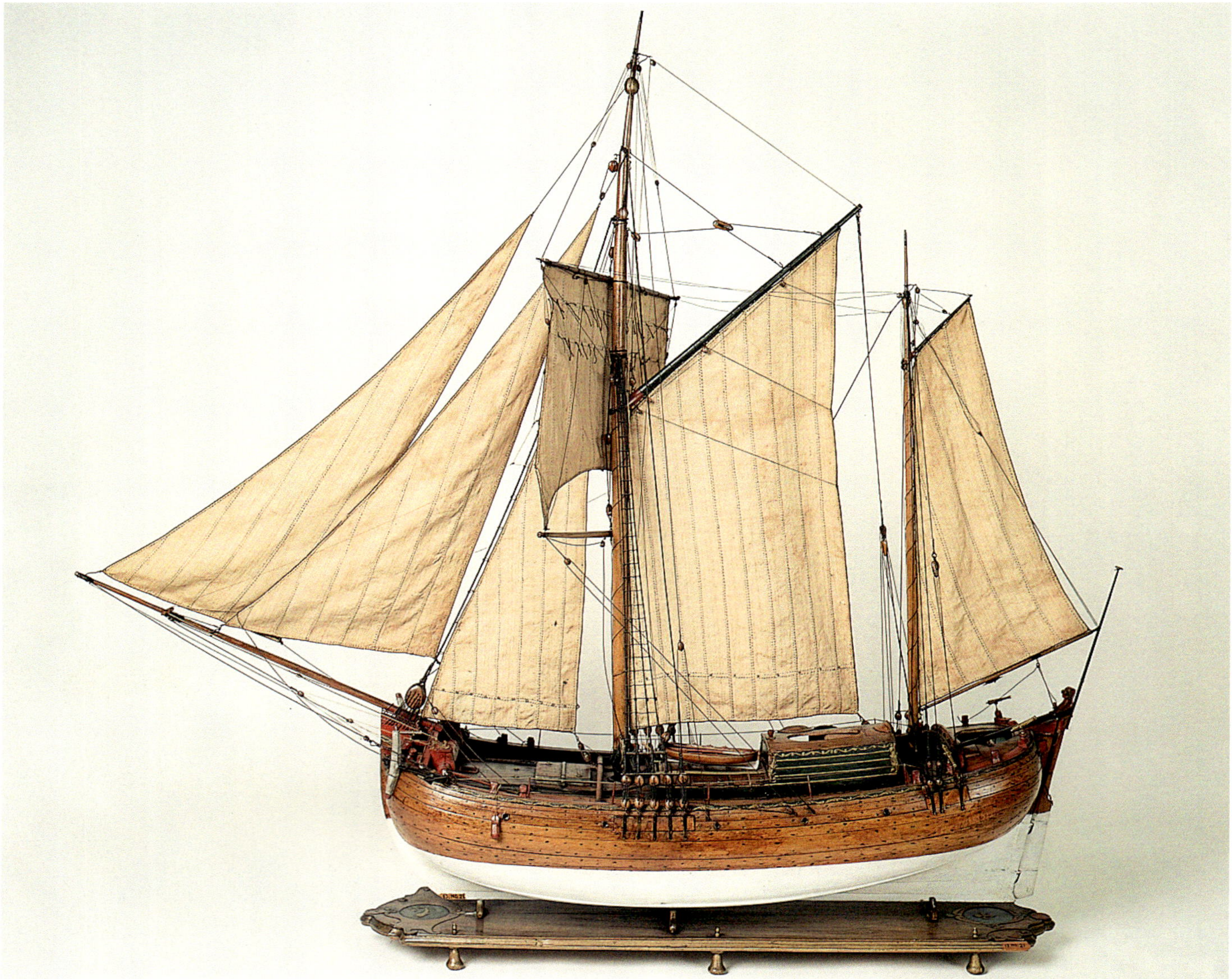

Le Vive le Roi

Model of a Flemish galliot ▪ Circa 1718 ▪ Wood, iron, brass, plant fibres ▪ 104 x 112 x 45 cm ▪ Entered museum collections 1886 ▪ MnM 13 MG 21

According to tradition, this model was offered to the boy Louis XV by the city of Dunkirk (possibly in 1718 when the burgomaster Faulconnier presented to the king the sad state of the city, ruined by the Treaty of Utrecht). This probably explains the decorative ornamentation, unusual on a cargo boat.
With its fat-bellied hull and rounded bow and stern, the ship is typical of Flemish boats. It is lightly armed with six pierriers mounted on a pivot set on the bulwark fore and aft. F. C.

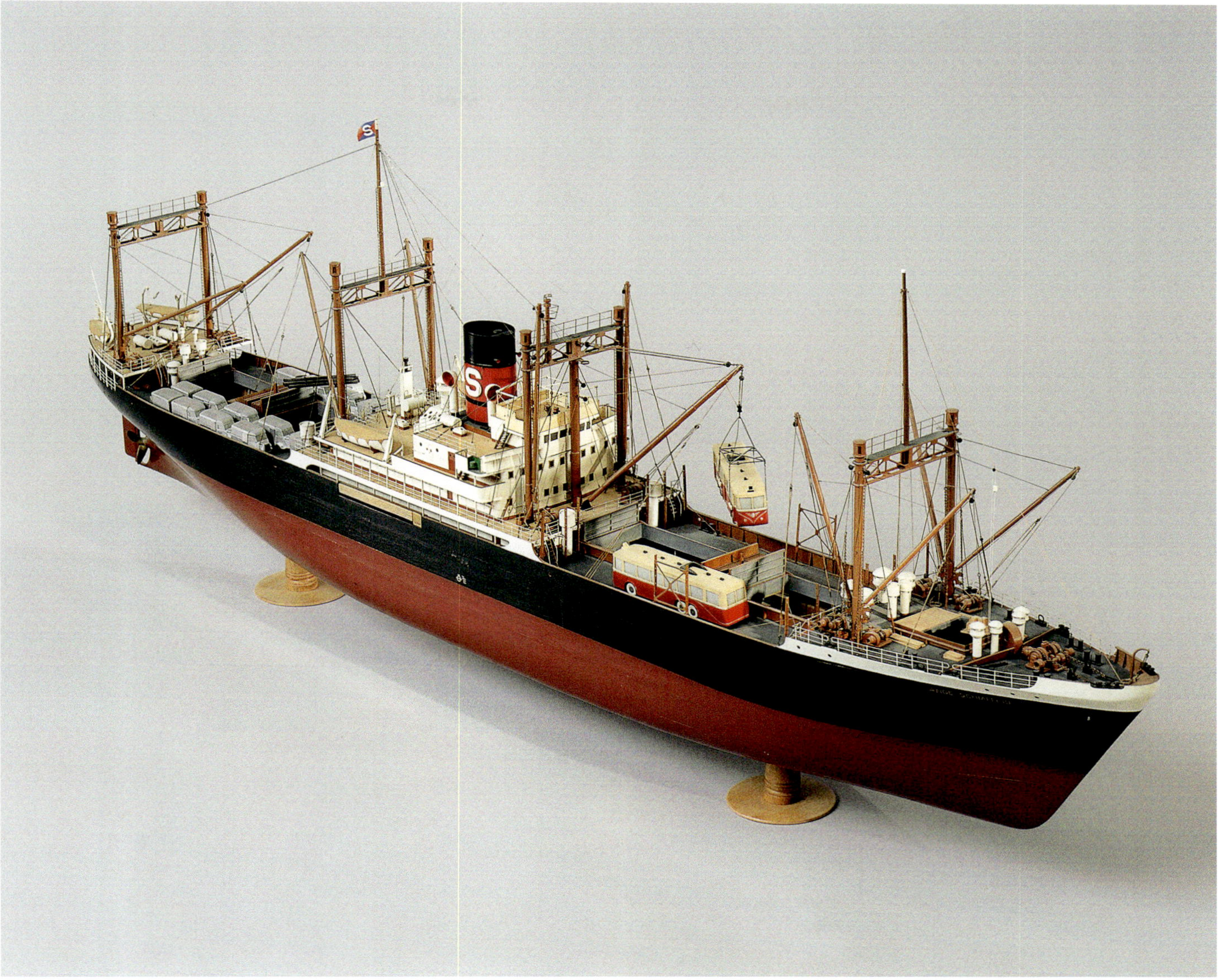

Cargo ship *Ange-Schiaffino*

Shipyard model of the cargo ship commissioned in 1951, 1:100 scale . Constructed at the Caen-Blainville dockyards . 1951 . Wood and composite materials . 41.5 x 124 x 18 cm . Entered museum collections 1991 . MnM 7 MM 61

This model is one of the five given to the Musée National de la Marine by the Société d'Armement et de Navigation Charles-Schiaffino. The heyday of this shipbuilding company, which operated mostly in trade between the French ports and Algeria, was between 1920 and 1978. Laurent Schiaffino, the son of the founder, remained at the head of the company throughout this period. For each contract drawn up with a shipyard, he negotiated the construction of a reduced-scale model of the ship. Thanks to this initiative, we today have valuable and well-documented records of this family-run company, which played a major role in the commerce of France at a particular time in its history. M. M.

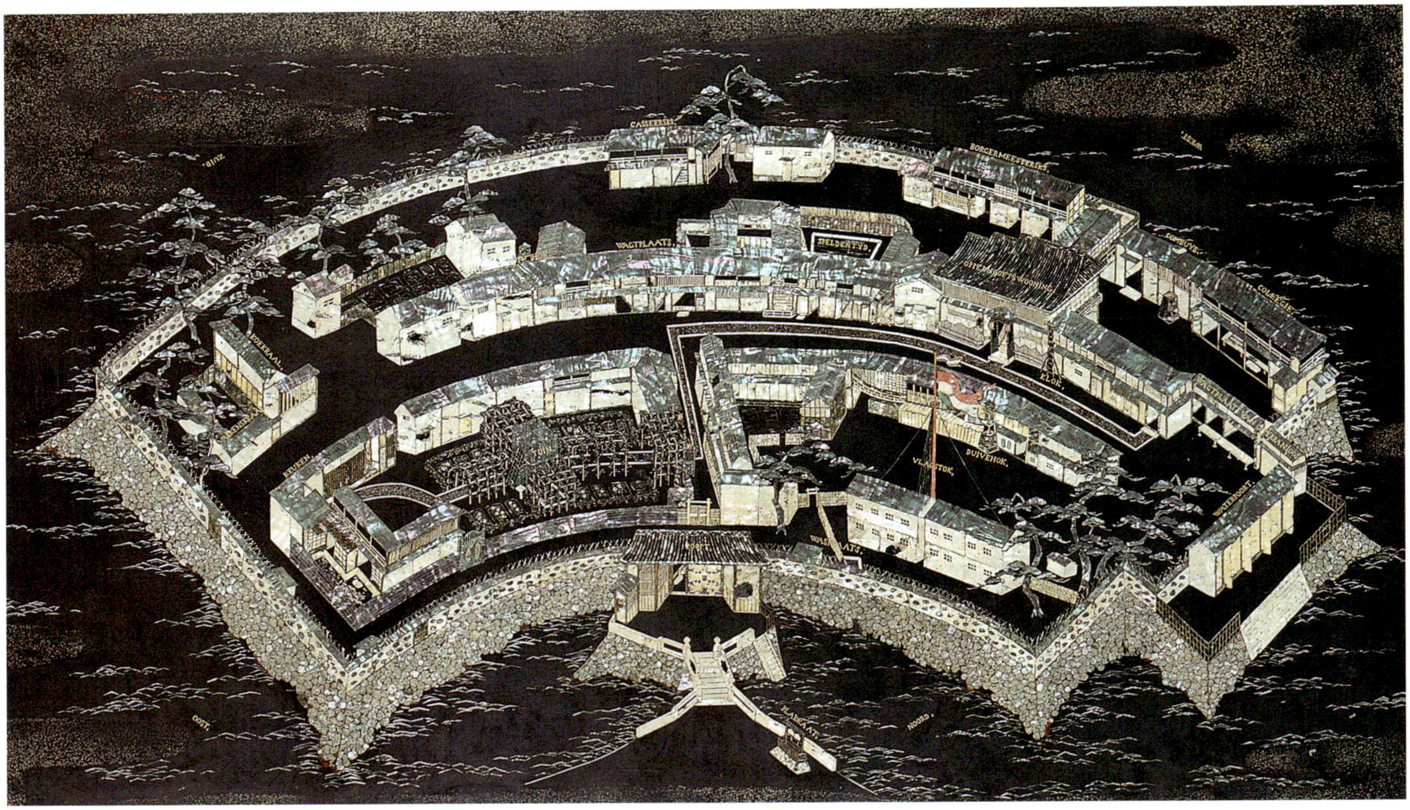

The Dutch trading post at Deshima, Nagasaki

Japan, early 19th century . Lacquered wood, mother-of-pearl inlay . 78.5 x 126.5 cm . Entered museum collections 1946 . MnM 49 OA 3

In the mid-16th century, Nagasaki was one of the first Japanese ports open to Western trade. The Jesuits had the monopoly there, but the Japanese, fearing the spread of Christianity, put an end to the commercial activities of the Portuguese in 1639. Curiously, while Japan remained closed to the outside world, the Protestant Dutch were tolerated. In 1641, their trading post was transferred to the small island of Deshima. For two centuries, all trade between Japan and the West was carried out here. This exceptional panel illustrates this period. F. C.

Dish with crab decor

China, East India Company, circa 1760 . Porcelain . H. 2.1 cm x Ø 21.2 cm . Entered museum collections 2002 . MnM 2002.4.48

This porcelain dish with a crab motif is of the 'blue and white' type, decorated with enamelwork. It was probably made especially for export to Europe in Jingdezhen, which had become the porcelain capital of China. It was discovered among the cargo of the British East India Company's ship *Griffin*. The wreck of the ship, which sank in 1761 on the reefs of the Philippine islands, was discovered and excavated in 1986 by a team of archaeologists headed by Franck Goddio. This dish is part of the large donation made by Goddio to the Musée National de la Marine after the excavation. F. C.

Dish with the Danycan coat of arms

China, East India Company, 18th century . Commissioned china . H. 3 cm x Ø 25 cm . Entered museum collections 1988 . MnM 47 OA 152

This dish decorated with the Danycan arms reflects the power of this family of wealthy merchants from Saint-Malo, several members of which were officers of the French East India Company's ships in the 18th century. F. C.

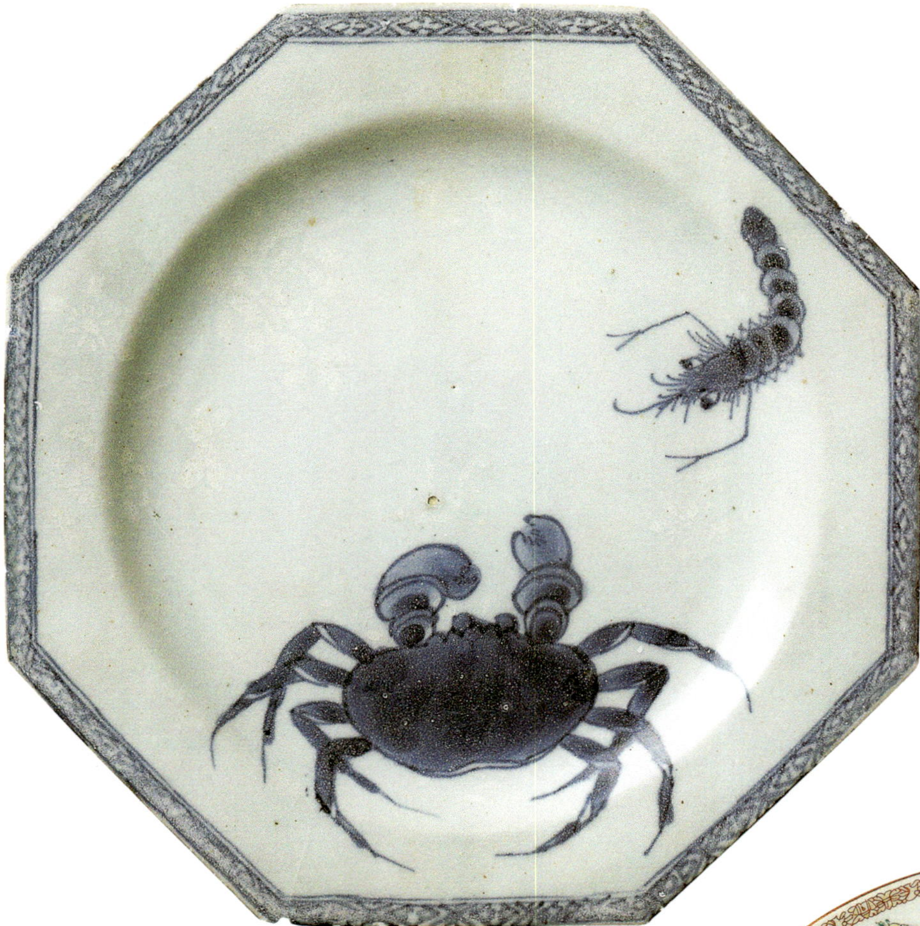
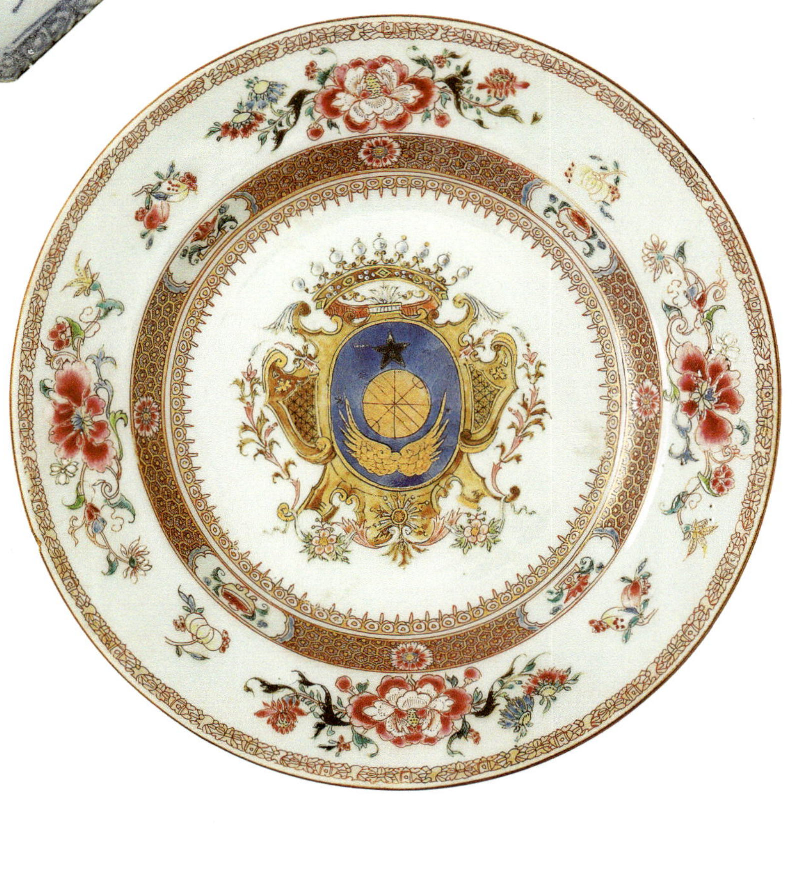

Yachting and pleasure boating

There is no lack of historical evidence of the taste for nautical pleasures and festivities in past times. At Versailles, the Grand Canal was used for reconstructions of naval battles for the entertainment of the king and his court, or simply for royal rides in boats among intimates. Marie-Antoinette had a number of barges built. Water jousting and racing were also highly popular activities.

Pleasure boating and sailing developed from the mid-19th century on along the coasts and at more sheltered freshwater sites. Numerous regattas took place over the years. The simple pleasures of boating along the Seine and Marne rivers, an activity boosted by the health-giving properties associated with the practice of sport, gave rise to a whole lifestyle celebrated by painters and writers alike.

The same period saw the rise of luxury yachting. Nautical rivalries between crowned heads have gone down in history: at the Cowes Regatta, the crew of the emperor William II competed against that of William's uncle King Edward VII. The rich had their own yachts built, boats that were ever more luxurious and technologically advanced.

In France, it was after World War II that sailing became accessible to all, notably with the opening of Les Glénans sailing school in Brittany. Simpler craft were designed and safety procedures at sea improved. The French developed a keen interest in the sea and sailing. The victories of Éric Tabarly from the 1960s onwards popularised the big single-handed and crewed sailing races. French shipyards are at the cutting edge of technological innovation.

Royal barge

Model of a royal pleasure launch . 18th century . Wood, gilt wood, cotton . 15 x 60 x 13 cm . Entered museum collections 1836, former Salle de Marine Collection . MnM 13 PL 1

This flat-bottomed pleasure boat, magnificently decorated with gilded sculptures at the bows and stern, has a movable mast and a dozen oars. This model is probably that recorded in the 1783 inventory of the Salle de Marine at the Louvre as the 'king's barge at Choisy'. A. N.

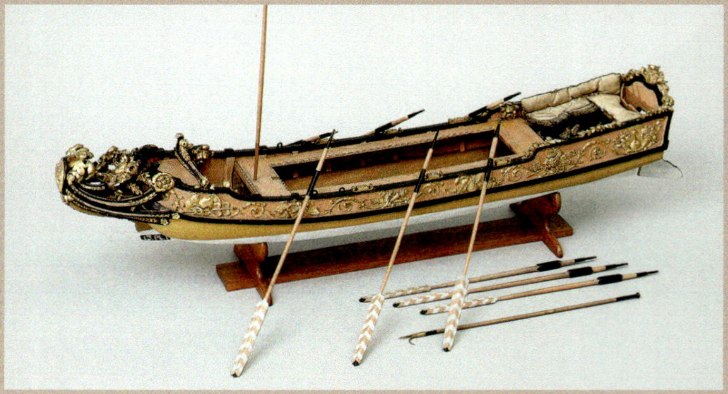

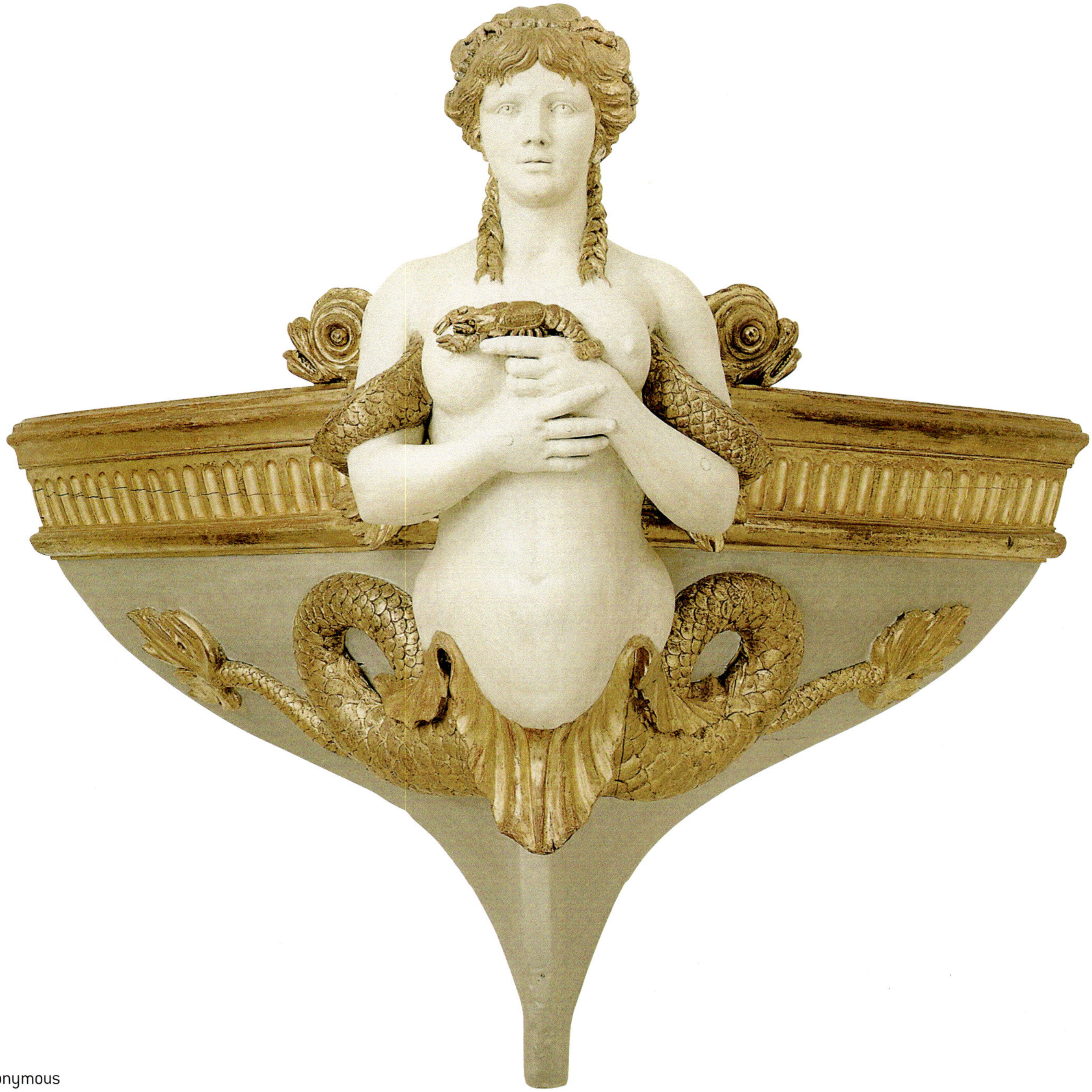

Anonymous

Prow of Queen Marie-Antoinette's pleasure barge

1777 . Painted and gilded wood . 1.80 x 1.68 x 0.86 m . Entered museum collections 1894 . MnM 39 OA 7.1

Queen Marie-Antoinette liked to go for rides down the Grand Canal at Versailles aboard this lavishly decorated open boat, of which the bow and stern are unfortunately all that remain. A remnant of those exclusive and frivolous pleasures in which the royal court was well versed, the queen's boat was part of a miniature flotilla that dated back to 1669. The place where this flotilla of boats was maintained soon earned the nickname 'Little Venice', in honour of the gondolas, with gondoliers, that were given to Louis XIV by the Serenissima. **M. M.**

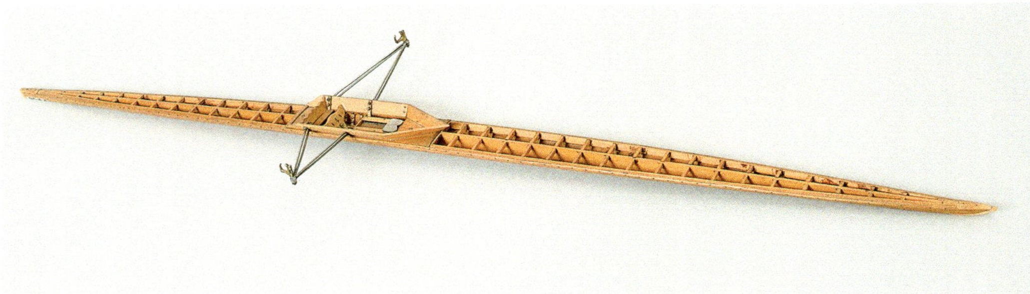

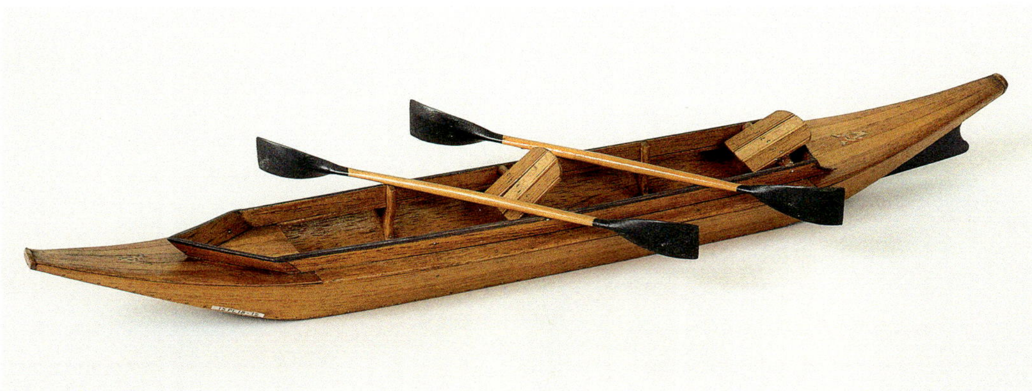

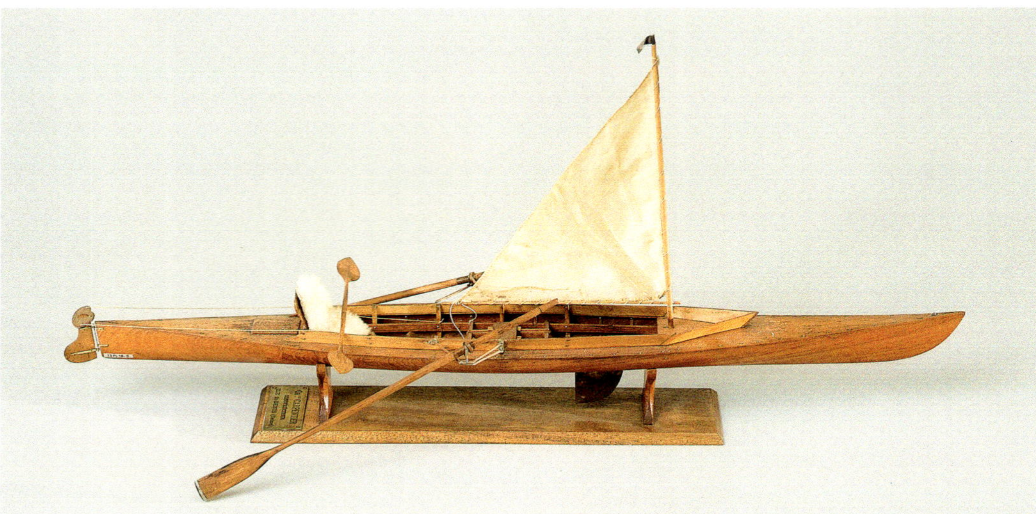

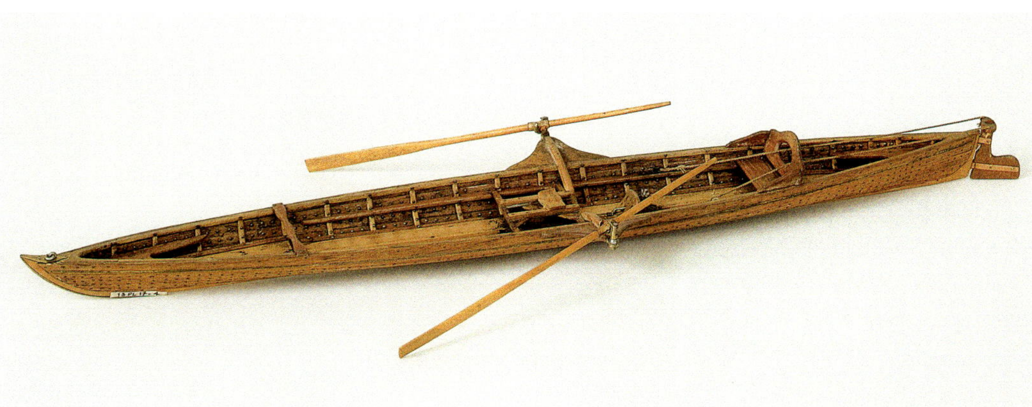

Racing skiff

Model, circa 1905 ▪ Mahogany, steel, brass ▪ 3.15 x 76.5 x 15.5 cm ▪ Entered museum collections 1932 ▪ MnM 13 PL 18.14

Marne River pleasure boat

Model, circa 1905 ▪ Mahogany, pitch pine, beech ▪ 5.4 x 53.8 x 8 cm ▪ Entered museum collections 1932 ▪ MnM 13 PL 18.12

Sailing canoe

Model, circa 1904 ▪ Mahogany, pitch pine, cotton ▪ 4.5 x 35 x 8 cm ▪ Entered museum collections 1932 ▪ MnM 13 PL 18.5

Pleasure skiff

Model, circa 1905 ▪ Mahogany ▪ 4 x 41.5 x 6 cm ▪ Entered museum collections 1932 ▪ MnM 13 PL 17.4

These pleasure skiffs used for river boating are part of a group of around thirty miniature boats, on a presumed scale of 1:10, constructed for the Canoë-Club de France in the very early years of the 20th century. The complete flotilla, presented in 1907 at the Exposition Maritime de Bordeaux, was described at the time as 'a résumé of the best types of pleasure boats today'. **M. M.**

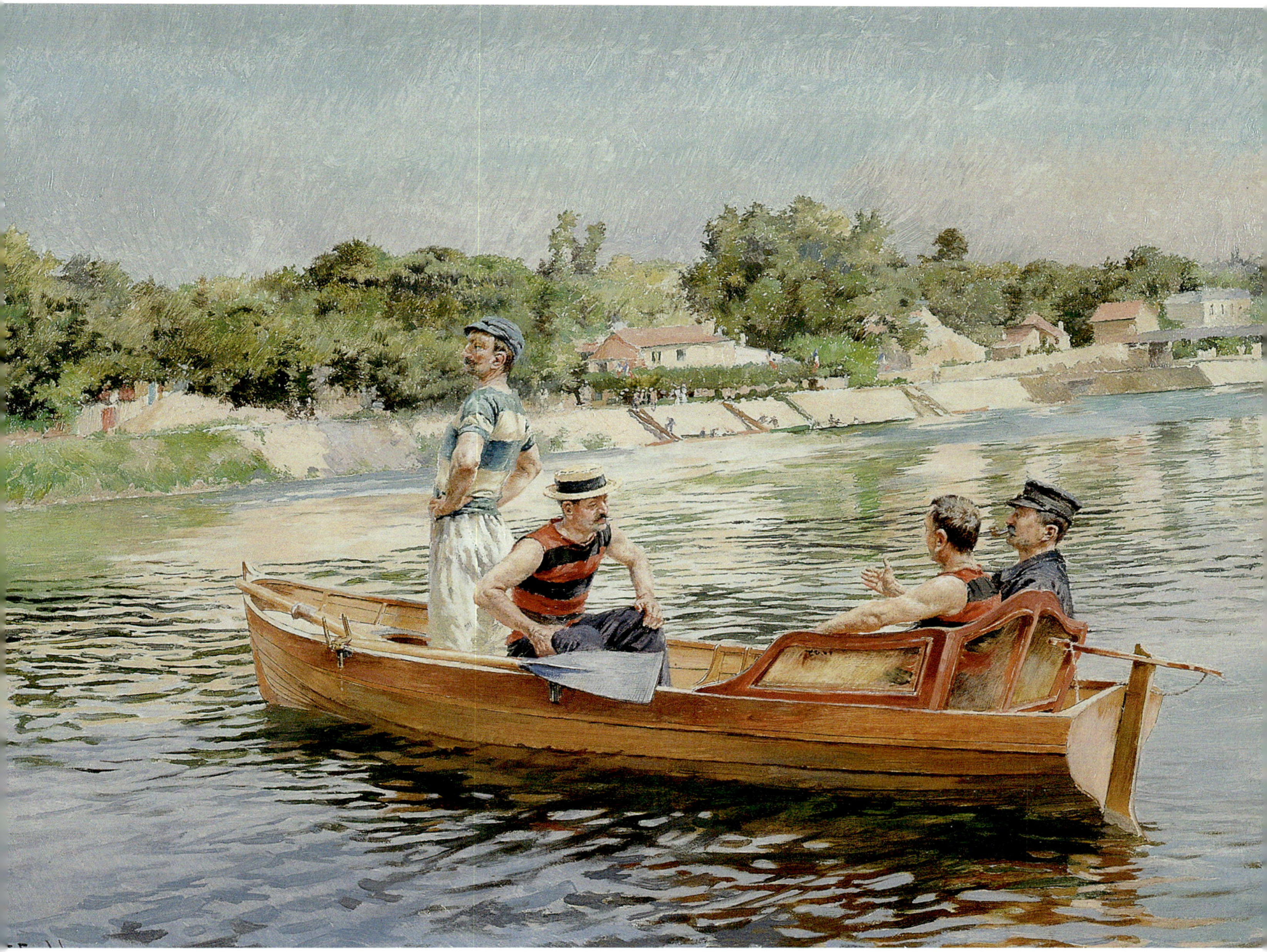

Ferdinand Gueldry (1858–1945)

A Ride in a Skiff

Circa 1906 . Oil on canvas . 46 x 61 cm . Signed on lower left . Entered museum collections 2001 . MnM 2001.17.1

The painter Ferdinand Gueldry was a keen oarsman. A member of the Société Nautique de la Marne at Joinville-le-Pont, he won many skiff races with his brother. In his studio at Bry-sur-Marne, the artist painted in great detail the boating scenes he knew so well. The changing light on the banks of the Marne lent a particular transparency to the water that Gueldry treated with masterly technique, close to impressionism. M. M.

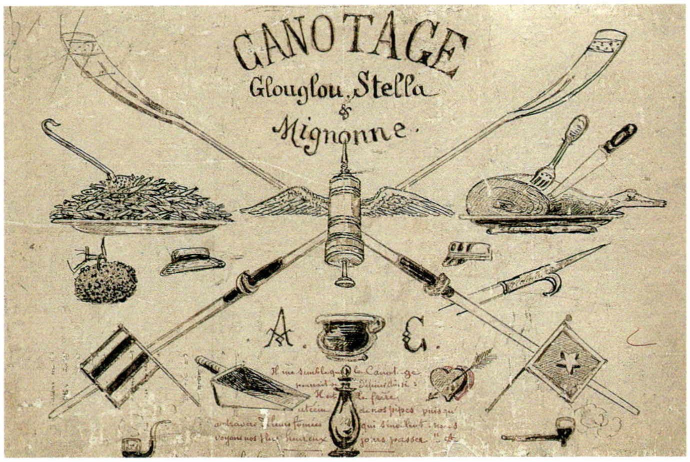

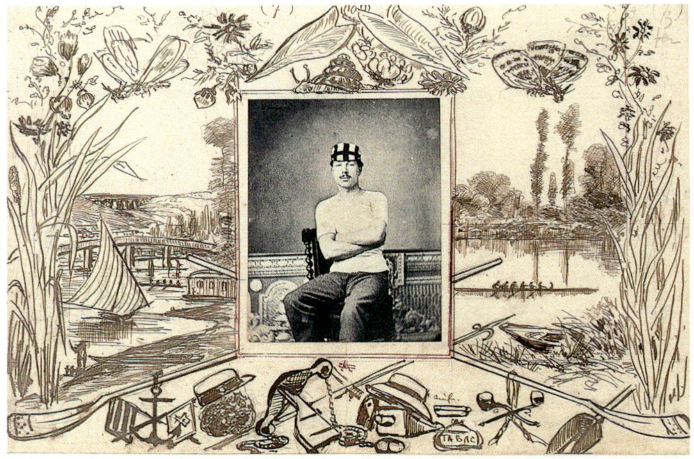

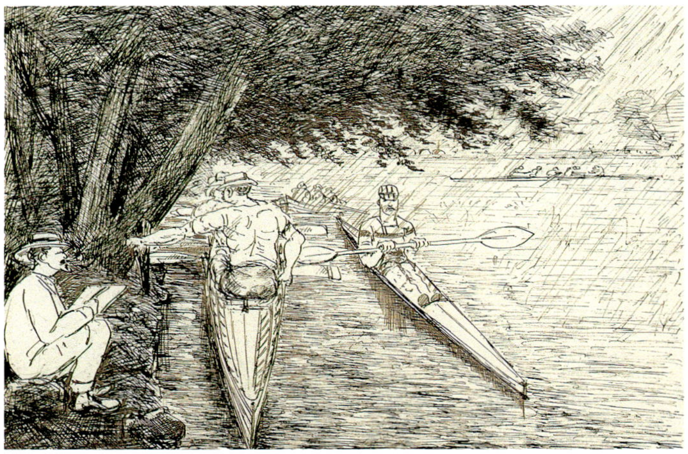

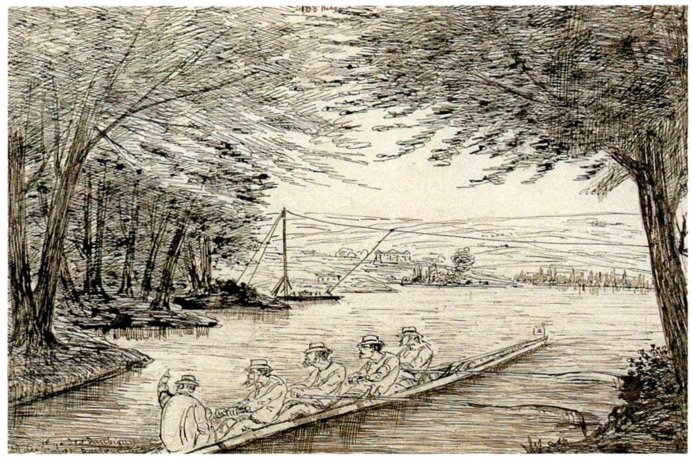

Alain Chartier (fl. mid-19th century)

Canotage. Glouglou, Stella & Mignonne

Seven plates . 1845–1875 . Album of 285 pen-and-ink drawings on paper . 35 x 50 cm . Entered museum collections 1973 . MnM B2829

In these scenes of three boats and their crews on the Seine, Alain Chartier shows us the world of boating before it became a regulated activity. Donated to the museum by Georges Thierry, president of the Yacht-Club de France, this album illustrates, in the manner of a strip cartoon, the pleasurable world of the ancestor of water sports, and the first modern leisure activity. M. -P. D.

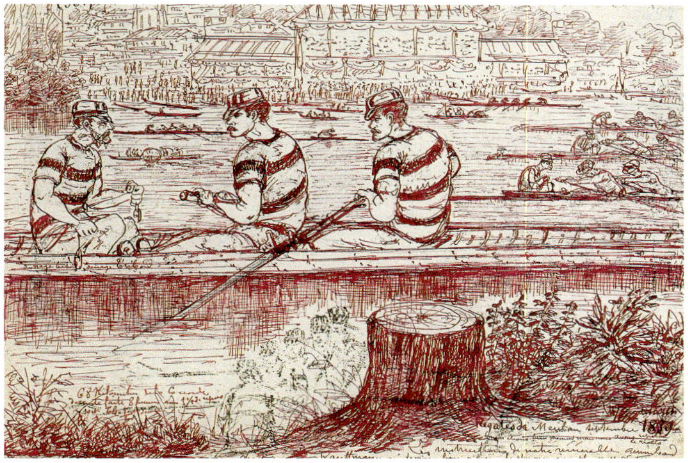

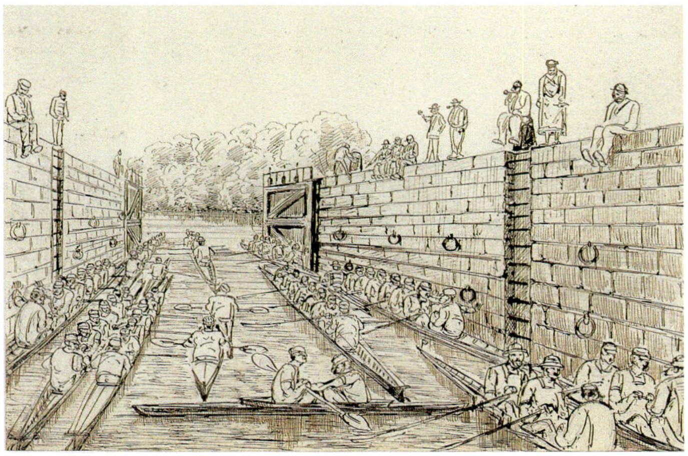

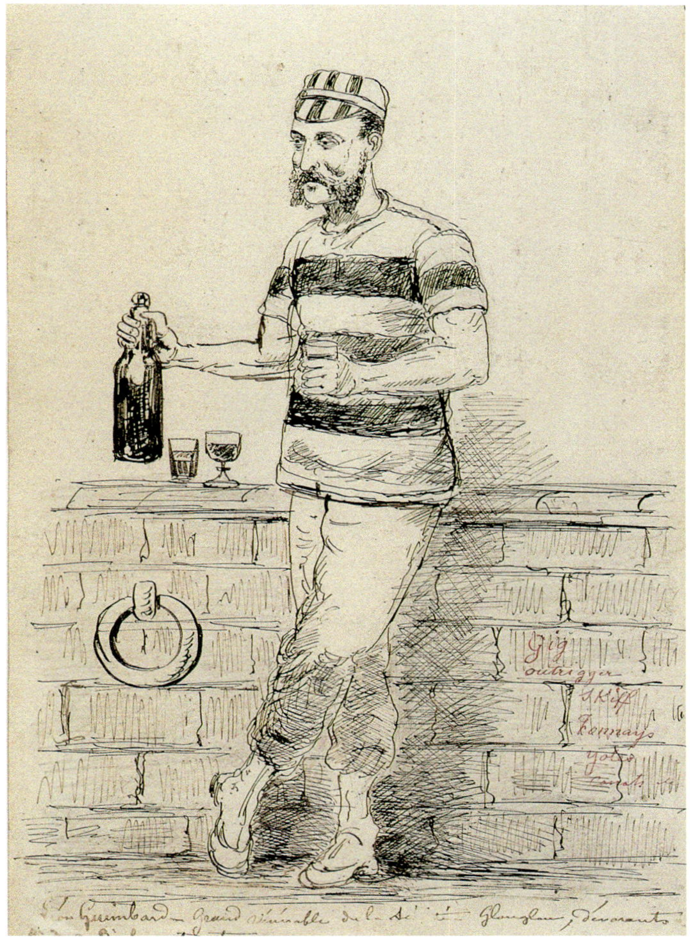

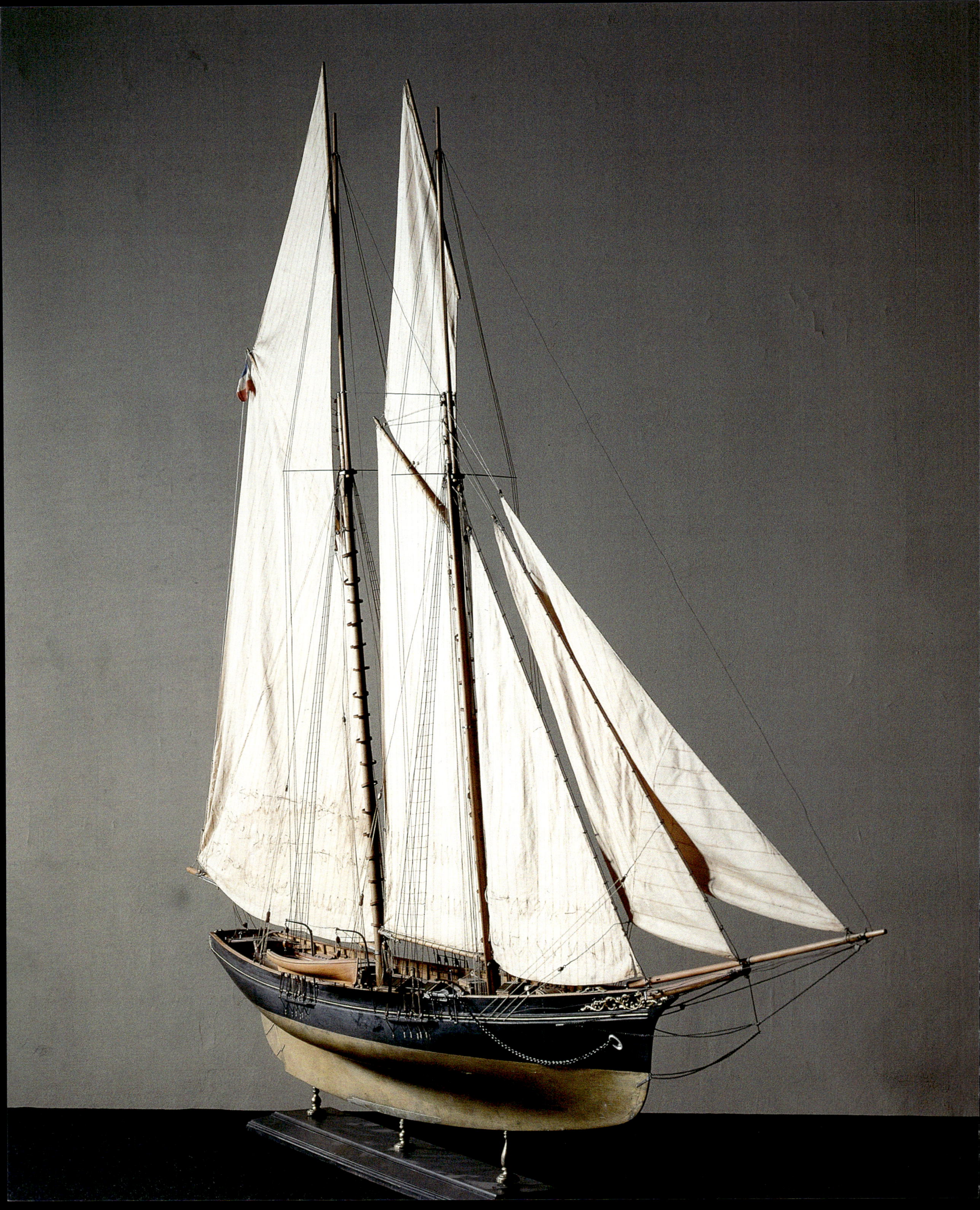

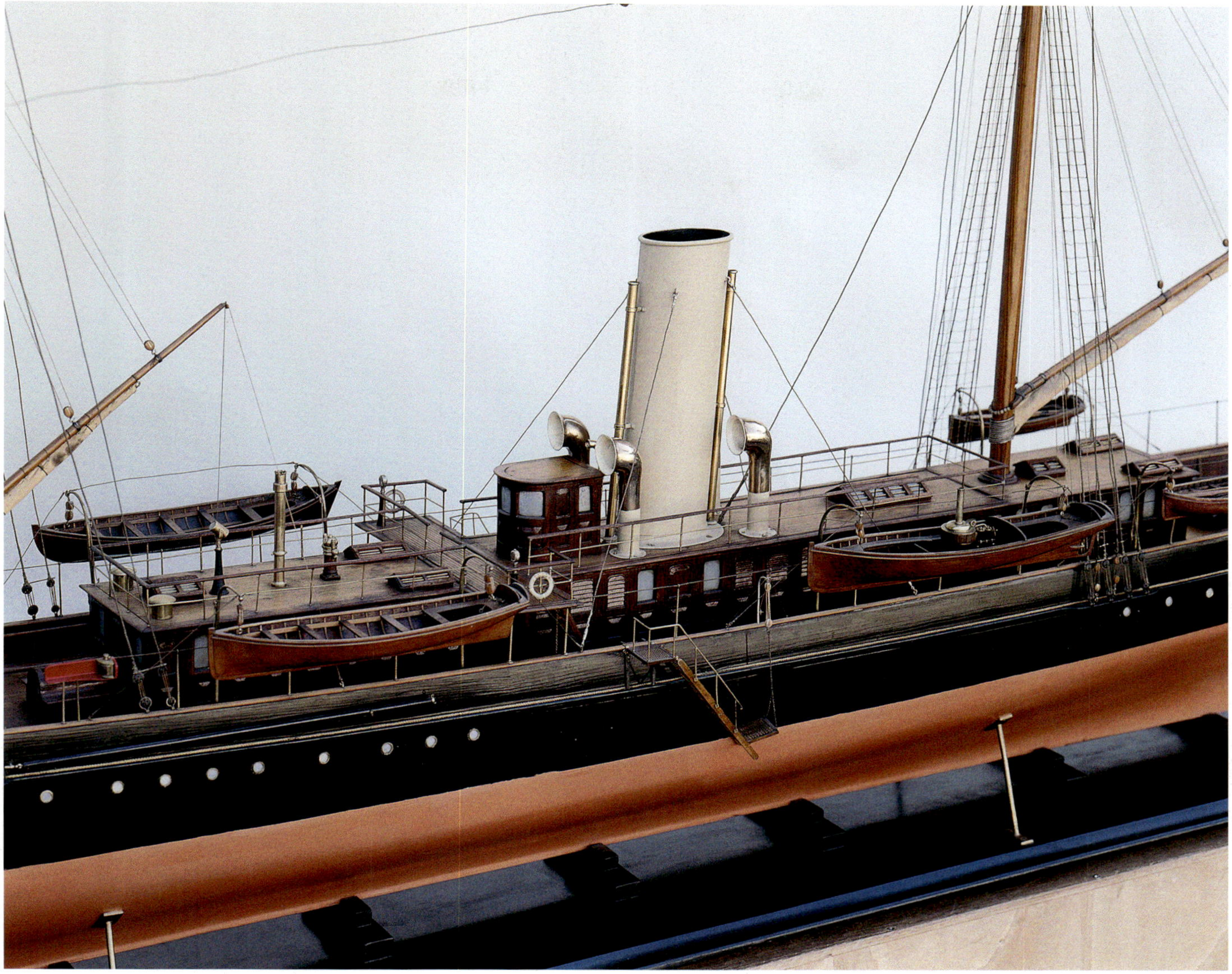

Velox

Model of the pleasure schooner Velox, 1:25 scale ▪ Constructed by Édouard Hamelin (?–1906), Paris and the Augustin-Normand shipyard, Le Havre ▪ After drawings by Jacques Augustin Normand (1839–1906) ▪ 1903–1907 ▪ Wood, canvas, plant fibres ▪ 189 x 240 x 52 cm ▪ Entered museum collections 1906 ▪ MnM 7 PL 4

The model of the *Velox* was completed in 1907 at the Augustin-Normand shipyard in Le Havre just after the deaths of the model maker Édouard Hamelin, head of the model workshop at the Musée de la Marine, and the ship's designer, Jacques Augustin Normand. The latter had, in 1875, drawn up highly original drawings for this now legendary boat. At the time, the *Velox* was the largest pleasure schooner ever built in France. Designed for racing, it was capable of reaching speeds of over fourteen knots thanks to its 1,481 square meters of rigging. Paradoxically, this yacht never sailed in a race and was used only as a cruising yacht by its three successive owners until its unfortunate demolition in 1913. M. M.

Éros II

Model of the yacht Éros II, formerly the property of Baron Arthur de Rothschild, 1:24 scale ▪ Anonymous ▪ Circa 1885 ▪ Wood, maple, mahogany, iron, steel, bronze, brass, cotton ▪ 172 x 340 x 82 cm ▪ Entered museum collections 1889 ▪ MnM 9 PL 3

The object of a very costly commission in England in 1885, the sail- and propeller-powered *Éros II* was in its time the archetypal luxury cutting-edge long-range yacht. Built of steel, it featured sumptuous cabin quarters and electric lighting, and required a 44-strong crew. Its owner, Baron Arthur de Rothschild, donated this model to the Musée de la Marine following its presentation at the 1889 World's Fair. A. N.

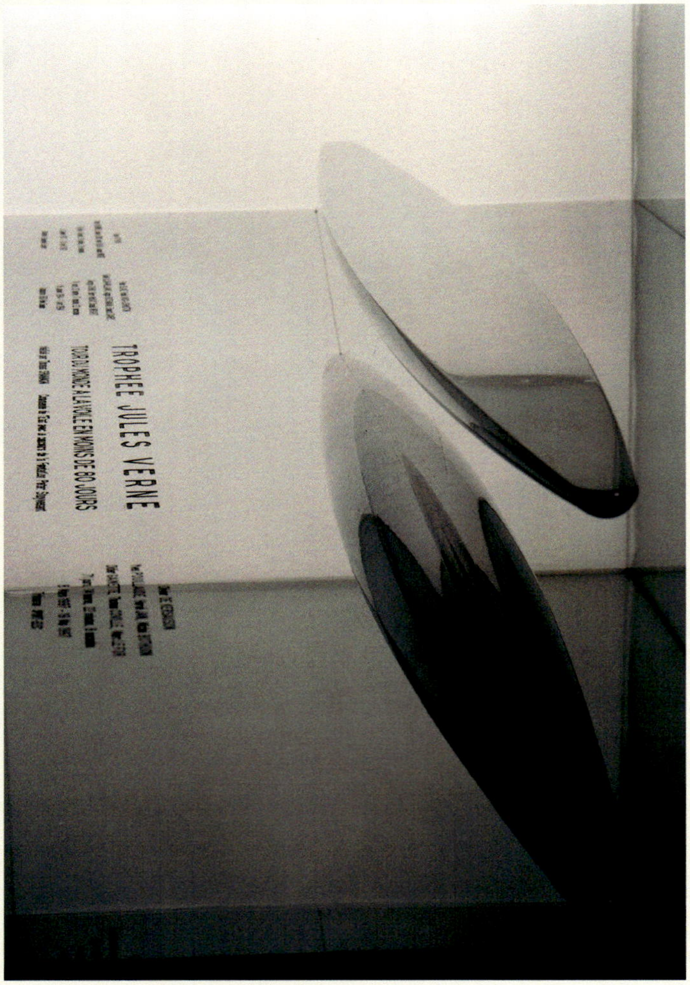

Thomas Shannon (born 1947)

Jules Verne trophy

1993 . Cast polished aluminium, glass . 180 x 260 x 80 cm . On loan from the Fonds National d'Art Contemporain (inv. 93627.1 to 6), 1994 . MnM D2240

The American artist Thomas Shannon was commissioned to design the Jules Verne trophy. Placed in a magnetic field, the hull-shaped sculpture hovers in space. Its forms are defined by a series of curves proportional to the circumferences of the sun, the earth and the moon, celestial bodies that influence the tides and navigation at sea.

The unique Jules Verne trophy is awarded to the challenger who succeeds in beating the round-the-world crewed record. **M. M.**

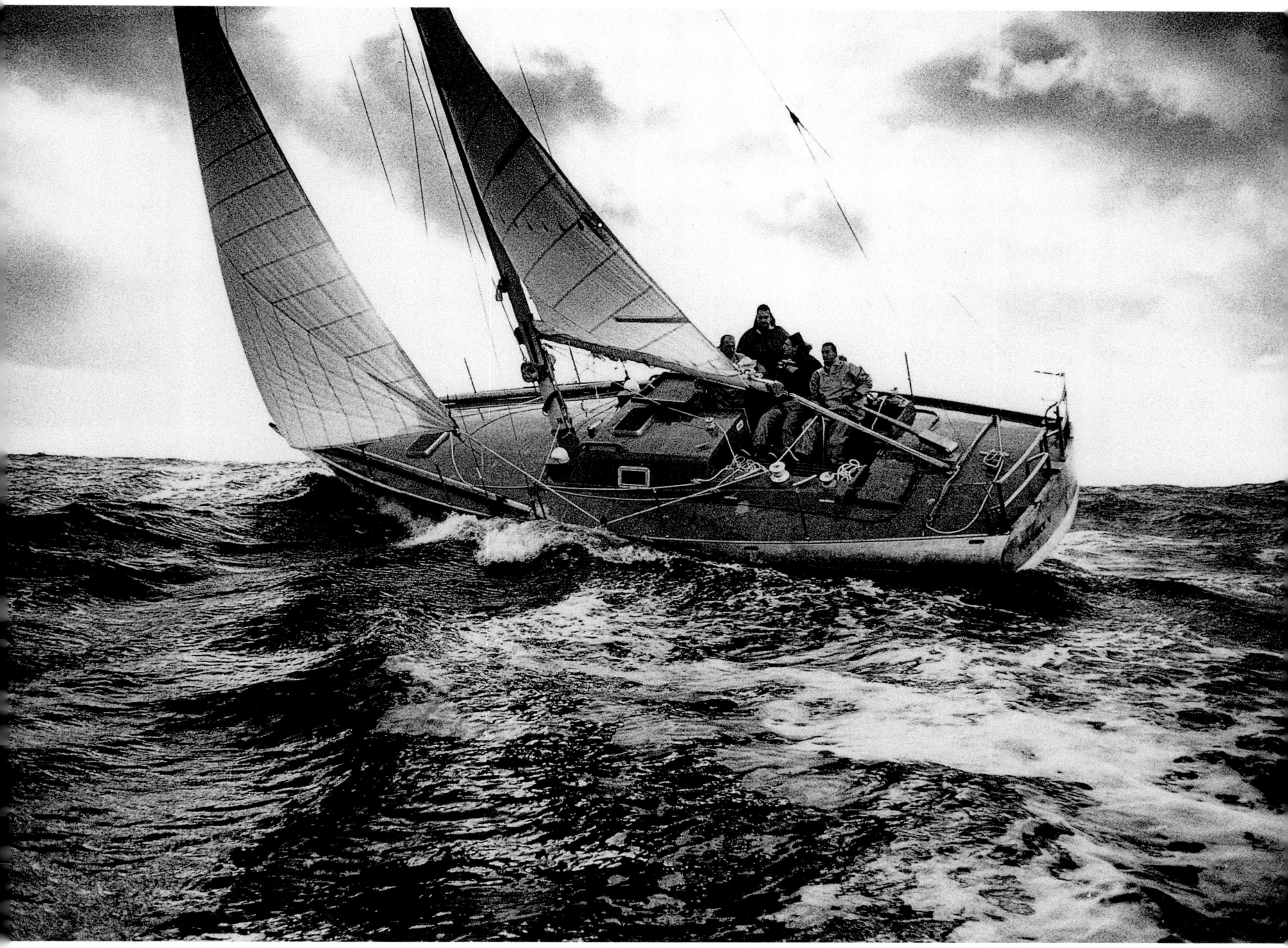

Pen-Duick V

Monohull built by the Chantiers et Ateliers de La Perrière, Lorient, after drawings by Michel Bigoin and Daniel Duvergié ▪ 1969 ▪ Aluminium (hull) ▪ L. 10.67 x W. 3.50 m, draught 2.30 m, sail surface 63 m² ▪ Entered museum collections 1992 ▪ MnM 1 PM 21

Designed in collaboration with Éric Tabarly (1931–1998), *Pen-Duick V* was built in record time for the first Transpacific Race (Mars–April 1969), a single-handed race between San Francisco and Tokyo, which Tabarly won easily. Tabarly came up with an ingenious system of water ballasts integrated into the hull that increased the boat's stability and compensated for list without adding weight.

Saved by the Musée de la Marine which purchased it in 1992, *Pen Duick V* was restored respecting its original design with the support of the Fondation Jean-Pierre et Marie-Thérèse Le Roch – Les Mousquetaires. The yacht is now based at the École Nationale de Voile (the French national sailing school) and continues to sail.
This photograph was taken by Erwan Quéméré in 1968 during trials off the coast of Lorient. H. T.

The seafarers

Fishermen, engineers, captains, sailors, adventurers, galley slaves... What do we know about the daily life of mariners of the past, a life, more often than not, of effort, suffering and extraordinary danger?

Until the 19th century, a sailor's entire fortune often amounted to a chest or a bag in which he kept a few personal items, eating utensils and some clothes. These fragile and not especially characteristic material traces of sailors' everyday lives are today very rare. Under Louis XIV, the authorities sought to standardise naval officers' uniforms, without concerning themselves with those of plain sailors, albeit the most numerous category of personnel aboard. Not until the 1870s did painters began to take an interest in the living conditions of sailors. An officer's coat, an admiral's baton, a sailor hat are so many precious records of the lives of these mariners.

What seafarers feared most, however, is better documented, for the dread of sinking and shipwreck is always with the sailor. This was a dramatic subject that inspired numerous painters: Joseph Vernet in the 18th century and, in the following century, the Romantics Eugène Isabey and Théodore Gudin. In the face of peril at sea, man has always found recourse, whether spiritual or pragmatic. The ex-voto offering was the expression of a sailor's religious devotion, with which he could give thanks for or request divine intervention; but the building of a network of lighthouses and setting up of rescue service stations constituted, in the 19th century, a more rational response to the dangers at sea. From ex-votos to lifeboats, all these objects, charged with a unique, emotional quality, are testimony to the courage of seafarers.

Sailor's chest

17th century . Cembro pine, polychrome decor . 50 x 114 x 46 cm . Entered museum collections 1995 . MnM 49 OA 230

This chest comes from a family of sailors from the Rochefort region. The hand-crafted metal elements and the carved decor would appear to date it from the 17th century. The pictorial decoration, executed in different periods and probably in different places (Portugal and Marseilles), is mostly religious in inspiration, making this sailor's chest, a symbolic item of life at sea, a rare and original piece. M. M.

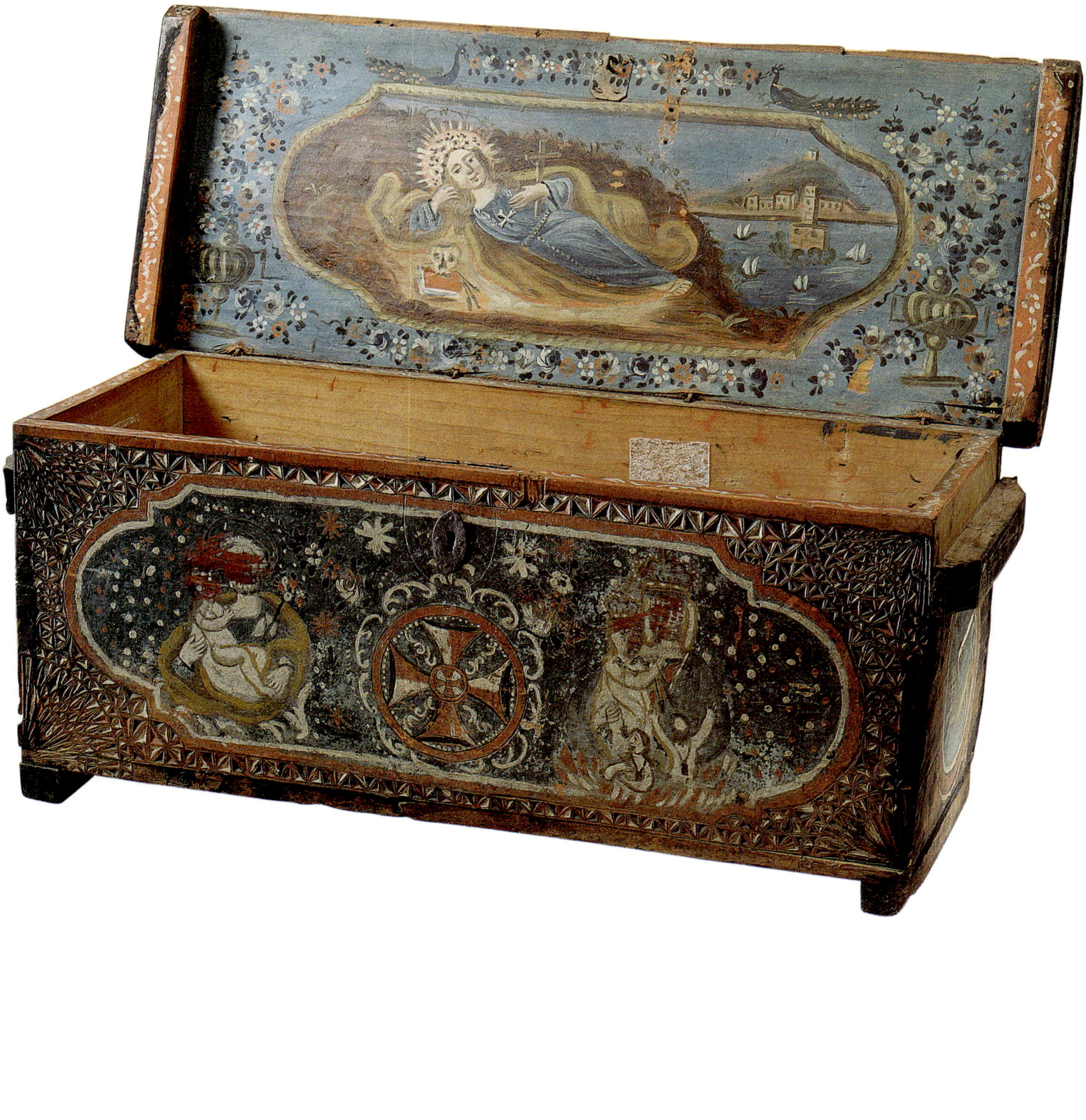

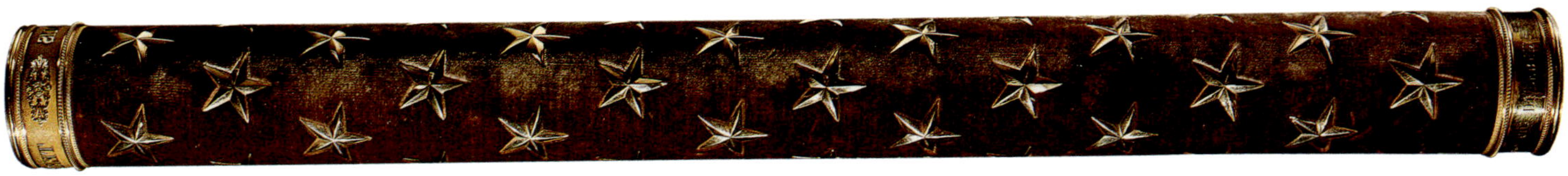

Baton of Amiral Duperré

1830 . Wood, velvet, gold . L. 49 cm x Ø 5 cm . Entered museum collections 1983 . MnM 7 SO 244

Baron Victor Guy Duperré (1775–1846) was the first person to hold the dignity of Amiral de France created on 13 August 1830 by order of King Louis-Philippe and comparable in every respect to the rank of Maréchal de France. Duperré earned this reward as commander-in-chief of the remarkably well-organised victorious expedition to Algiers. The baton is identical to that of the Maréchaux de France. A precious insignia of office, it is the earliest example of a very short-lived tradition in the French navy. F. C.

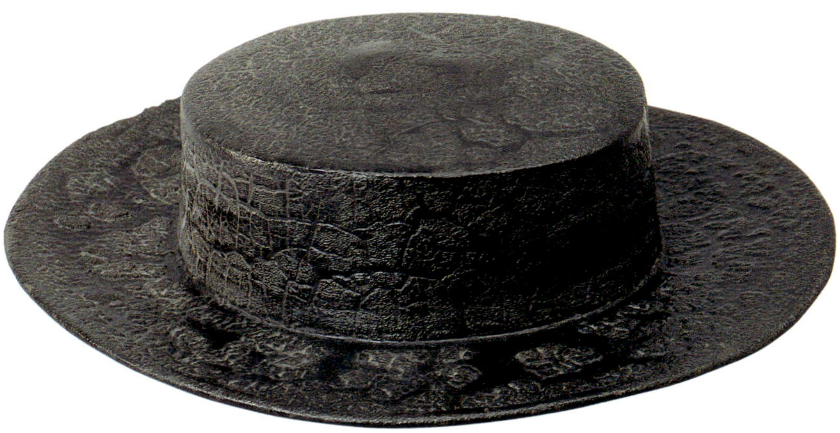

Sailor hat

Circa 1836–1858 . Straw, plant fibres, wax . H. 7.5 cm x Ø 33.5 cm . Entered museum collections 1994 . MnM 49 AR 95

This is one of the first and extremely rare regulation sailor hats made according to the French law of 11 October 1836: "Straw hat covered with blackened and waxed canvas, trimmed with a ribbon stamped with the name of the ship and the number of each man's company'. The ribbon has been lost, but it still has tying straps plaited into a cord. The shape of this hat was later abandoned in the 1858 regulations, and replaced by one with a narrow, turned-up brim. F. C.

Full dress uniform of Major Général d'Escadre Liberge de Granchain de Sémerville (detail)

Circa 1788 . Wool, silk, cotton, linen, copper, silver . 114 x 54 cm . On loan from the Vicomte Amaury de La Barre de Nanteuil, 1990 . MnM D 2201

These items of uniform belonged to the rear admiral Guillaume Liberge de Granchain de Sémerville (1744–1805). His research into astronomy, navigation and hydrography, and his fundamental role in the American war campaigns, make him one of the most brilliant naval officers of the second half of the 18th century. He was a prominent member of the Académie de Marine. F. C.

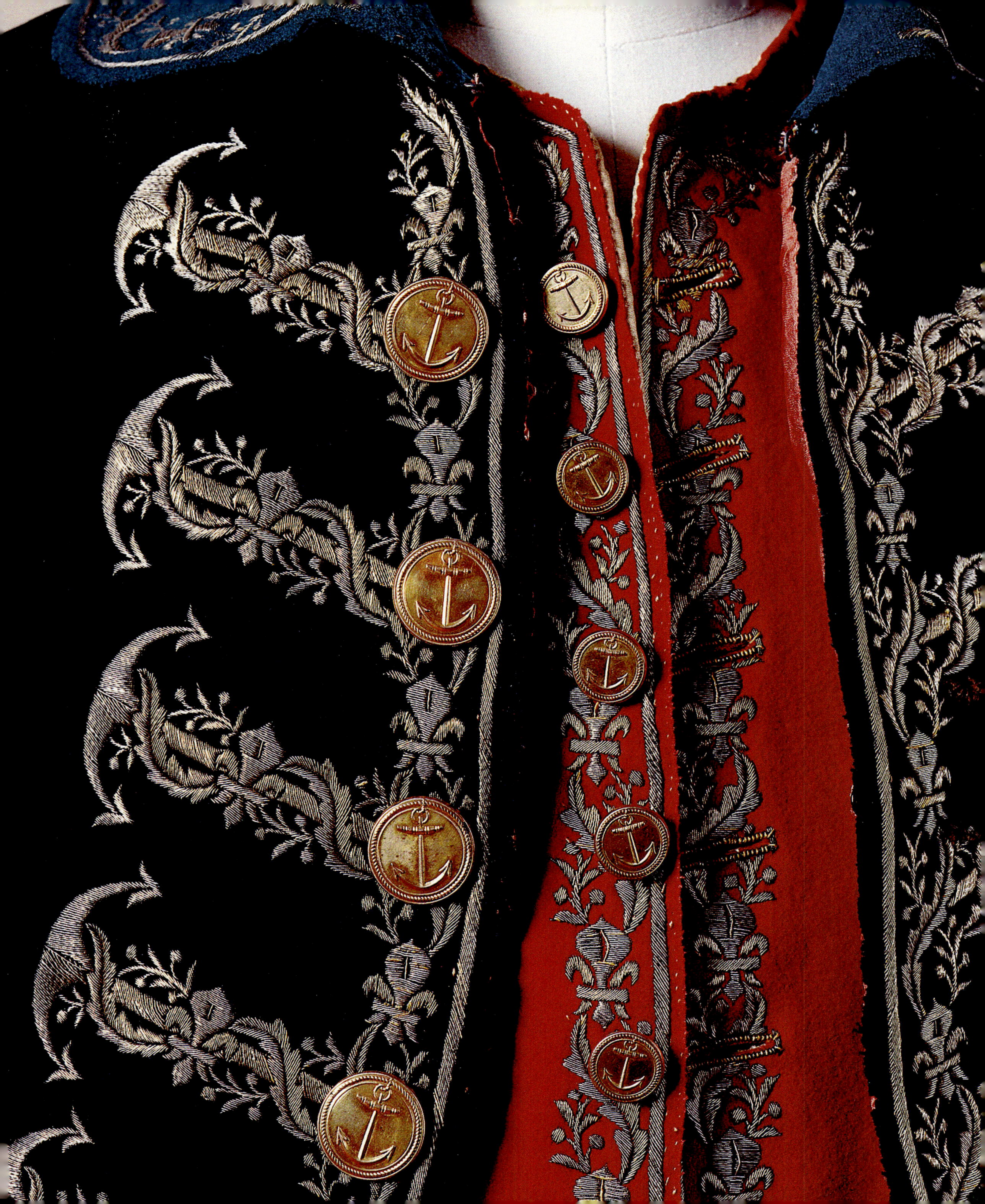

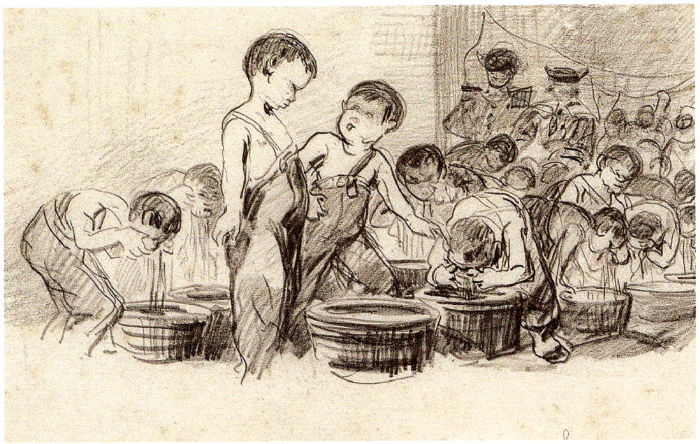

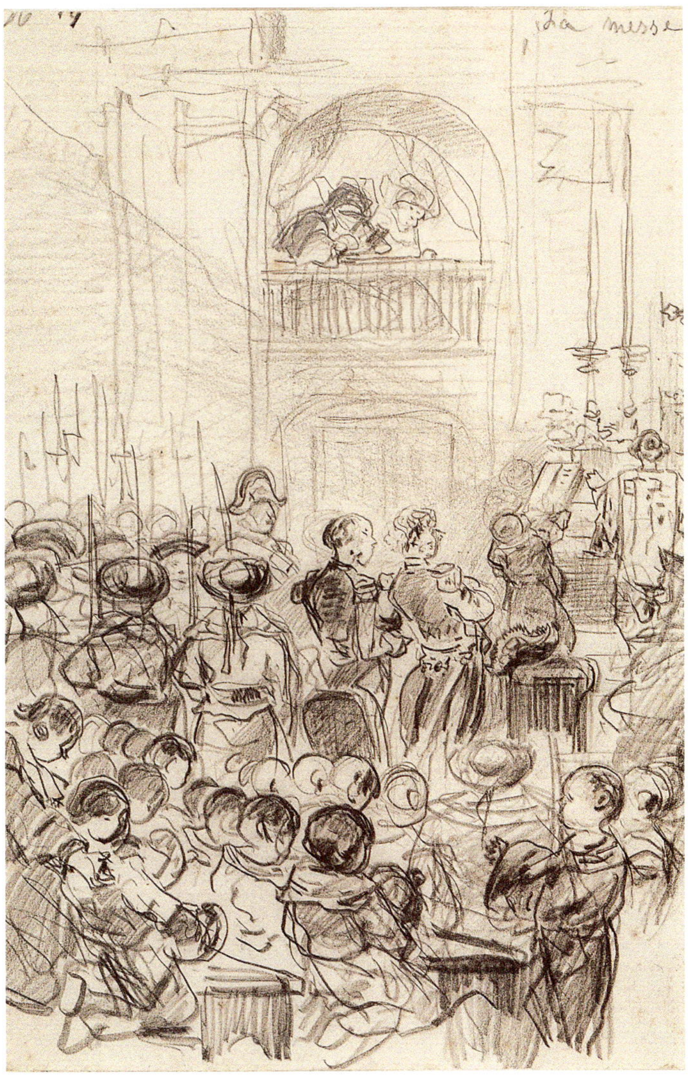

Jules Noël (1810–1881)

Navy Orphans. Wash time.

Circa 1866 ▪ Graphite with black chalk heightening on paper ▪ 14.5 x 23.5 cm ▪ Entered museum collections 2004 ▪ MnM 2004.40.8

Jules Noël

Navy Orphans. Mass.

Circa 1866 ▪ Graphite with black chalk heightening on paper ▪ 23.5 x 15.5 cm ▪ Entered museum collections 2004 ▪ MnM 2004.40.2

Jules Noël

Navy Orphans. First Steps.

Circa 1866 ▪ Graphite with black chalk heightening on paper ▪ 14.5 x 20 cm ▪ Entered museum collections 2004 ▪ MnM 2004.40.10

An esteemed marine painter, Jules Noël was also an excellent draughtsman and a gifted illustrator who contributed regularly to popular magazines. On 25 August 1866, he published an article in *L'Illustration* on the 'pupilles de la Marine', navy orphans, with hand-drawn illustrations. The thirteen original drawings from this series were recently discovered and purchased by the Musée National de la Marine. They are rare, moving images, sketched from life with a firm stroke, depicting various moments in the everyday life of these small children aged 7 to 13 whom Jules Noël described as the 'spoilt navy kids'. Their school, founded in Brest by imperial decree on 15 November 1862, was at the time run by the Frères des Écoles Chrétiennes (Brothers of the Christian Schools). **M. M.**

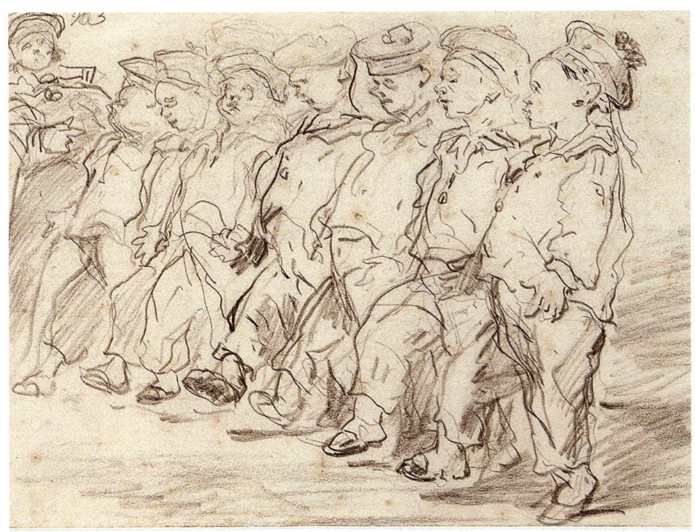

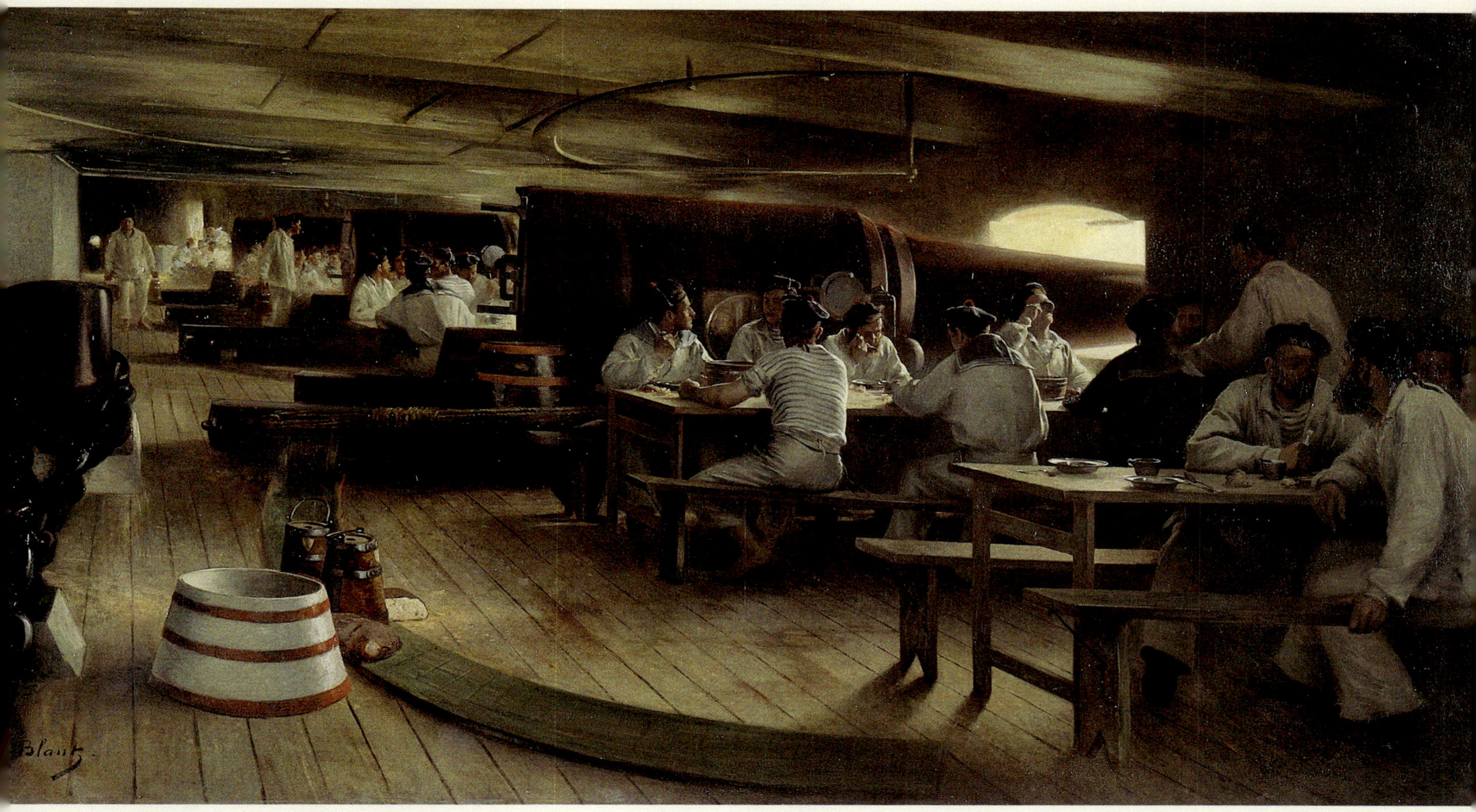

Julien Le Blant (1851–1930)

Crew Eating a Meal

1884 . Oil on canvas . 121 x 224 cm . Signed on lower left . On loan from the Fonds National d'Art Contemporain, 1944 . MnM 11 OA 1 D

From a very young age, Julien Le Blant was interested in both peasant life and military subjects. In this painting the artist seems to have combined his two favourite themes, since he depicts an intimate moment in the life of the crew on board a battleship: the sharing of a meal. Very few artists treated the daily life of sailors in the 19th century in their work. Julien Le Blant's painting provides us with valuable information on the subject. M. M.

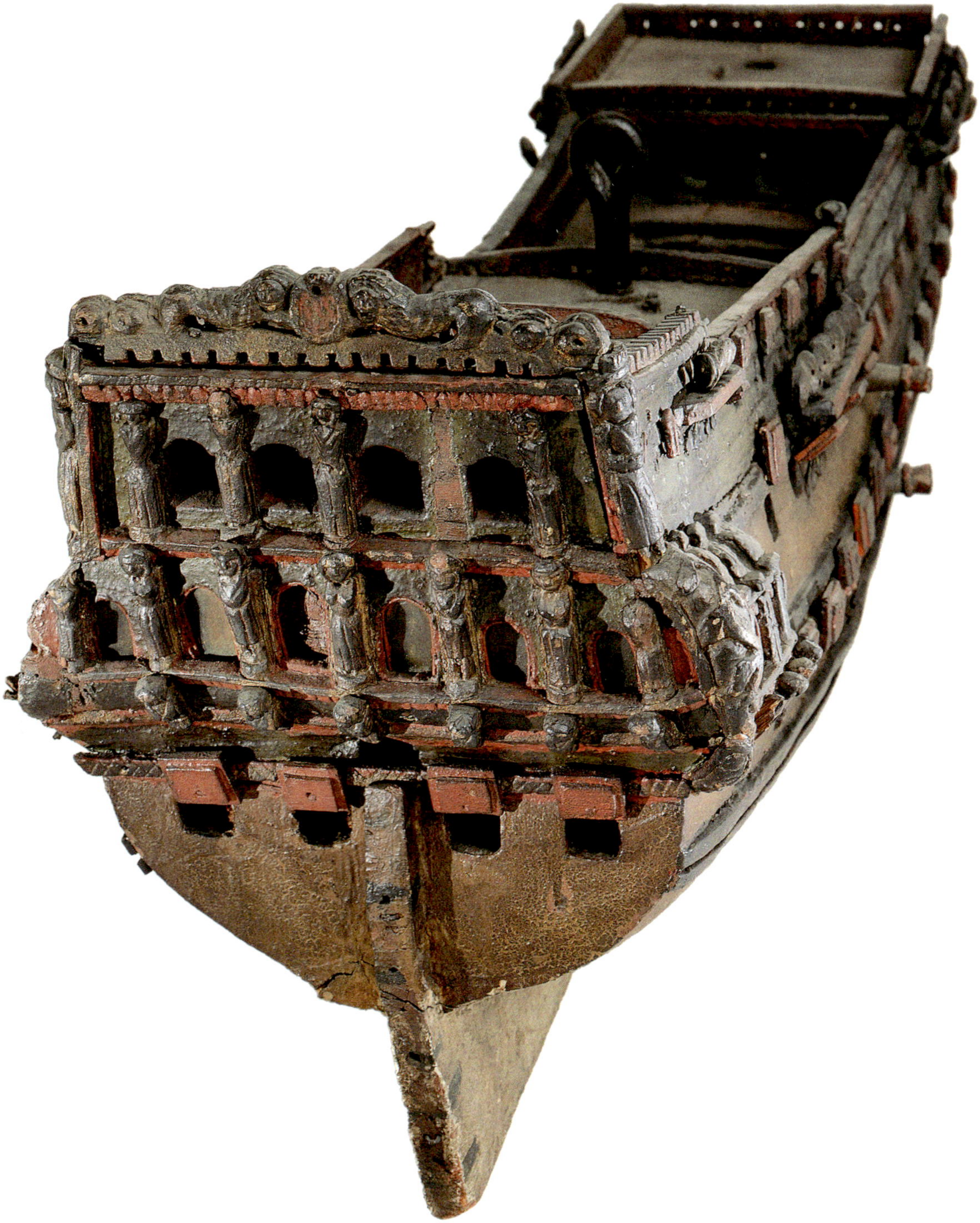

Ship's hull

Ex-voto . Second half of 17th century . Wood . 40 x 98 x 28 cm . Entered museum collections 1909 . MnM 1 BF 2

This ex-voto offering comes from a chapel in Brittany, where it was probably hung from the vault. The shape and decor of this unrigged two-deck, 72-gun vessel, are characteristic of the ships of the second half of the 17th century. The sea decor on the lower hull is found on other representations from the same period in France and abroad. F. C.

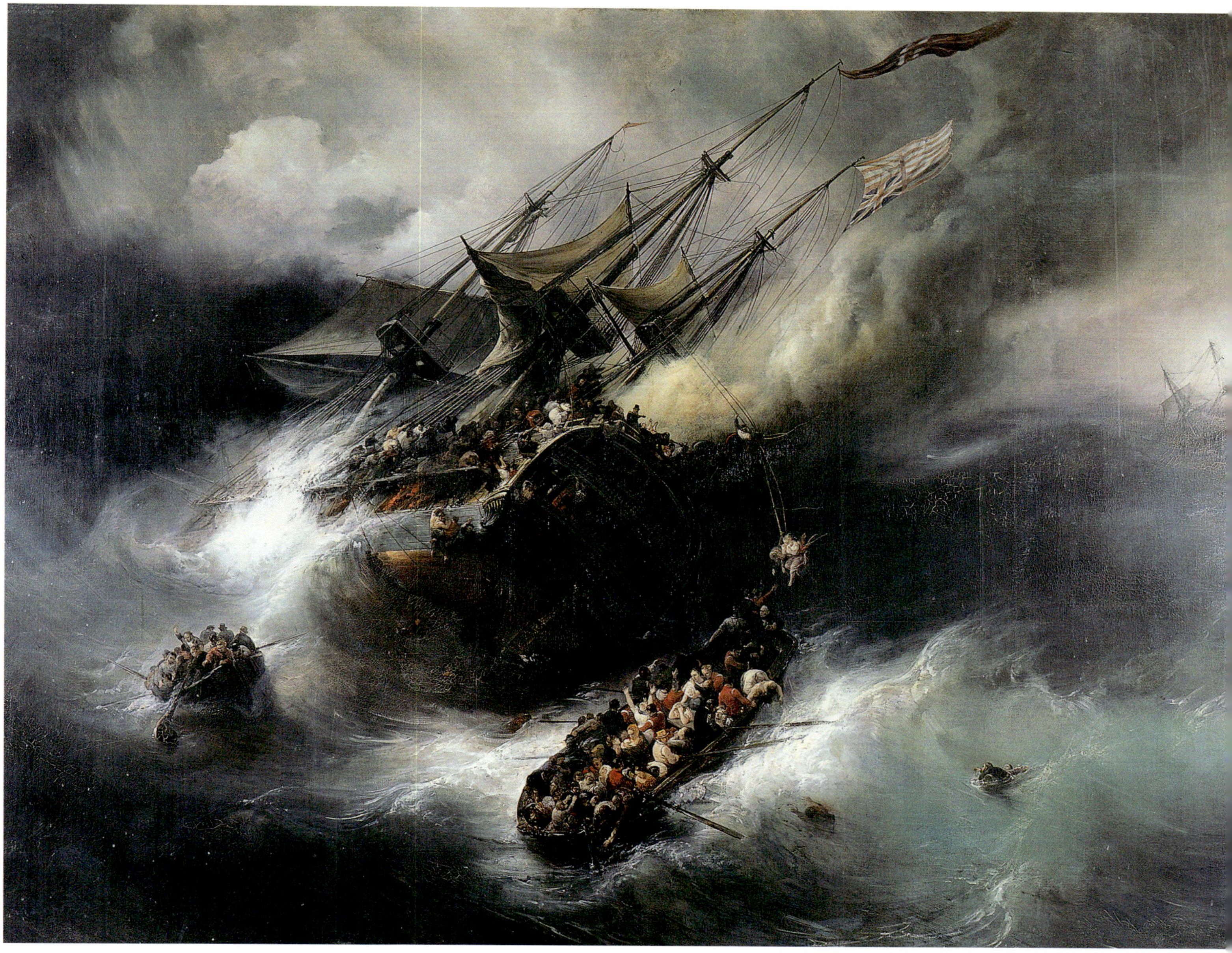

Théodore Gudin (1802–1880)

The Burning of the Kent, 28 February 1825 (detail)

1827 . Oil on canvas . 259 x 417.5 cm . Signed on lower right . On loan from the Department of Paintings, Musée du Louvre, 1903 (RF 90) . MnM 9 OA 34 D

This large composition presented at the 1827 Salon shows Gudin's talent and spirited style. The combined effects of the storm and fire make this a horrifying scene. The dramatic event had taken place two years before, in the Gulf of Gascony. A fire broke out on the *Kent*, a ship of the British East India Company that was on its way to Bengal. Over 650 people were on board, including around one hundred women and children. The English brig *Cambria* did its utmost, amidst the raging elements, to transfer as many passengers as possible. M. M.

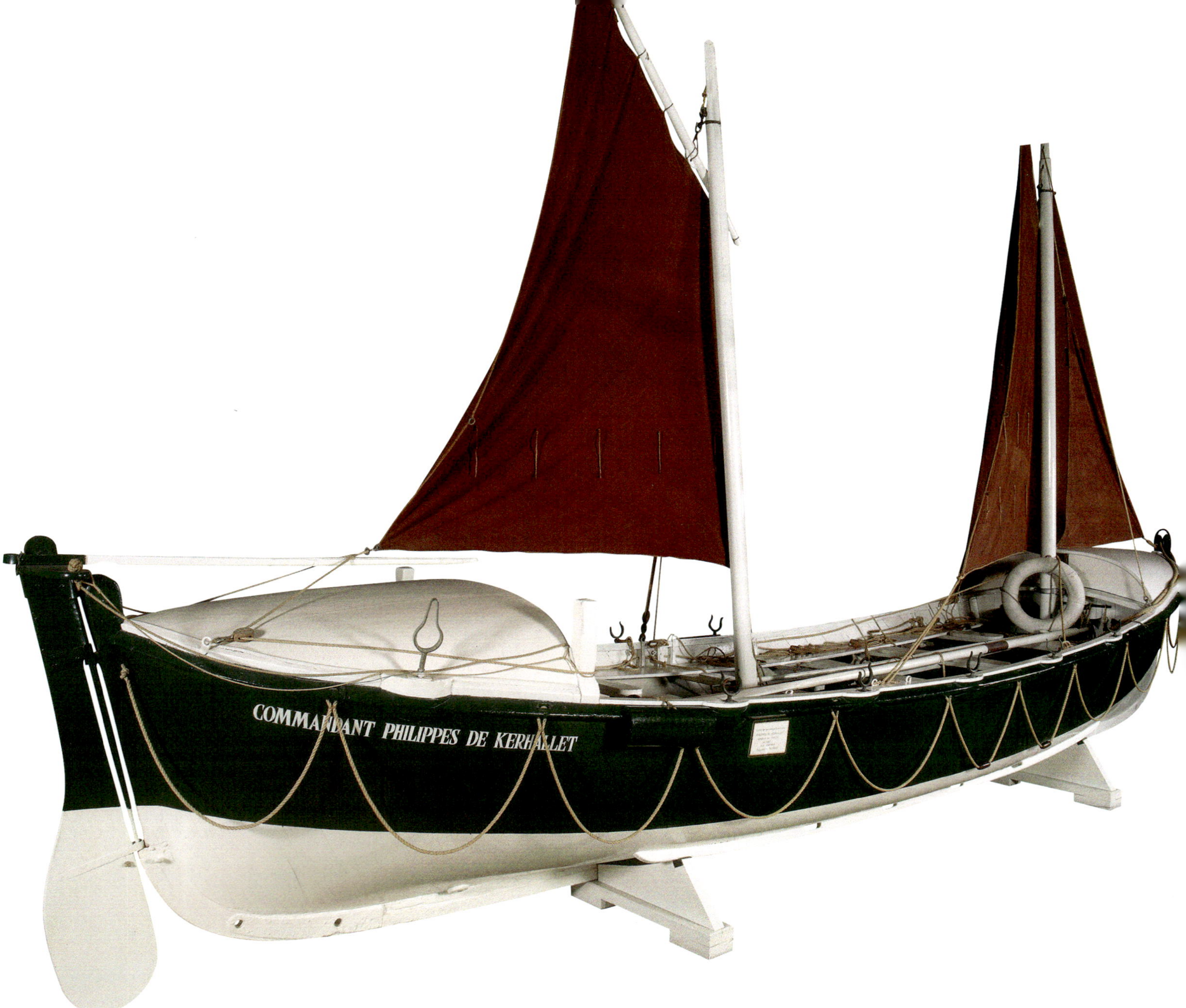

Commandant Philippes de Kerhallet

Lifeboat . Built by the Augustin-Normand boatyard, Le Havre . 1897 . Teak, hemp, steel, brass . 10.10 x 2.27 m . Entered museum collections 1976 . MnM 2002.35.1

The 10.10-meter lifeboat series equipped many sea rescue stations in France from the 1880s to the eve of World War II. This one was in service at the Roscoff station from 1897 to 1953. After its sale in 1953, its whereabouts were unknown. Rediscovered in 1974 and saved from destruction by an enthusiast, Docteur Jean Pillet, who had it restored, it is today the last remaining French lifeboat from the heroic period of oar-powered sea rescue. F. C.

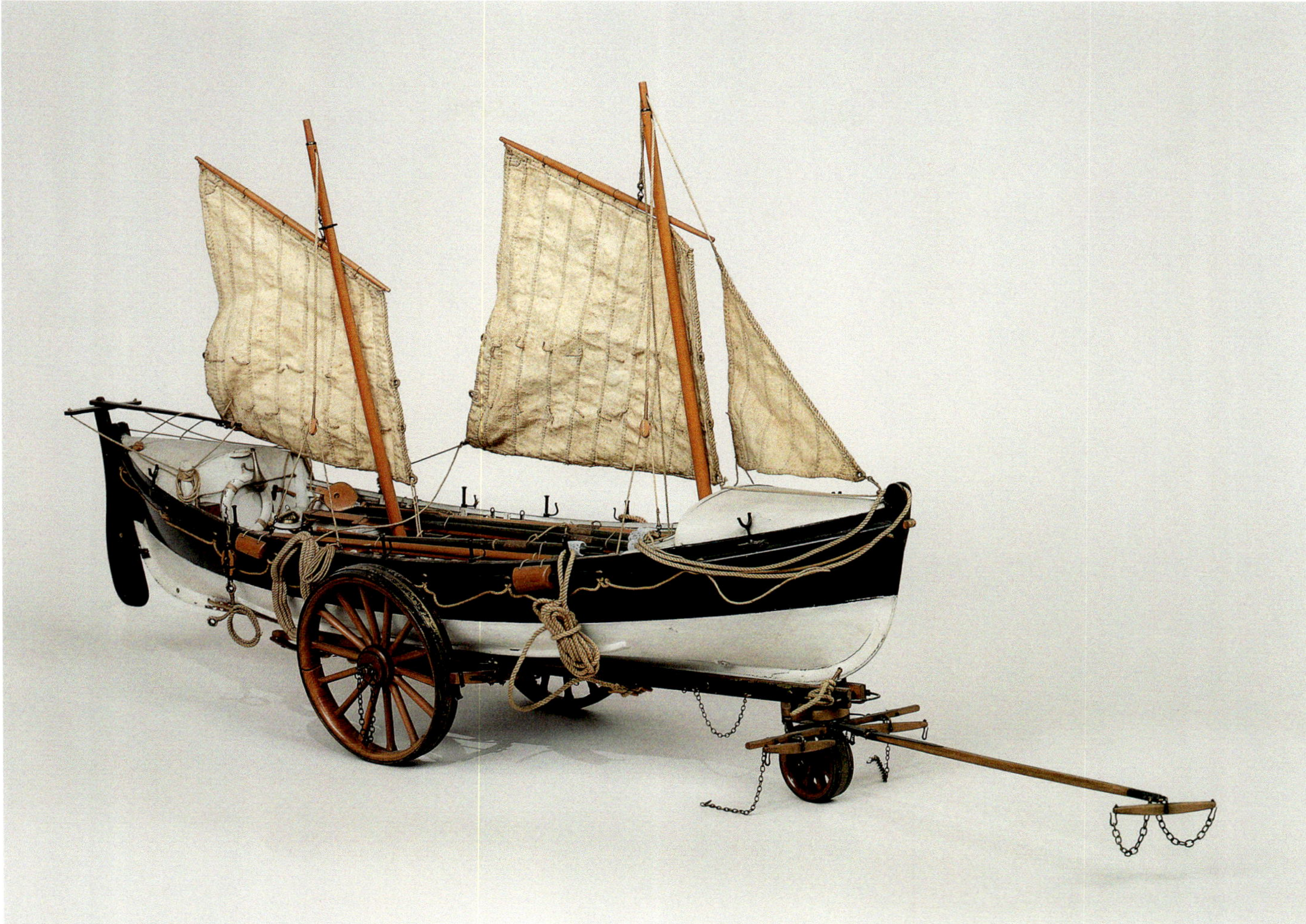

‘Pulling and sailing’ lifeboat

Model of a 9.78-meter lifeboat, 1:16 scale ▪ Before 1879 ▪ Wood, brass, plant fibres ▪ 33 x 61 x 14.5 cm ▪ Entered museum collections 1879 ▪ MnM 3 BS 4

This was the first lifeboat chosen in 1865 by the SCSN (Société Centrale de Sauvetage des Naufragés) to equip its lifeboat stations. Based on a British model, it was almost perfect in its design, fulfilling three essential qualities of a lifeboat: it was insubmersible (28 buoyancy compartments), self-righting (ballast tanks fore and aft), and self-bailing (six vertical valves in the hull). It was manned by a twelve-strong crew: ten oarsmen, the coxswain aft at the tiller and the second coxswain at the bow. F. C.

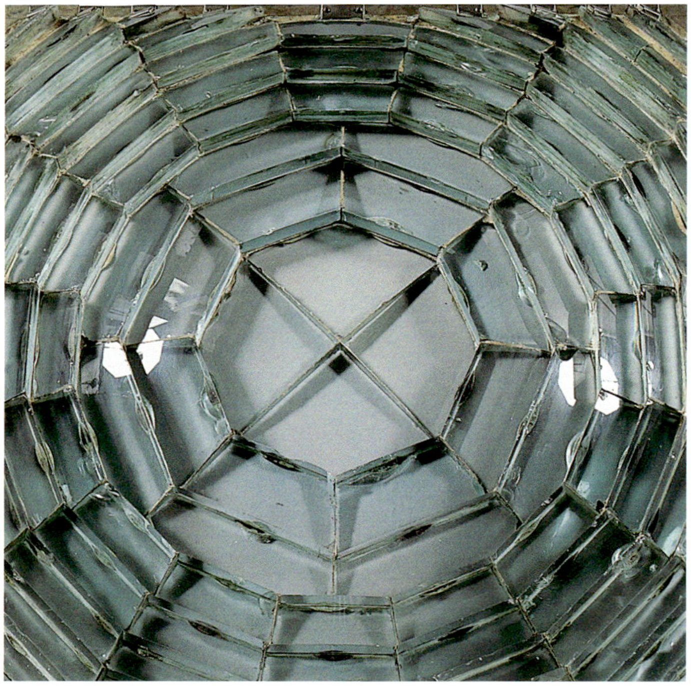

Prototype polygonal stepped lighthouse lens for flashing light (Fresnel lens)

Augustin Fresnel (1788–1827), inventor . François Soleil (1775–1846), constructor . 1821 . Glass, bronze . 81 x 78 cm . On loan from the Bureau des Phares et Balises, 1973 . MnM 19 PA 42 D

The stepped lens, invented by Buffon in around 1740, was applied in 1820 by Augustin Fresnel to the projection of beams of light from a lighthouse. Its highly characteristic beehive design enabled the use of thinner glass, thus substantially reducing the absorption of light by the lens material. In 1821, an octagonal rotating device two meters in diameter made up of eight similar lenses and lit by a four-wick oil lamp was tested on the Arc de Triomphe, in Paris. Eventually, this innovation replaced all previously used reflectors. F. C.

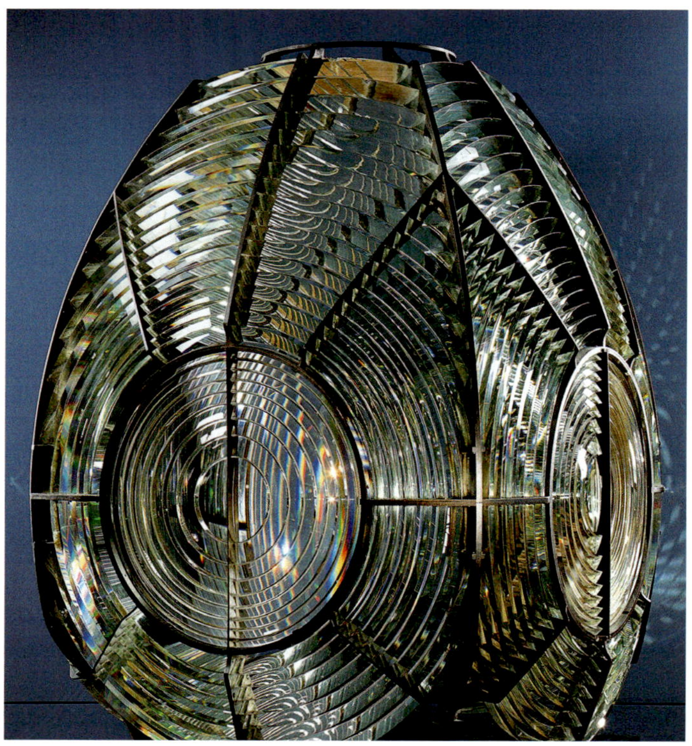

Large optic for a first-order lighthouse (overall view and detail)

Attributed to the Établissements Barbier, Bénard and Turenne . April 1894 . Glass, bronze, putty . H. 254 cm x Ø 198 cm . On loan from the Bureau des Phares et Balises, 1973 . MnM 19 PA 51 D

This is a large fixed light optic with a regular flash, made up of four 1:4 facets at a focal length of 92 cm. It was installed at the Hourtin lighthouse (Gironde) in April 1894 and originally floated in a vat of mercury. It is one of the largest lighthouse optics preserved in France. F. C.

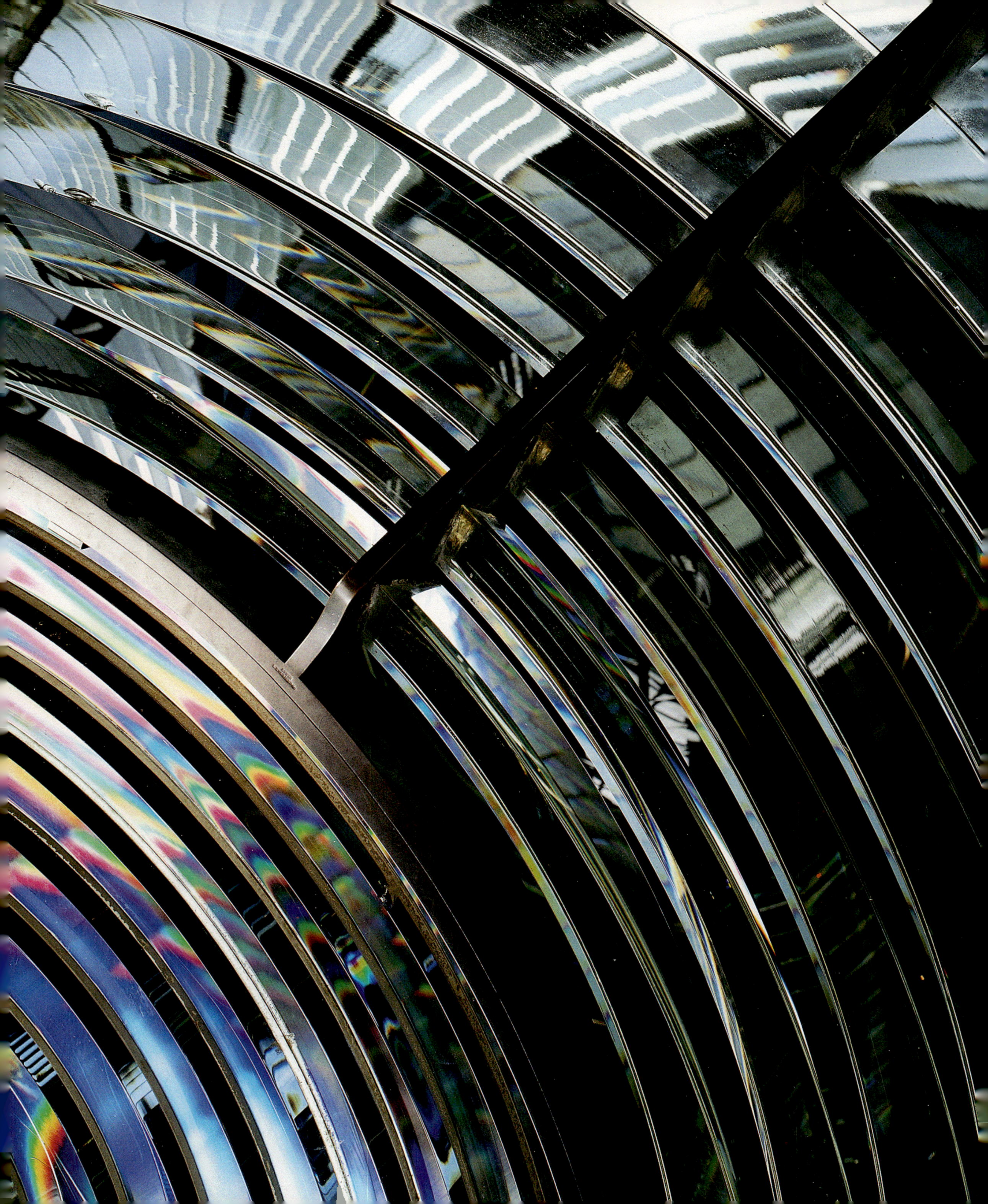

Manuscripts and records

The collection of publications and manuscripts, originally a research tool for the museum curators, reflects and complements the objects and works of art on display. It was constituted thanks to private initiatives, notably that of Amiral François Edmond Pâris, who considerably enriched the collection by contributing his own documentation and generating significant donations from his many relations. In the early 20th century, his successor Jean Destrem, who headed the museum from 1901 to 1929, worked on its classification and drew up the catalogue, organising the material into a library. The manuscripts in the library cover a whole range of subjects: records of professional and family practices, reflections of a policy to promote political awareness of maritime issues, memoirs of bygone institutions, accounts of a life devoted to the navy related in a private journal. They provide an insight into maritime history in all its richness and diversity. More significantly, they are the expression of a human, individual, often moving vision of the sea and seafaring, and of their authors' desire to pass on this maritime heritage.

Augustin Hyppolite Alexandre Reynaud (1780–?)

Journal historique du bagne ou Événemens marquants qui ont eu lieu pendant l'administration du commissaire Reynaud [Historical journal of the penal colony or Important events that took place under the administration of Commissaire Reynaud]

Title page and three plates . Toulon, 1821–1827 . 3 vols., bound, 73 pl., 127 manuscript pages . Black ink, watercolour . 32 x 21.5 cm . Entered museum collections 1957 . MnM J2445, J2446, J2447

In a lively, detailed daily account, illustrated with watercolours executed by the convicts themselves, the journal of Commissaire Reynaud draws us into the world of the penal colony at Toulon and its prisoners, colourful figures with tragic fates. 'I have given a carbon-copy description of remarkable events and men of an exceptional nature, in whose midst I lived; I have noted the transformations of the institution, its days of grandeur and of decadence'. This is how the author describes his journal, a precious record of a bygone place of confinement and hard labour. M.-P. D.

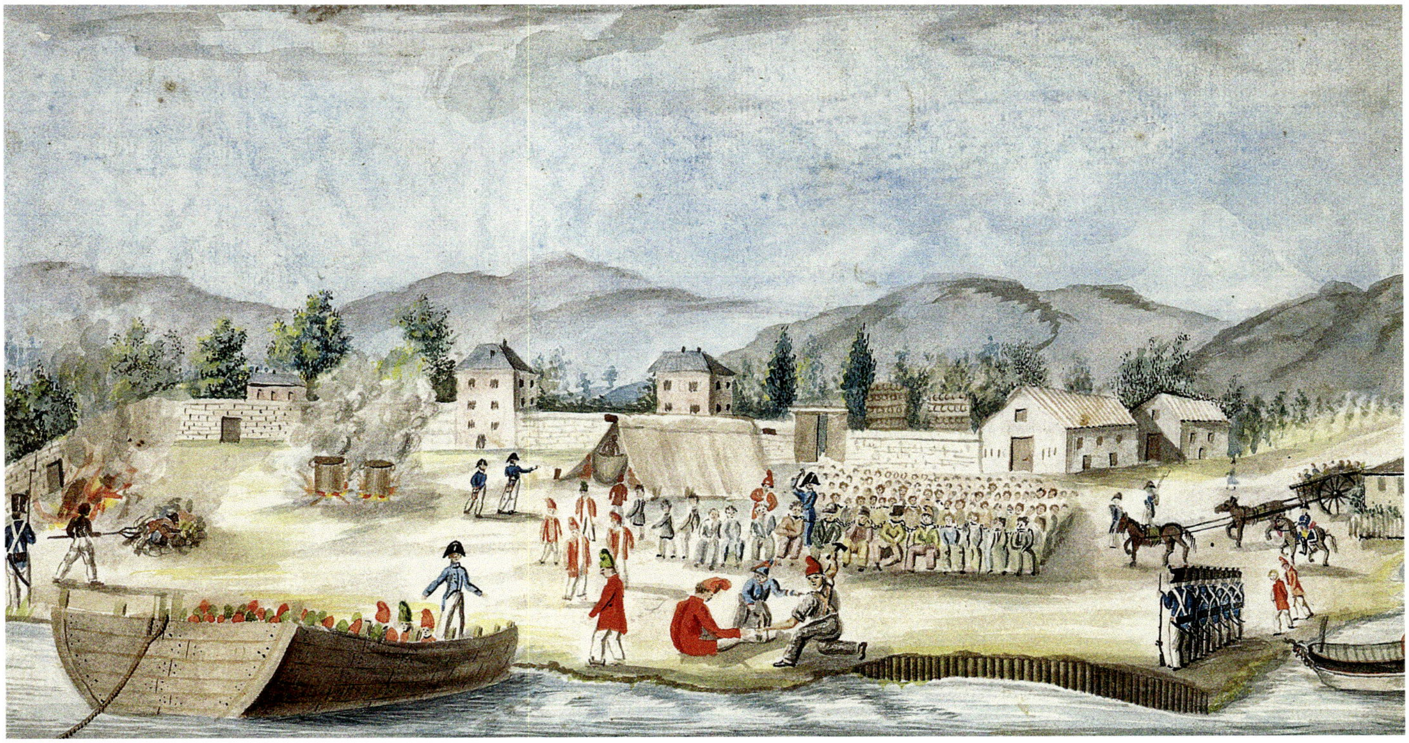

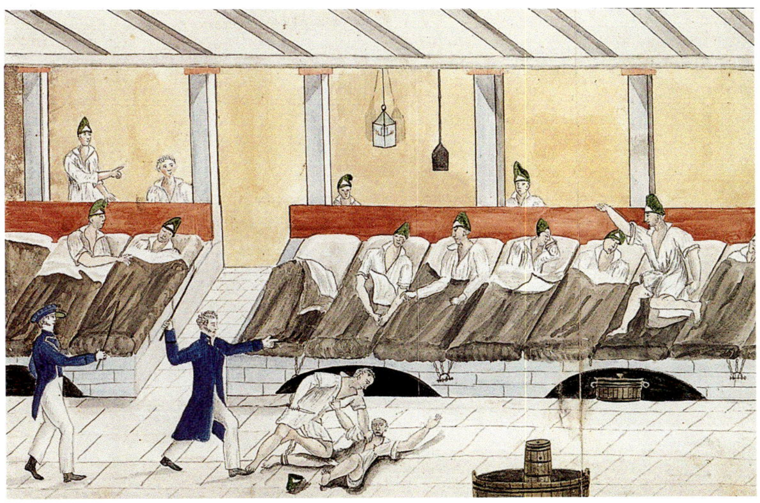

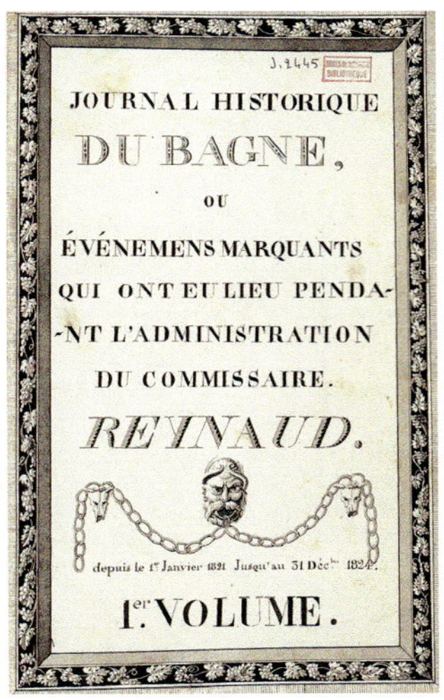

JOURNAL HISTORIQUE

DU BAGNE,

OU

ÉVÉNEMENS MARQUANTS QUI ONT EU LIEU PENDA-NT L'ADMINISTRATION DU COMMISSAIRE.

REYNAUD.

depuis le 1er Janvier 1821 Jusqu'au 31 Décbre 1824.

1er VOLUME.

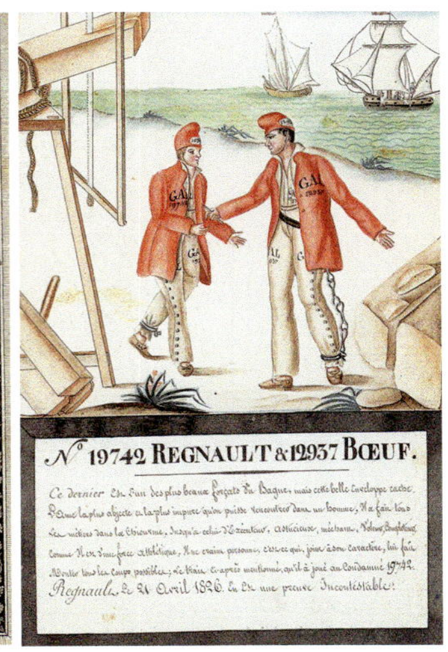

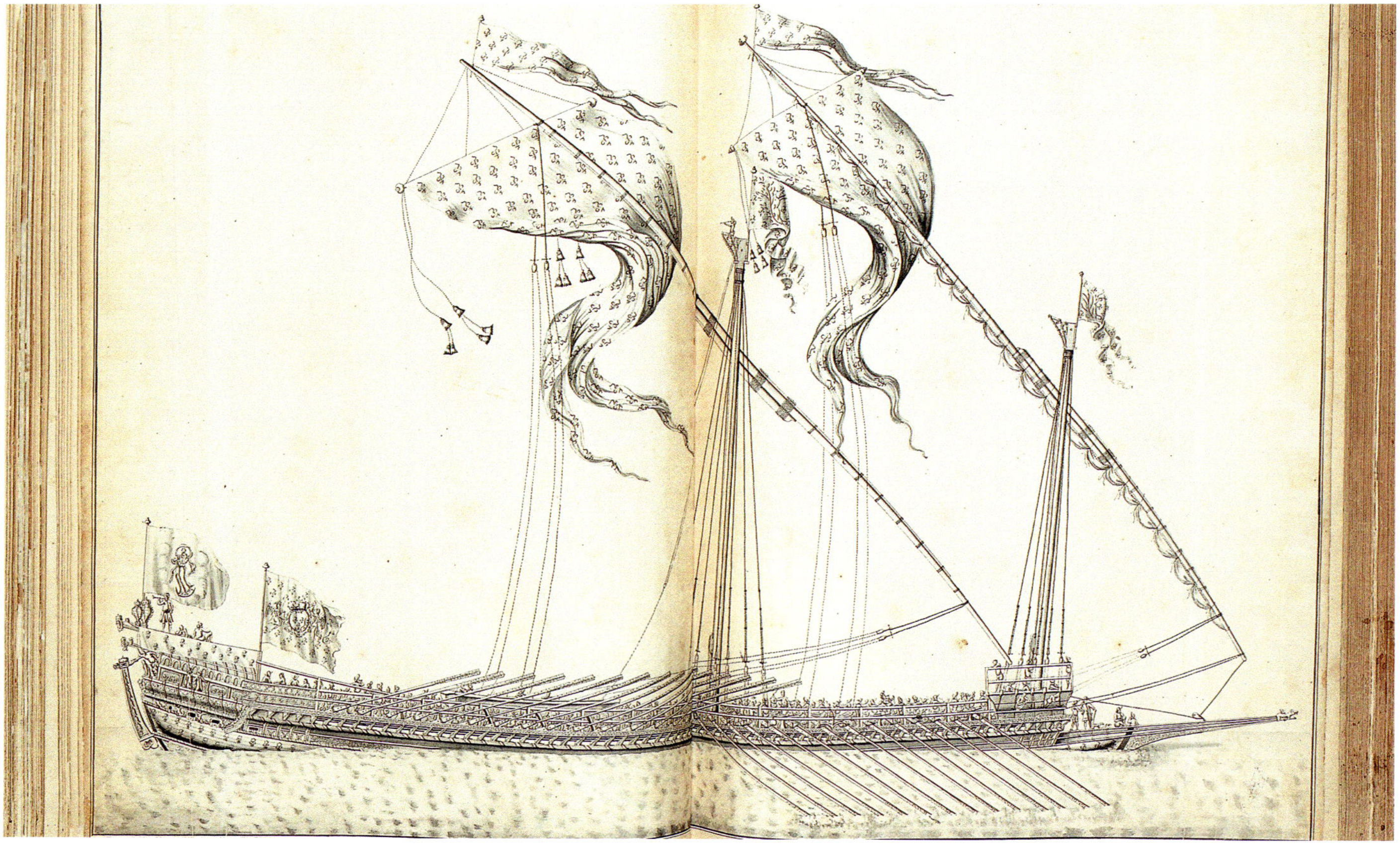

Jean Antoine Barras de La Penne (1654–1730)

La science des galères qui renferme tout ce qui regarde la construction l'armement la manœuvre le combat et la navigation des galères [The science of the galleys comprising all that concerns the building the arming the manoeuvring the fighting and the navigation of galleys]

Marseilles, 1697 . 3 vols.; 25 pl.; 278 manuscript pages; 72 ms. pp., in-text drawings . Black ink, ink wash on paper . 67 x 49 cm . Entered museum collections 1912 . MnM B1125

This manuscript addressed to Louis XIV is part of the prolific work of Barras de La Penne. Constantly in search of protectors who might advance his career in the galley corps, Barras de La Penne was the author of many papers, maps and drawings, and of a *Dictionnaire des galères* that remained unfinished. Here he paints a complete and superbly illustrated portrait of the navy in the late 17th century: ship construction, seamanship, history, vocabulary, etc. All aspects are looked at, by a professional, which makes this a document of great historical and factual interest. M.-P. D.

François Coulomb (1654–1717)

Construction 1690

[Toulon], 1690 . Black ink on paper . 30 x 22 cm . Entered museum collections 1912 . MnM J355

A master shipwright responsible for teaching the art of shipbuilding to trainee officers at the port of Toulon, the author belonged to a family that left a strong mark on naval architecture until the end of the Ancien Régime. This professional manual, written for Coulomb's son, shows the importance of the family heritage in the shipbuilders' training. M.-P. D.

Laurent Coulomb (?–1696)

Flute

Crayon, ink, ink wash on paper . 55 x 91 cm . Entered museum collections 1913 . MnM Plan-7439

When Colbert issued his new building recommendations in 1671, shipwrights were required to provide an estimate and a template when presenting their ship projects, like this cargo corvette, or 'flute'. The use of a drawing only became widespread later, in 1710–1719, owing to the shipwrights' lack of scientific and mathematical training. The Musée National de la Marine has some thirty of these rare drawings, dating from 1679 to the end of the century. In some cases relatively finished, but often clumsy or incomplete, they provide evidence of a decisive change in the way ships were designed at the time. M.-P. D.

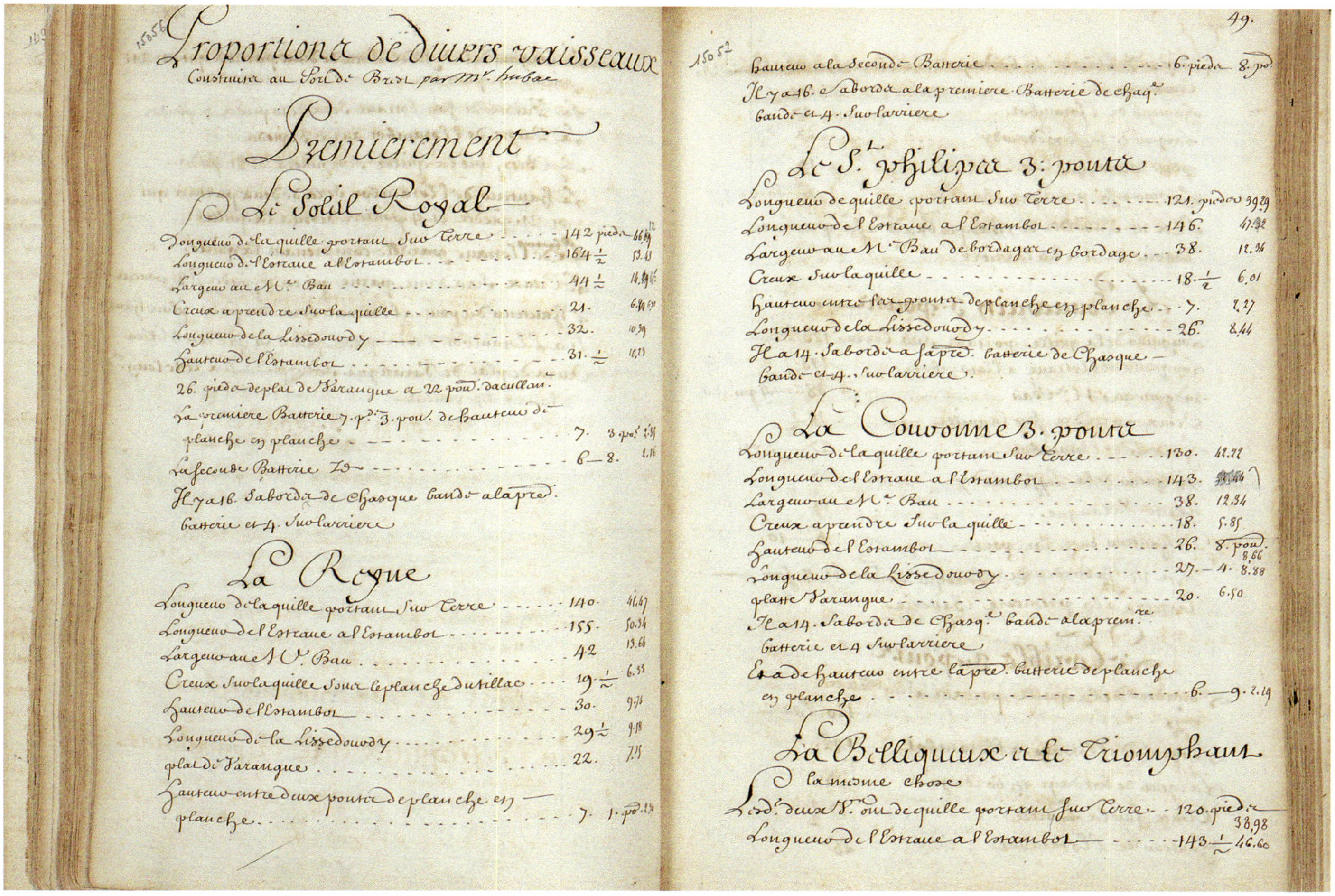

15056

Proportions de divers vaisseaux

Construits au Port de Brest par Mr. Hubac

Premierement

Le Soleil Royal

Longueur de la quille portant sur terre .... 142 pieds 46.19
Longueur de l'Estrave a l'Estambot .... 164 $\frac{1}{2}$ 53.43
Largeur au Mre. Bau .... 44 $\frac{1}{2}$ 14.45
Creux a prendre sur la quille 21. 6.82
Longueur de la Lisse de hourdy 32. 10.39
Hauteur de l'Estambot .... 31. $\frac{1}{2}$ 10.23
26. pieds de plat de Varangue et 22 pou. d'acculem.
La premiere Batterie 7. pds. 3. pou. de hauteur de planche en planche .... 7. 3 pos. 2.35
La seconde Batterie Id .... 6 — 8. 2.16
Il y a 16. Sabords de chasque bande a la pre. batterie et 4. sur l'arriere

La Reyne

Longueur de la quille portant sur terre 140. 45.47
Longueur de l'Estrave a l'Estambot 155. 50.34
Largeur au Mre. Bau 42 13.64
Creux sur la quille sous le planche du tillac .... 19 $\frac{1}{2}$ 6.33
Hauteur de l'Estambot 30. 9.74
Longueur de la Lisse de hourdy .... 29 $\frac{1}{2}$ 9.58
plat de Varangue 22. 7.15
Hauteur entre deux ponts de planche en planche .... 7. 1. po. 2.34

49.

15052

hauteur a la seconde Batterie .... 6. pieds 8. po.
Il y a 16. sabords a la premiere Batterie de chaqe. bande et 4. sur l'arriere

Le St. Philippes 3. ponts

Longueur de quille portant sur terre .... 121. pieds 39.29
Longueur de l'Estrave a l'Estambot 146. 47.32
Largeur au Mre. Bau de bordage en bordage 38. 12.34
Creux sur la quille .... 18. $\frac{1}{2}$ 6.01
hauteur entre les ponts de planche en planche 7. 2.27
Longueur de la Lisse de hourdy 26. 8.44
Il a 14. sabords a la pre. batterie de chasque bande et 4. sur l'arriere.

La Couronne 3. ponts

Longueur de la quille portant sur terre 130. 42.22
Longueur de l'Estrave a l'Estambot .... 143. [illegible].44
Largeur au Mre. Bau 38. 12.34
Creux a prendre sur la quille 18. 5.85
Hauteur de l'Estambot .... 26. 8. pou. 8.66
Longueur de la Lisse de hourdy .... 27. — 4. 8.88
platte Varangue 20. 6.50
Il a 14. Sabords de chasqe. bande a la premre. batterie et 4 sur l'arriere
Et a de hauteur entre la pre. batterie de planche en planche .... 6. — 9. 2.19

Le Belliqueux et le Triomphant

la mesme chose

Losd. deux Vx. ont de quille portant sur terre .... 120. pieds 38.98
Longueur de l'Estrave a l'Estambot .... 143. $\frac{1}{2}$ 46.60

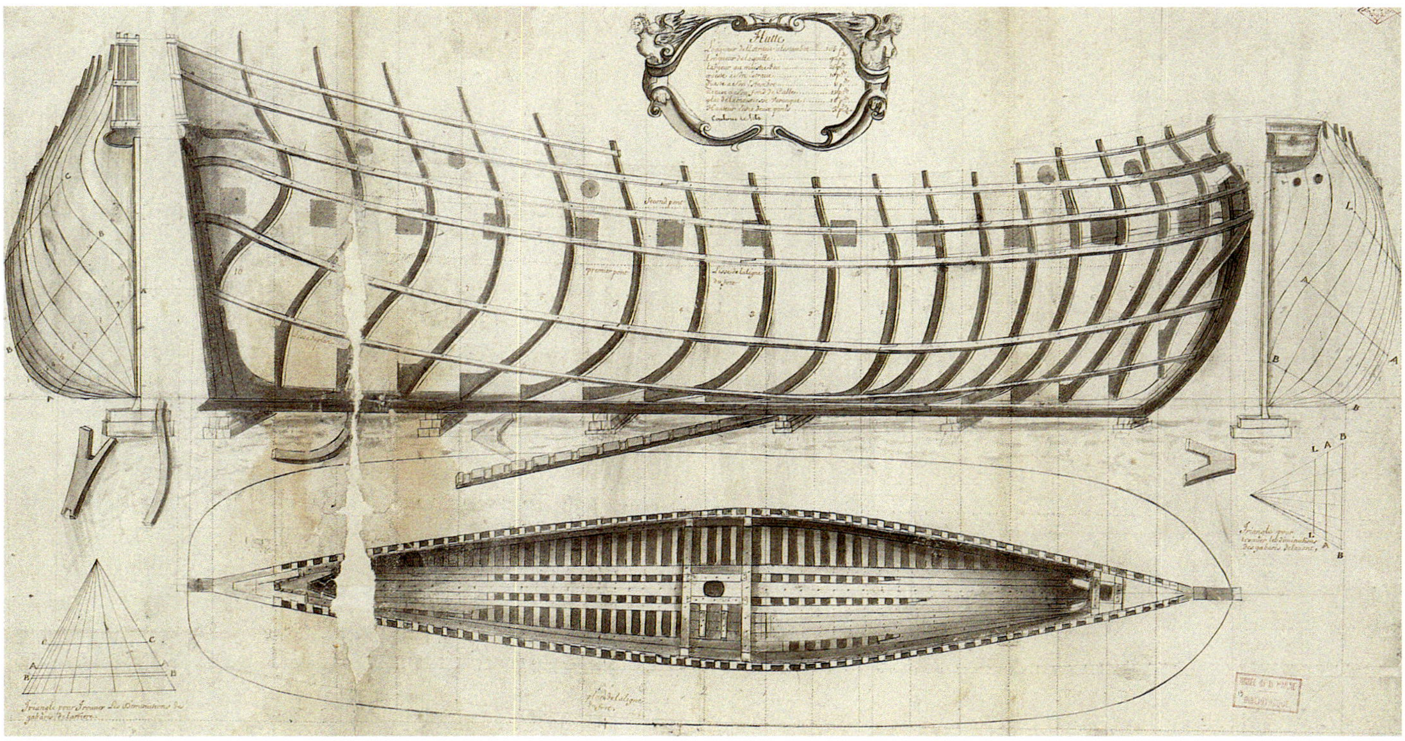

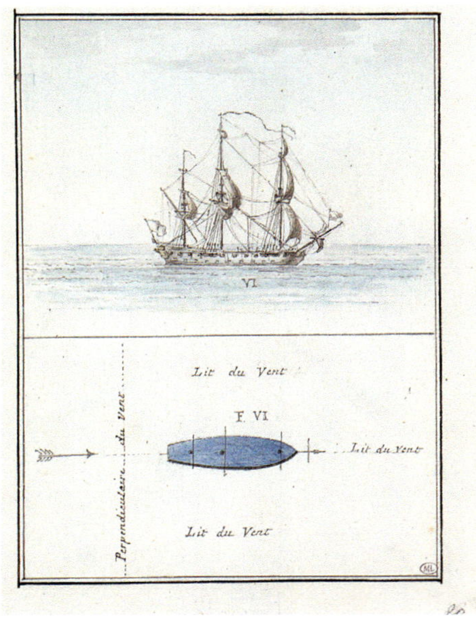

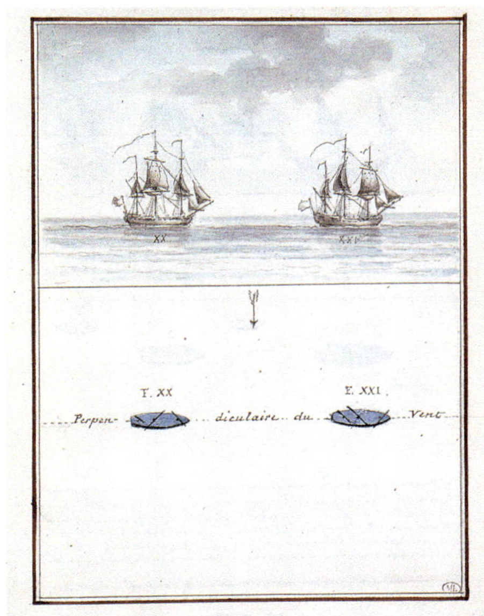

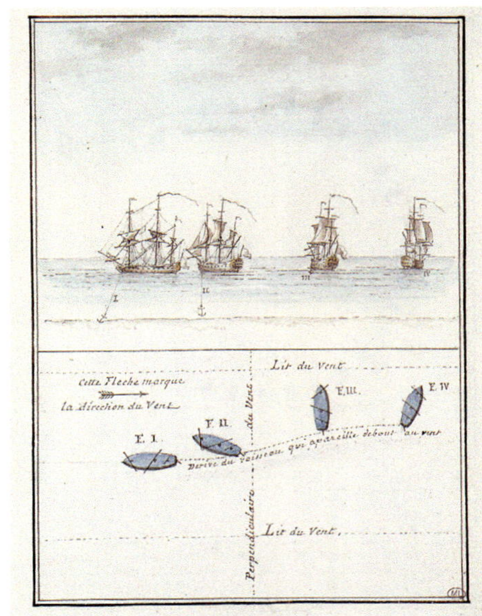

Nicolas Marie Ozanne (1728–1811)

Les évolutions du vaisseau démontrées par les plans et desseins [The movements of a ship shown in diagrams and drawings]

Circa 1770 . Black ink, watercolour and wash on paper . 23 x 18.5 cm . On loan from the Musée du Louvre, 1921 (inv. 32048 à 32055) . MnM R167

This document is part of a series of works and manuscripts used for the maritime training of the future Louis XVI and his brothers. In 1769, Nicolas Ozanne, draughtsman, engraver, shipwright and marine engineer, was employed to provide the royal children with this education. The programme included a number of subjects, notably the construction and manoeuvring of ships. For the latter, Ozanne made this illustrated manuscript on which he based the theoretical part of his lessons, completed with practical exercises on the boats on the Grand Canal at Versailles. M.-P. D.

François d'Orléans, Prince de Joinville (1818–1900)

Journal in manuscript (details)

1835–1858 . 6 vols., 27 x 23 cm each . Entered museum collections 1965 . MnM J3305 à J3309, J3755

François d'Orléans, third son of King Louis-Philippe, devoted himself with enthusiasm to his maritime career, which coincided with the early days of steam-powered ships. In his texts he describes with wonder the fine sailing ships on which he sailed, but he had a forward-looking mind and supported and encouraged innovation. His most famous campaign is the return of Napoleon's ashes from Saint Helena in 1840. A gifted draughtsman and watercolourist (he was a pupil of Gudin and of Ary Scheffer), he carried his sketchbook everywhere he went. In this journal he evokes his exile after the 1848 revolution, omitted from his autobiographical work *Vieux souvenirs*, published in 1894. M.-P. D.

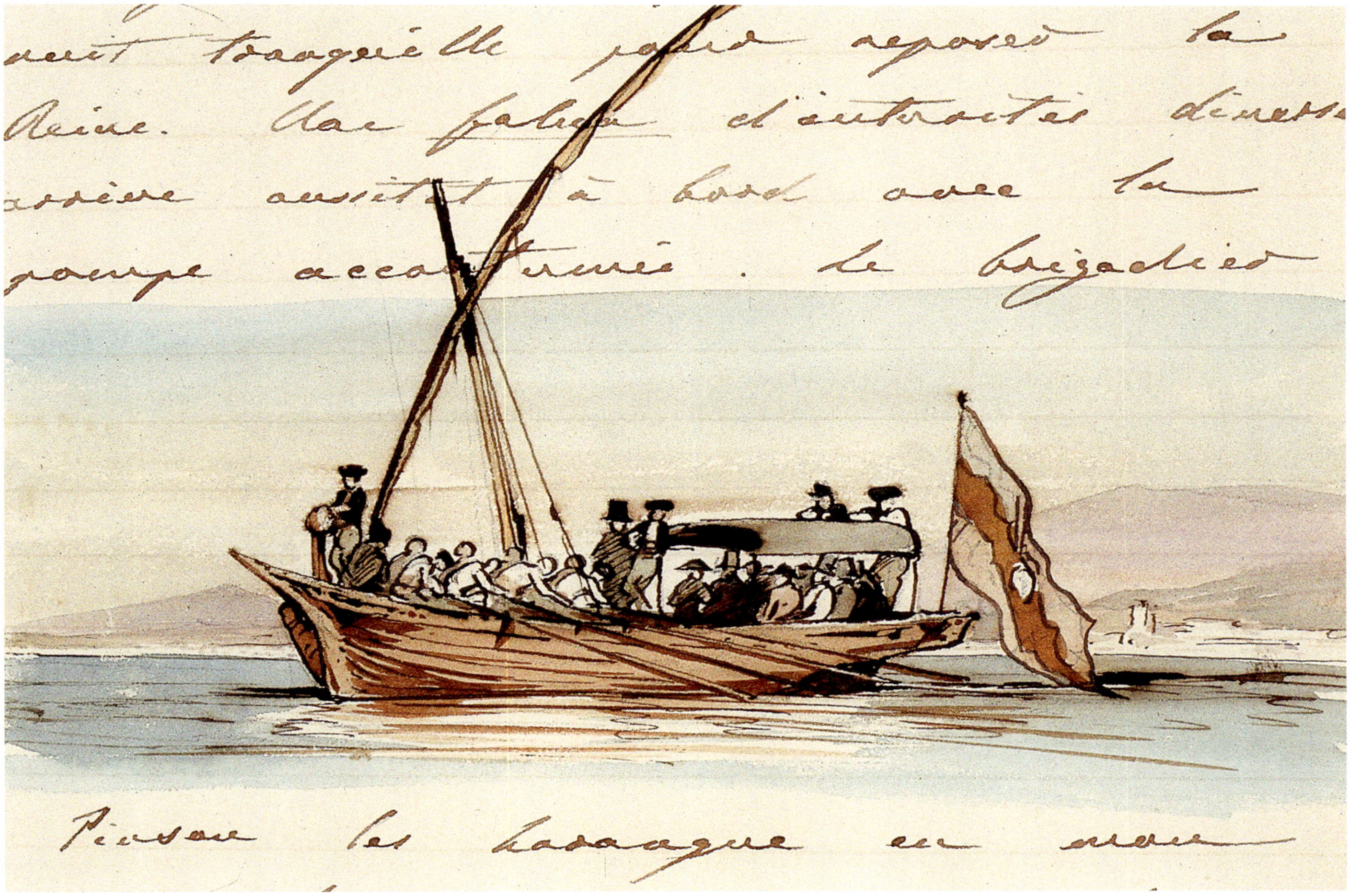
avait tranquille pour reposer la
Reine. Une falua d'autorités diverses
arrive aussitôt à bord avec la
pompe accoutumée. Le brigadier
Pinson les harangue en

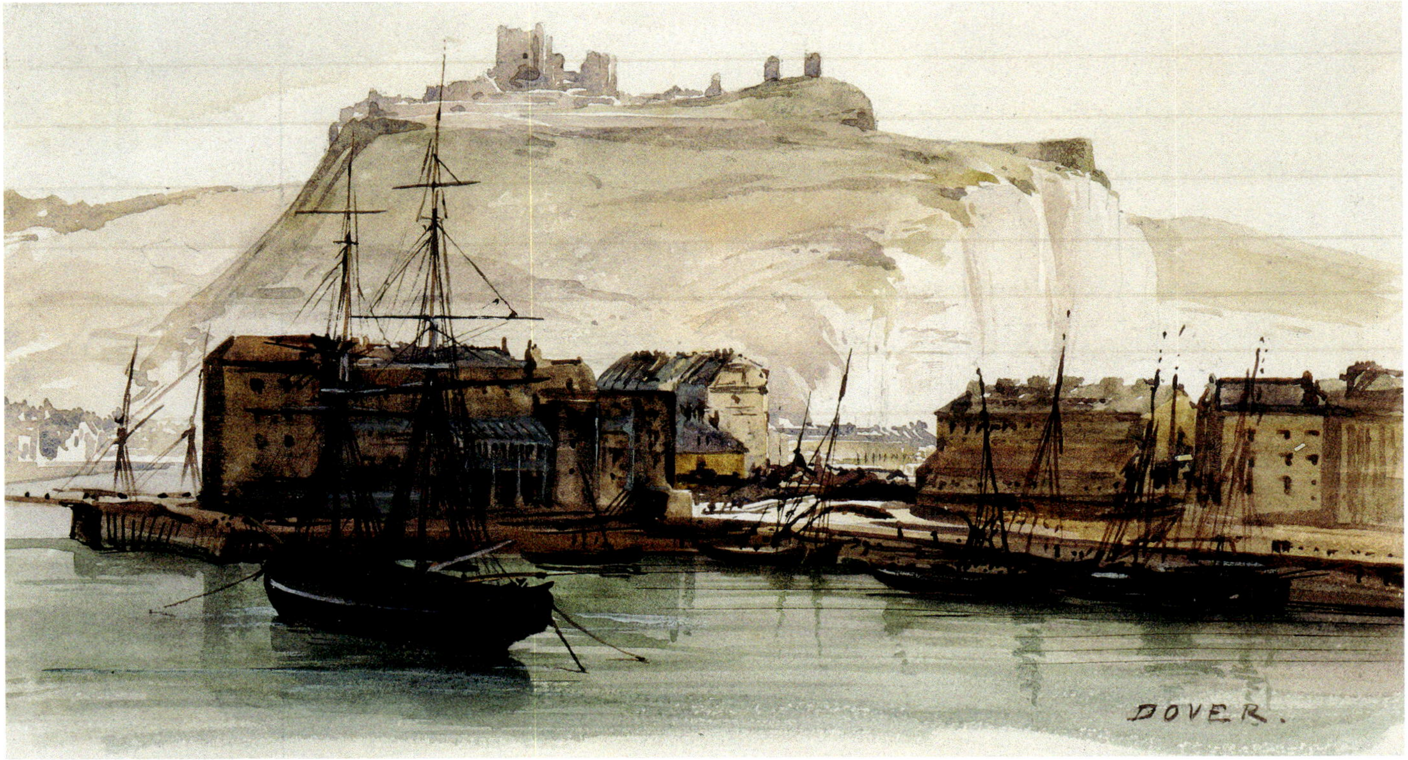
DOVER.

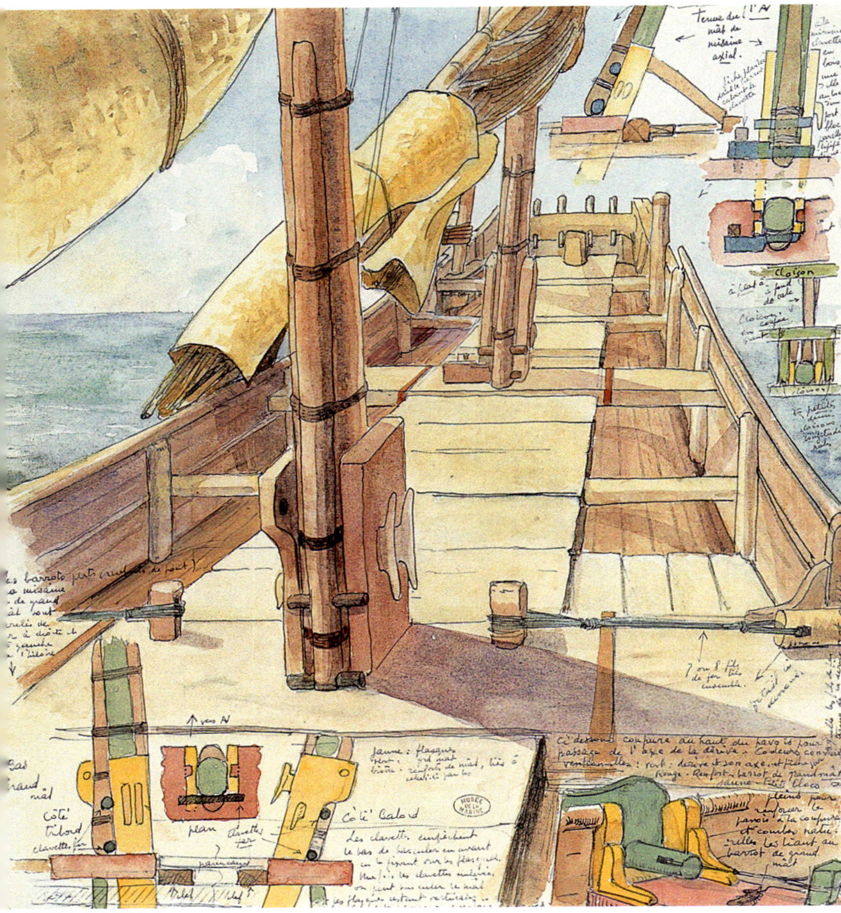

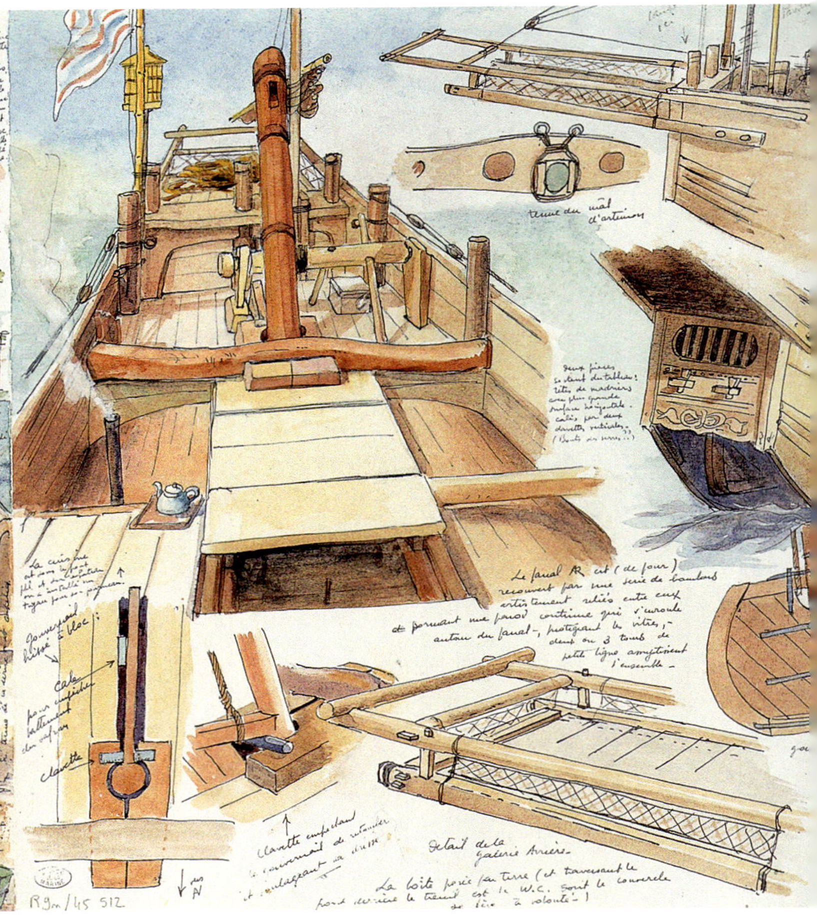

Étienne Sigaut (1887–1983)

Four-masted junk from Shandong

Folio 1 verso, folio 2 recto . 1944 . Ink and watercolour on paper . 33 x 30 cm . Entered museum collections 1960–1970 . MnM ico 45512.5 .

Étienne Sigaut

Small fishing junk from Shitang (detail)

Folio 3, detail . 1944 . Ink and watercolour on paper . 33 x 30 cm . Entered museum collections 1960–1970 . MnM ico 42551

Étienne Sigaut was not a sailor. An employee at the Compagnie des Messageries Maritimes and later an independent broker, he made several trips to Shanghai, where he developed a keen interest in the traditional boats that could be seen moored in the docks of the port. Wishing to record them for posterity, he observed, drew, photographed and analysed them, collecting very extensive documentation that he passed on to the Musée National de la Marine from the 1960s up to the 1970s. His approach, similar to that of his precursor Amiral Pâris, stems from his undeniable artistic qualities and scientific rigour. M.-P. D.

se trouvant
avant la sec à
possible de ~~po~~ voir
sont elle toute

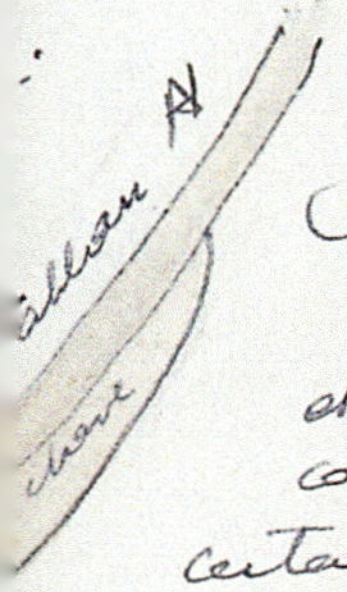

(a)

et non
comme dans
certaines autres
jonques du Sud Chekiang
ou Foukien

reste droite sur
joint sans
ve :

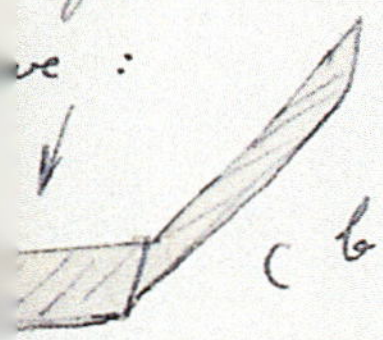

(b)

e et aussi haute
e pour les jonques

tes jonques du même
res (arrière avec cadre
é de la petite jonque
égalemenl la grille

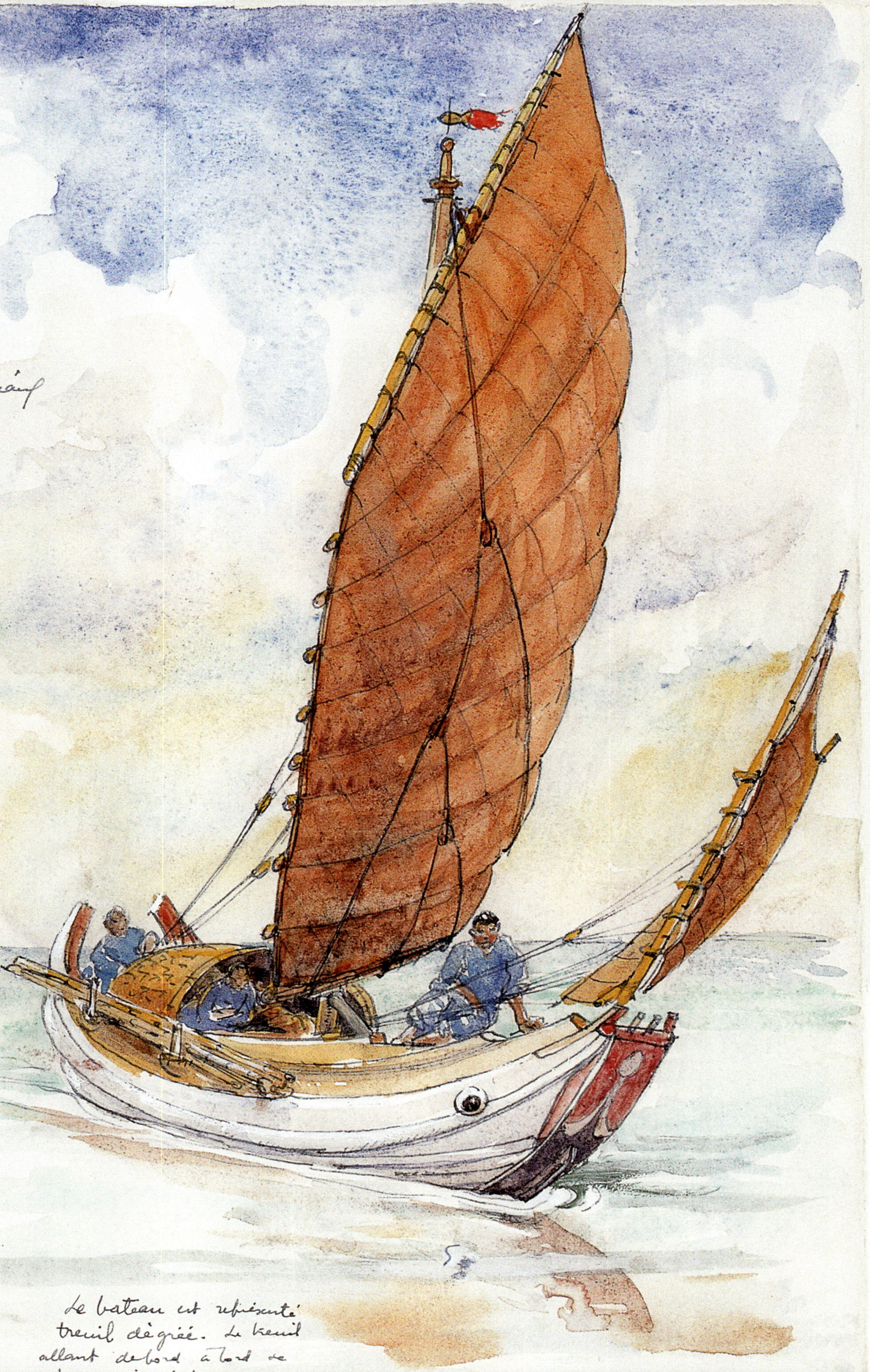

Le bateau est représenté
treuil dégréé. Le treuil
allant de bord à bord de

Distant shores

A great many seafarers participated in the making of French maritime history from the 16th to the 20th centuries: Jacques Cartier, Cavelier de La Salle, Bougainville, Lapérouse, Dumont d'Urville, Charcot, among others. Their voyages of exploration reflected a political desire to explore the world and extend France's influence, and to push back the frontiers of human knowledge.

When it first opened in the Louvre palace, the Musée de la Marine presented the latest geographical discoveries, displaying numerous objects brought back by explorers. On his return from his first journey around the world aboard *L'Astrolabe* in April 1826, Dumont d'Urville gave the museum the ethnographical pieces that had been collected in unknown regions of Oceania. He also deposited several objects from the wrecks of Lapérouse's frigates, which joined those found by Peter Dillon. In addition, the ethnographical collection of Vivant Denon (the Louvre's first director), purchased by the State in 1826, was allocated to the Musée de la Marine. In the last third of the 19th century, however, the development of anthropology as a scientific discipline set these objects aside from the maritime context, investing them with an identity of their own. The original ethnographical collection was divided up between several French museums.

Today, the history of exploration at the Musée National de la Marine is reflected in personal objects belonging to the explorers, in the vestiges and models of some of their vessels, and in the drawings, prints, paintings, maps and atlases related to the expeditions. A very few important ethnographical pieces were left to the museum after the dispersion of the original collection. To these has been added the collection of the former school of naval medicine in Rochefort, administered since 1986 by the Musée National de la Marine. These objects, some of which are extremely rare, were collected by the physicians and surgeons of the French navy.

A third field of geographical discovery emerged in the late 19th century: deep-sea exploration. The Carmagnolle diving suit, a fascinating prototype, and the bathyscaphe *FNRS III* are important landmarks in this scientific quest.

Robert Gessain (1907–1986)

The 'Pourquoi-Pas?' in the Bay of Tasiusaq

1934 . Modern baryta print after a 6 x 6 cm negative . 22.5 x 22 cm . Negative entered museum collections in 1999 . MnM Photographs collection

In 1934, a research team from the Musée d'Ethnographie du Trocadéro sailed to the east coast of Greenland aboard the *Pourquoi-Pas?*, the polar exploration ship of Commandant Charcot. In the course of this first French anthropological survey in the region, four young researchers (Victor, Gessain, Pérez and Matter) spent fourteen months at Ammassalik, where they collected an invaluable amount of documentation concerning the Inuits. This encounter rich in discoveries and emotions is here symbolised by a child contemplating the three-master at anchor in the Bay of Tasiusaq. A. M.

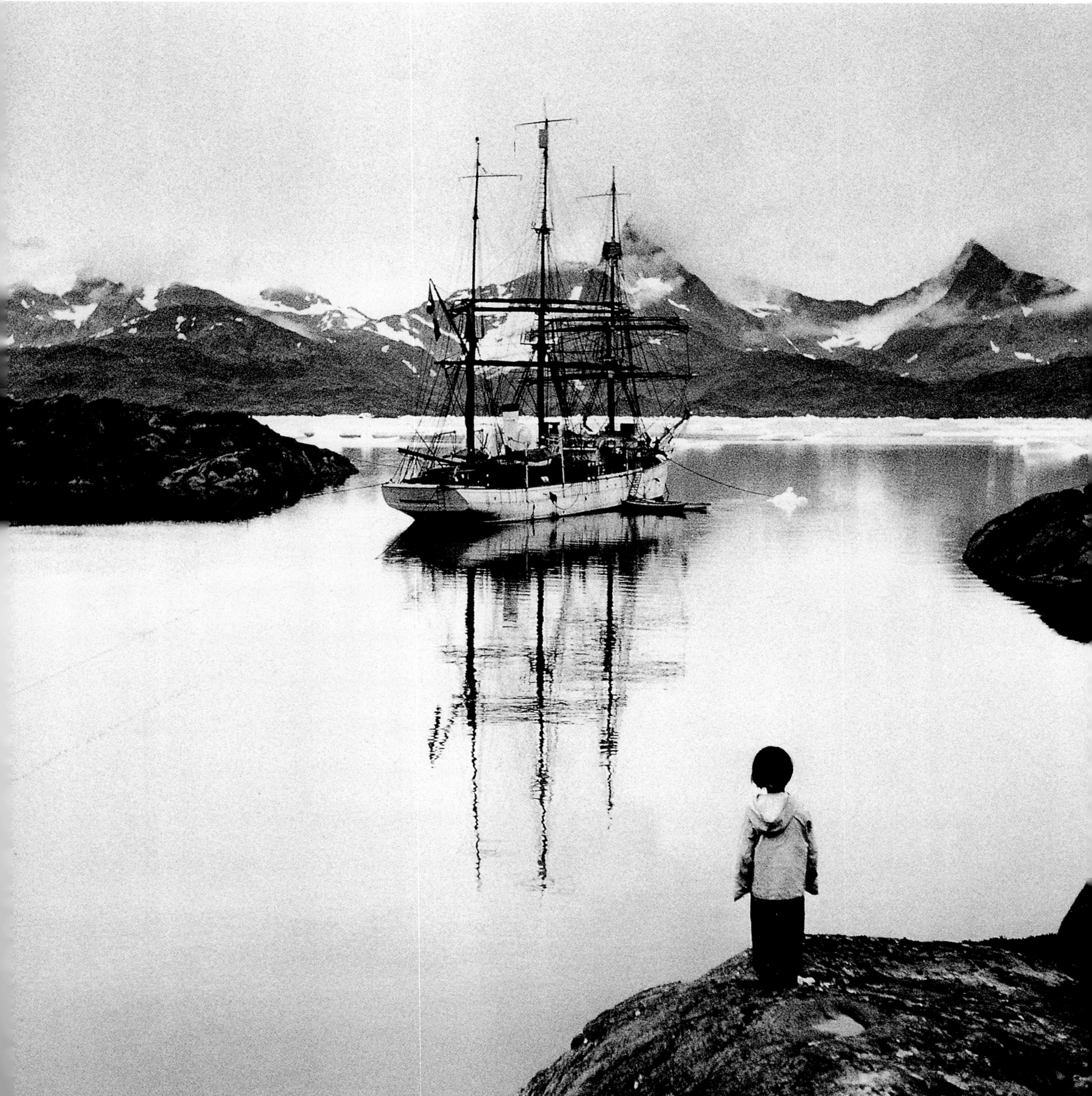

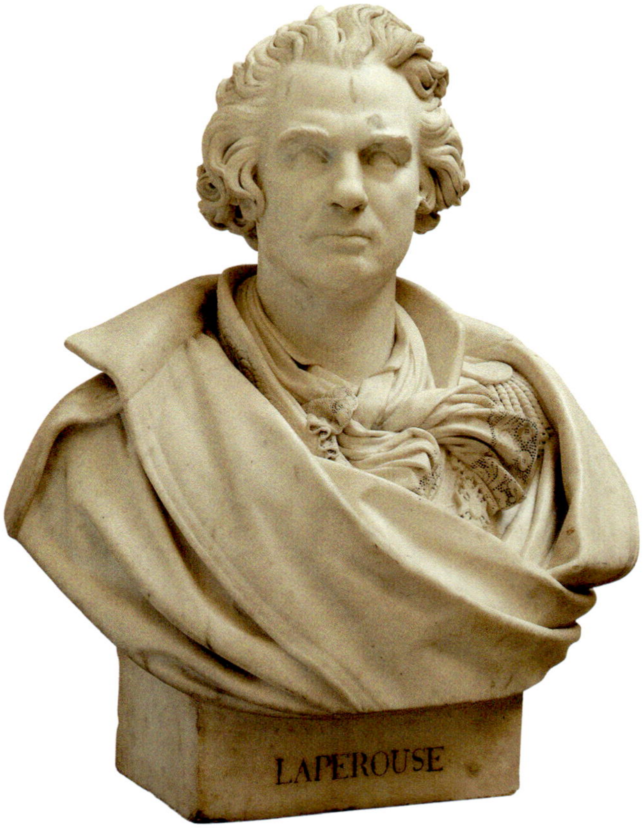

François Rude (1784–1855)

Bust of Jean-François de Galaup de Lapérouse (1741–1788)

1828 . Marble . 84 x 66 x 48 cm . On loan from the Department of Sculptures, Musée du Louvre (CC 0261), 1846 . MnM 41 OA 34 D

On 1st August 1785, *La Boussole* and *L'Astrolabe* cast off from Brest under the command of the ship's captain Jean-François de Galaup, Comte de Lapérouse, for a great voyage of exploration of the Pacific ordered by Louis XVI. Lapérouse had planned to return to France in July 1789, but, from February 1788, no further news of the expedition was received. Forty years later, the wrecks of the two ships were finally identified in Vanikoro in the Solomon Islands. In 1828, François Rude executed this bust of the famous lost mariner, of whom no known portrait exists. M. M.

Stern escutcheon of *L'Astrolabe or La Boussole*

Fragment of stern decor . Carved wood . 35 x 110 cm . Entered museum collections 1828 . MnM 5 SO 2.100

This fragment of decor was discovered by Peter Dillon in September 1827 in a village in Vanikoro (Solomon Islands). It had been used as a barrier in the doorway of a house. Adorned with a fleur-de-lis, it probably comes from one of the two wrecked ships of Lapérouse's expedition. It is fragmentary but unique evidence of the simple ornamentation of these cargo ships. H. T.

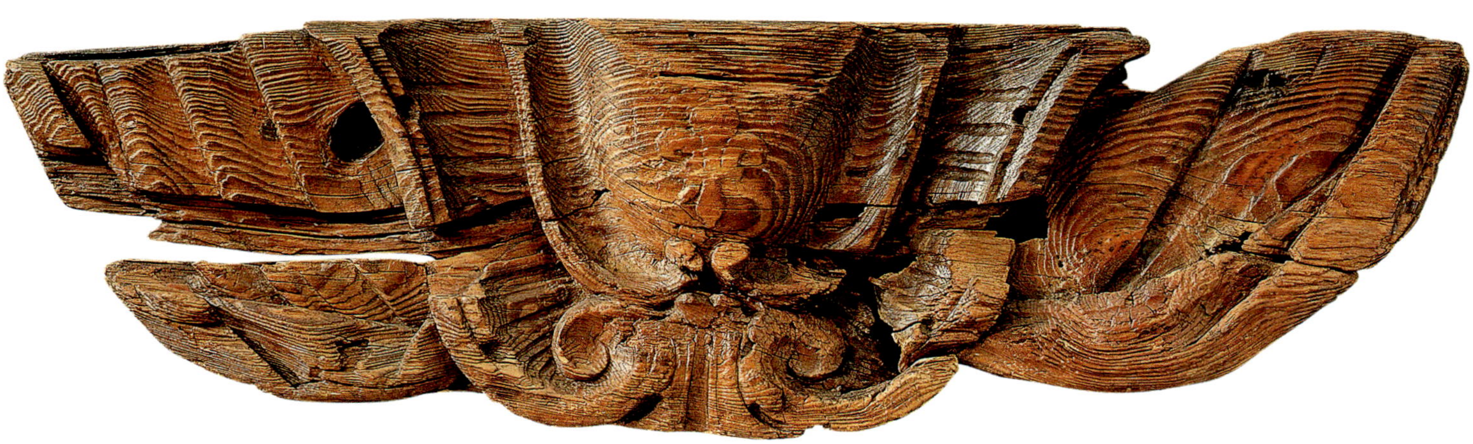

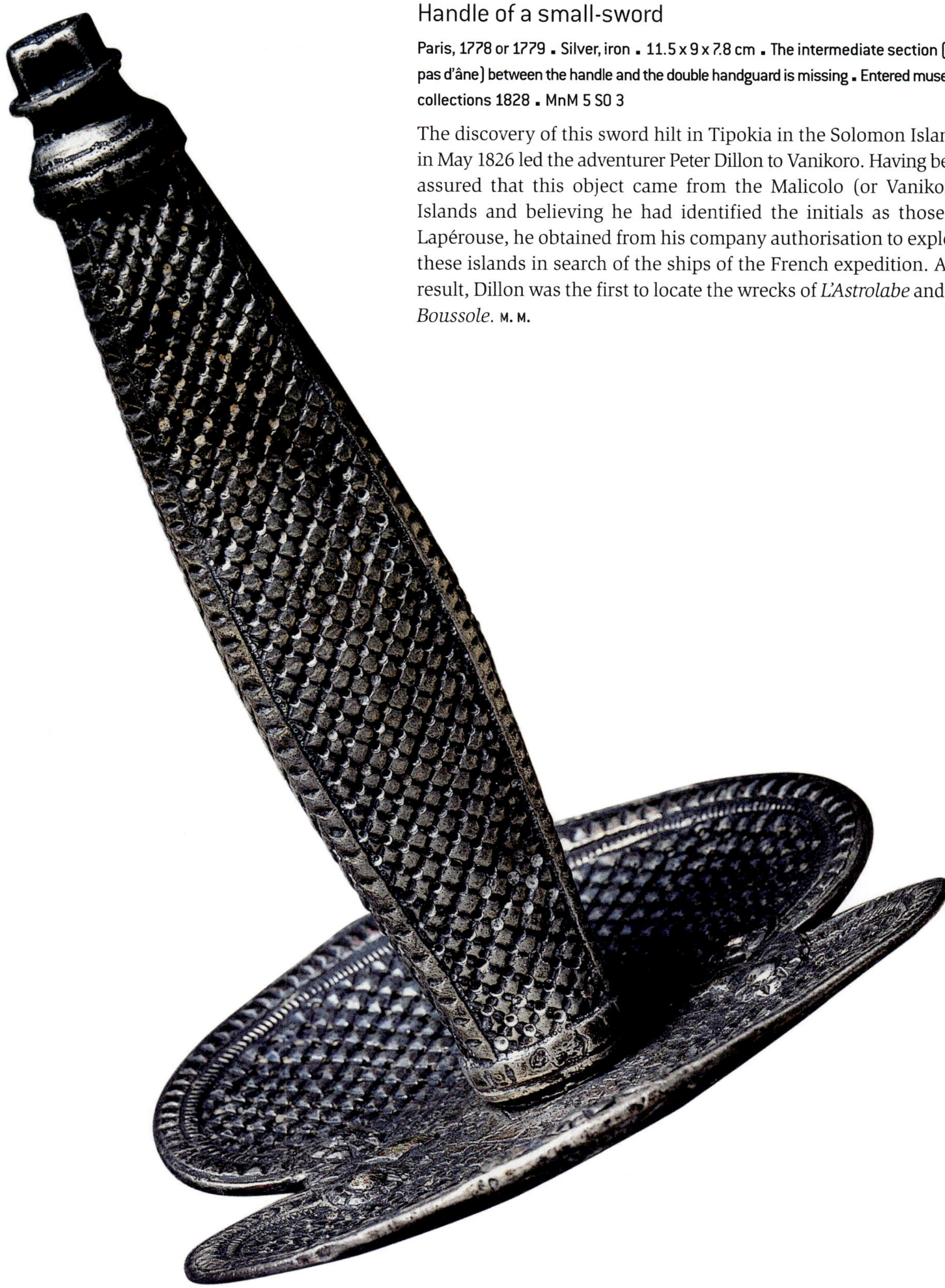

Handle of a small-sword

Paris, 1778 or 1779 ▪ Silver, iron ▪ 11.5 x 9 x 7.8 cm ▪ The intermediate section (the pas d'âne) between the handle and the double handguard is missing ▪ Entered museum collections 1828 ▪ MnM 5 SO 3

The discovery of this sword hilt in Tipokia in the Solomon Islands in May 1826 led the adventurer Peter Dillon to Vanikoro. Having been assured that this object came from the Malicolo (or Vanikoro) Islands and believing he had identified the initials as those of Lapérouse, he obtained from his company authorisation to explore these islands in search of the ships of the French expedition. As a result, Dillon was the first to locate the wrecks of *L'Astrolabe* and *La Boussole*. M. M.

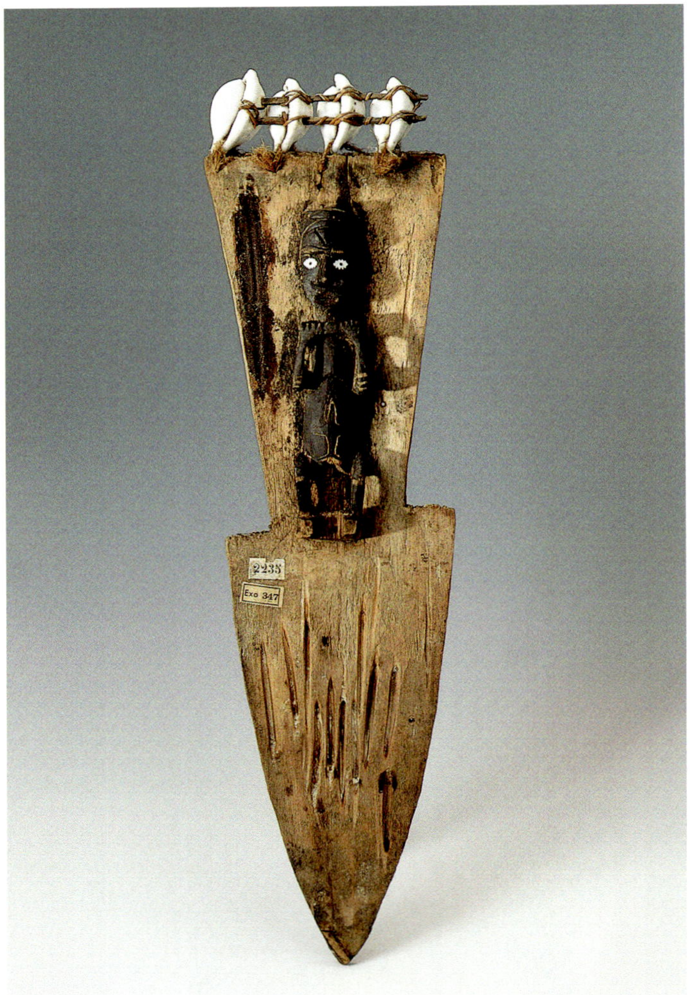

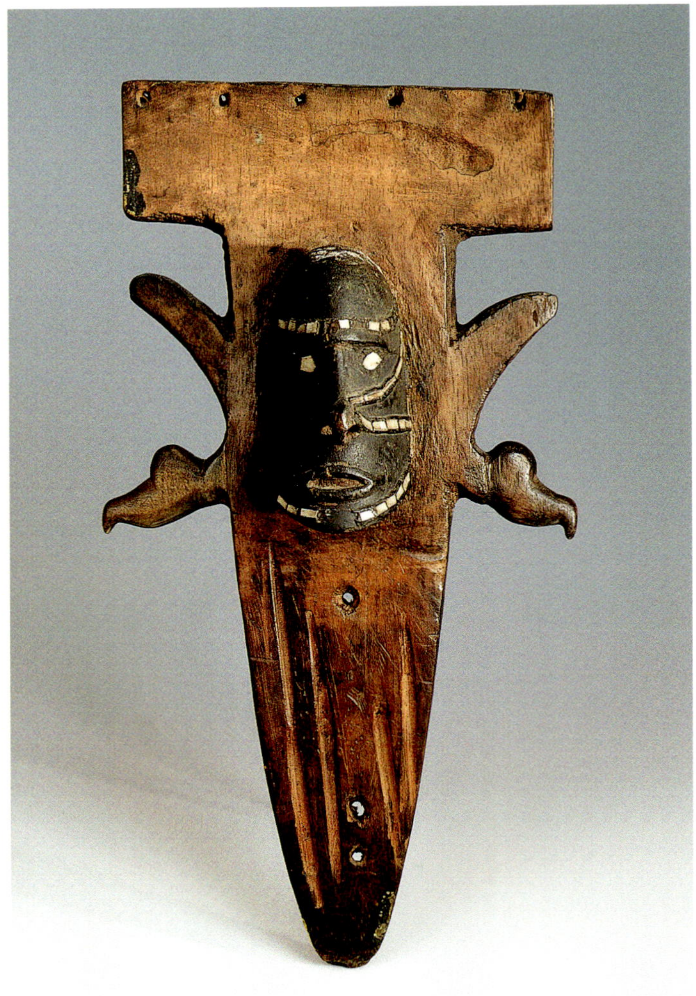

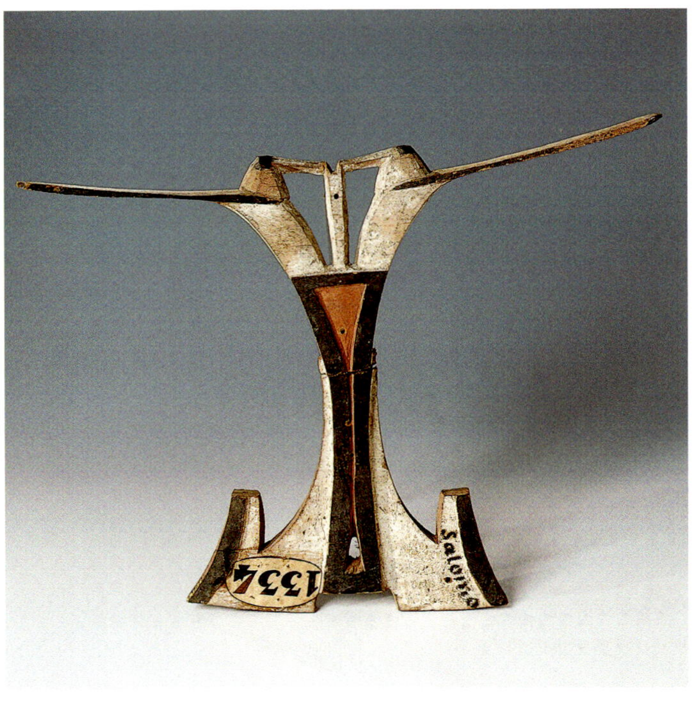

Canoe ornament from the Solomon Islands

Solomon Islands, before 1840 . Wood, shell . 86 x 22.5 x 5.5 cm . Entered museum collections 1843 . MnM 39 EX 6

Canoe ornament from the Solomon Islands

Solomon Islands, before 1840 . Wood, shell . 47 x 23 x 7 cm . Entered museum collections 1843 . MnM 39 EX 7

Canoe ornament from the Caroline Islands

Caroline Islands, before 1840 . Wood . 44.5 x 58.5 x 5 cm . Entered museum collections 1843 . MnM 39 EX 9

These artefacts from native boats were collected during Dumont d'Urville's last voyage, in the Pacific and Antarctic Oceans (1837–1840). Of all the ethnographical objects donated to the museum on his return they are among the rare original pieces to have remained at the Musée National de la Marine. They illustrate the important role of naval officers in our knowledge of Pacific populations and their way of life. H. T.

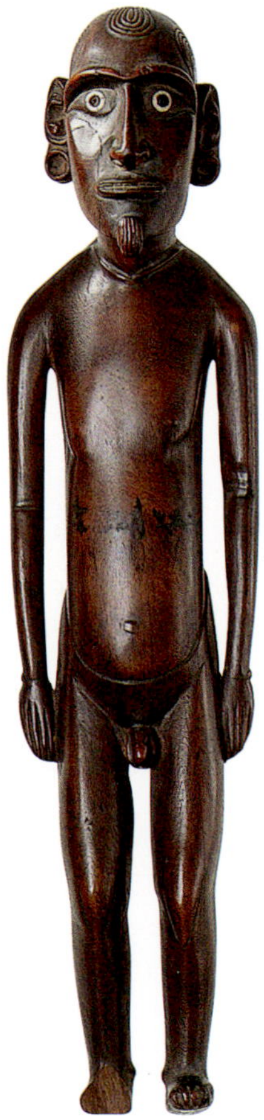

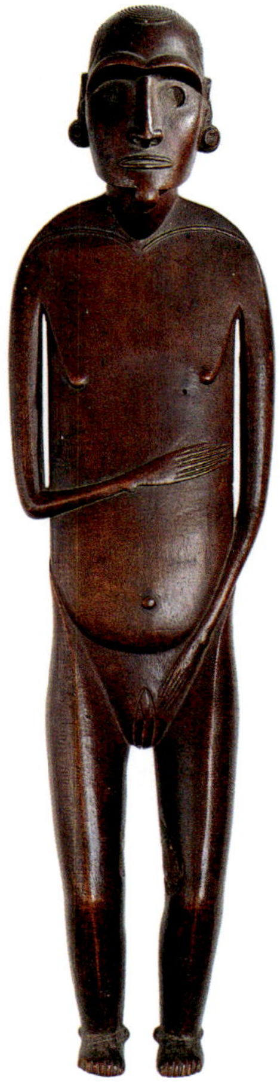

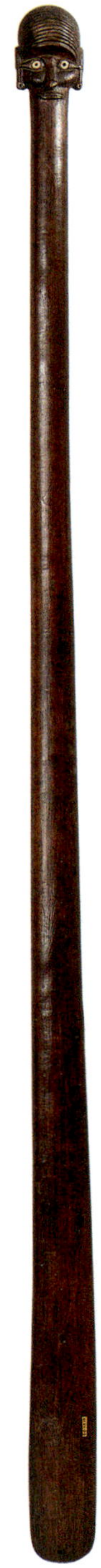

Moai tangata

Male statuette . Easter Island, 17th-18th century? . Sophora toromiro wood, obsidian and bone (eyes) . H. 46 cm . On loan from the Direction Centrale du Service de Santé des Armées (former school of naval medicine in Rochefort), 1986 . MnM 39 EX 28 D

Moai Papaa

Female statuette . Easter Island, before 1872 . Wood (toromiro) . H. 47.5 cm . On loan from the Direction Centrale of the Service de Santé des Armées (former school of naval medicine at Rochefort), 1986 . MnM 39 EX 29 D

This female statuette was given in 1872 to the naval school of medicine at Rochefort. Three other objects from Easter Island came with it, including an exceptional male statuette in wood, today on loan to the Louvre Museum for the room devoted to the arts of Africa, Asia, Oceania and the Americas. The donator, physician-in-chief Aze, headed the Service de Santé de la Marine in Tahiti from 1868 to 1872, where he probably purchased them. It shows an elderly woman of androgynous appearance, emphasised by her goatee beard. This type of wooden statuette charged with symbolic meaning was worn around dancers' necks at public celebrations. Only a few rare specimens have come down to us. H. T.

Ua staff

Ceremonial baton . Easter Island, before 1857 . Wood (marukuru), coral, obsidian . 203 x 11 cm . Entered museum collections 1857 . MnM 41 EX 23

The Ua sceptre, or staff, was probably a royal insignia, carried by the king at festivities. It is decorated at one end with a carved double-faced human head. The other end is flared and flattened. The flat end was probably used for delivering death blows. H. T.

Carmagnolle diving suit

Alphonse et Théodore Carmagnolle (fl. ca. 1882), inventors ■ Circa 1882 ■ Steel, glass ■ 190 x 92 x 97 cm ■ Entered museum collections 1939 ■ MnM 1 PA 20

From the mid-19th century on, in their quest to find a way to dive deeper than was possible with devices consisting in a rubber suit and helmet, inventors developed an all-metal, watertight, articulated diving suit. This diving suit, designed to descend to depths of two hundred meters, was the result of a series of prototypes whose patents were registered between 1866 and 1882. But the numerous ball-and-socket joints interconnected with impermeable canvas did not prove sufficiently watertight, and the device was not used. F. C.

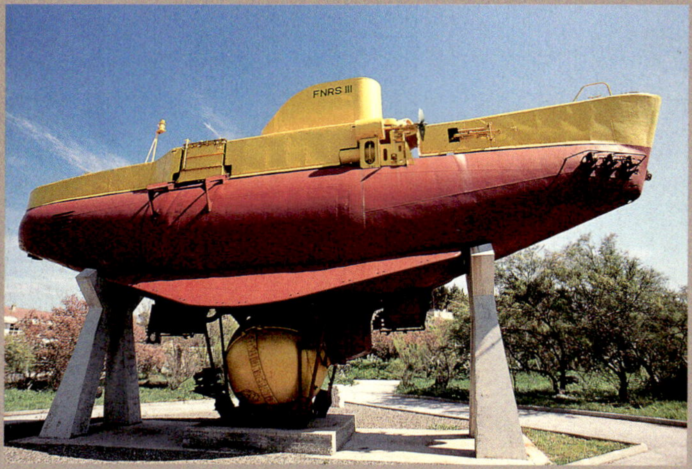

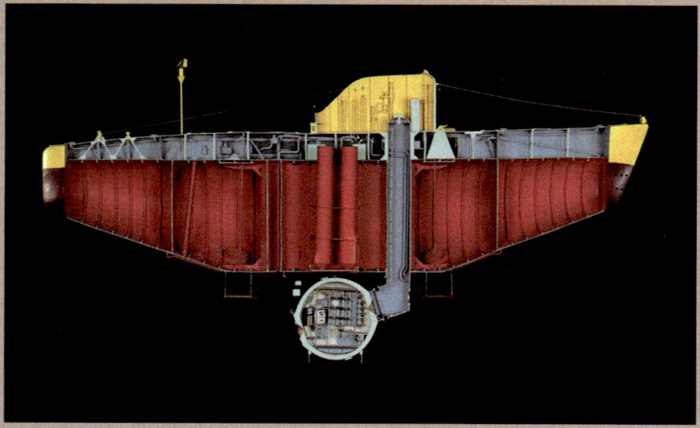

The FNRS III

Bathyscaphe designed by Auguste Piccard (1884–1962) ■ After drawings by André Gempp for the float ■ Built by par DCN Toulon (float) and the Établissements Georges L'Hoir, Liège, Belgium (sphere) ■ 1948–1953 ■ Steel ■ 16.40 x 7.70 x 5.50 cm ■ Entered museum collections 1996 ■ MnM 5 BS 8

The *FNRS III*

Cut-away model of the bathyscaphe *FNRS III*, 1:20 scale ■ Constructed by M. Tribet 1954 ■ Metal, brass, wood ■ 60 x 81 x 21 cm ■ Entered museum collections 1954 ■ MnM 31 MG 17

The *FNRS III*, designed by Professeur Piccard and launched in 1953, was the first self-propelled bathyscaphe (submersible) capable of diving to great depths. It consisted of a spherical cabin (from the *FNRS II*, a Belgian bathyscaphe built in 1948) and a float filled with petrol, lighter than water. On 15 February 1954, the *FNRS III*, manned by Commandant Houot and the engineer Willm, dived to the record depth of 4,050 m off the coast of Dakar. A. N.

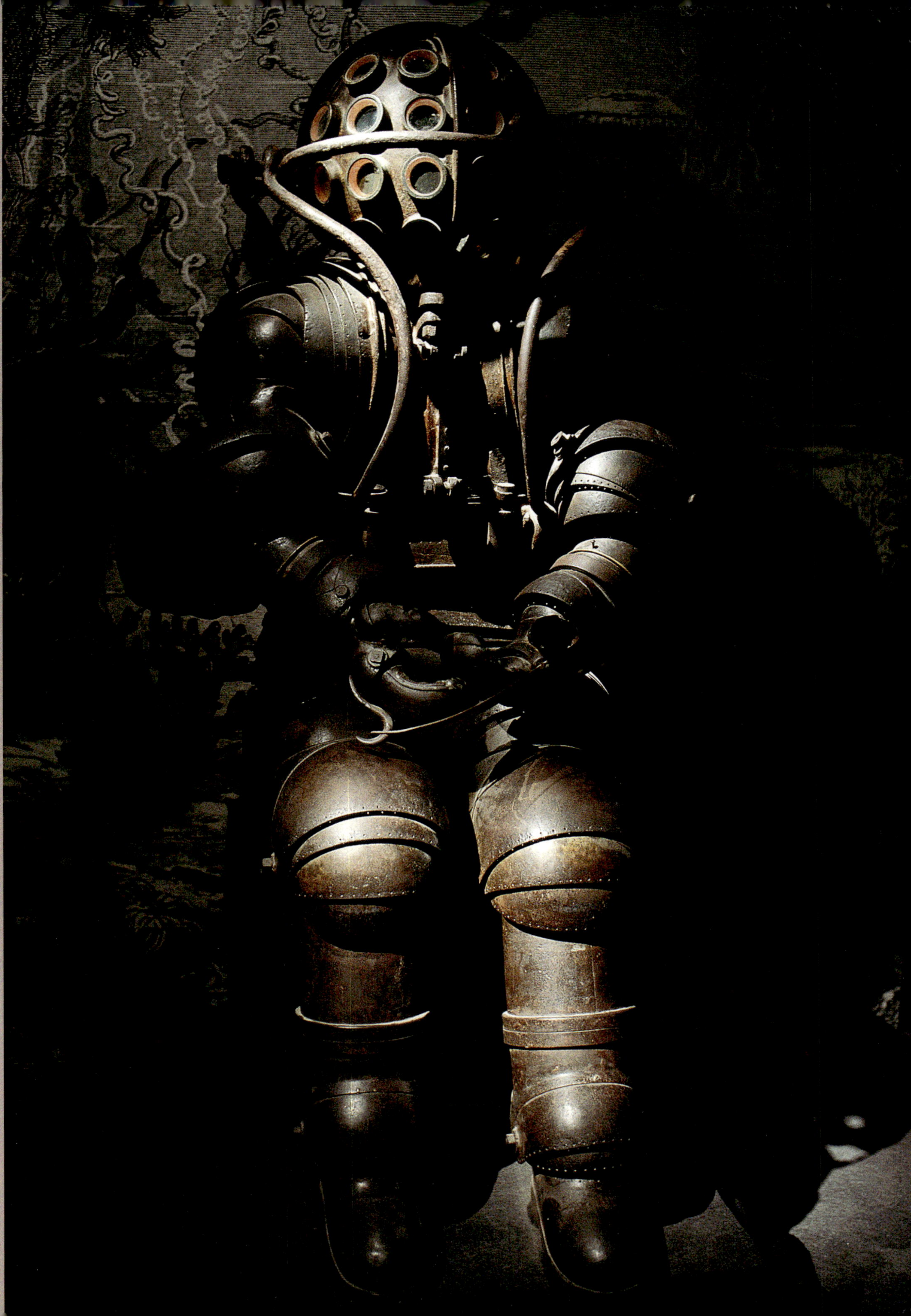

A ship in the mind's eye

Scale models, children's toys, models in bottles: more than any other manmade object, the ship has been the object of artistic representation and miniature reconstruction.
These singular objects, made of straw, wood, bone, white metal, and silver, or ivory – like *La Ville de Dieppe*, an imperial gift – or even cloves, are in a class of their own in the museum's collections, yet familiar to all. Beyond the use of precious materials, it is often the virtuosity of the execution that makes them worthy of our admiration: many are veritable feats reflecting the extraordinary skill of the artist; others are mass-produced objects, such as the toys, of which the museum has a very large collection.
Some of the objects are made by sailors, reflecting the qualities for which they are renowned: manual dexterity and patience. But they are also found in circles outside maritime spheres, and the model ships are often somewhat fanciful. But accuracy is not what counts here. It matters little how many guns are shown, the exact position of the masts, the order of sails and the shape of the hull. The aim is not to make a perfectly faithful reproduction of a real ship, but to communicate the *idea* of a ship. These objects, more than any other, are the makings of dreams. They are made to fire the imagination. And that is why, for centuries, they have graced chests and mantelpieces, be it in the home of an empress of France, a small boy in the 20th century, or a gentlemen of the 19th century.

Corvette, 'hulk work'

Model of a corvette from the First Empire . Between 1805 and 1814 . Wood, straw, silver . 14 x 17 x 6 cm (corvette); H. 2.5 cm, Ø 17 cm (stand) . Entered museum collections 1985 . MnM 1 BF 82

Three-deck British ship

Model of a three-deck British ship, late 17th century–early 19th century . First Empire . Bone, ivory, wood, straw . 7.8 x 9 x 4.4 cm (ship); 11.2 x 14.4 x 9.4 cm (showcase) . Entered museum collections 1975 . MnM 1 BF 70

These two minuscule models of ships were executed respectively in wood and bone. The first was embellished with a stand decorated with straw marquetry; the second was placed in a showcase. These delicate, meticulously executed objects were *travaux de ponton*, 'hulk works', made in England by French soldiers and sailors who had been captured during the Napoleonic Wars and imprisoned on hulks, old ships lying at anchor whose masts had been removed. A. N.

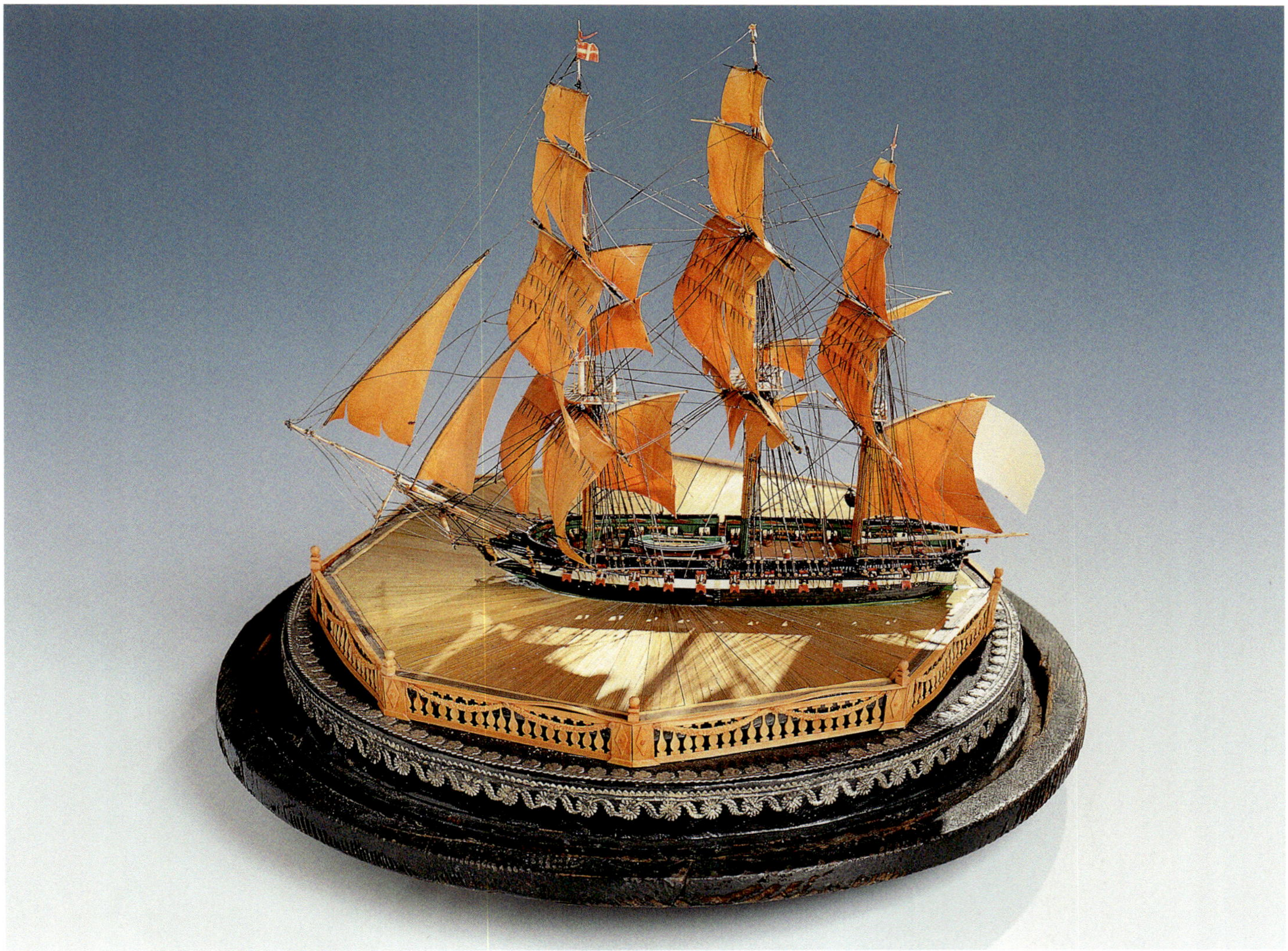

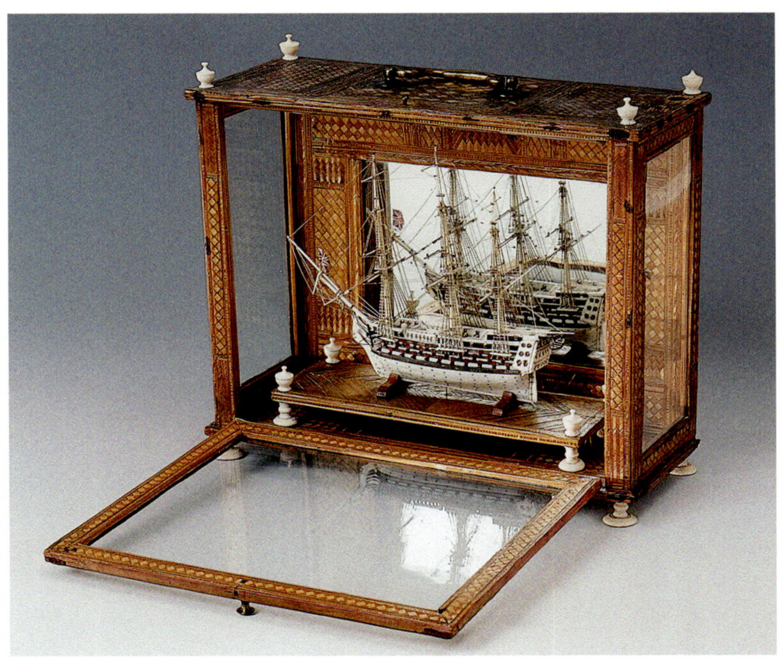

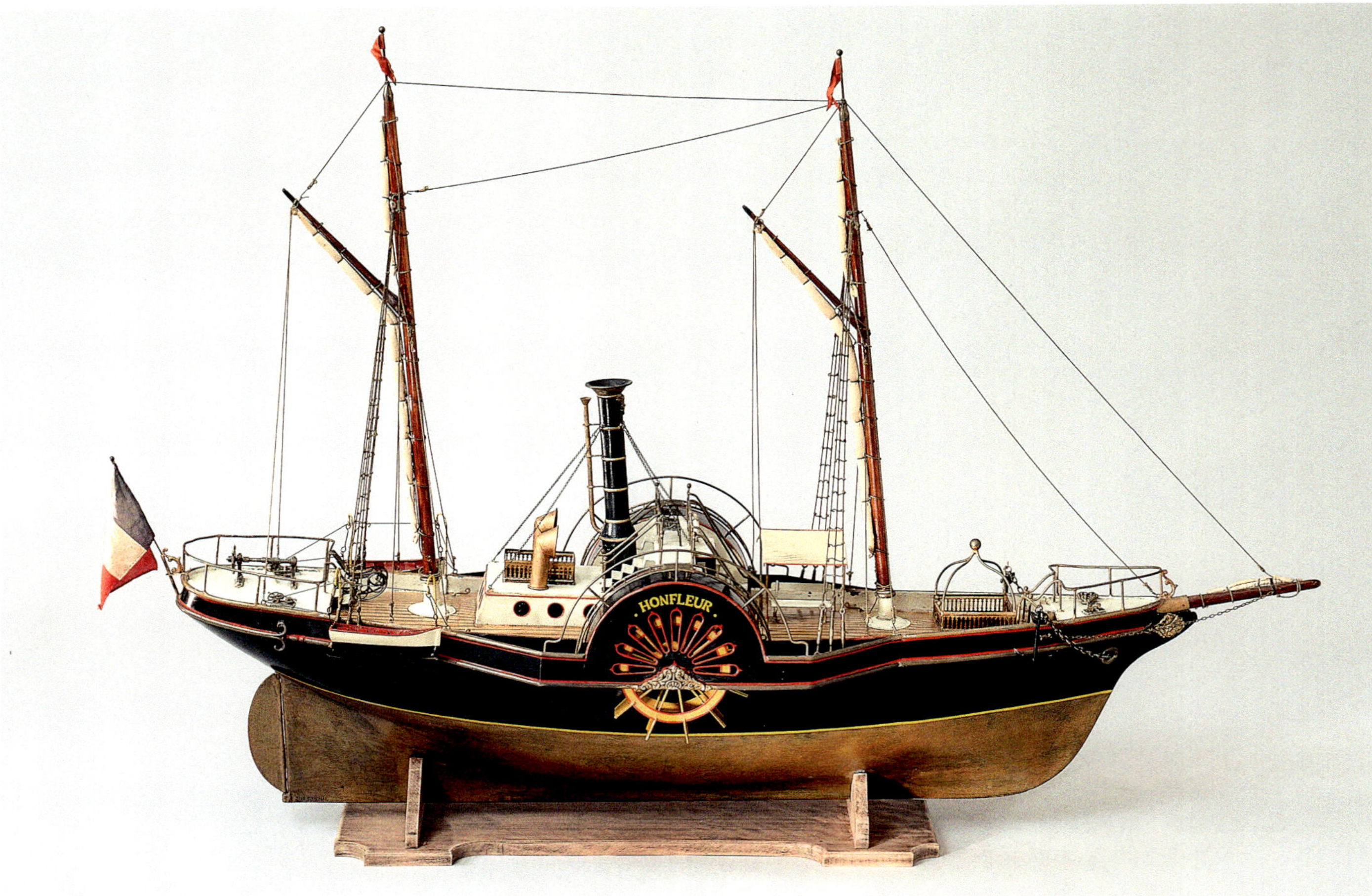

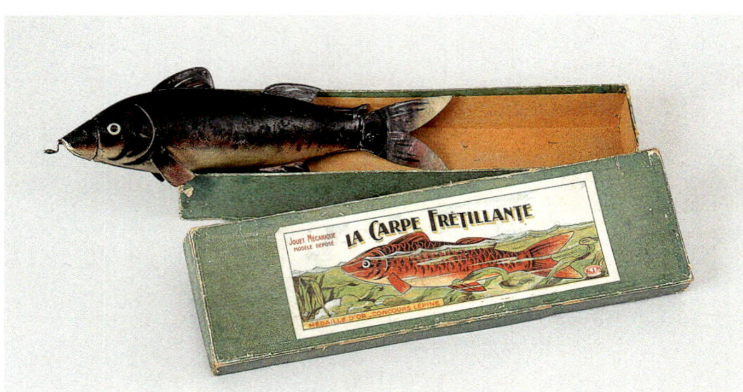

Honfleur

Toy ship ▪ Last quarter of the 19th century ▪ Iron, zinc ▪ 97 x 135 x 40 cm ▪ Entered museum collections 2005, former collection of Jac Remise ▪ MnM 2005.25.44

This toy boat on wheels is remarkable not only in its size but also because of its technical components. It has a steam engine with a horizontal boiler and gauge (an element rarely found on toy boats), a piston system and a pendulum regulator. It is also equipped with two burners for producing steam that provide a power supply lasting half an hour, exceptionally long for this type of toy. A. M.-V.

La Carpe Frétillante (The Quivering Carp)

Toy ▪ Fernand Migault, maker ▪ 1924 ▪ Sheet metal ▪ 11 x 43 x 4.8 cm ▪ Entered museum collections 2005, former collection of Jac Remise ▪ MnM 2005.25.103

As indicated in the instructions, 'The Quivering Carp is propelled by the alternative movement of its tail, powered by a rubber-band motor. If the latter snaps it may be replaced, by separating the body and head simply by pulling on the latter'. Fernand Migault, who was one of the three leading toy makers in France at the time, received the Gold Medal of the Lépine Competition for this device. A. M.-V.

La Salamandre

Toy boat ▪ Radiguet, maker ▪ Late 19th or early 20th century ▪ Copper, iron painted black, brick red and ochre ▪ 90 x 105 x 33 cm ▪ Entered museum collections 2005, former collection of Jac Remise ▪ MnM 2005.25.142

This battleship attributed to Radiguet is driven by a powerful steam engine. On board are 32 sailors and a mechanical launch. The Radiguet firm was founded in Paris in 1892 and was famous for the quality of the materials used in its boats (mahogany decks). Note the detail of the boilers and the metalwork, particularly the guard rails. A. M.-V.

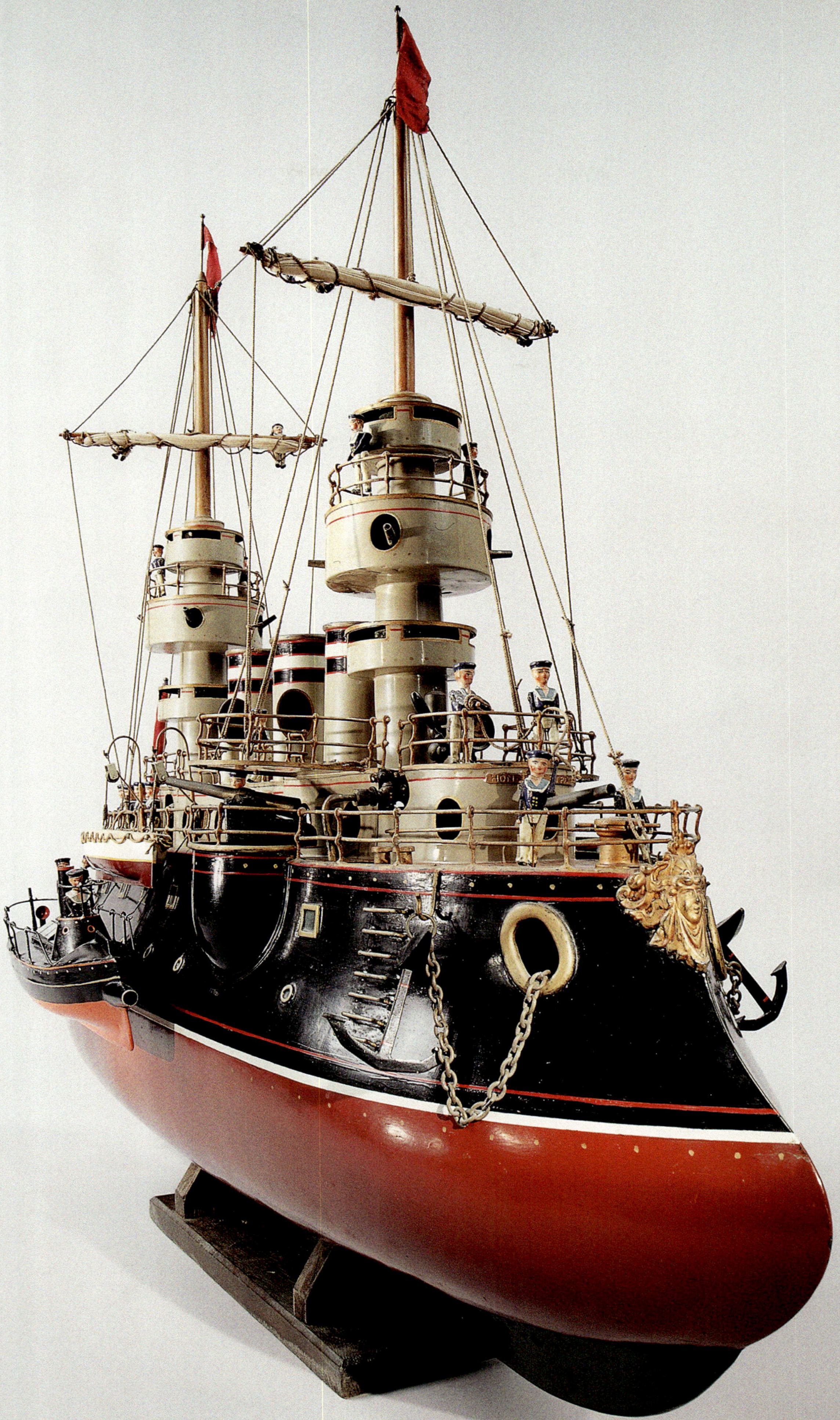

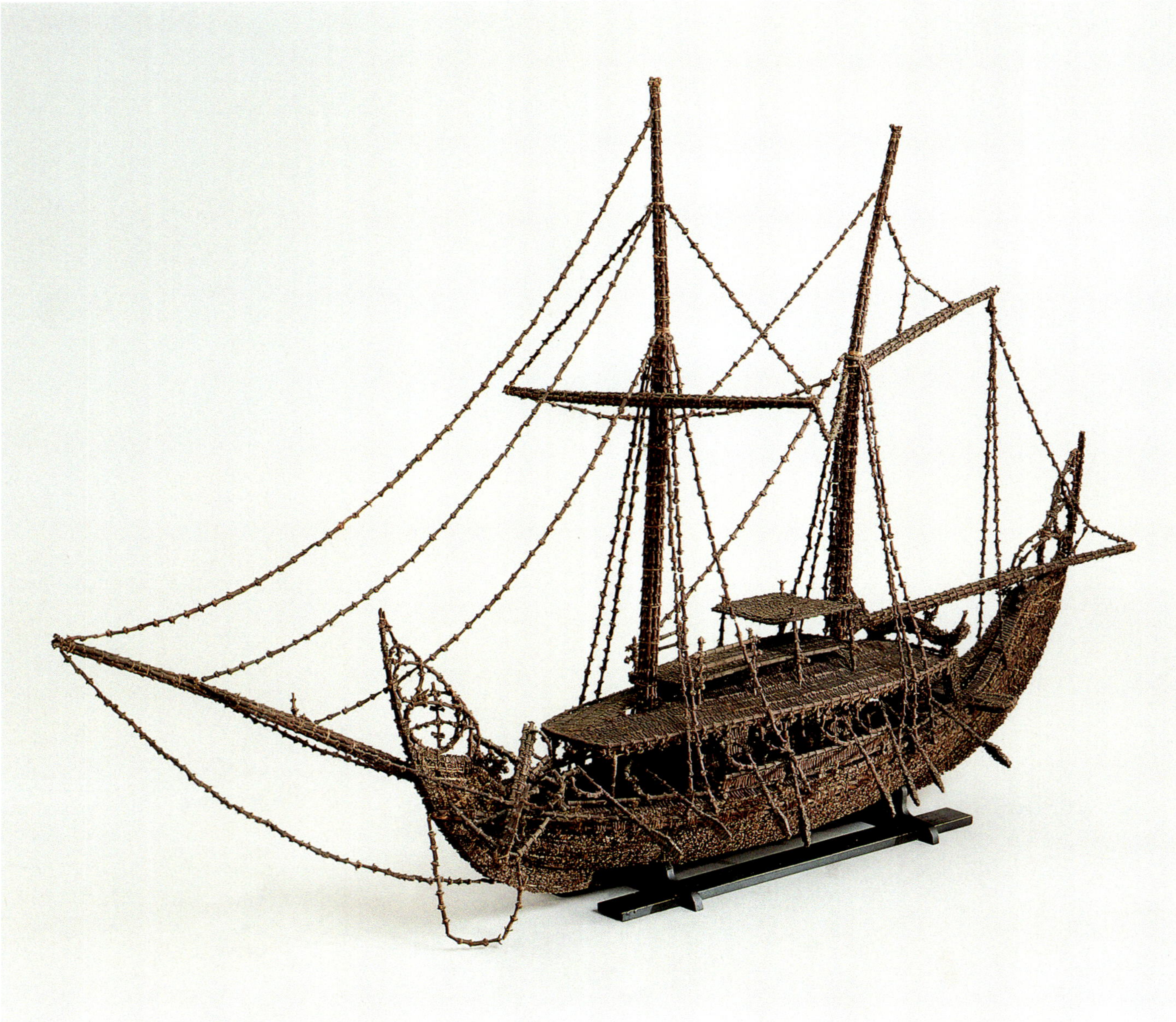

Boat from the Molucca Islands

Model, 1:16 scale ▪ The Moluccas, before 1842 ▪ Cloves, tropical hardwood, plant fibres ▪ 73 x 100 x 37 cm ▪ Entered museum collections 1845 ▪ MnM 1BF 22

This object is typical of the Moluccas, the world's largest producer of cloves. This curious two-masted ship also has fourteen paddlers, and an openwork central cabin. The vessel resembles an official boat, perhaps the 'governor's canoe', a drawing of which was printed by Dumont d'Urville in the *Voyages de la corvette [...] 'L'Astrolabe'*. F. C.

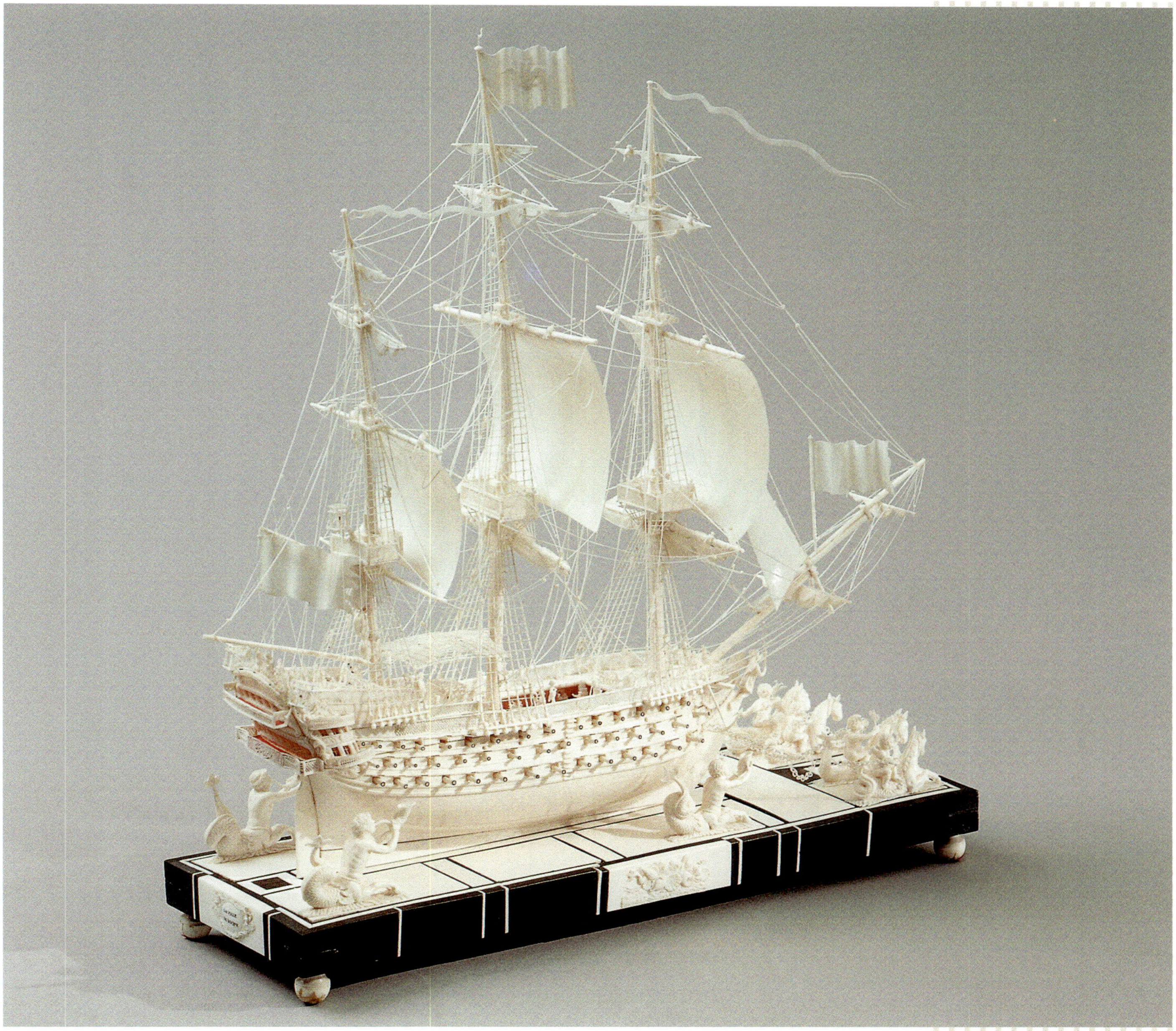

La Ville de Dieppe

Model of a three-deck ship from the 18th century ▪ Attributed to Louis Charles Vincent Belleteste (1757–1819) ▪ First Empire ▪ Ivory, ebony ▪ 38 x 38 x 11 cm ▪ Entered museum collections 1846 ▪ MnM 1 BF 8

A masterpiece of virtuosity executed by a great ivory sculptor from Dieppe, this model of the ship *La Ville de Dieppe*, brought to life with around one hundred tiny figures, was given to Napoleon I and Empress Marie-Louise during their visit to Dieppe on 27 May 1810. The stand, which features carved motifs symbolising the recent marriage of the imperial couple, was probably made at a later date. A. N.

A network of museums

The Musée National de la Marine is a network of six establishments in Paris and on the Atlantic and Mediterranean coasts.

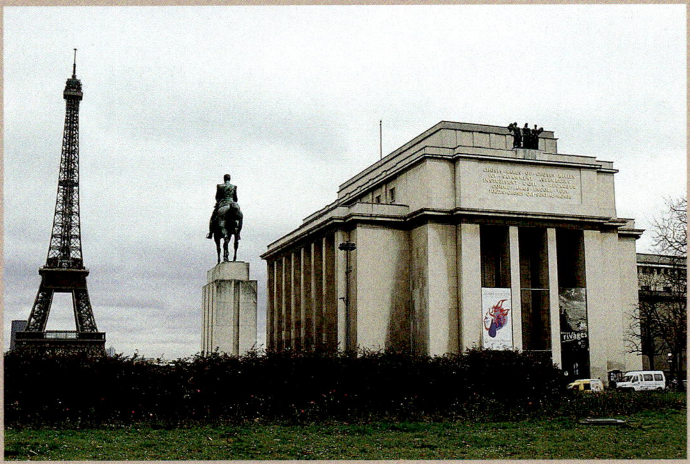

Paris, Palais de Chaillot

Located in the centre of Paris, facing the Eiffel Tower and the Champ de Mars, the museum is housed in one of the largest monuments in Paris, the Palais de Chaillot, built for the 1937 World's Fair. It is also the administrative headquarters of the Musée National de la Marine, founded in 1827 under the name Musée Naval and housed at the time in the Louvre palace.

The permanent collections and regular temporary exhibitions evoke the wealth and diversity of the French maritime heritage, in particular those of the five naval fleets: warships, merchantmen, scientific exploration vessels, fishing vessels, and yachts and pleasure boats. This history charts the passion of shipbuilders, inventors and seafarers of yesteryear through to the present day.

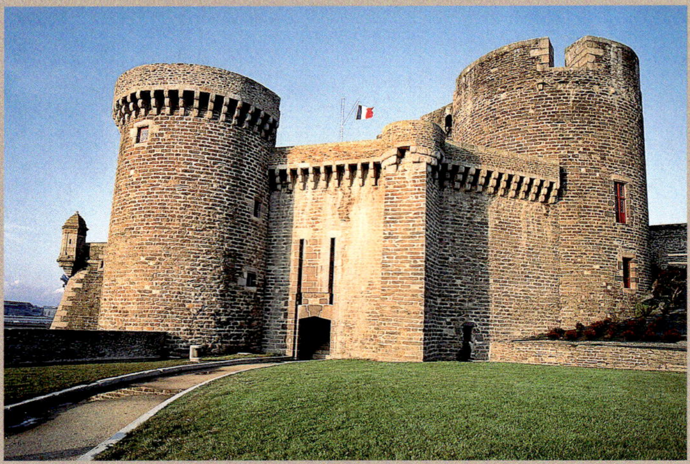

Brest, Château de Brest

The Musée National de la Marine in Brest, on the north-west coast of France, is the successor of the Models Room opened in 1826 in the dockyard, where models and elements of naval decoration were displayed at the time. Evacuated to Morlaix during World War II, in 1958 the collections were moved to the château, one of the very few monuments of the city to have escaped the bombings at the Liberation.

Modified many times, the Château de Brest has kept the appearance of an impressive medieval fortress. It has been the historic heart of the city for seventeen centuries. Restoration work carried out by the Ministries of Defence and Culture has enabled the museum to enhance the oldest parts of the building.

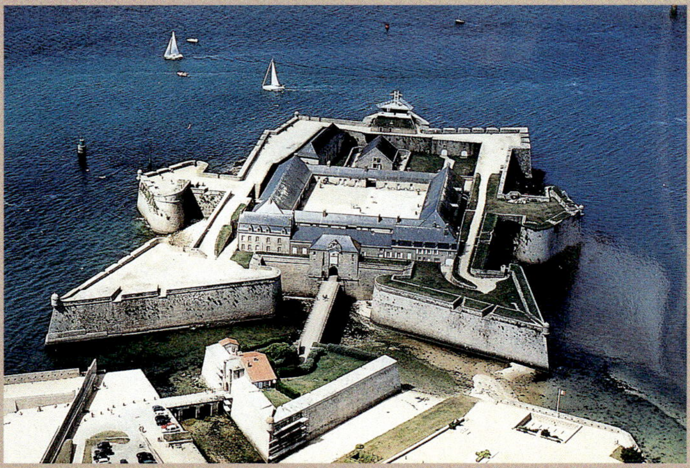

Port-Louis, Citadel

A magnificent example of military architecture, the Port-Louis citadel, near Lorient on the north-west coast of France, was founded by the Spanish during the Wars of Religion and its construction completed under Louis XIII. Its history is linked to that of the Compagnie des Indes (the French India Company), which in the 18th century enriched the city with the development of the port of Lorient. Major donations have enabled the renovation of the exhibition areas of the Musée National de la Marine. These are organised around two themes: 'Ocean Treasures', which presents underwater archaeology on the route to India, and 'Sea Rescue', which pays tribute to the dedication of the men who braved the perils of the sea. The citadel houses not only the Musée National de la Marine but also the Musée de la Compagnie des Indes, run by the City of Lorient.

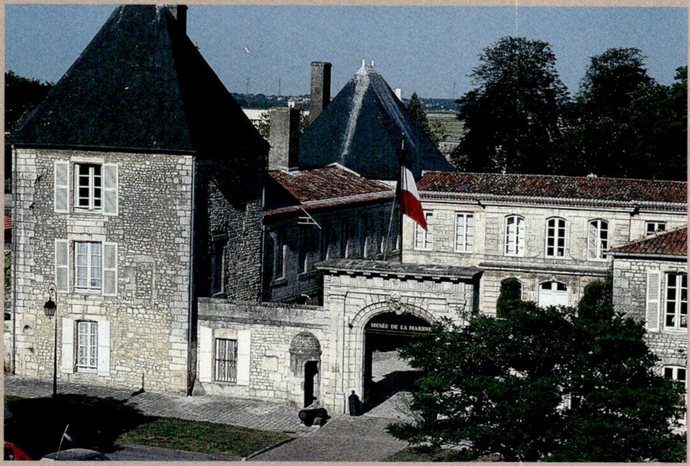

Rochefort, Hôtel de Cheusses

The Hôtel de Cheusses is undoubtedly the building that best illustrates the history of the city of Rochefort, on the Atlantic coast. When the dockyards were developed by Colbert, this early 17th-century manor house became the residence of the squadron commanders, and was extended and modernised. In the 19th century, the royal ropeworks housed a museum 'of small models', which presented historic models of ships and shipyard machinery, as well as a fine ensemble of wooden carvings. In 1936, this museum was transferred to the Hôtel de Cheusses, a move that saved its collections from destruction, the ropeworks having been burnt down at the end of the war. The museum reopened in 1973 after major rebuilding and renovation work.

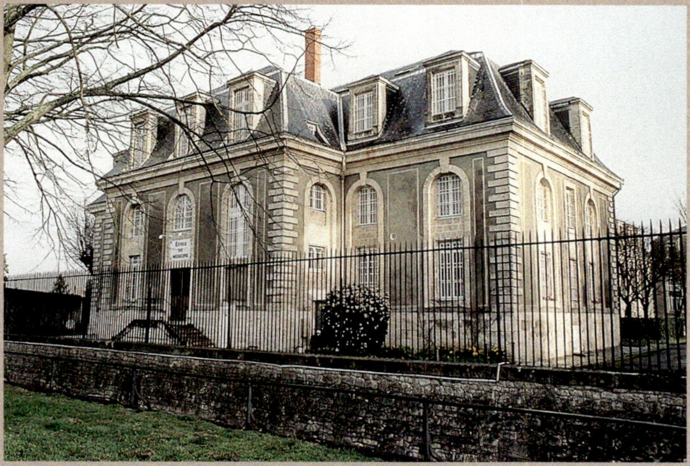

Rochefort, former School of Naval Medicine

In 1722, the first School of Naval Medicine opened in Rochefort, housed from 1788 in the new maritime hospital. The school's golden age was in the 19th century, at the time of the voyages of exploration. The arrangement of the building dates from this period: the large reading room in the library and the 'museum', designed as much as study room as a cabinet of curiosities.
After the closure of the hospital, in 1986 the French Armies Health Service entrusted the Musée National de la Marine with the task of preserving this exceptional heritage. A major restoration programme was undertaken to safeguard the spirit of the place. It opened its doors to the public in June 1998.

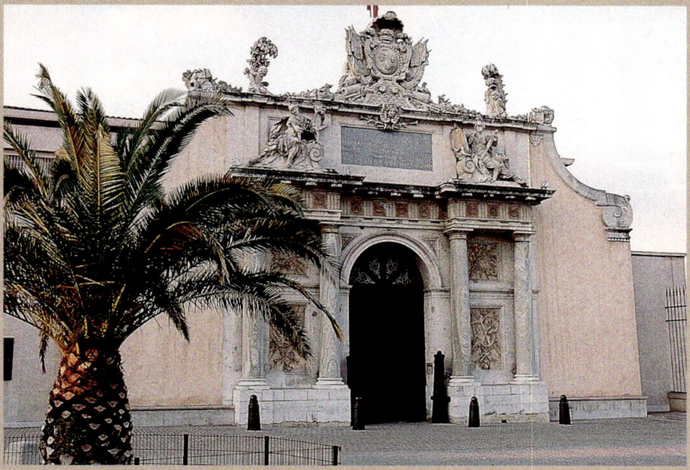

Toulon, Place Monsenergue

This museum in Toulon on the Mediterranean coast is entered by the former ceremonial gate of the dockyards, built in 1738 and today standing in the façade of one of the wings of the new *préfecture maritime* (police port authority). The original museum, founded in the late First Empire, opened to the public in 1813. It was housed in several different places, but its collections have remained intact. They present the navies of the Levant, notably the galley corps, and the history of the dockyards.

Selected bibliography

Bayle, L.-M. (ed.), introd. by Conisbee, Philip, *Joseph Vernet 1714–1789*, exh. cat., Paris, Musée de la Marine, 1976.

Bayle, L.-M., Mordal, J., *La marine en bois*, Paris, Fayard, 1978.

Bayle, L.-M., Mordal, J., *Le musée de la Marine*, Rennes, Ouest-France, 1980.

Béland, M., Mourot, M. (ed.), *Les Génies de la mer: chefs-d'œuvre de la sculpture navale du musée national de la Marine à Paris*, exh. cat., Québec, Musée du Québec, Paris, Musée National de la Marine, 2001.

Bellec, F., *Catalogue des collections du musée de la Marine. Instruments scientifiques*, Paris, 1988. Typed text, 2 vols.

Bellec, F. (ed.), *Quand voguaient les galères*, exh. cat., Paris, AAMM, 1990.

Bellec, F. *Le musée de la Marine, Palais de Chaillot, Paris*, (n. p.), Franco Maria Ricci (FMR).

Boudriot, J., Berti, H., Dantec, P., *Modèles historiques au musée de la Marine*, Paris, ANCRE, 1997. Publication of vol. 2 scheduled for spring 2006.

Boudriot, J., Demarcq, M.-P., *Musée de la Marine. Architecture navale française XVIIe, plans et dessins*, Paris, ANCRE, 1998.

Burlet, R., *Les Galères au musée de la Marine*, Paris, Presses de l'Université Paris-Sorbonne, 2001.

Demarcq, M.-P., 'Les traités de construction navale français de 1750 à 1850 dans les collections du musée national de la Marine', *Le Livre maritime au siècle des Lumières*, Paris, Presses de l'Université Paris-Sorbonne, 2005.

Demarcq, M.-P., Frémond, D., Tromparent, H. (ed.), *Jules Verne, le roman de la mer*, Paris, Seuil, Musée national de la Marine, 2005. Ill. book for exhib.

Demarcq, M.-P., Préneuf, J. de (ed.), *Mémoires de la mer*, Paris, L'Iconoclaste, 2005.

Destrem, J., 'Le musée de la marine au Louvre', *Gazette des Beaux-Arts*, Nov.–Dec. 1919.

Destrem, J., Clerc Rampal, G., *Catalogue raisonné du musée de la Marine*, Paris, Imprimerie Française, 1909.

Finamore, D., Tromparent, H., *Rendez-vous with the Sea: the Glory of the French Maritime Tradition*, Salem, Peabody Essex Museum, 2002.

Humbert, J.-M., 'Le Musée national de la Marine à Brest et à Port-Louis: l'évolution d'un réseau', *Musées et Collections Publiques de France*, no. 231, Sept. 2002.

Humbert, J.-M., Ponsonnet, B. (ed.), *Napoléon et la mer*, Paris, Seuil, Musée National de la Marine, 2004. Ill. book for exhib.

Lamy, J.-P., 'Les collections du musée national de la Marine: du plan du maître constructeur aux archives de chantier naval', *La Construction navale et sa mémoire: archives et patrimoine*, Rouen, Archives Départementales, 2005.

Manœuvre, L., Rieth, É., *Joseph Vernet 1714–1789, les ports de France*, Arcueil, Anthèse, 1994.

Morel-Fatio, L.-A., *Notice des collections du musée de marine exposées dans les galeries du Musée Impérial du Louvre*, Paris, Vinchon, 1853.

Mourot, M., 'L'inventaire administratif des collections du musée de la Marine', *Neptunia*, no. 214, 1999/2.

Mourot, M., Cohen, F., Baron, C., *Navires à la mer dans les collections du musée national de la Marine et dans le fonds Augustin Normand*, exh. cat., Le Havre, Ville du Havre, 1999.

Musée de la Marine, *Loisirs sur l'eau. Histoire de la plaisance en France 1640–1940*, exh. cat., Paris, Musée de la Marine, 1979.

Musée de la Marine, *La généreuse et tragique expédition Lapérouse*, exh. cat., Paris, Musée de la Marine, 1985.

Musée de la Marine, Bibliothèque nationale, *Océans des hommes*, exh. cat., Paris, Musée de la Marine, Bibliothèque Nationale, 1987.

Musée de la Marine, Bibliothèque nationale, *A la rencontre de Sindbad, les routes maritimes de la soie*, exh. cat., Paris, RMN, Musée de la Marine, 1994.

Musée de la Marine, *Le temps des clippers*, Paris, Musée de la Marine, 1996. Journal d'exposition.

Musée de la Marine, *De la Gloire au Charles de Gaulle*, Paris, Musée de la Marine, 1997. (Journal d'exposition, 1.)

Musée national de la Marine, *Voyages de rêve*, Paris, Musée de la Marine, 1999. (Journal d'exposition, 2.)

Musée National de la Marine, *Sur cale: regards sur la construction navale 1880–1914*, Paris, Musée National de la Marine, 2000. (Journal d'exposition, 3.)

Musée National de la Marine, *Trésors d'océans, l'archéologie sous-marine sur la route des Indes: Port-Louis*, Paris, Musée National de la Marine, 2002. (Les Carnets de bord, 1.)

Musée National de la Marine, *Joseph Vernet 1714-1789: les ports de France*, Paris, Musée National de la Marine, 2003. (Les Carnets de bord, 2.)

Musée National de la Marine, *Sauvetage en mer*, Paris, Musée National de la Marine, 2005. (Les Carnets de bord, 3.)

Musée National du Louvre, Miot, P.-E. (attrib. to), *Promenade au musée de la Marine*, Paris, Librairie Imprimerie réunies, (n.d.).

Niderlinder, A., 'Le musée de la Marine et ses collections', *Neptunia*, no. 193, 1994/1; no. 194, 1994/2; no. 195, 1994/3; no. 197, 1995/1.

Pâris, F.-É., *Le musée de marine du Louvre: histoire, description, construction, représentation, statistique des navires à rames et à voiles, d'après les modèles et les dessins des galeries du musée du Louvre...*, Paris, J. Rotschild, 1883.

Paris, F.-É., *Souvenirs de marine. Collection de plans ou dessins de navires et de bateaux anciens et modernes, existants ou disparus, avec les éléments numériques nécessaires à leur construction*, Paris, Gauthier-Villars, 1882–1908.

Paris, F.-É., *Souvenirs de marine conservés, ou Collection de plans de navires et de bateaux de tous les pays...*, Paris, Imprimerie de Monrocq, 1877.

Pâris, F.-É., Rieth, É., *Souvenirs de marines conservés*, abridged with notes; Douarnenez, Chasse-Marée/Armen, 1999, 2 vols.

Pâris, F.-É., Rieth, É., *Le Voyage de la Favorite, collection de bateaux dessinés d'après nature, 1830–1831–1832*, Arcueil, Anthèse, 1992.

Ravel, P. de, Thoisy-Dallem, A. de (ed.), *Canoë et Kayaks, à la découverte d'un nouveau monde*, Paris, Musée National de la Marine, 2004. Catalogue/special survey.

Rieth, É., 'Les cahiers manuscrits d'Étienne Sigaut', *Techniques et Culture*, no. 35, 2000.

Rieth, É., 'La collection de maquettes du fonds Amiral Pâris au musée national de la Marine, l'exemple des bateaux de l'Inde', Paris, RFHOM, 2001.

Serna, V., 'L'élaboration des collections documentaires au musée national de la Marine', *Neptunia*, no. 220, 2000/1.

Trésors du musée national de la Marine, Québec, Musée de la Civilisation, Paris, Musée National de la Marine, 2000. Ill. book for exhib.

NB: Each issue of the magazine *Neptunia*, published by the Association des Amis du Musée de la Marine (AAMM), contains a wealth of information. Special issues have been devoted to the museum, its collections and its exhibitions: no. 192 (Musée de la Marine), no. 196 (Rochefort), no. 202 (Brest), no. 212 (250th anniversary of the collections), no. 213 (little-known treasures of the Musée de la Marine), no. 226 (Académie de Marine exhibition).

This book is co-published by the Musée National de la Marine and the Réunion des Musées Nationaux

For the Musée National de la Marine
Editorial management and coordination, Cultural Department:
Bruno Ponsonnet, Head of Department
Virginie Duchêne, Publications Manager

For the Réunion des Musées Nationaux
Publications Director: Pierre Vallaud
Head of Book Department: Catherine Marquet
Editorial coordination: Laurence Posselle
Head of Production: Isabelle Floc'h

Design and layout: Mateo Baronnet
Translation from the French: Alexandra Keens

Texts set in Conduit and Slimbach
Photoengraving by Ex Fabrica/Edilog, France
Printed in June 2006 by Egedsa, Spain

Dépôt légal: June 2006
ISBN RMN (English edition): 2-7118-5096-X
RMN no.: GK 19 5096
ISBN MnM (English edition): 2 901421 29 6
EAN MnM: 9782901421290